Music for Three or More Pianists
A Historical Survey and Catalogue

by
Grant L. Maxwell

The Scarecrow Press, Inc.
Metuchen, N.J., & London
1993

This book was originally submitted as a thesis to the Faculty of
Graduate Studies and Research at the University of Alberta, Edmonton,
Alberta, Canada in the spring of 1992 in partial fulfillment of the
requirements for the degree of Doctor of Music.

British Library Cataloguing-in-Publication data available

Library of Congress Cataloging-in-Publication Data

Maxwell, Grant L. (Grant Lyle), 1960-
  Music for three or more pianists : a historical survey and
catalogue / by Grant L. Maxwell.
      p.   cm.
  Includes bibliographical references and index.
  ISBN 0-8108-2631-3 (acid-free paper)
  1. Piano ensembles—History and criticism. 2. Piano
ensembles—Bibliography. I. Title. II. Title: Music for 3 or
more pianists.
  ML700.M39 1993
  785.62—dc20   92-37842

This book is dedicated to Ernesto Lejano, my musical mentor who suggested the topic of the original dissertation. His enthusiasm, encouragement, generosity and assistance inspired me from the beginning to its completion and will not be forgotten.

CONTENTS

PREFACE

This survey and catalogue of music for three or more pianists evolved from my experience as founder, performer, librarian, repetiteur, producer and director of PIANoRAMA, an ensemble consisting of four pianos that was created for Edmonton's 1989 summer Fringe festival. Initially this ever-increasing involvement with repertoire for four pianists commenced with Gustav Martin Schmidt's transcription of Beethoven's *Septet, Op. 20*, for eight hands at two pianos (discovered in a second-hand music store in Bloomington, Indiana in July of 1983). The existing published sources were eventually examined: Frederic Chang and Albert Faurot's *Team-Piano Repertoire: A Manual of Music for Multiple Players at One or More Pianos* (1976); *The Pianist's Resource Guide, 1978-79: Piano Music in Print and Literature on the Pianistic Art [by] Joseph Rezits and Gerald Deatsman*; and Maurice Hinson's *The Piano in Chamber Ensemble* (1978), *Music for More Than One Piano* (1983) and *The Pianists' Guide to Transcriptions, Arrangements and Paraphrases* (1990). Although these recent bibliographies were beneficial, they are by no means complete or comprehensive. Noteworthy compositions such as Igor Stravinsky's *Les noces*, Antheil's *Ballet mécanique* and Orff's three cantatas *Veni Creator Spiritus, Der gute Mensch* and *Vom Frühjahr, Öltank und vom Fliegen* were not included, unfortunately. The Canadian literature is ignored. Hence I saw the need for a more detailed catalogue.

After correspondence with composers, music publishers, parent companies/agents, libraries, and national/international information centres, I collected, classified and catalogued voluminous original and transcribed/arranged scores--in manuscript, published and unpublished or no longer in print. This preparatory work was augmented by an enlightening research trip to the Library of Congress, the Peabody Conservatory of Music, the New York Public Library at Lincoln Center, the Eastman School of Music and the University of Michigan in Ann Arbor. The Library of Congress, alone, had forty-eight boxes of uncatalogued scores; the First Piano Quartet collection in the New York Public Library had approximately three hundred arrangements for four pianos.

The historical survey is a distillation of original compositions from the catalogue that, in my view, were significant in the development of this performance medium.

Numerous individuals have assisted me in preparation of this book. I gratefully acknowledge the help from the Department of Music of the University of Alberta:

my Supervisory Committee, and the invaluable assistance of James Whittle of the Music Resources Centre. Many composers have responded to my project with enthusiasm; John Beckwith, Jack Behrens, John Cage, Gaby Casadesus (on behalf of the late Robert Casadesus), Brian Chapple, George Crumb, Emma Lou Diemer, Morton Gould, Jane Smith Hart, Michael Horwood, Talivaldis Kenins, Patricia W. King, Ladislav Kupkovič, Alcides Lanza, Otto Luening, Bruce Mather, Lubomyr Melnyk, Marjan Mozetich, Raymond Parfrey, Steve Reich, Russel Riepe, Peter Schickele, Elliot Schwartz and John Winiarz. I was overwhelmed by the support given by the staff at music libraries: in particular, the Music Division of the Library of Congress, the Lila Acheson Wallace Library of the Juilliard School, the Sibley Music Library at the Eastman School of Music, the Music Library at Arizona State University, the Music Library at Indiana University, the British Library, the Friedheim Library of the Peabody Conservatory of Music, the Music Library of Yale University, the Eda Kuhn Loeb Music Library of Harvard University, the American Music Center and the various Canadian Music Centres. My musical mentor Dr. Ernesto Lejano was overwhelmingly helpful and supportive. Donna Wilton of "Chapter 7" and Don Sutton of "Novel Horizons" have not only named their professional wordprocessing companies after certain chapters of this book, which is quite flattering, but also made possible the preparation of the document throughout the past years. I am very grateful for the uncommon support and patience of my parents, Bob and Elaine Maxwell. Special thanks is extended to Joyce Oliver of Oliver Music in Edmonton, for inspiring a great love of musical scores since my childhood.

All have, in some way, contributed to a foundation vital for climbing the steps of Parnassus. Robert Schumann once wisely declared that nothing becomes of an art without enthusiasm. In this case, how right he was.

PART I

HISTORICAL SURVEY

INTRODUCTION

The purpose of this historical survey is to trace the development of music for three or more pianists, beginning with three multiple harpsichord concertos of Johann Sebastian Bach, *c.* 1730, and the *"Lodron" concerto, K. 242* by Wolfgang Amadeus Mozart. The nineteenth and twentieth centuries produced a considerable volume of significant works for three and more pianists, with or without other acoustic instruments and/or singers.

There are a number of reasons for the largely twentieth-century attention and attraction to original team piano repertoire for three or more players. The instruments used before Cristofori's invention of the *Gravecembalo col piano e forte,* instruments such as the virginal, spinet, harpsichord and clavichord, were too limited in size and compass to accommodate two or more players comfortably. For example, the keyboard of a sixteenth-century virginal measured approximately two feet from end to end, so two performers would have been uncomfortable playing side by side. In early times, the necessary intimacy of the performers' bodies had been thought indecorous by some, and the voluminous clothing of the period had also been a deterrent.[1] The tone of the early keyboard instruments was too thin to benefit appreciably from increasing the number of players. Even two players could hardly have increased the dynamic level to any perceptible extent. Nevertheless, the gradual extension of the range, dimension and sonic capacity of these instruments, especially with the added resonance of the damper pedal that activated more overtones, created the possibility for increased sonorities with the addition of more pianists. The increased appetite for larger instrumental forces in the nineteenth century encouraged the rise of team piano repertoire--for instance, in one essay Berlioz proposed an orchestra of 465 players that included 30 pianos. Also, the growth of the publishing industry, the rise of a wealthy and professional merchant class and the rapid development, deployment and availability of the fortepiano and pianoforte encouraged the rise of team piano repertoire from ca. 1775.

---

[1]   Don Michael Randel, ed. "Piano duet," *The New Harvard Dictionary of Music* (Cambridge, Mass.: The Belknap Press of Harvard University Press, 1986):636.

By the mid-1800s, Broadwood was making about 2,300 pianos per year, Collard 1,500, France approximately a third of the entire English total, and Vienna had 108 piano makers alone.

> . . . The piano was so firmly entrenched in amateur musical life that chamber music had drifted out of the home and was becoming the preserve of ensembles of professional players like the Joachim Quartet . . .[2]

With this rapid development and growth came virtuoso performers: Kalkbrenner, Liszt, Czerny, Moscheles, Smetana, Gottschalk, Glazunov and Rachmaninov, to name but a few. And with these brilliant players came occasions and opportunities to compose for varying teams of keyboard performers. Under certain circumstances, for particular occasions and when the conditions for the availability of multiple pianos and pianists were favorable, the composer/performers collaborated with colleagues, acquaintances, friends, family and pupils in the performance of music for three or more pianists. Occasionally legions of pianists were enlisted in the multiple piano cause for charity events or spectacles.

Any pianists who have performed both duets and music for two pianos will appreciate the difference in character, musical style, and public presentation between the two media. With the duet repertoire the close proximity of the performers at the same instrument leads to an intimate atmosphere and interplay, while the repertoire for two players at two pianos permits a greater musical independence, accompanied by increased physical and technical freedom. Naturally the differences between duets and duos are reflected in the compositions written for them. While duets generally lean toward an intimate chamber music style (with exceptions like Schubert's *Grand Duo* and *Fantasy in F Minor*), two-piano literature tends toward greater technical and musical complexities. Of course the differences between music for two pianists and music for three or more pianists are obvious. The latter, in general, is more orchestral and virtuosic sounding because of the added pianos and players.

---

[2]   Henry Raynor, *Music and Society Since 1815* (New York: Barrie & Jenkins, 1976):61-62.

Nineteenth-century concerts that included multiple pianos began to take place in various capitals of Europe, such as Vienna and Paris. For instance, the first concert featuring masses of multiple pianos and pianists was organized in Vienna on April 4, 1830. Instrument availability was not a consideration.

As early as the 1830s, Mendelssohn had written to Zelter
that there were 10,000 pianos in Vienna.[3]

With all the pianos and budding virtuosi then in one city, it was only a matter of time until someone decided to organize a multiple-piano concert.

In Paris on Sunday, February 26, 1832, Friedrich Kalkbrenner--one of the foremost pianists and pedagogues in Europe at that time, who also was a part owner of the famous Pleyel piano company--arranged a debut recital at the Salons Pleyel for Chopin. One of the works on the celebrated program was Kalkbrenner's *Introduction, March and Grande Polonaise for six pianos*, performed by Chopin, Hiller, George Osborne, Albert Sowinski, Camille-Marie Stamaty and Kalkbrenner himself.[4]

Franz Liszt and Felix Mendelssohn sat in the front row and
applauded the loudest.[5]

Multiple piano concerts spread, and began to be organized in Canada as well as the United States by the 1850s. Mass piano performances have taken place throughout Canada's comparatively brief musical history, particularly in Toronto. In *A History of Music in Canada*, Helmut Kallmann makes a passing reference to a Toronto monster concert in the 1850s; arrangements included Rossini's *Overture to La gazza ladra* for six pianists and Mendelssohn's *Overture to A*

---

[3]   Henry Raynor, *Music and Society*:62.

[4]   William Atwood, *G. Frideryk Chopin: Pianist From Warsaw* (New York: Columbia University Press, 1987):n.p.

[5]   Tom Prideaux, *Frédéric Chopin* (New York: Time-Life Records, 1976):11.

Midsummer Night's Dream for four pianists.[6] Formed in 1926, a group called the Five Piano Ensemble[7] regularly presented team piano programs. In 1931, the Torontonian Mona Bates assembled her leading students to create and sustain her Ten-Piano Ensemble. They successfully raised money for financially deprived individuals, and later contributed towards the war effort in the 1940s. The Royal Conservatory of Music in Toronto has presented its finest students in well-received monster concerts in Massey Hall from 1941 to 1990.[8] In Saskatoon, Saskatchewan, on May 9, 1928, the Lyell Gustin Piano Studios organized a four-piano recital. Evelyn Eby, Millicent Lusk, Alma Brock-Smith and Reginald Bedford performed pieces by J.S. Bach, Chopin, Saint-Saëns and Tchaikovsky.

Since 1945, numerous professional four-piano ensembles have emerged on the American concert circuit. A list of four-piano groups[9] includes the Original Piano Quartet/First Piano Quartet and the American Piano Quartet.[10] Since 1989, this writer's four piano

---

6   Helmut Kallmann, *A History of Music in Canada 1534-1914* (Toronto: University of Toronto Press, 1987):109.

7   The members of the Five Piano Ensemble of Toronto were Albert Guerrero, Viggio Kihl, Ernest Seit, Norah de Kresz and Reginald Stewart.

8   In 1941, 1943, 1958, 1980 and 1990, Massey Hall in Toronto, Ontario, Canada, has been the venue for monster concerts by staff and students of Toronto's Royal Conservatory of Music. Eugene List, an adamant exponent, performer and organizer of monster concerts, was a guest at the Massey Hall Monster Concert on October 31, 1980. William Shookoff (who has made one of the few existing monster concert recordings) directed the Royal Conservatory's "Awakening of the Monster" Concerts on October 28 and 29, 1990.

9   Recordings of these three, four-piano groups are listed in the discography.

10   Members of the Original Piano Quartet were pianists Adam Garner, Frank Mittler, Edward Edson and William Gunther. In the later First Piano Quartet, Glauco D'Attili replaced William Gunther while

group, PIANoRAMA, has been stimulated and enriched by the proliferation of the available multiple piano literature. Numerous performance activities have fostered musical discoveries as well as developed keyboard musicianship. "Through the group setting musical growth can flourish to new heights."[11]

The following statements by Maurice Hinson (*Music For More Than One Piano*) on "synergism" sums up the multiple piano experience:

> The sense of *synergism* that comes to a player in a multi-piano team is a special feeling. It is similar to what orchestral musicians may experience when they hear the instrumental drama taking place around them. (Webster's defines *synergism* as 'cooperative action of discrete agencies such that the total effect is greater than the sum of the . . .effects taken independently.' In other words, the whole is greater than the sum of the parts.) Almost all music can be performed by twenty [and more] fingers. In fact, the natural tendencies of multi-piano playing make it a symphonic medium.[12]

All these factors have led to a flourishing repertoire of music for three or more pianists, as demonstrated by the accompanying catalogue. This essay is primarily a survey of the repertoire written expressly for the multi-piano medium involving three or more players. The study aims at providing a historical perspective on noteworthy original compositions. A number of minor composers who have contributed interesting compositions will be considered alongside masters like Stravinsky, Dallapiccola and Cage. Little attention will be

---

Adam Garner, Frank Mittler and Edward Edson remained. The American Piano Quartet's members are Paul Pollei, Mack Wilberg, Jeffrey Shumway and Del Parkinson, and have been active performing and publishing multiple piano scores since the 1980s.

[11]   David A. Karp, "Teaching Musicianship Through Piano Ensemble," *Clavier* (May-June 1982):31.

[12]   Maurice Hinson, *Music For More Than One Piano* (Bloomington, Indiana: Indiana University Press, 1983):ix.

given to transcriptions or arrangements for three or more pianists of
works written for other media, and no attention will be given to salon
works. Sometimes exceptions will be made for transcriptions or
arrangements that are of special interest, such as Bach's multiple
keyboard concertos and Glazunov's *La mer*, but these are clearly
special cases.

"In this age of musical rediscovery when even the most trifling
composers of the Baroque era have been able to attain a respectable
place in the Schwann catalogue of recorded music, perhaps the time has
come at last to take another look at some of the neglected masterpieces
. . . . "[13]

13   Ernest Lubin, *The Piano Duet: A Guide for Pianists* (New York:
Da Capo Press, 1976):1.

Chapter 1. THE MULTIPLE KEYBOARD CONCERTOS

Johann Sebastian Bach is regarded as the first major composer of keyboard concertos, and the first to exploit multiple keyboards as a performance ensemble. Among his fourteen harpsichord concertos are three for three and four keyboards: the *Concerto in D Minor for Three Harpsichords, BWV 1063*[14]; the *Concerto in C Major for Three Harpsichords, BWV 1064*[15]; and the *Concerto in A Minor for Four Harpsichords, BWV 1065*. (Technically speaking, four and five harpsichord players are needed to realize these works if one includes the *basso continuo* group of instruments with the *concertino* groups.)

> Bach probably wrote his concertos for two, three and four harpsichords for the Leipzig Collegium Musicum of which he was director from 1729 to 1739.[16] More recent dating of the oldest extant manuscript source for [the Concerto in A Minor] (non-autograph, three solo parts only, Mus. ms. Bach St 378) suggests that the manuscript belongs to the (or an) original copy made in © 1730. Perhaps the concertos were made for the concerts in one of Zimmermann's public rooms; they could also have been part of the more advanced musical instruction for such pupils as the composer's two sons W.F. Bach and C.P.E. Bach, as the more-or-less contemporary compilations of the Six Sonatas for organ probably were.[17]

---

[14] The source is unknown; see *NBA* VII/vii, cc.

[15] Perhaps transcribed from Bach's lost *Concerto in D Major for Three Violins*, reconstructed in *NBA* VII/vii.

[16] Arnold Scherin, ed. *Johann Sebastian Bach's Concerto for 4 Harpsichords and Strings, BWV 1065* (London: Ernst Eulenburg Ltd., 1933):iii.

[17] Peter Williams, ed. *Johann Sebastian Bach: Concerto for 4 Harpsichords and Strings, BWV 1065* (London: Ernst Eulenburg Ltd., 1980):iii.

Around 1730, Bach was in charge of the Telemann Society, one of whose purposes was to introduce the New Collegium Musicum of Leipzig University to new music. Bach and his two elder sons, Wilhelm Friedemann and Carl Philipp Emanuel, performed new solo and ensemble works for the Telemann Society's concerts and chamber music *soirées*. There were also many accomplished students who performed, and it was easier at that time to assemble numerous keyboards in one room due to the lighter physical dimensions of the harpsichord.

The harpsichord perhaps no longer completely satisfied the requirements of fine musicians of the baroque, despite the many technical innovations made to it. By using numerous combinations of harpsichords for the *concertino* group in Bach's multiple keyboard concertos *BWV 1063, 1064* and *1065* (not to mention the three contemporaneous concertos for two harpsichords, *BWV 1060, 1061* and *1062*), Bach achieved rich and precedent-setting contrapuntal complexities, sonorities and effects. The movements of the keyboard concertos follow the standard scheme adapted by Vivaldi and other masters of the Italian violin school: a slow movement is framed by two *allegros*. The quick movements are in *ritornello* form in which the solo instrumental groups (concertino) contrast with an orchestral ensemble. The second movement is a richly harmonized adaptation of an old leisurely and lilting dance form.

The origins of the *Concerto in D Minor for Three Harpsichords and Strings, BWV 1063* are still mysterious and vague. There is no autograph score of this work in existence. "Be this as it may, it numbers among Bach's most beautiful creations, according to Albert Schweitzer who can hardly be suspected of indulgence for Bach's works of this type."[18] Although all Bach's multiple keyboard concertos offer the soloists the opportunity to express themselves in a variety of combinations, the *Concerto in D Minor* gives more attention to the first harpsichord, particularly in the first two movements. Perhaps J.S. Bach himself performed this virtuoso part, replete with thirty-second note figurations (in all movements), cadential passages and solo episodes (measures 139-166 in the third movement) that are

---

[18]   Jacqueline Malaurent, *J.S. Bach: The Concertos for 3 & 4 Claviers* (liner notes for Capitol Records, Inc., 1981).

reminiscent of the *Fifth Brandenburg*. In the brilliant *allegro* finale, each member of the *concertino* emerges as equal partners; each of the three soloists has a passage of *basso continuo* accompanying the florid display. *Tutti* passages, particularly in the opening and close of the first movement *Allegro* and throughout the second movement *Alla Siciliana* are played by the *concertino* in unison. Obviously this unconventional "doubling" of parts increases the dynamic level in these moments. This textural device, orchestral in nature, becomes popular for the production of larger sonorities in future multiple keyboard ensembles. Furthermore, the alternation of unison and polyphonic textures creates interest. Textural contrast and heightened awareness of the independence of instruments is achieved with the ever-changing conversational character of the solo instruments, alternatively performing in unison (with the strings) and a complex fabric of contrapuntal thought.

The *C Major Concerto for Three Harpsichords* is an imposing, "majestic and forceful work of great dignity."[19] From the onset, greater independence is given to the string orchestra, and Bach generally grants no special attention to the first harpsichordist (aside from the thirty-second note figurations). Instead of opening in unison with the *concertino*, as in the *D Minor Concerto*, the *ripieno* opens more contrapuntally independent and assertive. The equality of the harpsichord writing is seen throughout, particularly with passages written in imitative counterpoint and the episodes in the final movement.

Albert Schweitzer wrote, in describing Bach's two concertos for three harpsichords, "The tonal and rhythmical effects that Bach has achieved with three claviers are indescribable. At every hearing of these works we stand amazed before the mystery of so incredible a power of invention and combination."[20]

The *Concerto in A Minor for Four Harpsichords* is the only one of this instrumental combination in Bach's *oeuvre*. It is derived

---

[19]   Karl Geiringer, *Johann Sebastian Bach: Culmination of an Era* (New York: Oxford University Press, 1966):327.

[20]   Albert Schweitzer, *J.S. Bach* (Vol. 1. London: A. & C. Black, Ltd., 1923):415.

from Antonio Vivaldi's *Four Violin Concerto in B Minor, No. 10* from
Op. 3, which was originally entitled *L'Estro Armonico Concerti
Consacrati All' Altezza Reale Di Ferdinando III Gran Prencipe di
Toscana Da Antonio Vivaldi . . . , Opera Terza Libro Primo. A.
Amsterdam. Aux depens d'Estienne Roger Marchand Librairie . . . No.
50.* Bach admired the Venetian master's concertos and paid tribute to
him by transcribing a number of his compositions. *BWV 1065* "is the
grandest and most exciting of all J.S. Bach's Vivaldi transcriptions."[21]

Originally, the seventeenth century witnessed the rise of the
instrumental concerto in Italy,[22] particularly with the success and
popularity of the approximately five hundred concertos of Vivaldi. As
part of his learning process, Bach frequently transcribed works of other
composers (as well as his own) for other media. A few concertos of
Vivaldi served as his compositional models.

> In 1711, Estienne Roger, the Amsterdam publisher,
> brought out what was to become the most influential music
> publication of the first half of the eighteenth century;
> Vivaldi's **L'estro armonico, Op. 3**, dedicated to
> Ferdinand, Grand Prince of Tuscany . . . The change to
> the Roger firm from local publishers . . . reflected not only
> the printing from type still normally used in Italy (a
> superiority acknowledged in Vivaldi's preface of **L'estro
> armonico**), but also the enormous growth in demand for
> the latest Italian music in northern Europe. Nowhere was
> the enthusiasm for Vivaldi's concertos stronger than in
> Germany.[23]

In the German city of Pommersfelden the Schönborn family
collected Vivaldi manuscripts, especially when Rudolph Franz

---

[21]   Maurice Hinson, *Music for Piano and Orchestra*
        (Bloomington,Indiana: Indiana University Press, 1981):17.

[22]   Refer to Eugene Wolf, "Concerto," *The New Harvard Dictionary of
        Music* (Cambridge, MA: The Belknap Press of Harvard University
        Press, 1986):186-191.

[23]   Michael Talbot, "Antonio Vivaldi," *The New Grove Italian Baroque
        Masters* (New York: W.W. Norton and Co., Inc., 1958):277-278.

Eberwein was the family head. Rudolph and his brother Johann Philipp Franz (Provost of Würzburg Cathedral) were constantly ordering scores from Ragaznig, a Venetian merchant. On February 27, 1710, in a letter from Rudolph to Johann, he specifically asked his brother to bring back some more Vivaldi manuscripts.

> . . . Vivaldi was in the habit of selling his manuscripts, so it is not surprising that so many of them have been discovered in rather odd or remote places.[24]

The nineteenth-century Vivaldi revival was a consequence of the Bach renaissance. With the revival of Bach's music (begun chiefly by Felix Mendelssohn in 1829), the collecting of Bach's manuscripts for eventual publication became a primary concern. With this research came the initial rediscoveries of the Vivaldi-Bach concerto transcriptions. A collection (dated 1739, and entitled *XII Concerti di Vivaldi elaborati di J.S. Bach*) was discussed along with another collection entitled *Concerto del Sigre. Ant. Vivaldi accomodato per l'Organo a 2 clav. e ped. del Sigre. Giovanni Sebastian Bach*. Marc Pincherle, a Vivaldi scholar, writes:

> Initially these works were given little notice because they were considered . . . academic exercises. Eventually the transcriptions began to be respected as works of art, but it was not until the beginning of the twentieth century that Vivaldi was credited as a precursor to whom Bach owed in part his introduction to such important forms of instrumental music.[25]

The publication of *L'estro armonico* established Vivaldi's international reputation. This collection was printed in two sets of six

---

[24]   James Welch, "J.S. Bach's *Concerto in D Minor, BWV 596*, after Vivaldi," *Diapason*, Vol. 74 (May 1983):6.

[25]   Marc Pincherle, *Vivaldi, Genius of the Baroque* (Translated by C. Hatch. New York: W.W. Norton and Co., Inc., 1962):13-14.

concertos each.[26] Its title has been translated variously as *"The harmonic fancy," "rapture"* or *"a rage to harmonize."*

Experimentation in various media seems to have delighted J.S. Bach. He refined and nurtured his compositional style at this time by imitating and transcribing accessible models. During his tenure as organist and concert master in Weimar, he focused primarily on Italian music; he studied the scores of Giovanni Legrenzi, Archangelo Corelli, Tomaso Albinoni and Alessandro and Benedetto Marcello, and in 1714, copied Girolamo Frescobaldi's *Fiori musicali.* Also through the influence of his cousin Johann Gottfried Walter (1684-1748), who was a devotee of Italian music, Bach adopted the Vivaldian concerto design and familiarized himself with the genre by transcribing the following concertos by Vivaldi:

| Bach Transcriptions | | | | | | Vivaldi Originals | | | |
BWV	Key	Instrumentation	Op. and Rinaldi	Fanna	Tomo	Pincherle	Ryom	Key	Concertino
593	a	organ	Op. 3, No. 8	F.I, 177	413	2	RV522	a	2 violins
594	C	organ	Op. 7/ii, No. 5	F.I, 206	452	151i	RV208	D	1 violin
596	d	organ	Op. 3, No. 11	F.IV, 11	416	250	RV565	d	2 violins
972	D	harpsichord	Op. 3, No. 9	F.I, 178	414	147	RV230	D	1 violin
973	G	harpsichord	Op. 7/ii, No. 2	F.I, 203	449	102	RV299	G	1 violin
975	g	harpsichord	Op. 4, No. 6	F.I, 185	423	328	RV316	g	1 violin
976	C	harpsichord	Op. 3, No. 12	F.I, 179	417	240	RV265	E	1 violin
978	F	harpsichord	Op. 3, No. 3	F.I, 173	408	96	RV310	G	1 violin
980	G	harpsichord	Op. 4, No.1	F.I, 180	418	327i	RV381	b♭	1 violin
1065	a	4 harpsichords and orchestra	Op. 3, No. 10	F.IV, 10	415	148	RV580	b	4 violins

Illustration 1.   J.S. Bach's transcriptions of some Vivaldi compositions.[27]

---

[26]   Marc Pincherle, *Vivaldi, Genius of the Baroque*:65.

[27]   Grant Maxwell, "The *Concerto in D Minor, Op. 3, No. 11*: Transpired by Vivaldi; Transcribed by Bach." Term Paper, Music 606, University of Alberta (April 21, 1987):4.

"There is probably no better tribute to the vitality of Vivaldi's music than the fact that it found favor with J.S. Bach."[28] Bach's compositions for keyboard, and his acquaintance with works such as Vivaldi's concertos proved to be an experience which shaped his whole creative output.[29] Alan Kendall, a Vivaldi scholar, states that:

> J.S. Bach was not consciously trying to improve the Vivaldi concertos, let alone pass them off as his own work. He was simply retaining them for his own reference in an age when copying or outright purchase were the only means available to him, and he was certainly not interested in what posterity might think of his choice, let alone his contemporaries. Vivaldi's published music was only a small fraction of what he actually wrote, and circulating in northern Italy, in Bohemia and around Dresden and even as far afield as Sweden, were many manuscripts acquired by those who admired Vivaldi's music . . . Bach never went to Italy, and so these works were in some way models. He not only transcribed, but he also imitated.[30]

An analysis of *BWV 1065* requires a comparison of the original Vivaldi *Op. 3, No. 10*, with Bach's adaptation to four harpsichords and strings: it is not a literal transcription. The following is a summation of the most notable alterations Bach made to Vivaldi's original concerto. He transposed from b minor to a minor in order to make it technically more suitable for the harpsichords--with the harpsichord range in mind (contra F to F ||||). As in *BWV 1063*, the first harpsichord is given predominance in the first two movements, but all *soli* parts are equalized in the third movement. For the *Largo*, Bach wrote out in full what Vivaldi suggested in baroque musical shorthand, particularly in the middle section. Widely spaced intervals and leaps in the violin parts are removed and rewritten as idiomatic arpeggiated chords. Due to the harpsichord's inability to sustain tones, the longer

---

28   Welch, "J.S. Bach's *Concerto in D Minor, BWV 596*, after Vivaldi,": 6.

29   Geiringer, *Johann Sebastian Bach: Culmination of an Era*:262-263.

30   Alan Kendall, *Vivaldi* (London: Chappell and Co., 1978):104.

violin notes are converted into trills in all Bach's keyboard parts. Here and there he further enhanced Vivaldi's polyphony, ornamenting the linear shape and introducing occasional contrapuntal and rhythmical details. For the sake of converting solo violin lines into two-stave harpsichord parts, naturally counterpoint was added. Bach created a richer contrapuntal texture and sonority by enriching Vivaldi's harmonies. At times, in Vivaldi's *Stile concitato*, fast repeated notes are recomposed by Bach as arpeggiated figures--masterfully adapting the violin writing for harpsichord.

Overall Bach avoided interference with the score, but also made changes in which his taste differed from Vivaldi. For example, the first three beats of the third from last measure are filled in with sixteenth notes in the string parts.

Bach was perhaps primarily concerned with making the work readily performable on four harpsichords, rather than creating a work of new character. Even though Vivaldi originally conceived the *Op. 3, No. 10*, for string, *concertino* and *ripieno*, Bach effectively arranged this composition for four harpsichords and maintained much of its character in the transcribing process. This is perhaps evident in the respect for the character of Vivaldi's themes, the tripartite design of the *largo* and the powerfully stated rhythmic scheme. Although this transcription might have been used for Bach's own compositional, structural or stylistic instruction, it most certainly was used as entertainment. It is a testimony to Bach's great interest in the Italian concerto and his ability to transcribe a fresco of contrasts transpired by another culminating figure of baroque music.

The cultivation of the duet literature[31] and pioneering

---

[31]   Dr. Charles Burney (1726-1814), musical historian and composer, claimed that his two published sets of *Four Sonatas or duets for two performers on one pianoforte or harpsichord* (London: R. Bremmer, 1777) were the first that have appeared in print, of this kind.

At about the same time, Franz Joseph Haydn (1732-1809) composed his two duets: the *Partita in F Major* (in two movements) and *The Master and Scholar [or the Pupil]* (a set of variations).

Johann Christian Bach (1735-1782) published five, two-movement duets as part of three volumes of instrumental pieces suitable for playing in the home (*No. 1: Op. 15;*

additions to the multiple keyboard literature were contributed by renowned composer-performers. Shortly after his twentieth birthday, Wolfgang Amadeus Mozart, arguably the greatest of all duet composers, wrote the *Concerto* No. 7 in F Major *Lodron, K. 242,* for three fortepianos.[32]

The *Concerto, K. 242,* was commissioned by one of Mozart's patrons and pupils--the Countess Maria Antonia Lodron, *née* Countess d'Arco, a prominent personality in Salzburg and the sister of Mozart's employer, Count-Archbishop Hieronymous von Colloredo.[33] Maria Lodron's husband had a resident position at the Salzburg court. It was written for performances by the Countess[34] and her two daughters, the

---

Nos. 2 and 3: Op. 18; and Nos. 4 and 5 without opus number).

Along with writing sixty-two pianoforte sonatas, Muzio Clementi (1752-1832) wrote 7 duets (*Op. 3, Nos. 1-3; Op. 6, No. 4; Op. 7, Nos. 5 and 6, and Op. 14, No. 7*) and [*Trois*] *rondeaux agréables, Op. 41.*

Ludwig van Beethoven (1770-1827) composed five duets (WoO 67; Op. 6; WoO 74; Op. 45; and Op. 134, an arrangement of Op. 133--*Grosse Fugue*).

[32] The autograph manuscript of *K. 242,* is in the Prussian National Library, West Berlin. Facsimiles of this autograph are found in:

   a) Ludwig Schiedermain, *W.A. Mozarts Handschif in zeitlich geordneten Nachbildungen,* (Bückegurg: Leipzig, 1919): Tafel 22.

   b) Georg Schunemann, *Musiker-Handschrifen von Bach vis Schumann* (Berlin; Zürich, 1936): Tafel 40. It is scored for 2 oboes (2 flutes in the second movement), [bassoon ad. lib.] 2 horns and strings.

[33] On August 21, 1772, the new archbishop Count Hieronymous von Colloredo (reigned 1772 to 1801) guaranteed Mozart's post as concert master and payed him a yearly salary of 150 gulden.

[34] From about the same time, two *Divertimentos, K. 247* and *K. 287 (271b, 271H)* were written for the name day of Countess Maria Antonia Lodron (1738-1786). Her Salzburg home provided a frequent venue for private concerts.

Countesses Aloisia and Giuseppina Lodron. All three were amateur fortepianists of modest proficiency. The fact that the third fortepiano part is distinctly easier indicates that the younger daughter, Giuseppina, was the least technically accomplished musician of the family keyboard ensemble. Fortepiano I is the most involved, and Fortepiano II is assigned an important role. No record exists of the Lodrons ever having performed *K. 242* in public, although one can assume that it may have been performed for a private function or for their pleasure. The dedication reads as follows:

> Dedicated to the incomparable merit of Her Excellency the Signora Contessa Lodron and her two daughters, Countesses Aloisia and Giuseppina, by their most devoted servant Wolfgang Mozart.

Mozart's *K. 242* (the third of his original piano concertos) was composed in February of 1776, shortly after the completion of the last of his five violin concertos and the *Piano Concerto in B-Flat Major, K. 238*. It belongs to a productive period when he was actively composing works typical of the gallant, courtly style favored by the "London Bach," Johann Christian Bach, the most influential composer of Mozart's formative years. The entertaining, elegant style of *K. 242* was without doubt inspired by the gallant orchestral-chamber music style keyboard concertos of J.C. Bach. The main purpose of these compositions was to give pleasure and enjoyment to the performers and listeners.

"The idea of three pianos in one concerto makes us think at once of [J.S.] Bach and the rich contrapuntal effects he drew from this combination."[35] Mozart's *K. 242*, on the other hand, does not utilize complex polyphony; instead one sees the influence of J.C. Bach's rococo-early classical style. The music is uncomplicated, the best effects achieved with an economical amount of material. The solo keyboards continuously and alternately pass main melodic material with one another, supported at times by an unobtrusive orchestra.[36]

---

[35]   Cuthbert M. Girdlestone, *Mozart's Piano Concertos* (London: Cassel & Company, Ltd., 1958):88.

[36]   The orchestra is comprised of 2 oboes, 2 horns and four-part strings.

The concerto is in the customary three movements. The statement of attractive themes in the opening orchestral *ritornello* of the first movement *Allegro* leads to a *tutti* presentation of the opening *marziale*-like theme by all soloists and instrumentalists (at the opening of the second exposition). This unison writing recalls the opening of J.S. Bach's two concertos for three harpsichords. A contrasting phrase ensues--a lyric, thinly textured and highly contrasting motive played solo by the first fortepiano. The three fortepianists continue and develop the material as a team, constantly passing the main melodic material to one another.

The cadenzas in the first two movements are by Mozart, and feature cleverly wrought imitative writing. Accuracy in the performance of the runs in thirty-second notes could be problematic for a less than experienced team of three pianists.

The second movement is Mozart's only slow movement, aside from *K. 488*, to be marked *Adagio*. The fortepiano's inability to sustain tones influenced the writing, replete with flowing thirty-second notes in the first and second fortepiano parts. This typically florid, inspired Italianate writing was favored by many composers of the period. By balancing the registral placement of the three soloists and by carefully monitoring the dynamic levels and scoring, Mozart avoided an unneeded thickness of texture (inappropriate for the *gallant* mood of this movement). Mozart's solution was the use of *con sordino* (muted) strings throughout this movement. "With the interests of three soloists to consider, perhaps it was inevitable that Mozart made the musical argument largely their concern, leaving the orchestra for long periods in the role of accompanist."[37]

Mozart finds many assets in the combination of three fortepianos, and makes special use of echo effects, shared passage work, antiphonal effects and the distribution of thematic, motivic and accompanimental material among the three soloists. For these reasons, this movement remains unprecedented and unrivalled, in this writer's assessment, in the music for three or more pianists. "Throughout the movement the chromaticisms and appoggiaturas are very characteristic of Mozart's maturest style and decorative passages are never

---

[37]   Roger Hellyer, *Mozart: Wind Concertos/Early Piano concertos* (Liner notes. Alexandria, Virginia: Time-Life Records, 1981):22.

mechanical. The return of the first theme, in particular, is beautifully contrived."[38]

The third movement, marked *Rondeau: Tempo di Menuetto* in 3/4 meter, was influenced by the many minuet finales of the period. As with the finale of the *Flute Concerto in G Major, K. 313*, this is correctly described as a sonata rondo (with the d minor central developmental section imbued with some *Sturm und Drang* elements). The first and second fortepiano parts contain three of Mozart's *Eingänge*[39]; the third *Eingang* is for both the first and second fortepianists. The elegant and engaging rondo theme appears four times, always performed by the soloists and answered by an orchestral *tutti*. There are subtle changes at each repetition, creating a variety of presentation: the first time heard on two fortepianos; the second and third times on only one fortepiano, but with alterations in the harmonic and rhythmic writing, and finally presented by all three soloists delicately accompanied by *pizzicato* strings. Once again, Mozart avoids a thickness of texture by considering a careful balance of sonority.

The premiere performance took place in Augsburg on October 22, 1777, when Mozart and his mother stopped en route from Munich to Mannheim and Paris. The distribution of the parts for the soloists was thus: fortepiano I played by Johann Michael Demmler, who was active as a fortepianist and composer in Augsburg where, from 1774, he was also Cathedral organist (Mozart, in fact, supported his candidature for the organist's post at Salzburg Cathedral in 1778); fortepiano II by Mozart; fortepiano III played by Johann Andreas Stein, the fortepiano manufacturer, whose instruments Mozart praised in letters to his father, Leopold, dated October 14 and 17, 1777.

The concert was a fair success, even though, according to Mozart, the Augsburg orchestra was of poor quality, and Demmler continually disrupted rehearsals by cursing and laughing. On October 28, 1777, the concert was reviewed in the *Augsburgische Staats-und Gelehrten Zeitung*, a portion of which reads:

---

[38]   Philip Radcliffe, *Mozart's Piano Concertos* (London: BBC Music Guides, 1978):13.

[39]   In a classical concerto, a short *cadenza*-like passage for the soloist(s) that precedes and leads into a solo section.

> Augsburg, 24 Oct. The evening of Wednesday last was
> one of the most agreeable for the local music lovers. Herr
> Chevalier Mozart, a son of the famous Salzburg musician,
> who is a native of Augsburg, gave a concert on the
> fortepiano in the hall of Count Fugger. As Herr Stein
> happened to have three instruments of the kind ready, there
> was an opportunity to include a fine concerto for three
> claviers, in which Herr Demmler, the Cathedral organist,
> and Herr Stein himself played the other two clavier parts.

Of historical interest, the other works on this all-Mozart
program included: two symphonies, a solo fortepiano concerto (*K.
238*), an improvised *Fantasy in C Minor* and an improvised *Piano
Sonata in C Major*. An additional performance of *K. 242* (without
Mozart's participation) took place in Mannheim on March 12, 1778.

A version for two fortepianos also exists, catalogued as *K.
242a*. Mozart perhaps supervised, or did himself, a transcription ©
1779, making the *"Lodron" Concerto* more readily available and
accessible for future performances. This alternate, second version was
performed by Mozart and his sister Maria Anne,[40] (Nanerl) in
Salzburg on September 3, 1780, recalling the years when brother and
sister were taken on tours of the various European courts by Leopold
Mozart.

---

[40]   H.C. Robbins Landon, ed., *The Mozart Compendium: A Guide to
Mozart's Life and Music* (London: Thames and Hudson, 1990):265.
The *Neue-Mozart Ausgabe* and *Breitkopf und Härtel* editions contain
the alternate arrangement for two fortepianos, *K. 242a*.

Chapter 2. PIONEERING PIECES

In the nineteenth century, Carl Czerny, Franz Liszt, Ignaz Moscheles, Bedřich Smetana, Alexander Glazunov and Sergei Rachmaninov, among others (refer to "Nineteenth-Century Works" in the Catalogue) experimented with various permutations and combinations of music for three or more pianists during their careers. With the rapid development of the pianoforte during the nineteenth century came the virtuoso pianists and the increasing popularity of original and transcribed repertory for team pianists.

Carl Czerny—the Viennese piano pedagogue, virtuoso pianist and writer on music—was the first to contribute a substantial number of compositions for three or more pianists.[41]

From the *New Grove Dictionary of Music and Musicians:*

> As Beethoven's student [from 1800 to 1803, who could perform all Beethoven's piano *oeuvre* from memory] and the teacher of Liszt, he occupies a unique position among 19th-century pianists, not only as a transmitter of ideas from one great master to another but also by virtue of his extraordinary productivity during the decades that embraced the most dramatic changes in technique and literature for his instrument.[42]

Nicolas Slonimsky writes about Czerny:

> [He] was unexpectedly revealed to be a musician of imaginative fancy and engaging pedantic humor, as for

---

41   According to Maurice Hinson and Eugene List, photocopies of Czerny's music can be obtained through Lotte and Helmut Riesberger at the *Gesellschaft der Musikfreunde* in Vienna. The Newberry Library in Chicago has an unusually rich collection of Czerny's music, and is perhaps the best source of his one-piano, six hand scores. The Music Division of the Library of Congress and the New York Public Library at Lincoln Center have good collections of Czerny (particularly the four-and six-hand music).

42   Alice L. Mitchell, "Carl Czerny," *New Grove Dictionary of Music and Musicians* (. . . 20 Vols. London: Macmillan, 1980), Vol. 5:38.

instance in his Brobdingnagian arrangements of Rossini's *Overture*[s] to [*Semiramide* and] *William Tell* for 16 pianists playing four-hands on eight pianos, pieces for three pianists playing 6-hands on a single keyboard instrument, etc.[43]

Czerny himself admitted that aside from a few serious works (such as the piano sonatas), most of his compositions were not substantial.[44]   Some noteworthy contemporaries such as Chopin maligned his multiple piano compositions.   When Chopin was in Vienna, he often visited Czerny and frequently performed two-piano compositions with him.[45]   Chopin wrote home:

> He is a good fellow but nothing more. He has arranged
> another overture for eight pianos and sixteen pianists, and
> seems quite happy about it.[46]

Czerny's original works for three or more pianists deserve recognition for their imaginative melodic treatment and technical brilliance.   As in the *Rondeaux brilliantes, Op. 227*, for three pianists at one piano, the equal participation of all players at all times results in an ensemble texture thicker and more virtuosic than Mozart's *K. 242*.   In these works, Czerny's concern was undoubtedly the practical training of his equally accomplished pupils through ensemble

---

[43]   Nicolas Slonimsky, *The Concise Baker's Biographical Dictionary of Musicians* (New York: Schirmer Books, 1988):274.

[44]   A work list is located in Carl Czerny, *Erinnerungen aus meinem Leben* (Baden-Baden: Valentin Koerner, 1968; 1st edition. London: Verlag Cocks & Co., c. 1860):55-76.

[45]   In 1837, even Queen Victoria performed piano duets with Czerny.

[46]   Henryk Opieński, *Chopin's Letters* (New York: Vienna House, 1971):124. (December 1, 1830, Vienna).

experience. His four-volume *Klavierschule* (Keyboard School),[47]
published in Vienna and London in 1839, incorporates suggestions for
pedagogues, including instructional piano ensemble playing in Volume
IV. In order to train and instill rhythmic sense in pupils, Czerny not
only suggested that the teacher count out loud while conducting, but
also emphasized the usefulness of four-hand music. He felt even
orchestral transcriptions for multiple players can be given to develop
musical joy and knowledge.[48] A list of his team piano works includes
the following:

> *Op. 18, Grande polonaise brilliante*, for four pianos, eight
> hands, or solo with an accompaniment for a second
> piano or both *ad. lib.* (c. 1820).
>
> *Op. 38, Première grand potpourri concertante*, for two
> pianos, six hands.
>
> *Op. 84, Deuxième grand potpourri concertante*, for two
> pianos, six hands.
>
> *Op. 212,No.? Grand potpourri brilliante et concertante*, for
> two pianos, six hands. (There are six pieces in this
> opus).

*Les pianistes associés, ou Compositions brilliantes et
concertantes pour un pianoforte à six mains.*

Op. 227, Book 1,   *Rondeaux brilliantes*, for one
                          piano, six hands (c. 1831).

Op. 228, Book 2,   *Variations brilliantes sur le thème
                          tyrolien, de l'opéra La fiancée*, for
                          one piano, six hands.

---

[47]   *Complete Theoretical and Practical Piano-Forte School, from the
       First Rudiments of Playing, to the Highest and most Refined state of
       Cultivation; with the requisite numerous Examples, newly and
       expressively composed for the Occasion, Opus 500* (London: R.
       Cocks & Company, 1839).

[48]   Maurice Hinson, "Carl Czerny Remembered (1791-1857)," *Clavier*,
       Vol. 24 (1965):18.

Op. 229, Book 3,	*Divertissement militaire,* for one piano, six hands.
Op. 230,	[*Première*] *Quatuor concertante,* for four pianos, eight hands. Also for solo or duet with orchestral or string quartet accompaniment [c. 1825]. "Some of his most effective compositions are in the genre of music for piano and orchestra."[49]
Op. 295,	*Variations brilliantes sur un thème de l'opéra, I Montechi e Capuletti [par Bellini]* for one piano, six hands.

Opp. 295, 296 and *297* combine to form *Op. 227, Nos. 1, 2* and *3* of *Les pianistes associés.*

Op 298,	*Troisième grand potpourri,* for one piano, six hands.
Op. 609,	from Part II, *La bibliothèque de pianistes: Les trois soeurs--Six rondinos,* for one piano, six hands.
Op. 689, Nos. 1 and 2,	*Deux grandes fantaisies sur l'airs de l'opéra, Norma* [by Bellini], for one piano, six hands.
Op. 741, Nos. 1-6,	*Les trois amateurs--Six fantaisies,* for one piano, six hands.
	1. *Fantaisie sur des thèmes d'opéras de Mozart*

---

[49]   Maurice Hinson, *Music for Piano and Orchestra* (Bloomington, Indiana: Indiana University Press, 1981):74-75.

	2.	*Fantaisie sur des airs écossais*
	3.	*Fantaisie sur des airs irlandais*
	4.	*Fantaisie sur des airs anglais*
	5.	*Fantaisie sur des airs d'opéras de Donizetti*
	6.	*Fantaisie sur des airs d'oratories d'Händel*
Op. 816,		*Deuxième grand quatuor concertante,* for four pianos, eight hands (see *Op. 230).*

The *Première quatuor concertante in C Major, Op. 230,* scored for four pianists at four pianos, is one of Czerny's most ambitious multiple-piano compositions. The one-movement work was written in 1825 for four Austrian, virtuoso female pianists: Frau v. Albrecht, Gräfin Julie v. Dietrichstein, Gräfin v. Lebzeltern and Frau Gräfin v. Taafe. (Gifted pianists and members of nobility lined up to study with Czerny, so he always had a large class of capable players.) The music is remarkably complex, technically difficult and highly sectionalized:

> *Introduzione: Andante maestoso*
> *Allegro moderato ma con anima (Pirata)*
> *Allegro vivo (La Muette de Portici)*
> *Andante con moto (La Muette de Portici)*
> *Allegretto (Paganini)*
> *Allegro (La Muette de Portici)*
> *Molto Allegro*
> *Allegretto con anima (Pasta)*
> *Molto Allegro seconda (Le Petit Tambour, Romance; Othello)*
> *Vivo (La Muette de Portici)*
> *Vivacissimo*
> *Presto*

The *Première quatuor concertante* incorporates quotations from contemporaneous operas: *Il Pirata (The Pirate),* an opera in two acts by Bellini; *La Muette de Portici (The Dumb Girl of Portici),* an opera in five acts by Auber; and *Othello,* an opera in three acts by Rossini.

Melodies composed for or made popular by legendary performers are also quoted: Nicolo Paganini's violin *Caprice No. 2, "La Campanella";* and fragments of arias once sung by the legendary Italian soprano Giuditta Pasta (1797-1865).

The four scores are thickly textured and filled with pyrotechnical display. Czerny included almost every possible technical and musical demand in all parts: sixty-fourth note runs and arpeggios marked *fortissimo*; thirty-second note staccato broken octaves and repeated notes; fast runs and arpeggios doubled in octaves; triple-forte orchestral tremolos and dotted-rhythm chordal sonorities; extreme contrasts in dynamic and expression marks; registral shifts and leaps, exploiting the entire range of the four keyboards; fast tempos; difficult *fioratura* cadenza-like ornamentation; double-third glissandos; swiftly changing textures and moods--brilliant technical display passages alternating with Italianate lyrical ones. Needless to say, Czerny's *Op. 230* requires the endurance and ultimate ensemble prowess of four equally skillful piano virtuosos.

The premiere performance given by four ladies must have made an overwhelming impression on the Viennese audiences. It is perhaps the most complex score for multiple pianos from the nineteenth century. According to Czerny:

> It is quite natural for a large and therefore mixed audience
> to be surprised by something extraordinary, and the surest,
> in fact only means of achieving this is--absolute bravura
> combined with good taste.[50]

Chopin labelled Czerny "Vienna's oracle in the manufacture of musical taste."[51] Czerny's extensive experience in proof reading, transcribing and arranging scores from orchestral literature came from his association with Beethoven. By 1802, he had copied several Haydn and Mozart symphonies, Beethoven's *First* and *Second Symphonies* and the *C Major Piano Concerto*. His *oeuvre* contains one-piano, six-hand

---

[50]   Grete Wehmeyer, *Carl Czerny: Absolute bravura combined with good taste* (Liner notes. New York: Sony Music Entertainment, Inc. SK 45936, 1991):4.

[51]   Henryk Opieński, *Chopin's Letters*:142. (May 28, 1831, Vienna).

arrangements of celebrated compositions by Handel (the *Hallelujah Chorus* from the *Messiah*), Thomas Arne (*Rule Britannia*) and various overtures and folk songs.

All the above works attest to the broad musical spectrum of his interests and activities involving one, two or more pianos. They were inspired by the generous quantity of fine pianistic talent he had at his disposal. Czerny's fine reputation as a pedagogue allowed him to be highly selective. He attracted an abundant array of the most gifted and brilliant pianoforte students of the time. He often taught up to ten hours a day, and spent the remaining hours writing with exceptional speed and facility. According to Ernest Lubin:

> [Czerny's] pioneering experiments in writing for six hands at one piano, which include [the] set of six excellent and somewhat extended pieces published under the general title of *Les pianistes associés*, [demonstrates that he] handled this novel medium very cleverly, giving each of the players his own chance to shine, and making the very most of the opportunities for virtuosity in this extremely limited medium. Although it is not easy to be serious about the thought of three players crowded together at one piano, it is tempting to imagine [how] three virtuosi--let us say Horowitz, Rubinstein and Serkin--might [have performed] these pieces.. . . [52]

The areas of music pedagogy (the studies) and music for the concert hall reveal two sides of Czerny. His didactic works helped to develop his style; his works for concert audiences, actually greater in number than the etudes, reveal a composer

> . . . whose melodic delight is astounding. Czerny's themes are like arias reminding us that he listened to many works by Rossini and Donizetti . . . unfortunately fail[ing] to become renowned . . . , even forgotten.[53]

---

[52] Ernest Lubin, *The Piano Duet: A Guide for Pianists* (New York: Da Capo, 1976):33.

[53] Grete Wehmeyer, *Carl Czerny: Absolute bravura combined with good taste*:4-5.

Carl Czerny made important contributions to the repertoire for three or more pianists. It is unfortunate that he is most often regarded as a composer only of vacant and inconsequential etudes.

Franz Liszt acknowledged that his pianistic success was, to a large extent, the result of Czerny's wise and prudent pedagogical guidance. Liszt often performed and praised Czerny's *Sonata No. 1 in A-flat Major, Op. 7* (1810), and dedicated his twelve *Transcendental Etudes* to him.

Liszt was aware of the possibilities of multiple pianos and pianists and occasionally took a subordinate role in performance. He performed two-piano music and works for three or more pianists with almost every accomplished pianist of his day. For example, in Paris on March 22, 1829, at a Pape *soirée musicale*, he participated in a three-piano, twelve-hand arrangement of Mozart's *Overture* to *Die Zauberflöte*; in Geneva, on April 6, 1836, at a *Salle du Casino soirée*, he performed Czerny's *Potpourri brilliante, pour six mains et deux pianos, sur des thèmes de Mozart et de Beethoven*, with pianists Hermann Cohen and Joseph Schad (a professor at the Conservatory); and in Milan on February 18, 1838, in La Scala's *Sala de Ridotto*, he once again performed in the *Die Zauberflöte Overture* arrangement, this time with Ferdinand Hiller, Johann Peter Pixis, Schoberlechner, Origgi and Pedronic. *La Moda*, March 12, 1838, reported that the "wonderful" performance of the Mozart overture was encored; Giacchino Rossini, who was in the audience, paid tribute to the performance with the loudest applause.

Liszt characteristically arranged and revised other composers' compositions as well as his own throughout his career. Ever the innovator, he arranged two marches for the unusual combination of one piano, eight hands: the Tscherkessenmarsch (March of the Chernomor) from Glinka's Russlan und Ludmilla in 1843; the Bülow-Marsch in 1884.

Prior to the creation of modern Czechoslovakia in 1918, and until recently, "Czech music has manifested the divergent traditions of the nation's three principal regions, the former Hapsburg territories of

Bohemia, Moravia and Slovakia. "[54] Until after World War II, Bohemia
and Moravia were the centre of Czech art music.

When the patronage system ended in Czechoslovakia in the late
1700s, many native sons emigrated elsewhere to study composition.
Ignaz Moscheles was one such composer who was also an illustrious
pianist and talented improviser. After intensive study of the keyboard
works of J.S. Bach, Mozart and Clementi,[55] he left for Vienna to study
with Johann Georg Albrechtsberger and Antonio Salieri. Among
Moscheles's best compositions are his piano sonatas for duet. His
Grande Sonata, Op. 47, was performed with Chopin before the
Flemish royal family in Paris in 1834. He left almost as many works
for piano duet as for piano solo in his copious output. Moscheles was
also fond of the two-piano medium, and first made his reputation as a
composer of his two piano *Hommage à Händel*.

The *Grand duo [concertante], Les contrastes, Op. 115*, was
originally intended as a duet, and later arranged by Moscheles for eight
hands at two pianos. It was likely composed in England, *c.* 1845, a
year prior to his appointment as principal professor of piano at the
Leipzig Conservatory by Felix Mendelssohn-Bartholdy, who respected
Moscheles's talent. Mendelssohn was a pupil, duo-piano partner and
close colleague of Moscheles. While in London, prior to the Leipzig
appointment, the Moscheles family was often host to Mendelssohn.
The Moscheles-Mendelssohn duo performed Mozart's *Concerto, K. 365*
for two pianos, and Mendelssohn's *Concerto in E-Flat Major* for two
pianos at the 1835 Gewandhaus concerts in Leipzig. The *Duo
concertante, Op. 87b*, was a compositional collaboration between both
composers on a theme by Weber, the *Gypsy's March* from *Preziosa*.

Les contrastes is a virtuoso, multi-sectional composition, not
unlike the formal design of a Baroque slow-fast-slow-fast *sonata da
chiesa—Andante con moto, ma ben accentuato*; *Fuga: Allegro
maestoso*; *Andante religioso*; and *Allegretto siciliano*. Although not
nearly as difficult as Czerny's *Quatuor concertante, Op. 230*, it

---

[54]   Don Michael Randel, ed.,"Czechoslovakia," *The New Harvard
Dictionary of Music* (Cambridge, Mass.:   The Belknap Press of
Harvard University Press, 1986):219.

[55]   Moscheles studied piano at the Prague Conservatory with Dionys
Weber.

provides plenty of technical display and musical challenges for each of
the four pianists. The melding of two duet teams at two pianos creates
a hybrid form of keyboard ensemble. The best traits of both media are
exploited and juxtaposed by Moscheles: the intimacy of duet literature
and chamber music is united with the orchestral tendencies and
possibilities of composition with two pianos. Contrapuntal
resourcefulness and intricacy is united with the technical standards and
romantic style of Moscheles's day: thirty-second note runs, tremolos
(and other orchestral effects), double third runs and figures, dynamic
extremes, detailed performance directions, intricate
elaboration/ornamentation, and so forth. The work represents an
amalgamation of all the elegant romantic attributes of the period with
techniques of the baroque and classical eras.

Moscheles had an interest in music of the past, and *Les
contrastes* is a reflection of this. After he moved to London in March
1825 to teach at the Royal Academy of Music, he founded a "classical
chamber concert" series or "historical *soirée*" in which he participated
in the rediscovery of early music. In February 1837 the first program
included authentic performances on a 1771 harpsichord of works by
Domenico Scarlatti and George Frideric Handel, vocal pieces by Henry
Purcell and three *Preludes and Fugues* by J.S. Bach from the *Well-
Tempered Clavier*. He was active as an editor and specialist in the
music of Handel, Haydn, Mozart, Clementi and Weber. *Hommage à
Händel, Op. 92*, for two pianofortes, "is a tasteful parody, showing his
interest in Baroque music."[56]

It is uncertain for what occasion *Les contrastes* was written--
perhaps for students at the Academy of Music or the Gewandhaus
Concert Series. Nevertheless, like so many of his pieces, it is
representative of the classical school and also the beginning of a new
epoch.

> In all his more serious works Moscheles was capable of
> skillfully wrought musical structures, in which a classical
> balance of thematic ideas is tempered with an early

---

[56]   Jerome Roch, "Ignaz Moscheles," *New Grove Dictionary of Music
        and Musicians*, . . . Vol. 12:600.

Romantic dynamism. Pathos and chromaticism . . . are
never overplayed, and his music is never sentimental.[57]

In 1845, the year Moscheles wrote *Les contrastes*, a piece
entitled *Skladba bez nadpisu, in G Minor (B. 47, T. 26)*[58] for two
pianos, eight hands,[59] was written by Bedřich Smetana—a noteworthy
spokesman of the Slavic spirit and Bohemian nationalism.

After an unsuccessful attempt to launch a solo piano career in
1848, Smetana needed to find some way to augment a meagre income.
After dedicating his *Six morceaux caractéristiques, Op. 1*, to Liszt,
Smetana asked him for some financial assistance for the establishment
of a music conservatory in Prague. Liszt complied with the request.
Two months after the June 11 Prague Revolution, Smetana opened his
Piano Institute on August 8, 1848.

The Piano Institute was successful and popular. A year later,
in 1849, he became financially secure enough to wed Kateřina Hradec,
an adequate pianist for whom Smetana wrote character pieces, and with
whom he played duets. It was also in 1849 when Smetana directed his
energies to composition and arrangement of pieces for the Institute.
Student concerts won local acclaim. The journal *Cecilia* declared them
an essential part of Prague's musical life, and they were apparently
worthy of praise for their innovative and unconventional programming.
As Smetana's class enrollment increased, so did the musical standard;
and so as to involve as many students as possible in the concerts, he
wrote several arrangements of celebrated orchestral scores for two to
four pianos. He commenced with eight-handed versions of famous
overtures, Beethoven's *Fideleo,* and *Coriolan* and Mendelssohn's
Fingal's Cave. Smetana followed these with Weber's *Jubel-Ouverture*
and Schumann's *Canonic Studies.* As his pianistic ensemble expanded,

---

[57]   Jerome Roch, "Ignaz Moscheles," *New Grove Dictionary of Music and Musicians,* . . . Vol. 12:600.

[58]   With regard to the cataloguing of Smetana's compositions, the "B" numbers represent the 1973 Fantišek Bartoš listing, and the "T" numbers represent the 1893 K. Teige listing.

[59]   In 1846, Smetana attempted to write a rondo for one piano, four hands; only a rough sketch of the duet exists.

he made sixteen-hand transcriptions including one of Wagner's *Prelude* to *Tannhäuser*, "which won enormous popularity."[60]

In 1849, Smetana wrote the dramatic *Sonata in One Movement, B. 70, T. 47*, for two pianos, eight hands.[61] Marked *Allegro energico* and in triple meter, it features challenging technical display (especially in the primo parts), interspersed with Slavic poetic and peasant-like sentiments, major-minor shifts of tonality and frequent irregularity of accentuation.   "Modeled on the Liszt *Sonata [in b minor]*, clever if not distinguished themes, plenty of zest."[62]

The following year, Smetana wrote an exuberant and spirited *Jugend-Rondo, B. 73, T. 57*, also for eight hands at two pianos. Subtitled *Mládi (Jugend* or *Youth)*, it was Smetana's homage to Mozart, thus its other popular subtitle: the *Mozart Rondo.* (On January 23, 1845, he wrote in his diary, "by the grace of God and with His help I shall one day be a Liszt in technique and a Mozart in composition."[63]) Marked *Allegro moderato* and in duple meter, this transparent and predominantly joyous team piano piece is imbued with vitality and Czech folk elements.

> Though in origin a *pièce d'occasion*, a by-product of the composer's work as a teacher at the Music School . . . , it mirrors in the most vivid fashion one of the sunniest periods in Smetana's troubled life, being written during the happy days that followed upon his marriage.[64]

---

[60]   Brian Large, *Smetana* (London: Ducksworth, 1970):50.

[61]   In 1851, Smetana began sketching another sonata for eight hands at two pianos, but the project was never completed.

[62]   Maurice Hinson, *Music for More Than One Piano*:186.

[63]   Quoted from the *New Grove Dictionary of Music and Musicians*, Vol. 27:392.

[64]   Georg Kuhlmann, ed., Smetana's *Sonata in One Movement* (London: C.F. Peters Corp., 1938):28.

Passionately fond of dancing himself, Smetana's *Rondo* is polka-like. Another compositional technique is featured from measures 92 to 116: an imitative, contrapuntal effect sequentially repeated with *forzato*, off-beat entrances.[65] Also in 1850, and as a way

> . . . to encourage and refresh pupils, Smetana wrote the *Well of Melody (Prelude, Capriccio and Finale)* for two pianos, eight hands . . . Though intended for home and school consumption, these [three original works for four pianists at two pianos] are raised to a level of distinction by the freshness of melodic ideas and ingenious distribution of texture.[66]

Although Smetana's catalogue includes nothing for piano duet, the aforementioned examples have the distinction of being some of the few original compositions for eight hands at two pianos.

After Alexander Glazunov's studies with Nicolai Rimsky-Korsakov (from 1879 to 1881), he rapidly became another one of Russia's important composers, and in the tradition of Mikhail Glinka, a forceful voice of the emerging Russian National School. Glazunov's talent attracted the attention of Mitrofan P. Belaieff, a patron of the arts, who used some of his immense fortune to promote and support the careers of promising young Russian composers, including Rimsky-Korsakov, Liadov, Borodin and Scriabin.[67] In 1885, Belaieff opened a publishing company in Leipzig, and soon arranged for publication of the young Glazunov's works. In 1889, M.P. Belaieff published Glazunov's two piano, eight hand arrangement of the single-movement programmatic symphonic poem *Fantaisie pour grand orchestre, La mer*

---

[65] Smetana used this effect earlier in his Berlioz-inspired *Overture in D Major*. He met Berlioz at an evening *soirée* of Joseph Proksch (1794-1864), his teacher, on April 10, 1846.

[66] Large, *Smetana*:50.

[67] The "Belaieff Circle," led by Glazunov, met weekly at the palatial home of M.P. Belaieff. According to Rimsky-Korsakov, the rival group—the "Balakirev Circle" or "Russian Five"—presented the more radical approach to Russian composition, whereas the "Belaieff Circle" represented the conservative approach.

in E Major, Op. 28, which is "well laid out for the instruments, sectionalized, traditional treatment of musical material."[68] The post-romantic orchestral virtuosity, evident in all parts, attests to the fact that *La mer* was originally conceived as a symphony. *La mer* is rhapsodic and programmatic in style, with the thick orchestral textures similar to Glazunov's two-piano *Fantasy in f minor, Op. 104* (1919-1920).

Glazunov heard the Russian production of Richard Wagner's *Der Ring des Nibelungen* in St. Petersburg in 1889. Wagner's progressive and revolutionary music impressed the young composer so much that he dedicated his *La mer* arrangement for eight hands at two pianos to the memory of Wagner's genius.[69] In the same year, 1889, M.P. Belaieff published another two-piano eight-hand transcription of Glazunov's symphonic poem *Fantaisie pour grand orchestre, La forêt in C-Sharp Minor, Op. 19* (1887), arranged this time by K. Tschernov. With these and other works,

> . . . he has a significant place in Russian music in that he
> reconciled Russianism and Europeanism. He absorbed
> Balakirev's nationalism, Rimsky-Korsakov's orchestral
> virtuosity, Tchaikovsky's lyricism, Borodin's epic grandeur
> and Taneyev's contrapuntal skill.[70]

In 1890 and 1891, the Russian composer and pianist Sergei Rachmaninov wrote two little pieces for six hands at one piano: a charming *Valse,* composed in Ivanovka from August 15 to August 27, 1890; and a nostalgic *Romance,* written in Moscow from September 20 to October 2, 1891. Both pieces were dedicated to Natalya, Lyudmila and Vera Skalon. The *Valse* was written while on a summer sojourn

---

68   Maurice Hinson, *Music for More Than One Piano*:72.

69   M.P. Belaieff had taken Glazunov on a trip to Weimar, where he met Franz Liszt, Wagner's father-in-law.

70   Stanley Sadie, "Alexander Glazunov," *The Norton/Grove Concise Encyclopedia of Music,* (New York; London: W.W. Norton & Co., 1988):294.

at Ivanovka when he was a fifth-year student at the Moscow Conservatory.

Ivanovka was a political estate owned by Rachmaninov's father's sister Varva Satina,[71] that comfortably accommodated the many guests who annually visited during the summer. In 1890, the summer guests included some distant relatives: Elizabeta Skalon and her three daughters Natalya, Lyudmila and Vera, Rachmaninov's cousins by marriage. All were passionately interested in music, and spent their time discussing and playing it with the seventeen-year-old Rachmaninov. While at Ivanovka he composed the one piano, six hand *Valse* for the three sisters to perform.[72] Rachmaninov composed another *Romance* for one piano, six hands, one week prior to the completion of the first movement of his *Symphony No. 1 in D Minor* and after finishing the two-piano *Russian Rhapsody* and the *Piano Concerto No. 1, Op. 1.* The introduction (measures 1 to 5) was used nine years later in the opening to the second movement of the *Piano Concerto No. 2, Op. 18* (1900) (measures 5 to 12).

The *Valse* and *Romance* for three pianists display Rachmaninov's early technical resourcefulness, and reveal the melodic invention and chromatic harmonies encountered in pieces such as the *Moments musicaux, Op. 16.*

---

[71]   Rachmaninov married his first cousin, Natalia Satina (whom he always called Natasha). The opulent Satina country estate Ivanovka was their home for many years.

[72]   Geoffrey Norris, *Rachmaninov* (London: J.M. Dent & Sons, Ltd., 1976):9.

Chapter 3. THE MONSTER CONCERT

An Entertainment: Wherein Divers Practitioners of the True Art of Playing the Klavier Render Various Compositions for the Pianoforte in Tandem, in Sextuplicate, and in Sundry Other Combinations Cunningly Devised to Tax the Credibility and Assault the Sensibilities of the Assembled Multitude.[73]

So wrote a nineteenth-century writer on the monster concert ideal ("monster" in this connection meaning "large"), a tradition nearly as old as the piano itself.

These concerts were a regular feature of music-making in the nineteenth century and reflect a taste to explore the grand spectacle that gave us many of the mammoth orchestral compositions of that century.[74]

The tendency towards gigantism was popular during the nineteenth century, but not unique to it. For instance, nearly every wind player in London must have participated in the monumental ensemble used for the premiere of the *Royal Fireworks Music* by George Frideric Handel. In April 1749 the Treaty of Aix-la-Chapelle, which restored peace in Europe following the eight years of the War of the Austrian Succession, was celebrated in London with a grandiose fireworks display. The instrumental forces utilized were twenty-four oboes, twelve bassoons, one contra bassoon, nine trumpets, nine horns, three timpani and side drums. Even though Handel's *Messiah* was intended for relatively modest forces, it was given mammoth performances on occasion. For example, the 1784 memorial concert in Westminster Abbey placed emphasis on grandiosity.

Louis-Hector Berlioz was renowned for his compositions for grandiose masses of instrumentalists, intended to *épater le bourgeois*.

---

[73] "Awakening the Monster: October [27 and 28] Massey Hall Concerts Continue Multi-Piano Performance Tradition," *Music Magazine, Royal Conservatory of Music, Toronto,* Vol. 13, No. 4 (September/October 1990):30.

[74] Ibid.

His colossal presentations of the *Requiem* (1837) and the *Te Deum* (1849) featured scores of performers at the climaxes. The *Requiem* is, in the sheer number of performers requested, one of Berlioz's largest undertakings—every one of the 190 instruments is doubled in the score (with thirty-eight in the brass section alone); there is a 210-member chorus and an unprecedented use of sixteen timpani. The *Te Deum*, similarly, is a massive choral work conceived for nearly one thousand individual performers. "Colossal Babylonian" Berlioz affectionately called it when he was able to get it properly performed in Paris six years after its completion in 1855. In his important and revolutionary *Treatise on Modern Instrumentation and Orchestration* (1844) (which alone would gain immortality for the composer), Berlioz envisioned his utopian ensemble of 467 virtuoso instrumentalists. This gargantuan orchestra included thirty harps, eighteen double basses, four octobasses (thirteen feet high with three strings), sixteen French horns, five saxophones and *thirty pianofortes*.

It was Carl Czerny, Louis Moreau Gottschalk and Percy Alderidge Grainger who had the strongest impact on the direction in which the use of massed multiple pianos in concert would develop into the twentieth century.

The first documented monster concert that used massed pianos was a special charity event at the Imperial Palace in Vienna on April 4, 1830, to aid victims of a Danube flood. It involved pianists from the Viennese nobility, including two from the Esterházy family. Carl Czerny, the first recognized exponent of piano monster concerts, was commissioned to arrange Rossini's *Overture* to *Semiramide* for sixteen pianists at eight pianos for this benefit performance. The "Rossini crescendo" must have been grandly kinetic. Czerny was involved with a second Viennese multiple-pianoforte extravaganza in 1837, in which his arrangement of the *Overture* to *Guillaume Tell* by Rossini was programmed. An impressive array of talent was assembled, including some of the finest pianists of the day--Thalberg, Chopin and Liszt.

Louis Moreau Gottschalk was one of the most colorful figures in the history of music in the United States. As a professional and practicing musician he was firstly a concert pianist. Not unlike other virtuosos of the day, he wrote his own material. He became a composer who introduced novel strains to the music of his time, anticipating many future trends--creole tunes and South American rhythms, for example.

Gottschalk became an ardent champion of the gigantic festivals in the Americas. It was Berlioz, one of his composition teachers, who gave Gottschalk the idea of producing and staging monster concerts. He assisted in some of Berlioz's mammoth festival productions in Paris. Gottschalk used a generous quantity of pianos and pianists--as many as possible or available on any given occasion--and allowed a sizeable number of pianists to perform any one of his compositions.[75]

> Gottschalk industrialized single concerts as well as tours; in dozens of monster concerts throughout the Americas, he offered a performer's vision of the mass-production future. Multiple-ensemble events had long been popular in Europe, but Gottschalk's approach was distinctive; rather than assembling a team of well-known performers to support his own playing, he submerged himself in local, amateur ensembles. Managing these situations required great ingenuity . . . Gottschalk seemed determined to envelop his own virtuosity in the collective, to become one among many, to lose his identity; . . . Such radical democracy was peculiarly American; in Europe, only Berlioz, Gottschalk's friend and supporter, pursued remotely similar aims. Gottschalk was the first pop superstar, an ambivalent virtuoso whose idolization became greater the more he tried to blend. He seems to have been convinced that music, the machine age and American democracy could be reconciled in a kind of manic multiplicity. To a certain extent, he was proven correct.[76]

After a lengthy tour of France and Switzerland in 1851, he entered into a year-and-a-half residency at the Spanish court of Queen Isabella II. After being invested with knighthood, decorated with the orders of Isabella and Charles III and given the sword of the country's most revered matador, Gottschalk embarked on a period of intensive composition. The music he wrote at this time reflected the legends and

---

[75]   Eugene List, *10 Pianos/16 Pianists: Monster Concert* (Liner notes. New York: Columbia Masterworks, M 31726, 1973).

[76]   Dominic Gill, ed., *The Book of the Piano* (Oxford: Phaidon Press Ltd., 1981):183.

rhythms of Spain. His two operas *Charles IX* and *Isaura de Salerno* are now lost, but his grand symphony for ten pianos, *El Sitio Zaragoza (The Siege of Saragossa)*, has survived through piano reductions and a piano duet. The pianist Eugene List performed a reconstruction of one of the movements of the original ten-piano version, a setting of the *Jota Aragonesa*. This ambitious composition quotes numerous other Spanish songs. When Gottschalk returned to the United States in 1853, he recomposed it as *Bunker's Hill Grand National Symphony for Ten Pianos* by substituting American tunes for the Spanish ones.

Early in 1960, he wrote about a monster concert which was to happen on February 17:

> I had, as I say, the idea of giving a grand festival, and I made an arrangement with the director of the Italian opera company, then in possession of the Grand Tacón Theater. He contracted with me to furnish his chief performers, all the choruses, and his whole orchestra on condition of having an interest in the result. I set to work and composed, on some Spanish verses written for me by a Havanese poet, an opera in one act, entitled *Fête champêtre cubaine*. Then I composed a *Triumphal Hymn* and a *Grand March*. My orchestra consisted of 650 performers, 87 choristers, 15 solo singers, 50 drums, and 80 trumpets--that is to say, nearly 900 persons bellowing and blowing, to see who could scream the loudest. The violins alone were seventy in number, contrabasses eleven, violoncellos eleven![77]

This extravaganza was so successful, apparently exciting the crowd to a frenzied demonstration, that it was followed by several encore performances, though by a more modest contingent of singers and instrumentalists.

The *Gaceta de la Havana* reported that a compositional technique used by Berlioz in his festivals would be used by the director, Gottschalk:

---

[77]   Louis Moreau Gottschalk, *Notes of a Pianist* (Translated and Ed. by Jeanne Behrend. New York: Alfred A. Knopf, 1964):27.

> . . . the principal phrase sung successively by soprano,
> tenor, and baritone would be sung by all the sopranos, all
> the tenors, and the baritones of the Maretzek' company,
> with members of chorus and orchestra joining in to make
> a thrilling crescendo.[78]

In a second *festival gigántica* at the Grand Tacón Theater on
April 17, 1861, Gottschalk's Cuban dances *La Gallina (The Hen)* and
Ojos Criollos (Creole Eyes), reflecting his fascination with the
seductive charmers of the Caribbean islands, were performed by 39
pianists. Other pieces on the program included *La nuit des tropiques*
(150 players), *Grande fantaisie triomphale sur l'hymne national
brésilien* and *Marcha Triunfal y Final de Opera*.

In the summer of 1865, he presented

> Two Grand Monster concerts and Musical Festivals with
> Ten Pianos, . . . the greatest musical success of the
> inimitable artist's career in California.[79]

Not all the throng of youngsters Gottschalk engaged for these
concerts were talented:

> In San Francisco in 1865, he found himself one pianist
> short for a scheduled performance of his fourteen-piano
> arrangement of the *March* from *Tannhäuser*, and he was
> urged to accept the services of the son of the manager of
> the concert hall, with much assurance of his extraordinary
> gifts. The boy announced that the part was so easy he
> would not have to rehearse at all, but when Gottschalk
> insisted on a rehearsal he discovered that the boy was an
> execrable pianist. Since Gottschalk did not feel he could
> offer the public only thirteen pianists when he had
> announced fourteen (and he could not offend the boy's
> father, either), his ingenious solution was to have the
> piano-tuner remove the interior mechanism of the
> instrument on which the lad was to perform. The keyboard

---

[78] Louis Moreau Gottschalk, *Notes of a Pianist*:27.

[79] Louis Moreau Gottschalk, *Notes of a Pianist*:316.

was itself left intact, and the young virtuoso attacked it
with a flourish; in the din of the thirteen "live"
instruments, no one beyond the stage could tell that one
was dead, and no harm was done (except to the young
man's self-esteem, and that was probably therapeutic).[80]

From May 30 to September 14, 1866, Gottschalk performed
fifteen concerts in Santiago, Chile. Three of these were monster
concerts using 350 musicians, with an assemblage of more than 3,500.
He conducted a Rio de Janeiro concert, three years later, that featured
40 young ladies on 25 pianos performing his *National Hymn, Op. 69,*
and the *Andante* from *La nuit des tropiques.*[81]

On October 5, 1869, Gottschalk conducted a *concerto monstro*
at the Theatre Lyrico Fluminense in Rio de Janeiro that involved 31
pianists at 16 pianos and 2 orchestras. Another concert was performed
with 56 pianists. Like Berlioz he dreamed of even larger instrumental
and vocal forces. In September of 1869 Gottschalk wrote to a friend
in Boston about organizing

. . . for the "bonne bouche", three grand festivals, with
eight hundred performers and eighty drums to lead, at
which I will produce my symphonies, and the *Grand
marche triumphale* I dedicated to the emperor.[82]

For these concerts, the "emperor" (presumably the President)
guaranteed the availability of all the military bands in the area, with
Gottschalk as their temporary director.[83]

The first program took place on the 24th November and
included the *Grande tarantella*, the *Andante* from *La nuit*

[80]   Eugene List, *A Gottschalk Festival* (Liner notes. Vox Box COX
5009, 1990).

[81]   Octavia Hensel, *Life and Letters of Louis Moreau Gottschalk* (Boston:
Oliver Ditson Co., 1870):174.

[82]   Octavia Hensel, *Life and Letters of Louis Moreau Gottschalk*:174.

[83]   Octavia Hensel, *Life and Letters of Louis Moreau Gottschalk*:173.

des tropiques and the *Grande marcha solemne*. The
performers totalled six hundred and fifty and the ticket
prices were equally inflated. The second festival scheduled
for 26th November included the same three orchestral
works.[84]

The audience reaction to the final number on the program, the
Grande marcha solemne (according to Gottschalk's biographer Octavia
Hensel), was as follows:

> It was received with much manifestations of approval as
> one rarely witnesses in a life-time. When, towards the
> close of it, was heard the well-known strains of the national
> hymn, which were so beautifully interwoven with the
> original theme of the composition, the effect upon the
> audience was electrical. All sprang to their feet and the
> wildest enthusiasm prevailed . . .[85]

Although Gottschalk was close to the point of exhaustion from
the pressures of preparing the festival, he had an obligation to honor a
contract to perform a solo recital at the Sociedade Philharmonic
Fluminense on November 25, 1869. It was during this concert that
Gottschalk collapsed while at the keyboard playing his piece *Morte*. He
was too ill to conduct a second festival program. It was cancelled, of
course. This last of two spectacles--for 31 pianists on 16 pianos and
18 orchestras totalling 650 performers--literally killed him.

George Percy Alderidge Grainger, the Australian composer,
pianist, editor, pedagogue and writer, had an important role in the
transition of the nineteenth-century tradition of the monster concert to
the prototypes of the twentieth century. A determined and adamant
exponent of amateur music-making, his approach to the mammoth
ensemble was a pedagogical one as well. His abundant, successful
compositions and "dishings-up" (arrangements) of folk songs and
dances for beginner to advanced "keyboard team-work" and "room-

---

[84]   T.C. Lange, "*Vida y muerte de Louis Moreau Gottschalk en Rio de
       Janeiro* (1869)," *Revista de estudios musicales II*, Vol. 5, No. 6
       (Mendosa, Argentina, 1953):332-334.

[85]   Octavia Hensel, *Life and Letters of Louis Moreau Gottschalk*:178.

music groups" (dance hall-like chamber ensembles) set a pedagogical precedent and gave him relative financial security throughout his life.

> They owe their potently affirmative qualities and their durability to the Bachian elements in their technique: the continuity of the beat, the consistency of the figurations, the polyphonic independence of the lines that cohere in the harmony . . . The bulk of Grainger's work is not original compositions, but arrangements of meander[ings] around traditional folk material . . [This is] not a consequence of deficient invention, but rather of the fact that for Grainger, a Global Village composer, old worlds had to be reborn, in the process . . . [making them] far more convincing . . . such pieces are poised between past and present . . . as is the extended passacaglia on *Green Bushes*, which embraces folk material within a . . . baroque convention . . .[86]

Grainger believed that ensemble experience was invaluable for all the performers and participants. In an article on "Community Music," he expounded on this philosophy:

> The art-music of Europe and America is based upon a long experience of many-voicedness, upon long-established habits of musical team work and cooperation. All our music for solo instruments more or less (usually more than less) reflects this rooted many-voicedness, so that it is impossible to do full justice even to the most soloistic music without knowledge and experience of many-voiced music. Therefore a wide familiarity with all kinds of musical team work is even more needful to the earnest music lover than any kind of soloistic study and practice ever can be.[87]

---

[86]   Wilfred Mellers, "Music Matters. New Worlds for Old, Old Worlds for New: Percy's Paradox," *Music and Musicians International*, Vol. 39, No. 2 (October, 1990):15.

[87]   Percy Alderidge Grainger, "Community Music," *Playground*, Vol. 24 (July, 1930):235.

The foreword to Grainger's *J.S. Bach for Keyboard Team-Work: [Organ] Toccata in F Major*, gives an account of his method of arrangement. For Grainger, the *F Major Toccata* arrangement was:

> . . . a sample of a normal way to transfer to 3 pianos any . . . 3-voice, or mainly 3-voice composition by Bach or other polyphonic composer--allotting to each of the 3 piano parts a voice of the original.
>
> Amateurs, piano teachers, piano students and organisers of massed piano programs need not wait for the appearance of 'arrangements' like this one, but can easily make their own arrangements along these and kindred lines . . . It is a good musical exercise for 3 pianists (or massed pianists) to extract their own part from the 3-voice . . . original score; it takes little practice and greatly develops score-mindedness . . . [88]

Although some of Grainger's methods might be questionable by today's musical standard--the use of "beat-counters" at every piano to whisper a conductor's beat to the pianist(s) when the ensemble suffers or the players cannot watch the conductor--he was a pioneer of piano ensemble for amateur group piano class instruction. "These ideas of piano pedagogy were ahead of their time. They certainly were designed to inculcate the musicality that only ensemble-work can provide: a feature often absent from piano lessons."[89] Group piano lessons and piano ensembles provide a foundation for the study of chamber music and training musicianship in the early years.

Massed multiple piano concerts have not been dominated by amateurs in the twentieth century. Monster concerts, performed by professional pianists, have also taken place throughout the twentieth century. For instance, Carnegie Hall's first-ever monster concert was in the 1921-1922 season. Fifteen important pianists joined forces for a benefit to raise money for an aging, penniless and seriously ill Moritz

---

[88]   Percy Alderidge Grainger, *J.S. Bach for Keyboard Team-Work: [Organ] Toccata in F Major* (New York: G. Schirmer, Inc., 1940, Pub. No. 38381 c):2-3.

[89]   Lewis Foreman, ed., *The Percy Grainger Companion* (London: Thames Publishing, 1981):118.

Moszkowski. Among them were Harold Bauer, Iganaz Friedman, Ossip Gabrilowitsch, Percy Grainger and Leo Ornstein (a futurist composer). The concert included transcribed works by Schubert, Saint-Saëns and Moszkowski.

> Chaos threatened until it was realized that all these egos needed a conductor, Walter Damrosch was brought in to provide order. The stage was so crowded that some of the pianists had to double up on their instruments, and Damrosch led the impromptu ensemble from the rear of the stage, facing the audience. Somehow it all came off.[90]

---

[90]   Richard Schickel and Michael Walsh, *Carnegie Hall: The First One Hundred Years* (New York: Harry N. Abrams, Inc., 1987):97.

Chapter 4. NOVEL HORIZONS

The twentieth century was a time of experimentation and exploration in Western European music. The creation and assimilation of novel ideas was a compositional concern. Prominent composers worked with new materials, structures and ideas. Experiments were undertaken, changing the course and the basis of musical composition: music using factory and city noises (the so-called "music of the future"), the microtonal school, which used quarter tones and even smaller intervals; primitivism; jazz; *Gebrauchsmusik* ("functional music"); neo-classicism (an objective, concentrated, sparse style recalling the forms and ideas of the classical period); the serial (twelve-tone) technique initiated by Arnold Schoenberg.

There is a sizeable repertoire of works for multiple pianos written during this period. Included here are discussions of works created by musicians of prominence: Charles Ives, Igor Stravinsky, Maurice Ravel, George Antheil, Carl Orff, Luigi Dallapiccola and Darius Milhaud, among others, wrote experimental works for three or more pianists and pianos. In particular, Stravinsky's *Les noces* proved to be a source of inspiration and influenced other composers of multiple piano works: Antheil, Orff and Dallapiccola. The multiple piano music of the early-twentieth century was also influenced by *avant-garde* ideologies and ideas--"the notion of the artist forging ahead in advance of public taste . . . "[91]

Charles Ives created some of

> . . . the most successful American compositions from the early twentieth century, and [was a] composer of a remarkable series of piano and chamber pieces, symphonies, choral works and [114] songs.[92]

---

[91]   Paul Griffiths, *Encyclopedia of 20th Century Music* (London: Thames and Hudson Ltd., 1986):22.

[92]   Don Michael Randel, ed., "United States," *The New Harvard Dictionary of Music* (Cambridge, Mass.: The Belknap Press of Harvard University Press, 1986):898.

After the completion of *Three Places in New England, The Fourth of July* and the *Second String Quartet* in 1912, Ives wrote the text[93] and music for a twenty-four measure song for three pianos and "Tenor or Soprano or together or in chorus," *Vote For Names*[94]--the first original multiple piano piece of the twentieth century.

Dissonant contrapuntal writing and clashing sonorities are distinctive marks of *Vote for Names*, used unsparingly to heighten and intensify the message of Ives' text. He may be using the strong dissonant statements to emphasize a political consciousness as expressed in his views quoted below:

> I feel strongly that the great fundamentals should be more discussed in all public meetings, and also in meetings of schools and colleges. Not only the students but also the faculty should get down to more thinking and action about the great problems which concern all countries and all peoples in the world today, and not let the politicians do it all and have the whole say. I have often been told that it is not the function of music (or a concert) to concern itself with matters like these. But I do not by any means agree. I think that it is one of the things that music can do, if it happens to want to, if it comes naturally, and is not the result of superimposition--I have had some fights about this.[95]

The ritualistic, primitive-sounding quality of Ives writing in *Vote For Names*, is enhanced by the scoring for three pianos (used

---

[93]   Text: "Vote for names! All nice men!! Three nice men: Teddy, Woodrow and Bill. After trying hard to think what's the best way to vote--I say--just walk right in and grab a ballot with eyes shut and walk right out again!" Charles Ives (1912)

[94]   The manuscript is in the "Music Division Archival Collections" of the New York Public Library at Lincoln Center in New York (Reel No. 6, 6792).

[95]   Charles Ives, quoted from Peter S. Hansen, *An Introduction to Twentieth Century Music* (3rd Ed. Boston: Allyn and Bacon, Inc., 1971):79.

percussively). This primitive quality is further emphasized by a basic structural technique of juxtaposition of three contrasting static layers of ostinato sound patterns set against one another in repetitive cycles which gain vitality by the use of shifting overlaps of phrase, meter, rhythm and accent. Piano I is assigned an ostinato, a widely spaced sixteenth-note arpeggiated chord on the notes: A♭ G G♭ F E G♭ G♮ A♭. Piano II enters in measure 2 with a *forte*, sixteenth-note ostinato on one chordal sonority: notes E G B D F♯ A♯ E♭. A clashing rhythmic ostinato is assigned to Piano III ($\frac{9}{16}$ ♫ ♪. ♪). The voice(s) open the song speaking the text on a B♮. From measure 11 to the end, the voice part is marked: "Free singing words without bar lines; without reference to pianos (no meter)." This part also features *portamento,* "tremble" and "chanted" notes.

The insistent vocal chanting and the ostinato accompaniment in Ives' *Vote For Names* (1912), is also coincidentally exploited in Igor Stravinsky's *The Rite of Spring* (1913). Ives insisted that he had never heard or seen the score of *Le sacre du printemps* as late as the 1930s.[96] Perhaps Ives copied Stravinskian compositional techniques in *Vote for Names*, and predated it before *the Rite of Spring*. Indeed, the central issue--the veracity of the datings of Ives' music[97]--was a very real one for Maynard Solomon:

> . . . the Russian painters Larinov and Goncharova, in order to establish their priority over Picasso and Braque in Cubist techniques, predated their works of 1912-13 to 1909-10. There is no reason to think that Ives . . . was immune to this commonplace temptation. And he was singularly well-placed to capitalize upon it, for there were few

---

[96] Maynard Solomon, "Charles Ives: Some Questions of Veracity," *Journal of the American Musicological Society,* Vol., XL, No. 3 (Fall 1987):451.

[97] See Maynard Solomon, "Charles Ives: Some Questions of Veracity," *Journal of the American Musicological Society*, Vol. XL, No. 3 (Fall 1987):443-470.

performances, publications, reviews, or descriptions of his works prior to the 1920's.[98]

Stravinsky's characteristic compositional techniques--insistent vocal chanting and ostinato accompaniment--can be seen in *Les noces* (1923). According to Eric Salzman, in a description of Stravinsky's dance-cantata *Les noces* (1923):

> This tendency towards clear, static, ostinato-based forms is also clearly evident in [Stravinsky's] last two works based largely on Russian materials: the burlesque opera *Renard* of 1916-1917 and the "choreographic scenes," *Les noces* . . . Both of these works use a high degree of static "color" dissonance combined with and set off from diatonic, "neo-Russian" melodic ideas . . . *Les noces* is the first of Stravinsky's works to re-establish an ancient and thorough-going tonal principle--tonality by assertion. These remarkable choral sketches of a Russian peasant wedding employ a simple yet effective melodic technique which juxtaposes brief melodic motives with ornamental figures and insistent choral chants, all set in cyclical patterns of repetition turning around one or two insistent pitches. The ritualistic quality of this writing, much enhanced by the remarkable [four]-piano-and-percussion orchestration, is further emphasized by a basic structural technique of juxtaposition of alternating and contrasting static layers of sound patterns . . . "[99]

Stravinsky's *Les noces* (*Svadebka, The Wedding*) is a ritualistic dance-cantata or ballet-cantata choreographed by Bronislava Nijinska and designed by Nathalie Gontcharova. The work had its premiere at the *Théâtre de la gaîté-lyrique* in Paris on June 13, 1923--an extravagant production of the impresario Diaghilev and his *Ballet*

---

[98]   Maynard Solomon, "Charles Ives: Some Questions of Veracity," *Journal of the American Musicological Society*, Vol. XL, No. 3 (Fall 1987):453.

[99]   Eric Salzman, *Twentieth-Century Music: An Introduction* (2nd ed. Englewood Cliffs, New Jersey: Prentice-Hall, Inc., 1974):45.

Russes. It was directed and choreographed by Nijinska, the set and costumes designed by Gontcharova and conducted by Ernest Ansermet. The four "elephantine" pianos were played by Marcelle Meyer and three members of *Les six*--Georges Auric, Darius Milhaud and Francis Poulenc.

The scenario of *Les noces* is a stern, austere stylization of a wedding in ancient Russia. Nijinska used a revolutionary choreography. In it she breaks with the soft rounded style, and used basic, bold motions to create a picture of the solemnity and humor of a Russian wedding. The principal dancers were Felia Duslrovska (the Bride) and Leon Woiikowsky (the Bridegroom).[100]

Of all Stravinsky's compositions *Les noces* had a lengthy history of prolonged revision and indecision in instrumentation. The idea for four "Russian choreographic scenes with song and music" about a peasant wedding came in 1912.[101] Stravinsky wrote the libretto and took over a decade to discover the correct medium for the ceremonial work. The first version for soloists and chorus, 1914 to 1917, was given orchestral accompaniment in 1917, then the work was rescored in 1919, and finally the voices were supported by percussion and four pianos (1921 to 1923).

---

[100]   Richard Burbank, *Twentieth-Century Music* (London: Thames and Hudson, 1984):108-109.

[101]   *Les noces* is a four choral tableaux:

Part I:	*Scene 1. The Bride's Chamber*, where she prepares herself with the assistance of the bride's maids.
	Scene 2. At the Bridegroom's House, where he asks for his family's blessings.
	Scene 3. The Bride's Departure, to the distress of two lamenting mothers.
Part II:	*Scene 4. The Wedding Feast*, where after much celebration and a vivid depiction of an intoxicated guest, the couple retire to the nuptial chamber. The work concludes with the husband's incantation of a love poem (accompanied by unison bells and pianos).

In May or June of 1914, after attending the London premiere of his opera *The Nightingale*,[102] Stravinsky travelled to Ukraine to search for folk material for the *Les noces* libretto. In Kiev, he located a published copy of the Ukrainian collection of popular poems, *Sobranniye Piesni* (10 Vols, Moscow, 1868-1874), by Piotr V. Kireievsky. It included an extensive group of poems and folk tunes of wedding songs and dances. Other sources of folk poetry which influenced *Les noces* were collections by Afanasiev and Sakharov. He returned to Paris with Dal's *Dictionary of Russian Phrases* (from his father's library) as ground work for the composition of this important dance cantata. The libretto for *Les noces* was adapted almost entirely from Kireievsky, according to the composer, by October 1914.

> Later, Stravinsky astutely compared the use of textual clichés and small-talk to a scene in James Joyce's *Ulysses*, where the reader seems to be overhearing scraps of conversation without the connecting thread of discourse. Certainly, there are many more elements in *Les noces* than the mere sequence of wedding preparations and festivities. Perhaps the composer is right in warning us that a knowledge of the cultural customs and even the language itself is essential for any true understanding of the work.[103]

According to Stravinsky, *Les noces* is a suite of typical wedding episodes told through quotations of typical talk of the bride, groom, parents or the guests--always ritualistic. Individual roles and proper names do not exist. His original idea was that the whole company of singers, dancers and musicians be on stage together as equal participants.

---

[102]   The sketches for Stravinsky's opera, *The Nightingale*, contains a theme that was incorporated into the fourth scene of *Les noces*.

[103]   James Wishart, *Stravinsky: Les noces* (Liner notes. Deutsche Grammophon, 423-251-2, 1988):3.

Most of the conversational *reparties* are literal quotations of folk-material sources.[104] The final version of the libretto was completed in 1914. Stravinsky made an adaptation from the original Russian words, and assisted his friend Charles-Ferdinand Ramuz in the French translation. The final version of the libretto was completed in 1914.

At its inception, the score for *Les noces* seemed an easy task to complete. But soon complications arose:

> I am no longer certain how many versions I may have begun, or how extensive each fragment may have been; I have lately discovered a complete score for four pianos, without vocal parts, of which I had no recollection, and other scores and sketches may still be excavated among the manuscripts I gave to people in return for financial help. Nor am I certain of chronology . . . [105]

The first version, completed on October 11, 1917, was scored for 4 vocal soloists (soprano, mezzo soprano, tenor, bass), SATB chorus , and chamber orchestra: 3 flutes (including a piccolo), 3 oboes (including an English horn), 3 clarinets (including an E-flat clarinet and bass clarinet), 2 bassoons, 4 horns, 4 trumpets, 2 Flügelhorns, 3 trombones, 1 baritone horn in B-flat, bass tuba, 3 solo violins, 2 solo violas, 2 solo cellos, solo bass, harp, harpsichord, 1 piano, cimbalom, timpani, bass drum, tambourine, triangle and drum (without snare).

In 1919, Stravinsky revised *Les noces*, scoring it for 4 vocal soloists, SATB chorus and only five instrumentalists. This second version's instrumentation included 2 cimbaloms, pianola (or player piano), harmonium, 3 side drums (large, middle and small, all without snare), tambourine, bass drum, triangle and 2 small cymbals

---

104 Stravinsky suggests that the libretto contains a line or two of Alexander Pushkin. See Eric Walter White, *Stravinsky: The Composer and His Works* (Berkeley; Los Angeles: University of California Press, 1966):213-214.

105 Quoted from András Wilheim, liner notes for Igor Stravinsky's *Les noces* (Hungaroton, SLPD-12989 (D); CD-HCD-12989, 1988):4.

(suspended).   András Wilheim provides the following evaluation and judgment:

> Had it been completed and not interrupted after scene 2, it
> might have become the most exciting of Stravinsky's
> scores: he himself declared that the fragment was more
> polished and authentic, and in many ways better than the
> final version. Although work on this variant was
> interrupted by an urgent commission for *Pulcinella*, he
> must also have realized the practical difficulties it implied
> (it would have been hardly possible to find two good
> cimbalom players or to synchronize the live performance
> with the pianola).[106]

Two years after the second draft, in 1921, Stravinsky
announced that he was completely revising *Les noces*.   On April 6,
1923, the third and final version was complete and scored for 4 pianos,
4 vocal soloists, SATB chorus, xylophone, timpani, 2 crotales (B-
natural and C-sharp), 2 side drums (with and without snare), 2 drums
(with and without snare), tambourine, bass drum, 2 cymbals and
triangle. This version fulfilled all Stravinsky's expectations.

> It would be at the same time perfectly homogeneous,
> perfectly impersonal and perfectly mechanical.
>
> When I first played *Les noces* to Diaghilev--in 1915, at his
> home in Bellerive, near Lausanne--he wept and said it was
> the most beautiful and the most purely Russian creation of
> our Ballet. I think he did love *Les noces* more than any
> other work of mine. That is why it is dedicated to
> him.[107]

The work is saturated with the basic motive of bells--the
interval of a fourth made up of a minor third and a major second. This

---

[106]   András Wilheim, *Les noces*:5.

[107]   Igor Stravinsky, *Expositions and Developments*:130-134; quoted from
         Pieter C. Van Den Toorn, *The Music of Igor Stravinsky* (New Haven
         and London: Yale University Press, 1983):156.

provides the germ cell of *Les noces*, which is dominated by every possible variant of this basic sound. The block harmonizations of solo and choral voices are constantly contrasted and supported by a dense, rhythmically complex polyphonic texture of the many percussion instruments (some of definite pitches, and others of indefinite pitches) and the four pianos. There is an elemental mastery of and manipulation of fragments of the Russian folk wedding ritual; ancient religious and pagan symbols are cleverly absorbed into Stravinsky's novel compositional syntax.

Les noces represented Stravinsky's novel neo-classic syntax-- stripped of romantic pathos and sentiment. Many aspects of *Les noces* have been discussed at length elsewhere.[108] For Béla Bartók, the consummate master of the folk music expression, *Les noces* is

> . . . a profound and deep-felt experience [in which] the practically unfathomable spirit of folk music is manifest.[109]

Another early twentieth-century work not dissimilar to Ives' *Vote For Names* and Stravinsky's *Les noces* in its use of multi-layered ostinatos was written in June of 1918. Maurice Ravel wrote *Frontispice*,[110] a fifteen-measure piece for five hands at two pianos.

---

[108] For recent and detailed discussions/analyses of *Les noces* refer to Eric Walter White, *Stravinsky, The Composer and His Works* (Berkeley and Los Angeles: University of California Press, 1966):212-223; Minna Lederman, ed., *Stravinsky in the Theatre* (New York: Da Capo Press, 1975):32-38; Vera Stravinsky and Robert Craft, *Stravinsky in Pictures and Documents* (New York: Simon and Schuster, 1978):145; Pieter C. Van Den Toorn, *The Music of Igor Stravinsky* (New Haven and London: Yale University Press, 1983):155-177; Stephan Walsh, *The Music of Stravinsky* (London and New York: Routledge, 1988):53-85; Victor Belaiev, Igor Stravinsky's *Les noces*: The Outline (Trans. S. Pring, London: n.p., 1928).

[109] Wilheim, *Les noces*:5.

[110] The 1-page autograph is in a private collection in New York City, and is signed and dated June, 1918.

Although it has two parts for two pianists, it requires a third pianist to play a simple, single treble line marked *octava* (measures 6-10): an ostinato, five-note figure decorated with *acciaccaturas*. The left hand part of Piano I is assigned a hypnotic eighth-note ostinato: D♯ E G♯ F A. A rich contrapuntal texture is created with multi-layers of florid, ornamented melodies, repeated note figurations and ostinatos. The piece ends with ascending, parallel chordal sonorities played by the two main pianists.

The *Frontispice* has an interesting background. It was composed at the request of the Italian poet Ricciotto Canudo, to serve as a frontispiece for his *Le poème du Vardar Suivi de la sonate à salonique, S.P. 503*, a compilation of philosophically oriented, reflective memoirs based upon World War I combat experiences. It was first published in a collection, *Les feuillets d'art*,[111] that also included a portrait of Canudo by Pablo Picasso. In the preface, Canudo indicates that the *"S.P. 503"* refers to the postal sector of his combat division. It might be interesting to note that Ravel, like Canudo, had also served in the military. In 1915, Ravel enlisted in Military Transport, after trying unsuccessfully to join the infantry and air force, and became a munitions truck driver.

From 1924 to 1925, George Antheil began the composition of what has become one of the most "infamous" of noise pieces-- *Ballet*

---

[111]   *Les feuillets d'art (Les poètes de la Renaissance du livre)*.   Paris, 1923; Salabert, 1975.

mécanique.[112] The use of percussion effects was a current rage, and

---

[112]   George Antheil, *Ballet mécanique:*

> *No. 156a.*   Holograph score *(Ballet mécanique)* and instructions
> for cutting on pianola by Maison Pleyel, stamped 1924 on
> title page, signed, "Paris, 1925" on second page of
> instructions, Antheil estate. Composed to accompany the
> film of same name by Fernand Léger. Music and film
> never synchronized. First performed together in 1935 (see
> *156c*--number 3 below).
>
> In addition to scoring a pianola part, there are parts
> for wood airplane motor (probably propeller), steel airplane
> motor (probably propeller), and electric bells indicated on
> the score.
>
> Player piano rolls: #8983, 8984, 8985 *des Roleaux
> Pleyela*, Antheil Estate, Curtis Institute Library; three rolls,
> Box 185, Beach Collection.
>
> First version conceived for 16 pianolas run electrically
> from a common control (source: taped interview,
> Amirkhanian and Böski Antheil, 7.26.70, Antheil Estate).
> On the player piano rolls that Antheil sent to Mrs. Bok
> (Curtis), the composer stated that the work was originally
> scored for 16 pianolas, xylophones, drums and other
> percussion instruments. Performed in private concerts on
> one player piano at *Maison Pleyel* during 1925 and early
> 1926. (Sources: Bravig Imbs, *Confessions of Another
> Young Man*, New York: Henkle-Yewdale, Inc., 1936:56;
> *"Ballet mécanique* Has New Hearing," Review, Box 265,
> Scrapbook No. 1, Beach Collection; *"Ballet pour Pleyela
> par* George Antheil," *La Revue Musicale*, n.d., including
> in letter, A to B, Jan. 21, 1926; Irving Schwerké, "Notes
> of the Music World," Nov. [16, 1925], Scrapbook #1--this
> review was of a performance at the Conservatoire.)
>
> *No. 156b.*   Autograph score, *Ballet pour instrument mécaniques
> et percussion*, Antheil Estate c. 1926 (source: Letter, A to
> B, June 1, 1926)
>
> Scored for one pianola with amplifier, two pianos,
> three xylophones, electric bells, small wood propeller,
> large wood propeller, metal propeller, tamtam, four bass
> drums and siren.

Stravinsky's *Les noces* was one of the models of the early 1920s.

Performance---June 19, 1926, conducted by Vladmir Golschmann, *Champs Elysées Theatre*. (Source: *New York Herald* review, June 18, 1926, Scrapbook #2.)

Also performed on July 17, 1926, Vladimir Golschmann conducting, *Comédie du Champs-Elysées*, with three pianos. (Source: "Nobody Goes to Sleep at Second Mechanical Concert by Antheil," *New York Herald*, July 18, 1926, scrapbook #2, information on the three pianos, folder 28, Beach collection, announcement.)

No. 156c.   Published score, *Ballet mécanique*, by Templeton Publishing Co., 1959.

March 25, 1953, revision of photoreproduced holograph, copyright by Templeton, 1959. Scored for glockenspiel, small airplane propeller sound, large airplane propeller sound, gong, cymbal, woodblock, triangle, military drum, tambourine, small electric bell, large electric bell, tenor drum, bass drum, 2 xylophones and 4 pianos.

Performance--Feb. 21, 1954, Fifth Composer's Forum, Columbia University. (Source: pub. score, "Biographical Notes.")

Other performances:

1.   July 16, 1926, home of Mrs. Christian Gross, Paris, conducted by Vladimir Golschmann (source: announcement, Scrapbook #2), played by 8 pianos and an unspecified number of xylophones and percussion. (Source: BBm, 184-85.)

2.   April 10, 1927, Carnegie Hall, conducted by Eugene Goossens, played by 10 pianos, 1 mechanical piano (Antheil), 6 xylophones, 2 bass drums, a wind machine with a regulation airplane propeller and siren. (Source: program, Antheil Estate and Donald Friede, *The Mechanical Angel: His Adventures and Enterprises in the Glittering 1920's*, New York: Alfred A. Knopf, 1948; 50-61.)

3.   October 18, 1935, performed in version for pianola with Léger's film, Museum of Modern Art. (Source: program, Scrapbook #6.)

H.H. Stuckenschmidt, a George Antheil enthusiast, described the German/American pianist's *Ballet mécanique*--scored for four pianos and percussion--as:

> . . . rhythmically and dynamically of exciting, incessantly surprising precision, hard as metal, with lyrical sprinklings provided by a fanatic whose power and mechanical fluency are just as astonishing as the accuracy of both hands racing across the entire diapason of the [four] quivering grand piano[s].[113]

In a c. 1926 letter from Antheil to his American patron, Mrs. Mary Louise Curtis Bok (founder of the Curtis Institute of Music in Philadelphia), he wrote that:

> Stravinsky with his pure and sweet music, both artfully and artlessly carried out, with his absolutism, protected me, as the thought of it will always protect me, from the pseudo-nationalism of the European countries, or the philosophies and the metaphysics of particularly Central Europe, which have to do with things other than music, and [which] have not been tolerated by the true masters.[114]

The incessant, straightforward repetitiveness, both rhythmic and melodic, of *Ballet mécanique*

> . . . seeks to create a static music that derives from *Le sacre du printemps* [and *Les noces*] and is akin to the notions of Varèse. Satie's ballet *Parade* (1917) was a modest precursor of these experiments . . . it uses sirens and typewriters. Milhaud . . . [later used] fifteen

---

[113]   H.H. Stuckenschmidt, *Antheil: Ballet mécanique* (Liner notes. Telefunken 6. 42196, 1977).

[114]   Letter from George Antheil to Mrs. Mary Louise Curtis Bok, December 26, 1926, or January 1927. (Library of Congress): no file number. (Taken from George Antheil's *Bad Boy of Music*.)

percussion instruments in his ballet *L'homme et son désir* (1918).[115]

The three-part *Ballet mécanique*, originally entitled *Message to Mars*, embraced the anti-expressive, anti-romantic, coldly mechanistic musical aesthetic of the times. The controversy attending its premiere in Paris was not dissimilar to Stravinsky's *Le sacre du printemps:* fist fights erupted between audience members. *Ballet mécanique* was originally written for one of the first abstract motion pictures--also entitled *Ballet mécanique*--by the artist Fernand Léger.

The first version of *Ballet mécanique* was scored for sixteen pianolas (player pianos), operated from a master switchboard. When synchronization between the pianolas and Léger's film proved unsuccessful, both became independent works (until October 18, 1935, when the Museum of Modern Art in New York attempted the proper synchronization).

The first public performance was at the *Champs Elysées Theatre* on June 19, 1926, with Vladimir Golschmann conducting, and featured "a new and special arrangement--a reduction of the original score":[116] eight pianos, one pianola, four xylophones, two electric bells, tam-tam, four bass drums, an auto siren and two airplane propellers (whose noise creates an *orgel punkt*-like drone). The unusual and at the time outrageous combinations of instruments resulted in a scandal and public riot.

According to Antheil, the first *real* performance[117] (with the use of eight pianos) was on July 16, 1926, at the home of Mrs. Christian Gross, wife of an American diplomat. In his account of this first salon concert of *Ballet mécanique*, Antheil reminisced:

---

[115]   H.H. Stuckenschmidt, "*Unschau: Ausblick in die Musik*," *Das Kunstblatt VII* (July 1923):221-223.

[116]   Antheil in a letter to Mrs. M. Bok, June 1, 1926. (Location of letter not known. Taken from George Antheil's *Bad Boy of Music*.)

[117]   George Antheil, *Bad Boy of Music* (New York: Da Capo Press, 1981):184.

As I remember it now, her [Mrs. Gross's] house, large as it was, was not only filled with white-gloved butlers, guests, food, and wonderful champagne, but with grand pianos as well; the grand pianos literally hung from the ceilings. The *Ballet mécanique* is really scored for eight grand pianos, to say nothing of xylophones, percussion, and what not--although there were twice as many instruments in Carnegie Hall [April 10, 1927 American premiere].

Naturally, in this arrangement hardly any room remained for the guests--a slight oversight on our part. The eight grand pianos filled up the giant living room completely and without an extra inch of room, while the xylophones and percussion were located in the side room and on the giant staircase. Vladimir Golschmann, who conducted, stood at the top of the piano in the center. To this absolutely jammed-packed house, just add two hundred guests! Every nook and cranny between the pianos sheltered a guest; I think several even hung by the chandeliers--the Duchesse de Clermont-Tonnère in all probability; she was such an iconoclast! Ah yes, and add to all this the fact that it was summer and ultra-hot; in short, by the time we were ready to start, practically everybody in Paris seemed to have poured through a funnel in the chimney down into the house, where they were perspiring and waiting.

At the first chord of the *Ballet mécanique* the roof nearly lifted from the ceiling! The remainder of our guests squirmed like live sardines in a can; the pianos underneath or above or next to their ears boomed mightily and in a strange synchronization.

At the end of this most sweaty concert, champagne was served in great quantity, and people were very thirsty, not to say shaken and distraught.[118]

---

[118]   George Antheil, *Bad Boy of Music* (New York: Da Capo Press, 1981):184.

On April 10, 1927, a third expanded version was given at Carnegie Hall, funded by the zealous promoter Donald Friede. The carnival-like performance was conducted by Eugene Goossens, and became one of the most scandalous concerts in New York City's history--so poorly received by the press and audience that, much to his delight, Antheil was labelled the "Bad Boy of Music."

In his autobiography, *Bad Boy of Music*, Antheil had second thoughts about Stravinsky's influence during their Paris years:

> My original idea in writing the work was to both synthesize and expand the piano sonatas. Also to eliminate whatever effect *Les noces* might have made upon me through the first movement of the *First violin Sonata*--all this in a work of sufficient size that the public could . . . see it better.[119]

On February 21, 1954, for Columbia University's Fifth Composer's Forum in New York, Antheil made a final, condensed revision of *Ballet mécanique*. (The original first version is thirty minutes in duration, whereas the third version is eighteen minutes.) The *New York Times* reviewer reported that:

> The work which caused riots in Paris . . . and burst 'on startled ears' in Carnegie Hall, now sounds like an ebullient and lively piece that is actually pretty in places . . . Instead of riots there was a three-minute ovation that necessitated many bows from the composer . . . [120]

The work was rescored as *No. 156c*, for 4 pianos, 2 electrically amplified xylophones, bass and tenor drums, small and large electric bells (of the door-bell type), tambourine, military drum, triangle, woodblock, cymbal, gong, glockenspiel and small and large airplane propeller sounds (either taped or a loop of a sound track of two different types of propeller sounds).

---

[119]   Antheil, *Bad Boy of Music*: 184-185.

[120]   Antheil, *Bad Boy of Music*:139.

The music contains piano tone clusters and characteristic "Stravinskian" rhythmic ostinatos, frequently shifting meters and irregular accentuation. It begins with very loud, driving sonorities; alternating note passages abound in the piano parts of the opening section. Antheil provided comments in the published edition[121] of the final version of 1952 to 1953.

While Antheil was composing *Ballet mécanique* from 1924 to 1925, he was contemplating an enormous composition which would expand the structural principles of another work: a setting of an episode in Joyce's *Ulysses* called the *Cyclops*. It was intended to be four hours long and without interruption. The only surviving portion (part of the Antheil Musical supplement in a 1925 issue of *This Quarter*) indicates Antheil's conception of a revolutionary orchestration that includes an electrified percussion orchestra, electrically operated pianolas and xylophones accompanying electrically amplified vocal soloists and chorus, and electrically reproduced sounds of a traditional orchestra of acoustic instruments manipulated on an amplified phonograph:

> 16 Mechanical Pianos--operated from master roll and
>   controlled from a switchboard
> 8 Xylophones--controlled from a switchboard
> Amplified Gramophone --containing all of the ordinary
>   o r c h e s t r a l   i n s t r u m e n t s
>   registered upon a gramophone record--
>   amplified and controlled from a switchboard
> Auto Siren
> 4 Bass Drums
> 4 Electric Buzzers
> 4 Electric Bells
> 4 Pieces of Steel
> Electric Motor (wood attachment)
> Electric Motor (steel attachment)[122]

---

121   George Antheil, *Ballet mécanique, No. 156c* (Dubuque, Iowa: Templeton Publishing Co., Inc., 1959):n.p.

122   Linda Whitesitt, *The Life and Music of George Antheil: 1900-1959* (Ann Arbor, Michigan: UMI Research Press, 1983):110-111.

Antheil did not complete the work and *Cyclops* never became a reality.

The post-World War I period in Germany was one of artistic iconoclasm and excitement. Among the significant composers of the period were Paul Hindemith, Hugo Distler, Ernst Pepping and Carl Orff. The musico-dramatic works of Orff are indebted to Stravinsky's rhythmic revolution.

Orff's characteristic style was consolidated in the cantata *Carmina Burana* (1937), a setting of rowdy and ribald medieval German and Latin songs to rudimentary mechanical music derived from *Les noces*.

> Here was established his conception of music as part of a composite art form in which textural declamation assumes the dominant role. Simple syllabic settings are projected through elemental chant-like melodic figures, repeated incessantly to the percussive accompaniment of static triadic harmonies which themselves appear in recurrent, block-like patterns featuring highly rhythmic, though uncomplicated, ostinato figures. The closest musical precedent is Stravinsky, especially the Stravinsky of *The Wedding*; but the extremely differential compositional techniques of that work are here reduced to their most basic common denominator. Everything is contrived to produce a direct and instantaneous effect. The music gives something of the impression of a ritualistic incantation, but one that seems to have been purposely shorn of all mystery.[123]

Elements of Orff's mature style can be seen in his cantatas of 1929 and 1930. The foreword to the *Werkbuch* gives Orff's explanation of the purpose of this cantata series:

> The workbook includes choral and instrumental movements which, by their nature, do not derive from concert practice. They seek that spiritual attitude which must lead from the

---

[123]   Robert P. Morgan, *Twentieth-Century Music: A History of Musical Style in Modern Europe and America* (New York; London: W.W. Norton & Company, 1991):158.

subjectivity and isolation of the individual to a binding, universally valid sense of community. The simplicity of the construction and the choice of the means were the result of this attitude, and should make possible the greatest intensity, by renouncing anything which could render their practicability difficult.[124]

The first workbook, *Kantaten nach Texten von Franz Werfel* (1929), contains two cantatas--*Veni Creator Spiritus*[125] and *Der gute Mensch*[126]--scored for three pianos, percussion instruments and SATB chorus. These two cantatas were premiered in 1930.

Orff's second workbook of the series, *Kantaten nach Texten von Bertolt Brecht* (1931) contains one cantata--*Vom Frühjahr, Öltank und vom Fliegen*[127]--also scored for three pianos, percussion instruments and SATB chorus.

The chorus is given a significant role in these cantatas. The accompaniments are richly scored for percussion. The static, block harmonizations are used to underline highly accentuated choral rhythms. The percussive ostinato accompaniments anticipate *Carmina Burana*.

Another *Les noces*-inspired work for multiple pianos was written by Luigi Dallapiccola, born in Istria and settled in Florence in 1922. In spite of having been born of Italian parents, there is something Germanic in his upbringing and thinking. He was influenced by the music of Ferruccio Busoni, Alban Berg and Anton von Webern.

---

[124] Quoted from the preface to Carl Orff's cantata *Workbooks* (1929; 1931).

[125] The order of the three movements of the cantata *Veni Creator Spiritus* (1929) is: *Litanei; Nacht*; and *Veni Creator Spiritus*.

[126] The order of the three movements of the cantata *Der gute Mensch* (1929) is: *Lächeln, Atmen, Schreiten; Liebeslied;* and *Der gute Mensch*.

[127] The order of the three movements of the cantata is: *Vom Frühjahr (On Spring); Öltank (An Oiltank);* and *Vom Fliegen (Report on Flying)*.

From the mid-1930s, he became a principal proponent of the Schoenbergian twelve-tone system.

In Dallapiccola's early compositions, tone rows are occasionally used as a method of organizing the chromatic content of certain melodic sequences (without affecting vertical aspects and accompanimental figures). His initial conception of dodecaphony was open to tonal syntax (the Berg influence) along with strict canonic structures (the Webern influence). In explaining why he adopted the serial method, Dallapiccola states:

> What interested me above all in the dodecaphonic system were its expressive and melodic possibilities, a principle moreover, which I never abandoned in the works that followed in later years no matter how much more complex they may have been.[128]

The first purely instrumental composition of Luigi Dallapiccola, *Musica Per Tre Pianoforte (Inni)* (1935), is in three movements: *Allegro molto sostenuto*; *Un poco adagio; funebre*; and *Allegramente, ma solenne*.[129] The decision to score the work for three pianos came after he attended performances of Stravinsky's *Les noces* in Florence and Padua. The pianos assist in clarifying the contrapuntal texture, in keeping with his *purificarsi della materia* ("purification of material").

Dallapiccola's *Musica Per Tre Pianoforte (Inni)* is related to a carillon, or set of stationary bells normally in a tower or on a high outdoor frame. The work was awarded first prize at the 1936 Geneva Conservatory *Concorso Internazionale de Carillon* by the Chamber Music Society, and later premiered on March 30, 1936 by pianists M.

---

[128]   Luigi Dallapiccola, "On the Twelve-Note Road," *Music Survey* (October 1951): n.p.

[129]   From 1930 until his retirement in 1967, Dallapiccola taught piano (second study) at the Florence Conservatory.

Orloff, Dallapiccola and J.M. Pasche.[130] One of Dallapiccola's patrons subtitled the work "Le carillon," because the aural effect reminded him of Geneva's Carillon. One Parisian critic had the impression of hearing a group of carillonneurs striking the hammers and clappers of a carillon. Dallapiccola's score is replete with accents and indications to play *forte/fortissimo, molto sostenuto, non legato, pesante, lasciar vibrare, martellato sostenuto il suono*, among others-- all indicative of bells. *Musica Per Tre Pianoforte (Inni)* is part of a tradition that correlates the sounds of bells with the piano as in: Modest Musorgsky's *The Great Bogatyr Gate (at Kiev, the Ancient Capital)* from *Pictures at an Exhibition, Op. 11* (1874); Sergei Rachmaninov's *Russian Easter* from the *Fantasy, Op. 15* (1896); Maurice Ravel's *La valleé des cloches* from *Miroirs* (1905); Claude Debussy's *La Cathédrale engloutie* from *Préludes* (1910); the conclusion of Scene IV of Igor Stavinsky's *Les noces* (1923); Messiaen's *Cloches d'angoisse et larmes d'adieu* from *Préludes* (1930); and Otto Luening's *The Bells of Bellagio* (1967) for three pianists (discussed in Chapter 5).

The first significant, original work for multiple pianos by a French composer was written thirty years after Ravel's *Frontispice*. Darius Milhaud's programmatic suite in six movements for eight hands at four pianos, *Paris, Op. 284a*, was completed on May 18, 1948. The scoring was presumably influenced by Milhaud's performance of one of the piano parts for the 1923 premiere of *Les noces*.

The suite is a tribute to the French capital, written during his residence as Professor of Composition at Mills College in Oakland, California.[131] It is a musical depiction of six aspects of Paris and its lifestyle.

> . . . [Milhaud] acquired a patina of urban sophistication in
> Paris, and was happy enough to allow himself to be swept

---

130 See Maurice Hinson, *Music for More Than One Piano* (Bloomington: Indiana University Press, 1983):47, for a concise and condensed description of Dallapiccola's *Musica Per Tre Pianoforte (Inni)*.

131 From August 1947 until his retirement in 1971, Milhaud divided his teaching duties between the Paris Conservatoire, Mills College and the School of Music in Aspen, Colorado.

along by the currents of contemporary musical thought; his
contacts with Cocteau, Satie and Stravinsky and the
formation of "Les Six" encouraged his natural iconoclasm
in harmonic (that is, polytonality) and structural matters
(his waywardness in respect of the latter is frequently the
result either of a desire to allow the music to find the form
best suited to its own expression . . . or of an
impulsiveness that casts aside the predictable in favour of
the unexpected, regardless of context), his bias towards
popular music, even that of "low life," his delight in the
refurbishing of old music in present-day garb, and the
sometimes rather self-conscious cleverness of his own
technical facility, as in the oft-quoted case of those two of
his 18 string quartets which can be played separately or
together.[132]

The lively first movement, *Montmartre*, depicts a vivacious,
older section of the City (with narrow roads and charming
architecture), well-known for its numerous resident authors and
artisans. The serene second movement is entitled *L'ile Saint-Louis,* one
of the islands located on the Seine, where a portion of Paris is
constructed. Canon at the octave is an important compositional device
in this movement. The virtuoso third movement, *Montparnasse*,
captures the mood of this quarter of Paris, now a modern and trendy
section. This movement, the longest of the suite, is a rhythmic and
contrapuntal *tour de force*. Its parallel octave and chordal passages are
reminiscent of Stravinsky's piano transcription of the *Danse russe* from
Trois mouvements de Petrouchka (1921). The tranquil, atmospheric
fourth movement, *Bateaux-mouches,* evokes (as the title indicates) the
tourist boats that cruise the Seine. The brisk, densely contrapuntal fifth
movement, *Longchamp*, depicts the track in the centre of the *Bois de
Boulogne* area where Parisians race horses. As in the second piece in
the suite (*L'ile Saint-Louis*) it is written in canon at the octave. The
lively, blithe subject and the energetic contrapuntal writing creates
ensemble challenges with the multiplicity of rhythmic figures equally
divided among all four pianists. Multiple piano teams, in general, do
not use a conductor in any live performance. The unpianistic, difficult

---

[132]   Christopher Palmer, "Darius Milhaud," *New Grove Dictionary of
Music and Musicians*, Vol. 12:306-307.

writing perhaps led to Milhaud's orchestrated version, *Op. 284b* of *Paris*. The final piece of the suite, *La tour Eiffel*, is a "visual and photographic" depiction of the well-known landmark. The dramatic octave writing in canon captures the grandeur and majesty of Alexandre Gustave Eiffel's monument to mankind's industrial progress.

> [By beginning] in the bass register of the piano, [the movement] gradually progress[es] to the treble by the end, imitating the eye movement travelling from the base of the Eiffel Tower to the top of it. The frequency of octaves and the use of the dynamic "ff" seem to convey the strength of the steel tower, . . . a fitting end to a very skillfully written programmatic suite on Parisian themes.[133]

---

[133] Mary Jane Rupert, "The Piano Music of Darius Milhaud: A Survey." D. Mus. diss., Indiana University, December 1974:124-126.

Chapter 5. RECENT ECLECTICISM

In recent years, the rise of brilliant, highly trained solo pianists led to an increasing demand and interest for compositions for multiple pianos; hence the substantial growth of pieces for this medium.

The twentieth century has produced a generation of musicians who amalgamated and cultivated divergent musical styles. Out of this recent eclecticism comes a multinational *mélange* of music for three or more pianists. The main directions adopted and selected by composers of the international music community--for instance, electronic music, serialism, minimalism, indeterminacy, microtonalism--greatly influenced and encouraged multiple keyboard compositions. (Refer to sections 2 through 6 of the Catalogue.)

Selected Works for Three Pianists

There are many compositions for three pianists at one or two or three pianos with or without other acoustic and electronic instruments in the twentieth century. Works by Niels Viggo Bentzon, Stefan Wolpe, Johannes Georg Fritsch, Robert Casadesus, Wolfgang Fortner, Otto Luening, George Crumb and Mauricio Kagel will be considered in the following section.

Twentieth-century Danish composers have nearly all felt the impact of Carl Nielsen, Denmark's most important and influential composer. A post-Nielsen composer who came into prominence in his own country after World War II was Niels Viggo Bentzon (*b* 1919). Prior to his appointment at the Royal Danish Conservatory in Copenhagen, Bentzon, a prolific, self-taught composer, pianist, organist and writer on music, wrote *Chamber Concert No. 1 for Eleven Instruments, Op. 52* (1948). It is likely the first work involving multiple pianos from the twentieth century by a composer from Denmark, and is a formidable pianistic test.

Hindemith, Bartók, Schoenberg, jazz and popular music are amalgamated in the *Chamber Concert No. 1 for Eleven Instruments:*

> Powerful and often bombastic . . . , dissonant but tonal in
> concept, free-flowing with an almost improvisatory
> character . . . His intellectual curiosity and inventive

approach have caused him to experiment frequently, with
many avant-garde procedures . . .[134]

Bentzon's other multiple keyboard works are *Pezzo, Op. 99a*
(1954), for twelve pianos; the *Pièce héroïque, Op. 224* (1967), for six
hands at three pianos; and *Studie, Op. 398* (1977) for seven electronic
keyboard instruments.

Stefan Wolpe, a student of Webern, composed one of his most
important compositions, *Enactments* (from 1950 to 1953 in 4 extended
movements: *I. Chant; II. In a State of Flight; III. Held In; IV.
Inception; V. Fugal Motions)*, for six hands at three pianos. Dedicated
to Edgard Varèse, it represents a high point in Wolpe's first period of
composition while in America. (He settled in New York in the late
1930s.) During the 1950s, *Enactments* was admired for its virtuosic
ideas and length. It features the challenging juxtaposition of
compositional extremes: brilliant passage work, widely differentiated
tempos, multiplicity of expressive levels and moods, wide shifts in
register, rhythmic complexities, rapidly changing sonorities and textures
and a myriad of interpretative detail. Furthermore, his own high
regard for the work is expressed in the quote below:

> *Enactments* is, with all its tumults, vortexes, exuberances,
> simultaneities of multiple organic stages and states, terribly
> dear to me.[135]

Enactments was a compendium of a vision Wolpe described in
1952:

> For a first time (for years) I see a vast orbit possibly to
> write music existing (as definite totalities of organic modes)
> under the most different conditions of complex behavior.
> I came close to my ideal of writing a language with a

---

[134] William H. Reynolds, "Niels Viggo Bentzon," *New Grove Dictionary
       of Music and Musicians.* Vol. 2:511.

[135] Stefan Wolpe, quoted from liner notes by Eric Salzman, *Stefan
       Wolpe: Enactments* (Elektra/Asylum/Nonesuch Records, No.
       78824, 1984).

common-sense (and this in a sense of an all-union-of-the-
human-tongue). . . . *Enactments* doesn't mean anything
else but acting out, being in an act of, being the act
itself.[136]

Eric Salzman has observed that in the late 1940s, Wolpe
composed numerous works that culminated in the *Seven Pieces for
Three Pianos* (1950-1951), a preparatory study for *Enactments*, also
dedicated to Varèse. They are a set of exploratory studies in
expressive and structural interval complexes and spatial proportions,
arranged in order of increasing technical difficulty. Wolpe also
discovered how to generate an open, mobile space, how to create a
non-motive continuum and how to expand, contract, and overlap
musical ideas. The *Seven Pieces* are experiments in abstract
expressionism (not unlike the calligraphic studies of the avant-garde
visual artists Pollock, de Kooning, Rothko and Kline, when they
discarded figurative painting in the 1940s).[137]

The three pianos are protagonists who become
progressively more independent as they overlap and
interweave with the complex statements.[138]

"So that art may have the power to transform life,"[139] Wolpe
felt the greatest possible complexity and intensity must prevail in
composition. His philosophy and achievements brought the respect of
many, including Edgard Varèse:

He was one of the most remarkable composers of his
century, who introduced a totally original principle of

---

[136] Wolpe, *Stefan Wolpe: Enactments*, liner notes by Eric Salzman.

[137] Ibid.

[138] Ibid.

[139] Wolpe, *Stefan Wolpe: Enactments*, liner notes by Eric Salzman.

organizing the materials and forms of sound, profoundly
influencing the direction of music.[140]

The critic Eric Salzman reveals further observations on Wolpe:

> Wolpe had a decisive influence as composer and
> teacher, and was an intense presence in the New York
> musical scene. In the late forties, and early fifties, he
> developed a new and completely individual language
> parallel to--but not quite distinct from--the other leaders of
> the post-war avant garde. Along with Varèse, Babbit and
> Cage, Wolpe deserves to be ranked among the great
> innovators of our time.[141]

The German Johannes Georg Fritsch (*b* 1941) studied
composition with Karlheinz Stockhausen and played the viola in the
Stockhausen Ensemble from 1964 to 1970. In the late fifties and early
sixties, Fritsch represented not so much general trends in German
music as an individual mode of expression.[142] His ten-minute
virtuosic composition for three pianos, *Ikonen* (1964), was written for
the pianists Aloys, Alfons and Bernhard Kontarsky after studies at the
Darmstadt summer courses with Stockhausen. This avant-garde,
ametric work, in six clearly marked sections, contains elements of
pointillism, expressionism, indeterminacy, and is written in spatial
notation. It is characterized by frequent, extreme dynamic contrasts
(from *ppp* to *fff*), strummed glissandos on the strings and aleatoric
effects. *Ikonen*, like other pieces by Fritsch, has a pronounced
multiplicity of textures and unpredictable, impulsive shifts of mood.

French composer Robert Casadesus (1899-1972) was
commissioned to compose his only work for three pianists, the

---

140   Edgard Varèse, quoted from Nicolas Slonimsky, *The Concise Baker's
      Biographical Dictionary of Musicians* (New York: Schirmer Books,
      1988):1290.

141   Salzman, *Stefan Wolpe: Enactments*, liner notes.

142   Lichtenfeld, "Johannes Georg Fritsch," *New Grove Dictionary of
      Music and Musicians*, Vol. 6:723.

Concerto for Three Pianos and String Orchestra, Op. 65. It was written in the spring of 1964 in Paris and premiered at the French-American Festival on July 24, 1965, in New York's Philharmonic Hall. The soloists were Robert, his wife Gaby and his son Jean Casadesus;[143] the New York Philharmonic was conducted by Lucas Foss. "The *Concerto* was also performed in Paris on October 3, 1965, at the Théâtre du Châtelet (the Concerts Colone series) with Pierre Dervaux conducting"[144] the *Orchestre des Concerts Colonnes.*

The *Concerto* is in the traditional three movements, with the following indications: *I. Allegro marziale*; *II. Andante siciliano*; and *III. Presto spagnuolo.* The elements of Casadesus's style are embodied in the concerto. According to Gaby Casadesus:

> . . . his ideals . . . [are] classic structure [combined] with
> [the] modern idiom. Catalonian blood, coming from his
> grand father Louis Casadesus, still flows warmly in his
> veins and in the rhythms of his music.[145]

In the first and third movements, the pianos are treated as percussion instruments and the thematic material is often rhythmically brilliant, antiphonally treated and equally distributed between the soloists. The first movement *Allegro marziale* immediately opens *fortissimo* with the three pianos, followed by the main theme played by the strings, a brief introspective section, and finally a rhythmically exciting recapitulation of the main themes and a virtuoso coda. The second movement *Andante siciliano* provides a lyric foil and treats the pianos as *cantabile* instruments. The pianos enter one by one with a

---

[143] In 1950, the celebrated Casadesus Three-Piano Ensemble--comprised of pianists Robert, Gaby and Jean Michel Casadesus--came about after the suggestion by the Greek/American conductor, Dimitri Mitropoulos (1896-1960). They frequently performed the Mozart, Bach and Casadesus concertos on three pianos.

[144] Letter to Grant Maxwell from Michelle A. Mead, secretary of Madame Gaby Casadesus (December 12, 1990).

[145] Nancy K. Siff, *Casadesus: First Recording [of the] Triple-Piano Concerto* (Liner notes. Columbia Masterworks, M3211 0025, 1967).

subdued theme, followed by the strings. The movement concludes with
a repetition of the themes by the strings and pianos. As it decays with
ethereal string accompaniment and chains of trills, one piano maintains
a *basso ostinato* while the other two play the melody. The *Presto
spagnuolo* ("in a Spanish style") third movement features the pianists
performing an accentuated, syncopated rhythmic subject against a
percussive *basso ostinato*.

> A juxtapositioning by pianos and strings of multi-rhythms,
> combined with a moderately dissonant harmonic texture,
> creates a high volume of sound that belies the sparse
> orchestration, and the work ends in an expansive
> climax.[146]

Maurice Hinson adds that the Casadesus concerto

> . . . is a dazzling interplay between various forces . . .
> [requiring] first-rate pianistic ensemble technique.[147]

The German composer Wolfgang Fortner (*b* 1907) was an
influential teacher whose work underwent a transformation from the
aesthetics of the baroque to serial composition. He composed *Triplum*
(1965-1966), for three obbligato pianos and orchestra while he was
Professor of Composition at the Freiburg *Musikhochschule*. The three
movements of *Triplum* are *Giuoco*; *Intermezzo*; and *4 Variazioni*.

This is a dazzling, percussive, quite lengthy (c. 25 minutes)
composition. It includes aleatoric, pointillistic and expressionistic
passages, demonstrating Fortner's interest in assimilating and
amalgamating significant musical trends of the period.

> In the [neo-Baroque] generation after Hindemith he was
> probably the most learned and skillful artist in musical
> form [especially appropriated Baroque and pre-Baroque

---

[146]   N.K.Siff, *Casadesus: Concerto for Three Pianos and String
        Orchestra, Op. 65* (Liner notes. Columbia Records/CBS, Inc., LC
        73-752511).

[147]   Maurice Hinson, *Music for Piano and Orchestra*:60.

minor forms, and other kinds of symmetrical structures],
owing this to his varied practical experience [as composer
and teacher of students like Heinze]. From contrapuntal
thought [in the widest sense] and expanded tonality [i.e.,
twelve-tone method], he came to a specifically neo-classical
style, in which the influence of Hindemith was combined
with that of Stravinsky.[148]

Along with co-founding and co-directing the Columbia-
Princeton Electronic Music Center in 1950, with Milton Babbit,
Vladimir Ussachevsky and Roger Sessions, Otto Luening (*b* 1900) is
a distinguished educator, administrator, conductor, and flautist and is
regarded as one of the important composers of the formative years of
modern American music.

Luening's canonic *The Bells of Bellagio* (*I. Hail; II. Farewell*,
1967) was written for two or three players at one or two or three
pianos, and exemplifies his mastery of polyphonic procedures.[149]
Luening wrote the pieces when he

> . . . was a fellow of the Rockefeller Foundation Study
> Center in Bellagio, Italy, in 1967 . . . . Once there were
> three pianists there . . . , so I decided to write *The Bells of
> Bellagio* for them, inspired by the sounds from the bells in
> the village church. I'm a pretty good pianist--my wife is
> also--and Janet Payne the secretary was fair. In order to
> meet the abilities of the available performers, I wrote this
> canon in which the second piano is in diminution with the
> first, the third piano is in double diminution with the first.
> The erudition kept me from writing a piece that was too
> simple-minded and taking into account of the players'
> abilities enabled us to give a decent performance . . .[150]

---

[148] Hanspeter Krellmann, "Wolfgang Fortner," *New Grove Dictionary
of Music and Musicians*, Vol. 6:723.

[149] After investigating the music of Arnold Schoenberg, Luening went
on to study counterpoint with Ferruccio Busoni and composition with
Philipp Jarnach in his student years.

[150] Letter to Grant Maxwell from Otto Luening (December 11, 1990).

The American George Crumb (*b* 1929) and the Argentinian
Mauricio Kagel (*b* 1931) have composed curiosities for three pianists
at one piano that are not unrelated to Ravel's *Frontispice* (1918).
Crumb's *Celestial Mechanics: Cosmic Dances for Amplified Piano,
Four Hands* from *Makrokosmos IV* (1979) contains two movements
with "two short passages that require the page turner to act as a 3rd
pianist":[151] *III. Gamma Draconis* at rehearsal No. 42; and *IV.
Delta Orionis* at and prior to rehearsal No. 53. Kagel, who began
specializing in unconventional performance techniques during the
1960s, wrote a two-minute, thirty-second *Der Eid des Hippokrates*
(1984) for three pianists at one piano--one line of music each. One
hand can easily manage each part. Kagel's piece requires two of the
pianists to tap on a random spot on the piano case with the open hand,
fingertip, fingernail or knuckle. Upper partials are activated throughout
by the silently depressed bass key (held by the middle, sostenuto pedal)
that functions as a bass fundamental.

Selected Works for Four Pianists

Some twentieth-century composers continued the nineteenth-
century practice of scoring for four pianists at two or four pianos--with
or without an orchestra. This survey includes examples by Ingolf
Dahl, Morton Gould, Brian Chapple and Ladislav Kupkovič.

Ingolf Dahl (1912-1970) the Swiss/American composer,
conductor, pianist and music educator, wrote a team piano work skillful
in its idiomatic handling of American folk tunes and rhythms. The
Quodlibet on American Folk Tunes (1953), for eight hands at two
pianos, is based on numerous folk tunes contrapuntally combined in the
manner of a quodlibet. Four of the six tunes are spirited Virginia reels
or square dance melodies: *Boston Fancy, Devil's Dream, Old Fiddler's
Breakdown* (or *Arkansas Traveller*) and *Old Zip Coon* (or *Turkey in the
Straw*). Two slow folk tunes are also quoted: *Deep Blue Sea* (from
the hills of Tennessee) and *California Joe* (a narrative Western cowboy
ballad). Dahl used the words "Fancy", "Blue", "Devil's" and

---

151   Letter to Grant Maxwell from George Crumb (November 19, 1990).

"Breakdown" from these titles to create the subtitle--*Fancy Blue Devil's Breakdown.*

> . . . The tunes go their way merrily, yet they have been
> brought into a convincing interrelation. Above all, this
> work is a rhythmic *tour de force*, full of the bounciness of
> the fiddler's tunes.[152]

The work is in three sections: *Allegro leggiero*, *Poco meno mosso* and *Tempo I*.

The impact of the years of close collaboration with Stravinsky motivated Dahl to conduct and introduce *Les noces* (a work he admired) while teaching at the University of Southern California. Stravinsky's influence can be clearly felt in the *Quodlibet*; it is characterized by a skillful grasp of Stravinskian polyrhythmic and polymetric writing, with clear textures and instrumental virtuosity within the diatonic syntax.   Dahl must have been convinced of the work's value--the *Quodlibet on American Folk Tunes* was orchestrated in 1965.

In 1953, the year when Antheil's *Ballet mécanique, No. 156c*, and Wolpe's *Enactments* were completed, the American Morton Gould (*b* 1913) had a successful premiere of *Inventions* (*I. Warm Up; II. Ballad; III. Schottische, IV. Toccata*)--scored for four pianos and an orchestra of winds (2 flutes, 1 piccolo, 2 oboes, 1 English horn, 2 clarinets, 1 bass clarinet, 2 bassoons and 1 contra bassoon), brass (4 horns, 3 trumpets, 3 trombones and tuba) percussion and timpani. Steinway and Sons, to whom Gould dedicated *Inventions*, commissioned this multiple-piano concerto for their Centenary Gala Concert held in Carnegie Hall on October 19, 1953.[153]   The clever

---

[152]   Hinson, *Music for More Than One Piano*:47.

[153]   The anniversary event proved to be spectacular. A roster of Steinway Artists performed at ten, nine-foot concert grand pianos-- filling the celebrated stage. For an account, refer to Ronald V. Ratcliffe, *Steinway* (San Francisco: Chronicle Books, 1989):128- 132.

and effective work was premiered by the First Piano Quartet[154] and the Philharmonic-Symphony Orchestra of New York, conducted by Dimitri Mitropoulos.

Gould has composed equal, freely tonal parts for all four piano soloists, which are generally used as a group in contrast to the rest of the ensemble. A review by Howard Taubman of the successful premiere performance appeared in the *New York Times* on October 20, 1953, emphasizing the positive attributes of *Inventions*:

> Whatever one may think of the idea of an ensemble of four
> pianos, Mr. Gould made a virtue of his solo combination.
> He did not overload it with doublings or request it to pound
> out great gobs of sound. His writing was idiomatic, crisp
> and sprightly, and by dispensing with the string choirs of
> the orchestra, he complemented the four pianos with an
> instrumental background that was cool and tangy.[155]

The four-piano, eight-hand *Scherzos* by English composer Brian Chapple (*b* 1945) was written from 1969 to 1970. The premiere performance was given in the "Proms" 1976 in the Royal Albert Hall, London.[156] According to Chapple:

> The sources of inspiration for the piece's composition were
> various . . . [It has a] virtuoso potential, . . . rhythmic
> incisiveness and textural brilliance.
>
> *Scherzos* is a graveyard of any pianistic ambitions I may
> have had--the fragments quoted aleatorically in the three-

---

154   Adam Garner, Edward Edson, Glauco D'Attili and Frank Mittler, pianists.

155   Howard Taubman, "Thirty-Four Pianists Render Steinway Tribute," *New York Times* (October 20, 1953):35, Col. 1.

156   The pianists for the premiere were Susan Bradshaw, Richard Rodney Bennet, Anne Shasby and Richard McMahon.

minute central section[157] are predominantly from classic nineteenth-century piano masterpieces (Beethoven's *Sonata, Op. 109*; Liszt's *Gnomenreigen* and *Un Sospiro*; Brahms' *Handel Variations*; Chopin's *B-Flat Minor Scherzo*). The sound world of the work is characterized by the stylistic and tonal clash of these juxtaposed and superimposed quotations and pseudoquotations (from invented mock-Messiaen and from the work itself!) (e.g., predominant E major tonality versus B major or D-Flat major, or the note C).

The work also exuberantly exploits contrasting styles of composition: collage, on underlying twelve-note *cantus*, quasi-minimalist arpeggio and scale work and a hint of vaudeville histrionics in the four pianists' efforts at singing/shouting, as well as percussion effects.[158]

The Czechoslovakian composer Ladislav Kupkovič (*b* 1939)[159] has written two works for eight hands at four pianos: *Happy End* (1975-1976) and *Präludium und Fuga in Form einer Klavierübung* (1977). The demanding *Happy End* was a commissioned work for the Witten Festival of New Chamber Music. A recurrent, principal theme, according to Kupkovič

> . . . comes from Gustav Mahler, my daughter Ida composed the children's waltz, and then there is a Christmas carol (*O, Tannenbaum*).[160]

---

157   Two pianists perform--in any order--any or all of the quotations; the third pianist plays a slow moving and continuous solo that the fourth pianist regularly interrupts.

158   Letter to Grant Maxwell from Brian Chapple (November 18, 1990).

159   Ladislav Kupkovič has been Professor of Music Theory, Twentieth-Century Composition and Composition at the *Hochschule für Musik und Theater* in Hannover since 1976.

160   Letter to Grant Maxwell from Ladislav Kupkovič (November 17, 1990).

The main theme, itself developed, punctuates numerous episodes of increasing length and complexity, the majority of which are minimalist-inspired. The work is fifty minutes in duration and 262 pages long.

Kupkovič's *Präludium und Fuga in form einer Klavierübung* is modest in length compared to *Happy End* (64 pages of approximately only eight minutes duration). Kupkovič explains that he

> . . . used the four pianos in both pieces (particularly in the *Clavierübung*) on account of the polytonal passages (C Major, E-flat major, F-sharp major and A major, the four symmetrical keys). *Happy End* is perhaps more of a philosophy of music; but we were very successful with *Clavierübung* in concerts . . . [161]

Maurice Hinson supports Kupkovič's assessment of *Clavierübung*:

> Brilliant keyboard display with alternating chords, contrary and parallel scales, classic cadences, juxtaposition of keys, fugal polytonal textures, neo-Classic. Instruments are treated soloistically and sometimes orchestrally. Basically tonal with "foreign" keys briefly introduced. Would "bring down the house" when effectively performed.[162]

Indeterminacy and Multiple Pianos

The acceptance of indeterminacy--the intentional utilization of some degree of chance in performance and/or composition--by a broad spectrum of musicians during the 1950s came mostly from the influence of a single American composer, John Cage (*b* 1912).[163]

---

[161]   Ibid.

[162]   Maurice Hinson, *Music for More Than One Piano*:110.

[163]   Robert P. Morgan, *Twentieth-Century Music: A History of Musical Style in Modern Europe and America* (New York; London: W.W. Norton & Co., 1991):359.

Indebted to the composers Satie, Webern and Varèse,[164] Cage listed the"paths [his] musical thought has taken" as:

> . . . composition using charts and move thereon (1951); composition using templates made or found (1952-); composition using observation of imperfections in the paper upon which it is written (1952-); composition without a fixed relation of parts to score (1954-); composition indeterminate of its performance (1958-).[165]

After Cage wrote *Music of Changes* (1951),[166] a lengthy piano work in which all structural elements--amplitude, density, duration, pitch, silence and tempo--were selected by tossing coins and using charts derived from *I-Ching* (the Chinese *Book of Changes*), he wrote numerous works for varying numbers of pianists that involved indeterminate operations:

> . . . *Music for Piano* can be played by any number of pianists but as far as I know the most has been 4. *Winter Music* [is for] 1-20 pianists.[167]

---

164 Richard Kostelanetz, *John Cage* (New York: RK Editions, 1971):143.

165 John Cage, "Composition as Process," *Silence: Lectures and Writings* (Middleton, Conn.: Wesleyan University Press, 1961):18-55. (paraphrased)

166 Cage had radically altered his personal philosophical opinions about music after 1950--from Western to Eastern thought patterns. He attributed his novel ideas to an enlightened awareness of Eastern mysticism (especially Zen Buddhism), Indian music (improvised music based on prescribed scales and rhythmic formulas) and dadaism. [Used in connection with Satie's music in the dada epoch--the iconoclastic movement that flourished around 1917 to 1920, Cage directed the first New York performance of Satie's *Vexations* (c. 1893) in 1963, a twelve-hour-and-ten-minute realization.]

167 Letter to Grant Maxwell from John Cage (October 20, 1990).

In the *Music for Piano* (1952-1956) series, Cage determined individual pitches by invariant/indeterminate/chance operations.

> . . . Cage states that the number of sounds per page is determined from the *I Ching* by means of chance operations: 'a blank sheet of transparent paper is then placed so that its pointal imperfections may readily be observed. That number of imperfections corresponding to the determined number of sounds is intensified with pencil.' [*Silence*, 2nd ed., 1966, p. 60.] This page is then placed on a 'master page', staves and ledger lines inked in, and where a pencilled imperfection falls between two staves a crotchet without a stem is drawn, while in the other cases a whole note is inserted. The clefs are decided by tossing a coin . . .[168]

The role of indeterminacy was further extended to include decisions by performers. The tempo, accidentals, durations, dynamics, selection of pages and the way in which the piano is played (whether at the keyboard, muted or plucked on the strings) were decisions left completely up to the performer's improvisatory discretion, taste and instinct.

After having carried the quest for an absolute asymmetry as far as possible (like Webern with his atonal set pieces), Cage discovered symmetry and asymmetry to be complementary. Individually adapted pitch and interval micro-components, determined through indeterminacy, are organically adopted into the unpredictable macro-structure of a live performance. Multiplicative, microcosmic, symbiotic relationships discordantly and concordantly reside (like the sounds of nature)

> . . . within a universe predicted upon the sounds themselves rather than the mind which can envisage their coming into being.[169]

---

[168]   Sternfeld, F.W., ed., *Music in the Modern Age* (New York; Washington: Praeger, 1973):393-394.

[169]   Cage, "Composition as Process," *Silence: Lectures and Writings*:17-28.

> If. . . it is realized that sounds occur whether intended or
> not, one turns in the direction of those he does not intend.
> This turning is psychological and seems at first to be a
> giving up of everything that belongs to humanity--for a
> musician, the giving up of music. This psychological
> turning leads to the world of nature, where, gradually or
> suddenly, one sees that humanity and nature, not separate,
> are in this world together; that nothing was lost when
> everything was given away. In fact, everything is gained.
> In musical terms, any sounds may occur in any
> combination and in any continuity.[170]

Music for Piano, 4-19; 21-36; 37-52[171]; 53-68; 69-84 are
five sets of sixteen pieces each, and are

> . . . for any number of pianists . . . [and] which may be
> played alone or together . . . Their length in time is free
> and there may or may not be silence between them or they
> may be overlapped. Given a programmed time-length, the
> pianists may make a calculation such that their concert will
> fill it.

> A system (often incomplete) is two staves with [a] line
> between, notes above which latter are noises produced on
> the interior of the piano structure, below on the exterior,
> manually or with beaters.

> M = muted; P = *pizzicato*. (Free combinations and
> harmonics and pedals; duration of individual tones and
> dynamics also free.)[172]

---

[170]   Cage, "Experimental Music," *Silence*:8.

[171]   For a detailed discussion of *Music For Piano 21-36; 37-52*, refer to
John Cage, "To Describe the Process of Composition Used in *Music
for Piano 21-52*," Ibid., 60-61.

[172]   Cage, quoted from the Preface to *Music for Piano 69-84* (New York:
Henmar Press, Inc., 1960):1.

Winter Music (1957),[173] for one to twenty pianists, was written and performed in the same manner as the *Music for Piano* series. It consists mostly of chord aggregates with associated harmonics. The score contains isolated chordal sonorities which, because of the ambiguity of the clef signs, can be sounded in numerous ways. Owing to the number of pitches of these "skyscraper" chords, they are unplayable by a solo pianist, and must be distributed among members of the multiple piano ensemble. As in *Music for Piano*, the pianists determine the number of pages to be performed, dynamics, durations and tempos.

In a twenty-five year retrospective of his works held on May 15, 1958, at Town Hall in New York, John Cage stated his ideas on the aesthetic that led to the development of chance music:

> . . . in this music nothing takes place but sounds: those that are notated and those that are not. Those that are not notated appear in written music as silences . . . try as we may to make a silence, we cannot . . . Until I die there will be sounds. And they will continue following my death. One need not fear for the future of music.
>
> But this fearlessness only follows if, at the parting of the ways, where it is realized that sounds occur whether intended or not, one turns in the direction of those he did not intend . . . [174]

The title *HPSCHD* (1967-1969) is an abbreviated derivation of the word "harpsichord," the six-letter form that is the maximum necessary for computer coding. Enthusiasts hailed it as

> . . . one of the great artistic achievements of the decade . . . , a *Universe Symphony* in the distinctly American tradition dating back to Charles Ives, who spent the last

---

173   Cage's *Winter Music* may be played in whole or part with *Atlas Eclipticalis* (1961, for orchestra).

174   Cage, "Experimental Music," *Silence*:7.

forty years of his life on a similarly all-inclusive but unfinished work.[175]

Cage wrote this multi-media/mixed-media event or "happening" in collaboration with Lejaren Hiller. It was premiered in the 16,000-seat assembly hall at the University of Illinois in Urbana on May 16, 1969. It represented a culmination of the open form principle: a principle of structure in notated music in which the sequence and/or makeup of segments (at some level of the composition) is variable. It was a multimedia collage of sights and sounds, both indeterminate and predetermined. The production lasted about five hours, and involved seven harpsichord players performing seven solos; colored spotlights; fifty-one tapes (amplified, monaural and on fifty-eight channels) playing computer-generated sounds on fifty-one loudspeakers situated around the audience; fifty-two slide projectors showing multi-colored "psychedelic" slides; and six motion-picture projectors showing technological films, computer programs and foreign-language instructions. An audience of several thousand sat, danced, stood and browsed through the "environment."

The musical selections for *HPSCHD* and their organization were an extraordinary blend. One of the harpsichordists was free to select and perform any piece by Mozart. Three others played material based on Mozart's *Introduction to the Composition of Waltzes by means of Dice* on amplified harpsichords. Two other harpsichordists commenced with music by Mozart, and then performed works by Beethoven, Chopin, Schumann, Gottschalk, Ives, Schoenberg, Cage and Hiller. The seventh harpsichordist played a computer-generated repertory of music in equal-tempered twelve-tone tuning. Meanwhile, sound material based on a differing equal-tempered division of the octave, from five to fifty-six pitches, was produced by fifty-one tapes.[176] When a twenty-minute segment of *HPSCHD* was recorded by Nonesuch (H-71224), Cage and Hiller included a computer sheet

---

[175]   Kostelanetz, "Environmental Abundance," *John Cage*:177.

[176]   H. Wiley Hitchcock, *Music in the United States: An Historical Introduction* (2nd Edition. Englewood Cliffs, New Jersey: Prentice-Hall, Inc., 1974):271-272.

which enabled the listener to participate by manipulating knobs and buttons on the stereo set.

The aesthetic principles of Lejaren Hiller (*b* 1924),[177] Morton Feldman (1926-1987), Earle Brown (*b* 1926), Toshiro Ichiyanagi (*b* 1933) and Tōru Takemitsu (*b* 1930) were influenced by their close association in New York with John Cage, Christian Wolff (*b* 1934) and David Tudor (*b* 1926) in the 1950s and 1960s. They made up the first generation of chance composers.

> [Although] the compositions of Morton Feldman, [Earle Brown] and John Cage vary widely in style, . . . a common philosophy unites them: a concentration upon unfamiliar relationships of space and time, and sound and silence, rather than on new melodies and chords, and a conviction that all musical relationships, whether arrived at by chance or by design, have potential value and are worth examination. They all believe there should be more room in music for improvisatory factors, for the elements of casual choice and chance.[178]

Morton Feldman, who studied composition with Wallingford Riegger and Stefan Wolpe, produced a lengthy list of music for three or more pianists:

1)   *Extensions IV* (1952-1953), for three pianos

2)   *Piece for Four Pianos* (1957). As in all his music, the musical ideas of this "series of reverberations from an identical sound source"[179] (Feldman's description of the

---

[177]   Lejaren Hiller wrote a *Fantasy for Three Pianos* in 1951.

[178]   Henry Cowell, quoted from Kostelanetz, ed.,*John Cage*:366. Cowell was one of Cage's teachers.

[179]   Morton Feldman, quoted from Morgan, *Twentieth-Century Music*:366.

piece) are sparse, the tempo is slow and the dynamic level is subdued "with a minimum of attack."[180]

3)   *Trio for Three Pianos* (1957)

4)   *Two Pieces for Three Pianos* (1966)

5)   *First Principles* (1966-1967), for a chamber orchestra consisting of four pianos, two violins, three cellos, two basses, harp and two percussion instruments

6)   *False Relationships; Extended Ending* (1968), for three pianos, cello, violin, trombone and tubular bells (chimes)

7)   *Pianos and Voices I* (1971; premiere in West Berlin, July 16, 1972)

8)   *Pianos and Voices II* (premiere at Bavarian Broadcast Studios, München, August 31, 1972)

Feldman sought new kinds of sound relationships through indeterminacy and multiple pianos. In general, his music is quiet, open-textured and sometimes freely or elastically notated. Some of the multiple piano works require other instrumentalists,

> . . . and/or uninhibited, imaginative, gymnastic, contortionists capable of translating idiogramatic blueprints into sonic motion . . .[181]

Earle Brown's *Twenty-Five Pages* (1953), for one to twenty-five pianos and pianists, was not only his first study in open form, but the first open form work for piano (aside from a brief experiment by Henry Cowell). With this form, the visual ordering--in any sequence,

---

180   "Editorial," *The Piano Quarterly*, Vol. 16, No. 63 (1968):3.

181   Earle Brown, quoted from Morgan, *Twentieth-Century Music*:369-370.

any side up (due to the absence of clef signs) and combination of the twenty-five pages--is indeterminate and is an example of Brown's "space-time notation." It likens its process to Alexander Calder's suspended, mobile sculptures where the elements created by the artist are the same and constant, but their relationships are constantly changing.

After 1960, nearly all of Brown's compositions used open form and graphic notation. As early as *Folio* (1952-1953), an influential collection of seven pieces, Brown experimented with several kinds of notational approaches. Brown has summarized his reasons for becoming involved with new performance processes such as "mobility", "open-form" indeterminacy and new notational systems:

1. Belief that the complexity and subtlety of the desired sound results had passed the point at which standard notation could practically and reasonably express and describe the desired result.

2. The above belief led to a relaxation of finite notational controls and to the conscious inclusion of ambiguity in "generalized" notations with which the performer and the performance process could collaborate.

3. The search for inherent or "process" mobility in the work. The work as an endlessly transforming and generating "organism," conceptually unified in its delivery (the influence of the work of Calder).

4. The above necessitates a search for the "conditional" performance state of spontaneous involvement, responsible to the composed materials and to the poetic conception of the work; "work" in this case being the activity of producing as well as the acquisition of a finite result (the influence of the work of Pollock).

5. The fundamental motivation for all of the above: to produce a "multi-ordinal" communicative activity

> between the composer, the work, and the
> performer[s] and a similarly "open" potential of
> experience for the listener.

The complex word, "multi-ordinal" seems to me to contain
the basic character of communication and meaning to which
much of art is addressing itself today. (Joyce speaks of it
relative to concepts of Vico.) The effects of this concept
are overt in the work of Joyce, Mallarmé, Stein, Duchamp,
Ernst, Calder, Pollock (to mention only those who were my
primary contacts with it), and now in music.[182]

Brown's *December 1952* from *Folio* is representative of the
extreme application of indeterminacy, and is perhaps the earliest
instance of a completely graphic musical score for "one or more
instruments and/or sound-producing media. [It is] performed in any
direction from any point in the defined space for any length of time and
may be performed from any of the four rotational positions in any
sequence."[183] The piece can be realized with two or more pianos
and/or various instruments.

Brown's *Corroboree* (1963-1964), for three or two pianos, was
commissioned by Radio Bremen, Germany.[184] According to Brown
and *Webster's Dictionary*, *Corroboree* is defined as a nocturnal festivity
with songs and symbolic dances by which the Australian aborigines
celebrate events of importance.[185] This noisy festivity or tumult uses
five kinds of piano sonorities as the basic compositional material:
single notes, chords, cluster chords, plucked and muted sounds on the
strings. By means of tempo, frequency and spacing, these five piano

---

[182] Earle Brown, "The Notation and Performance of New Music," *The
Musical Quarterly*, Vol. 72 (1986):199.

[183] Hinson, *Music for More Than One Piano*:25-26.

[184] *Corroboree* was premiered by Aloys, Alfons and Bernhardt
Kontarsky in May, 1964.

[185] Preface to Earle Brown's *Corroboree* (London: Universal Edition,
1970):n.p.

sounds are assigned to each pianist to make "the continuity a kind of sonic-spatial 'conversation'."[186] Mobile structures within closed forms emerge. The pianists follow a predetermined sequence of events while the internal details remain indeterminate.

At the time when members of the New York School--Brown, Feldman, Wolff, Tudor and Cage--acquired ideas from the East, Japanese and some Korean composers were actively participating in Western musical developments. One of the best known of the Japanese Cage disciples who wrote team piano works is Toshiro Ichiyanagi.

Following his studies at the Juilliard School (1952-1961), Ichiyanagi returned to Japan as a recognized composer and organizer of new music concerts. He wrote two pieces for multiple pianos: *Prana* for five players at five pianos and *Music for Piano No. 4 for David Tudor*. The latter is a one page, note-less chance composition for any number of players on any number of pianos. According to Ichiyanagi, the pianists are only allowed silence(s) and sustaining sound(s) "in which no attack should be made." Only these words are provided on the score to direct the pianists in performance, who therefore must possess a tasteful plentitude of musically imaginative ideas. There is an absence of traditional or graphic notation.

Mostly self-educated, Tōru Takemitsu tempered European serialism with characteristics drawn from Asian music. He also used the indeterminate, open forms of the New York School. Takemitsu composed *Corona,* in which the number of participating pianists is variable. The score is graphically notated:

> five pages of coloured circles with 'solar flare' outgrowths
> are an exquisite [Asian] aestheticisation of Cage's *Fontana
> Mix*, with its dots and lines on transparent sheets,
> superimposable at will.[187]

The difference between *Corona* and Cage's *Fontana Mix* is that the former's notation is evidently an "art object" which, through refinement of its visual aspect, encourages the five pianists to display

---

186   Preface to Brown's *Corroboree*:n.p.

187   Richard Toop, *[Tōru Takemitsu.] Complete Piano Works (1952-
       1990): Corona* (Liner notes. Etcetera, 1990):6.

an equivalent amount of refinement in the realization. There is another
fundamental difference between Takemitsu and Cage. Takemitsu
indicates on the score, via its directions to the performer, that *Corona*
is a "Study in Expression:"

> . . . a far cry from Cage's willful eradication of the
> personal, subjective element in music-making.[188]

Since 1961, Takemitsu's music is often ametric. He uses
quasi-serial combinations, small cells and forms evolving from
perpetual variations of these small segments. The rests between
sections become as important as sounds. And like György Ligeti of
Hungary and Lutoslawski and Penderecki of Poland, for Takemitsu, the
search for novel sonorities and timbres was an important concern. In
1964, Takemitsu was invited by the East-West Center of Hawaii to
present a series of lectures in collaboration with John Cage. He said
of this East/West relationship that he:

> . . . would like to develop in two directions at once: as a
> Japanese with respect to tradition, and as a Westerner with
> respect to innovation. Deep down I would like to preserve
> both musical genres, each in its own legitimate form. But
> to take these fundamentally irreconcilable elements simply
> as a starting point for varied compositional uses is in my
> opinion no more than a first step. I would like the two
> forces to struggle with one another. In that way I can
> avoid isolation from the tradition and yet also push toward
> the future in each new work.[189]

Minimalism and Multiple Pianos

The term minimalism is not applied to music in which the
material is literally minimal, like Cage's *4'31"*, but to compositions

---

[188] Toop, *Complete Piano Works (1952-1990): Corona*:6.

[189] Tōru Takemitsu, quoted in Morgan, *Twentieth-Century Music*:422.

based on the repetition of short figures: as seen in the music of Terry Riley, Steve Reich and Philip Glass.

> There are adumbrations of this art in Cage (e.g. *Music for Marcel Duchamp*, 1947), but its more immediate sources were in the music created by Riley and Young in the mid-1960s, to which Reich and Glass in the late 1960s added a notion of process, or gradual change effected within ostinato textures . . .[190]

Steve Reich (*b* 1936) studied at Mills College with Darius Milhaud and Luciano Berio. Along with Philip Glass, Reich has been a leading exponent of the minimalist movement since the early 1960s. His *Music* (1964) for three or more pianos or piano and tape is an early example of minimalist music.

Reich participated in the premiere and first recording of Terry Riley's seminal work *In C*.[191] This score, for any number of melodic instruments, consists of fifty-three fragments notated on a single page and performed in sequence at the performers' own tempos.

Riley (*b* 1935) and Reich shared a similar compositional approach--both used repetition after experimenting with multiple tape loops and then applying similar methods to instrumental composition. Reich became fascinated with what he called the "phase shifting" possibilities of music; that is, the playing of two or more identical tape loops at slightly different speeds. "Phasing," according to *The New Harvard Dictionary of Music* (1986),

> is a technique developed by Steve Reich in which two subgroups of an ensemble begin by playing the same rhythmic pattern, but with one gradually accelerating until,

---

[190]   Griffiths, *Encyclopedia of 20th-Century Music*:121.

[191]   "Piano Circus" (Kirsteen Davidson-Kelly, Richard Harris, Kate Heath, Max Richter, Ginny Strawson and John Wood, pianists) recently recorded *Steve Reich's Six Pianos; Terry Riley's In C* (Argo, 430 380-2, Air Studios, London, January, 1990).

after a period of being 'out of phase,' the two are again playing the pattern simultaneously or 'in phase.'[192]

This rhythmic basis is primarily derived from Reich's interest and study of African and Balinese music.

Since 1970, Reich has written a number of minimalist works that can be performed by ensembles of multiple keyboards. *Four Organs* (1970) exploits the gradual lengthening in duration of individual pitches of an unchanging chord.[193] Reich continued to experiment with similar--albeit amplified forces--in *Phase Patterns* (1970) for four electric organs.[194]

Reich's *Six Pianos* was premiered at the John Weber Gallery in New York, May 1973, and was given its European premiere at the *Süddeutscher Rundfunk* in Stuttgart in January 1974. In Steve Reich's words:

> *Six Pianos* (1973) grew out of the idea I had for several years to do a piece for all the pianos in a piano store. The piece which actually resulted is a bit more modest in scope since too many pianos (especially if they are very large grands) can begin to sound thick and unmanageable. Using six smaller grands or spinet pianos made it possible to play the fast, rhythmically intricate kind of music I am drawn to while at the same time allowing the players to be physically close together so as to hear each other clearly.
>
> The piece begins with three pianists all playing the same eight-beat rhythmic pattern, but with different notes for each pianist. Two of the other pianists then begin in unison to build up gradually the exact pattern of one of the

---

[192]   Randel, ed., "Minimalism," *The New Harvard Dictionary of Music*:628.

[193]   *Four Organs* was premiered by Michael Tilson Thomas, Steve Reich and members of the Boston Symphony Orchestra in Boston's Symphony Hall, and then in Carnegie Hall.

[194]   *Phase Patterns* was presented at Pierre Boulez's first series of Perspective Encounter Concerts in New York.

pianists already playing by putting the notes of this fifth
beat on the seventh beat of their measure, then his first
beat on their third beat, and so on until they have
constructed the same pattern with the same notes, but two
beats out of phase. The end result is that of a pattern
played against itself, but one or more beats out of phase.
Though this result is similar to many older pieces of mine,
the process of arriving at that result is new. Instead of
slow shifts of phase, there is a percussive buildup of beats
in place of rests. The use of the pianos here is truly more
like sets of tuned drums . . .

This process of rhythmic construction is followed by a
doubling of the resulting patterns by one or two other
pianists and is then continued in three sections marked off
by changes in mode, key and, gradually, position on the
keyboard, the first being in D major, the second in E
dorian, and the third in B natural minor.[195]

Reich composed *Music for Mallet Instruments, Voices and
Organ* in 1973, scored for 4 maracas, 2 glockenspiels, metallophone,
3 female voices and electronic organ. The premiere took place at the
Tage der Neuen Musik in Hannover in January, 1974, under the
sponsorship of Radio Bremen. Reich indicates that *Music for Mallet
Instruments* can also be performed on six pianos. It is important to
note that in 1980, Reich released his scores for performance by any
combination or ensemble of instruments.

Music for Eighteen Musicians (1975), scored for four pianos,
violin, cello, 2 clarinets, 4 female voices, 3 marimbas, 2 xylophones
and metallophone, was a turning point for Reich:

. . . It introduced a new technique involving pulsed
durations determined by the breathing of the performers, .
. . and reflected his increasing interest in richer textures
and more full-bodied chordal sequences. The latter, though
simple and repetitive in the extreme, give rise to slow-
moving progressions with definite modal-tonal connotations

---

[195]   Steve Reich, *Six Pianos* (Liner notes. Deutsche Grammophon, 427
428-2 GC 2, 1974):n.p.

. . . As Reich commented: 'There is more harmonic movement in the first five minutes of *Music for Eighteen Musicians* than in any other complete work of mine to date' [quoted from liner notes for the recording, ECM 821-417-1].[196]

Additional minimalist works by Reich for multiple keyboards include *Variations for Winds, Strings and Keyboards* (1979, with chamber orchestra; 1980, with full orchestra); and *Music for Percussion and Keyboards* (1984). Steve Reich's summarizes his style in the following comments:

Performing and listening to a gradual musical process resembles pulling back a swing, releasing it and observing it gradually come to rest . . . turning over an hourglass and watching the sand slowly run through the bottom . . . placing your feet in the sand by the ocean's edge and watching, feeling and listening to the waves gradually bury them.[197]

Microtonality and Multiple Pianos

While Stravinsky was completing the final version of *Les noces* (1923), Ivan Wyschnegradsky or Vīshnegradsky (1893-1979)--the "great Russian pioneer of microtonal music"[198]--began the construction of a quarter-tone piano.

Wyschnegradsky studied composition at the St. Petersburg Conservatory with Nicolas Sokolov from 1911 to 1914, and then with Alexander Scriabin, whom he considered his musical and spiritual

---

[196]   Steve Reich, "Music as a Gradual Process," *Writings About Music* (Halifax, Nova Scotia: Nova Scotia College of Art and Design Press, 1974):9.

[197]   Steve Reich, "Music as a Gradual Process," *Writings About Music* (Halifax, Nova Scotia: Nova Scotia College of Art and Design Press, 1974):9.

[198]   From a letter to Grant Maxwell from Bruce Mather, the Canadian pianist and composer (November 13, 1990).

mentor.[199] His early compositions were influenced by Wagner and Tchaikovsky. His interest in the music and philosophy of Scriabin, together with religious experiences of "cosmic consciousness" in 1916 and 1918, led to the exploration of microtones within a tonal framework after 1918 (the extension of musical resources to include microtones had become symbolic of human consciousness expanding into the cosmic).[200] He used ultrachromatic scales (quarter-tone, sixth-tone, etc.), and as well, his compositions became "pantonal," or extended beyond the point at which they could, be said to be in a tonality or shifting in or out of many tonalities.

After the Russian Revolution of 1919, he emigrated to France in the hope of having his design for a quarter-tone concert piano built by the Pleyel firm. After settling in Paris, he continued experimentations with artificial modes and scales consisting of micro-tones and micro-intervals.

While in Germany, from 1922 to 1923, Wyschnegradsky collaborated with the microtonalists Richard Stein, Willi von Moellendorf, Jörg Mager and Alois Hába, in the construction of a workable quarter-tone piano. The construction of the microtonal keyboard was unsuccessful. Wyschnegradsky was discouraged from composing ultrachromatic works because a practical and feasible solution for their performance could not be found.

In 1936, even though Pleyel had finally constructed a three-manual quarter-tone piano from his plans, Wyschnegradsky came upon and discovered a solution: score two or more conventionally tuned instruments (in this case, pianos) which are tuned to different pitches (that is, a quarter-, sixth-, twelfth-tone above and below A=440, combined with the conventional tuning at A=440). Wyschnegradsky thereafter composed exclusively for pianos tuned a microtone (chiefly

---

[199]   Like Scriabin, Wyschnegradsky left instructions that his music be accompanied by colored lighting. His *La journée de l'existence* (1916-1917), an oratorio inspired by Scriabin's compositional influence for which he also wrote the text, dealt with the development of "cosmic consciousness."

[200]   John Vinton, ed., "Ivan Wyschnegradsky," *Dictionary of Contemporary Music* (New York: E.P. Dutton & Co., Inc., 1974):325.

a quarter-tone) apart and consequently revised previous works (such as *Ainsi parlait Zarathoustra*) to accommodate his new approach. On November 10, 1945, he presented a concert of his multiple-piano microtonal music, at which he conducted the premiere of *Cosmos* for four pianos.

After a brief hiatus, in the 1950s, Wyschnegradsky exploited the idea of, in his words, a

> . . . universe of sound which was in a state of permanence and which tended towards resolution within the sound continuum.[201]

This led him to a conception of "cyclic, non-octaval intervals"[202] on the basis of reduced or extended octaves. With this system, he created control over the extremes of ultra chromaticism as

---

[201] Taken from Detlef Gojowy, "Ivan Vïshnegradsky," New Grove Dictionary of Music and Musicians, Vol. 20:14.

[202] According to Bruce Mather, these "cyclic, non-octaval intervals" are cycles that repeat not at the octave, but at a slightly smaller or larger interval. For example, in Wyschnegradsky's *Dialogues à trois, Op. 51*, that interval is the major seventh or thirty-three, sixth-tones. This interval can be subdivided equally (11 + 11 + 11) in "perfect regular structure" (requiring three pianos), in "irregular structure--one color" (9 + 12 + 12, requiring one piano) or in "irregular structure--two colors" (10 + 11 + 12, requiring two pianos). Wyschnegradsky associated each piano with a color. In *Op. 51*, he also uses his system of *ultrachromatique rhythmique*, very subtle changes in tempo which are the counterpart of the smaller intervallic distances.

> Mather reduces this language to three primary compositional elements:
> 1. broken chords
> 2. repeated notes or chords
> 3. regular fluctuations between two chords.

> Source: Bruce Mather, liner notes for *Music for Three Pianos in Sixths-of-Tones* (Montréal: McGill University Records, 83017, 1985).

well as sixth- and twelfth-tones. However, in his principal compositions his organization of musical forms remained traditional.

The catalogue of Wyschnegradsky's works for three or more pianists is lengthy and impressive:[203]

> *Op. 14, Deux choeurs* (1927-1936) in quarter-tones, for four pianos and chorus on texts by A. Pomorsky.

> *Op. 17, Ainsi parlait Zarathoustra, Symphonie en système de quarts tons* (1929-1930); revised in 1936 for four pianos (two pianos are tuned to A=440; two are tuned a quarter-tone above A=440).

> *Op. 23, Premier fragment symphonique* (1934), revised in 1936 for four pianos in quarter tones (two pianos are tuned to A=440; two are tuned a quarter-tone below A=440); arranged for orchestra in 1967.

> *Op. 24, Deuxième fragment symphonique* (1937), for four pianos in quarter-tones (two pianos are tuned to A=440; two are tuned a quarter-tone below A=440).

> *Op. 25, Linnita* (1937), one-act pantomime for three women's voices and four pianos in quarter-tones (two pianos are tuned to A=440; two are tuned a quarter-tone below A=440). The text is by the composer's mother, S. Wyschnegradsky.

> *Op. 27, Acte choréographique* (1938-1940; revised 1958-1959), for bass baritone, chorus, percussion and four pianos (two pianos are tuned to A=440; two are tuned a quarter-tone below A=440). The text is by the composer.

---

[203]   All of Wyschnegradsky's compositions, except *Cosmos*, can be obtained from his son, Monsieur Dimitri Vicheney, 6 rue Plumet, 75015, Paris. *Cosmos* is published by Editions du Mordant (106 Blvd. Lefèvre, 93600 Aulmay sous Bois, France).

Op. 28, Cosmos (1939-1940) in quarter-tones, for four pianos (two pianos are tuned to A=440; two are tuned a quarter tone below A=440).

Op. 30, Prélude et fugue (1945) in sixth-tones, for three pianos.

Op. 32, Troisième fragment symphonique (1946) in quarter-tones, for four pianos (two pianos are tuned to A=440; two are tuned a quarter-tone below A=440).

Op. 37, Quatrième fragment symphonique (1956) in quarter-tones, for four pianos (two pianos are tuned to A=440; two are tuned a quarter-tone below A=440) and *ondes martenots*.

Op. 38, Arc-en-ciel (1956) in twelfth-tones, for six pianos.

Op. 45, Etude sur les mouvements rotatoires (1961), for two pianos in quarter-tones, four-hands each; arranged for orchestra in 1964.

Op. 46, No. 1, Composition (1961) in sixth-tones, for three pianos.

Op. 51, L'éternel étranger (1950s-1960s) in quarter-tones, for four pianos (two are tuned to A=440; two are tuned a quarter-tone below A=440), solo singers, chorus and percussion, to a text by the composer and subtitled an "*action musico-scénique*". Refer to catalogue 4.

Op. 51, Dialogue à trois (1973-1974) in sixth-tones, for three pianos. Refer to catalogue 2.

Opus Posthumous,   *Four Pianos* (one piano is tuned to A=440; one is tuned a sixth-tone above A=440; one is tuned a quarter-tone above A=440; and

one is tuned a sixth-tone below
A = 440).

The microtonal and theoretical writings of Wyschnegradsky
have been receiving wider recognition in recent years. For instance,
the 1974 issues of *La revue musicale* (Nos. 290-291) were devoted
entirely to his music, and featured his article *L'ultrachromatisme et les
espaces non-octaviants*. In 1977, two concerts honoring his music were
presented in Paris by Radio-France. The Canadian composer and
pianist Bruce Mather took an interest in Wyschnegradsky's music and
organized a concert of his compositions at McGill University in
Montréal that included three world premieres on February 10, 1977.
McGill University Records made the first recording (No. 77002, 1978)
of his quarter-tone music. In 1979, the *"Association d'Ivan
Wyschnegradsky"* in Paris produced additional recordings, as well as
concerts and publications of his music.

Wyschnegradsky dated his "awakening to ultrachromaticism"
November 7, 1918. The successful development of this "cosmic
consciousness," a concept that determined his future as a composer,
established him, in a statement by Nicolas Slonimsky, as a "figure of
legend."[204]

Canadian Composers

At McGill University in Montréal, a trio of Canadian
composer/pianists--John Winiarz (*b* 1952), Jack Behrens (*b* 1935) and
Bruce Mather (*b* 1939)--wrote and performed ultrachromatic, microtone compositions. Ivan Wyschnegradsky was their inspiration.

John Winiarz, born in St. Bonifice, Manitoba, was a student
of Bruce Mather. He wrote *Le parcours du jour* (1982-1983) for three
pianos tuned in sixths-of-tones. Winiarz describes the work as follows:

> Bruce Mather, who knew about my interest in
> microtonality from hearing my *Mikrotonos* for guitar in
> quarter-tones, invited me to compose a work for three

---

[204]   Nicolas Slonimsky, *The Concise Baker's Biographical Dictionary of
         Musicians* (New York: Schirmer Books, 1988):1382.

pianos having a special sixth-tone tuning arrangement. He was preparing the premières of music by the microtonal pioneer Ivan Wyschnegradsky that required this special tuning. Two pianos were tuned with their overall tuning flattened yet in equal temperament so the combination of three pianos would give 36 notes to an octave. Jack Behrens and Bruce Mather also composed new works for this piano ensemble. The music was performed . . . on Thursday, April 21, 1983 in Pollack Concert Hall of McGill University . . .

Le Parcours de Jour features Indian ragas, hence there is a lot of melodic writing with the notes passing about a lot between the three instruments. Synchronization difficulties were alleviated by the fact that Bruce Mather conducted the ensemble. The form of the piece is arch-like, with the final contrapuntal section (p. 15-16) acting as a kind of resumé of the entire piece (accented notes represent tonics of the different ragas). I considered the piano ensemble to be like one big piano subdivided into three instruments. Ideally, three identical grand pianos should be used so the timbre is uniform. The music was composed directly in sixth-tone tuning, and later notated to fit the three pianos. Because of [the] vast number of notes available due to the microtonal tuning, I intentionally limited the range of the music to about four octaves. Another consideration was that the ear is most sensitive to pitch in the mid-range. The entire piano range, therefore, was not used.[205]

Jack Behrens, born in Lancaster, Pennsylvania, and a student of Peter Mennin, Vincent Persichetti, Roger Sessions, Darius Milhaud, Stefan Wolpe and John Cage, teaches at the University of Western Ontario in London, Ontario. Behrens's *Aspects* (1983) is also a microtonal composition for three pianos in sixths-of-tones.[206] It consists of a Prologue, six Episodes and a Postlude. According to Behrens, *Aspects* is, in intent:

---

[205]   Letter to Grant Maxwell from John Winiarz (December 20, 1990).

[206]   Letter to Grant Maxwell from Jack Behrens (January 21, 1991).

. . . a work for one piano with enhanced pitch possibilities; that is, for the most part the work is not antiphonal, with one piano echoing or reflecting another. Against a static pitch centre the Prologue quietly explores the "feel" of microtonal possibilities; these are reaffirmed (with many octaves slightly enlarged) in the Postlude. In the body of the composition microtones are sometimes used to "color" pitches (especially in the final Prankish Episode) and are frequently treated as points of fluctuation (rather than steps) or as ingredients in clusters (Episode 1). In other instances spatial expansion (Episode 3) or interval expansion (Episode 5) is explored . . . [207]

Bruce Mather composed *Poème du délire* (1982) for three pianos in sixths-of-tones. For its organization of pitch, Mather:

. . . uses Wyschnegradsky's system of "non-octaviant spaces", modified to produce a scale of thirds- and sixths-of-tones. Formally it is a mosaic of six different textures: (1) monody; (2) a slow melody accompanied by complex broken chords; (3) a chorale with chords of 3, 5, 8 and 13 notes; (4) a melody of moderate pace accompanied by solid chords; (5) trills and chromatic (semitone) scales accompanied by slowly broken chords and (6) fast tremolos and ostinatos. *Poème du délire* is dedicated to the memory of A. Scriabin and his disciple Ivan Wyschnegradsky. In the title there is the allusion to Scriabin's *Poème de l'extase* and *Poème du feu*. The composer found a certain delirium in composing in sixths-of-tones.[208]

Prior to his appointment at McGill and a brief Parisian encounter with Ivan Wyschnegradsky in the early 1970s, Bruce Mather studied with a distinguished and impressive roster of Canadian, American and European composers/pedagogues: Godfrey Rideout, Roy Harris, Oskar Morawetz, Darius Milhaud, Pierre Boulez and Oliver

---

[207]   Letter to Grant Maxwell from Jack Behrens (January 21, 1991).

[208]   Bruce Mather, *Music for Three Pianos in Sixths of Tones* (Montréal: McGill University Records, 83017, 1985).

Messiaen. This is indicative, in general, of the cross-pollination of musical styles in Canada. The Canadian multiple-piano repertoire composed since the early 1960s is astonishingly rich and multifarious.[209]

---

[209] Parallel to diverse developments in the United States, Canada contributed an imaginative and substantial collection of repertoire for three or more pianists in a relatively short period of time.

CONCLUSIONS

The sizeable repertoire for three or more pianists of original and transcribed/arranged compositions--as shown by the accompanying catalogue, Part II of this study--began with J.S. Bach's three concertos for three and four harpsichords. Important multiple-piano compositions followed in the late-eighteenth and nineteenth centuries: Mozart's *Concerto, K. 242 ("Lodron")* for Three Fortepianos; Czerny's pioneering experiments for three or more pianists at one or more pianos; Kalkbrenner's multiple piano works composed for Chopin's premiere in Paris; and *oeuvres* by Liszt, Moscheles, Smetana, Glazunov and Rachmaninov, among others.

Music for three or more pianists became a commercial success relatively early in the 1800s. Along with the burgeoning pianoforte industry in the nineteenth century, promoted by popular touring virtuosos like Gottschalk and his insatiable appetite for piano monster concerts--an entertainment in the great American tradition that produced Barnum and Bailey, Macy's Thanksgiving Day parade, the Walt Disney Parks, Las Vegas and New York's Great White Way, Broadway--there was a healthy market for transcriptions and arrangements of symphonic, balletic and operatic material. Salon pieces with fanciful titles--*Cooing Dove Polka*, *Crimson Sunset*, *Flying Squadron Galop*-- were a music industry of their own for all ages and occasions.

Percy Grainger set a precedent for invaluable, didactic, pedagogically orientated and entertaining "fripperies" for "piano team-work," anticipating modern day beginner-to-intermediate piano class instruction and early childhood music education programs. Children could now participate in chamber music, honing their listening and technical skills from an early age and within a social environment.

The twentieth century witnessed a significant interest in the literature for multiple pianos and pianists. Important composers wrote for the medium, among them Ives, Ravel, Stravinsky, Antheil, Dallapiccola and Milhaud. Also, one can find noteworthy twentieth-century arrangements and transcriptions of staple, standard works which were readily accepted by the public. For instance, The First Piano Quartet had a weekly radio program from New York City in the 1950s of four-piano arrangements of serious and popular works which later produced numerous recordings. Hollywood captured the visual enticement of multiples of pianos, for example, with Warner Brothers' and Busby Berkeley's *Gold Diggers of 1935*, and the scene with José Iturbi in the Hollywood Bowl with rows of grands and pianists performing an arrangement of Liszt's *Hungarian Rhapsody No. 2*, in a musical *Anchors Aweigh* from the Metro Goldwyn Mayer studio. At the opening ceremonies for the 1984 Summer Olympic Games in Los Angeles, fifty white grand pianos were used for a live performance of an abbreviated version of Gershwin's *Rhapsody in Blue*. The public seems to enjoy monster-concert spectacles.

A rich variety of the literature for three or more pianists continues to increase at a healthy and respectable rate. Contemporary composers, in their constant search for novel sounds and syntax, and their exploration of the sonic capabilities and resources of the piano, have tended to favor unique instrumental combinations, and the multiple piano medium is no exception. The recent literature--in combination with other acoustic and electronic instruments, voice(s) and/or tape--is a testimony to twentieth-century experimentation, discoveries and eclecticism. Perhaps the ability to create orchestral sonorities and effects, the visual aspect, the pooling of talent and technical capabilities, the urge to share the experience of performing music with a larger-than-usual ensemble, have collectively ensured a consistent demand for, and continual, ever-increasing expansion of, the repertoire.

> Between the wars, persons concerned with the idiomatic purification of the piano as a concert instrument waged a highly successful revolt against the admittedly lush taste of the Late Romantic virtuosos, particularly in the matters of dynamic extremes and "unpianistic" coloration. We consequently abjured both the gnomic whispers of a de Pachmann and the cataclysmic thunderings of a Paderewski; we also learned to look with suspicion on the richly somber nightscapes of a Rachmaninoff and the delicate Fragonard coloring of a Gieseking. We made fashionable a severely defoliated piano style that is clinically pure in much the same doctrinaire sense that Corbusier's architecture is. Unfortunately, in practice this style has proved to be disappointingly monochromatic--and, in all but the most masterly hands, emotionally dull to boot.

Whatever else "Monster Concert" may be, dull it is not. .
. .[210]

The many-splendored sonorities of music for three or more pianists--on library shelves, second-hand book shops, in publisher's catalogues, in composer's portfolios, in local music stores--await discovery and rediscovery: the thoughtful and solemn, the lighthearted and frivolous, along with the educational and entertaining.

---

[210] Robert Offergeld, "A Monster Concert In the Great American Tradition," *Stereo Review* (April, 1973):108-109.

PART II

CATALOGUE

GUIDE TO THE CATALOGUE

The following sample illustrates the format for each entry.

1. Composer   2. Composer's Date(s)

GOULD, Morton (*b* 1913), American   **3. Nationality**
   N/A   N/A   **4. Transcriber(s)/**
                                             Arranger(s)
                                             5. Transcriber's/
                                             Arranger's Date(s)

6. Title of Composition
   Inventions, 4P8H, piccolo, 2 flutes, 2 oboes, English
                         horn, 2 clarinets, bass clarinet,
                         2 bassoons, contra bassoon, 4 horns,
                         3 trumpets, 3 trombones, tuba and
                         percussion
                               7. Number of Pianos and/or
                                           Pianists Required; Scoring

   1. *Warm-up*
   2. *Ballad*
   3. *Schottische*   **8. Movements (when**
   4. *Toccata*   **applicable)**

- S,G 1953 (17 ½*100)   **9. Publisher(s) or Manuscript**
   LC-M1045. G 715   **10. Publication and/or**
                                           Composition Date(s)
                                    11. Duration and/or Number of
                                         Pages
                                    12. Location(s) of Score

-Hin-*MPO*:115
-Letter from Gould, August 30, 1990
                                    13. Principal Source(s) of
                                      Information
   N/A   **14. Miscellaneous Information**

For further explanation:

1.   **COMPOSER'S NAME**

2.   **COMPOSER'S DATE(S)**
        Not all composers have divulged their date of birth.
        Others', like Fred T. Baker's, have disappeared
        without a trace.

3.   **NATIONALITY**
        The country of the composer's origin may also be
        given when it concerns foreign-born residents of a
        particular country.   For example Percy Alderidge
        Grainger became an American citizen, but was born
        in Australia.

4.   **TRANSCRIBER(S)/ARRANGER(S)**

5.   **TRANSCRIBER'S/ARRANGER'S DATE(S)**
        Similar to item No. 2.

6.   **TITLE OF COMPOSITION**
        This may include key and/or cataloguing number.

7.   **NUMBER OF PIANOS AND/OR PIANISTS REQUIRED;
        SCORING**
        The words "piano(s)" and "hand(s)" are abbreviated
        as "P" and "H" respectively. If a work is written for
        four pianos, eight hands (that is, four pianists), for
        example, it is abbreviated as "4P8H". All other
        instrumentalists, singers, . . . , are listed directly
        afterward.

8.   **MOVEMENTS**
        This may include title and/or tempo for each
        movement.

9.   PUBLISHER(S) OR MANUSCRIPT

Not all publishers indicated have a copy of the score for sale: some are on rental or some have discontinued printing or publishing the composition. (One should consult the publisher, whenever possible, to verify the score's availability.) If or when a composer can be contacted by mail, a photocopy of the manuscript perhaps could be obtained. Many addresses of Music Publishers, and Agents/Parent Companies of Music Publishers might be found in the current edition of *Musical America: International Directory of the Performing Arts* (New York: ABC Consumer Magazines, Inc., annually published in December), or through National Information Centres (such as the Canadian Music Centres or American Music Center).

10.   COMPOSITION DATE AND/OR PUBLICATION DATE(S)

If the date of composition is unknown or unavailable, a copyright date may appear with a ©.

11.   DURATION AND/OR NUMBER OF PAGES

The duration represents the approximate performance time of the composition because (needless to say) not all sources agree. The number to the left of the asterisk is the duration of the work (expressed in minutes); the number to the right of the asterisk is the number of pages of the work. For example, (17 1/2*100) represents a work that is of 17 1/2 minutes duration and is 100 pages in length.

12.   LOCATION(S) OF SCORE

Scores and manuscripts in libraries are listed when known. See page 121 for a list of abbreviations of not only music publishers and agents/parent companies, but also college and university libraries, public libraries and national/international information centres. The Library of Congress classification numbers, with their corresponding headings, are as follows:

Library of Congress Classification	Established Headings
M213	Canons, fugues, etc. (Six hands at One Piano)
M213	Overtures arranged for piano (Six Hands at One Piano)
M213	Piano Music (Five Hands at One Piano)
M213	Piano Music (Six Hands at One Piano)
M213	Piano Music, Arranged (Six Hands at One Piano)
M213	Piano Muisc (Eight Hands at One Piano)
M213	Harpsichord Music (Three Harpsichords)
M216	Harpsichord Music (Four Harpsichords)
M216	Overtures Arranged for Piano (Eight Hands at Two Pianos)
M216	Piano Ensembles
M216	Piano Ensembles, Arranged
M216	Piano Music (Five Hands at Two Pianos)
M216	Piano Music (Six Hands at Two Pianos)
M216	Piano Music, Arranged (Six Hands at Two Pianos)
M216	Piano Music, (Eight Hands at Two Pianos)
M216	Piano Music, Arranged (Eight Hands at Two Pianos)
M216	Rondos (Eight Hands at Two Pianos)

M216	Suites (Piano Ensemble)
M216	Symphonic Poems, Arranged (Eight Hands at Two Pianos)
M216	Symphonies, Arranged (Eight Hands at Two Pianos)
M216	Variations (Four Harpsichords)
M216	Variations (Eight Hands at Two Pianos)
M1005 and M1006	Three Organs with Orchestra
M1010	Suites (Three Pianos with Orchestra)
M1010 and M1011	Concertos (Four Harpsichords)
M1010 and M1011	Concertos, Arranged (Four Harpsichords)
M1010 and M1011	Concertos (Three Pianos)
M1010 and M1011	Four Harpsichords with Orchestra
M1010 and M1011	Three Pianos with Orchestra

13. PRINCIPAL SOURCES OF INFORMATION

14. MISCELLANEOUS INFORMATION

ABBREVIATIONS

A	Allan & Co. Prop., Ltd., Melbourne
AA	Author's Agency of Polish Music Pub., Warsaw
ACA	American Composer's Alliance/Composer's Facsimile Editions, New York
AgAu	Agencja Autorska, Warsaw
Aib	Joseph Aibl, Leipzig
Alf	Alfred Publishing Co., Inc.
AMA	W.A. Mozart, *Alte Mozart-Ausgabe*
AMC	American Music Center, New York
And	Johann André, Offenbach am Main
Ari	Ariadne, Vienna
arr./arrs.	arrangement(s) or arranger(s)
Art	Artia, Prague
ASCAP	American Society of Composers, Authors and Publishers, New York
Ash	Edwin Ashdown, Ltd., London
AshD	Ashley Dealers, Inc., Hasbrouck Heights, New Jersey
ASU	Arizona State University, Tempe: Music Library
Aug	Augener & Co., London
b	born
B&W	Balmer & Weber, St. Louis
Bar	Bärenreiter-Verlag
BBC	BBC, Central Music Library, London
BC	Banff Centre Library, Banff, Alberta
Bea	Beal & Co., London
Bel	M.P. Belaieff, Leipzig
Belw	Belwin Mills
Bes	W. Bessel et Cie., Moscow; St. Petersburg
BMC	Boston Music Co., Boston
Bo&Bo	Bote & Bock, Berlin (no longer in business)
Bo&H	Boosey & Hawkes, Inc., New York
Bol	H. Bollman & Sons, St. Louis
Bor	Borkey
Bos	Bosworth & Co., Ltd., London
BP	Bradley Publications, New York
BPL	Boston Public Library

Br & H	Breitkopf & Härte, Wiesbaden
Brai	S. Brainard's Sons, Cleveland
Bran	Brandus et Cie., Paris
Brau	Adolf Brauer/F. Plötner, Dresden
BrM	British Library/Museum, Dept. of Manuscripts/Music, London
Bro	Brodt Music Co., Charlotte, NC
BTG	Birch Tree Group (no longer in business; see Sengstack Group)
BU	Brandon University, John E. Robbins Library
BW	J.S. Bach, *Bach-Werke*
c.	circa
©	copyright
CAML	Canadian Association of Music Libraries, Music Division, National Library of Canada, Ottawa
Can	Canyon Press, Cincinnati
Car	A.G. Carisch, Milan
CeBeDeM	Centre Belge de Documentation Musicale, Brussels
Cha	Chappell, London; NY rental library: R.E.D. Bldg., Mitsubishi Center, NY.
Chu	John Church Co., Cincinnati
CM	J.W. Chester Music Ltd., London; New York
CMC-BC	Canadian Music Centre, Vancouver, B.C.
CMC-Nat	Canadian Music Centre, National Office, Toronto
CMC-P	Canadian Music Centre, Prairie Region, Calgary
CMC-Q	Canadian Music Centre, Québec Region, Montréal
CMP	Century Music Publishing Co., Inc.
Coc	Cocks Publishing Co. (no longer in business)
Col	Franco Columbo
Cole	Harry Coleman, Philadelphia
ConMC	Contemporary Music Center, Ltd., Dublin
Cos	Costallat et Cie., Paris
CPE	Composer/Performer Edition (Harrow); Composer to Player Edition
CPH	Concordia Pub. House, St. Louis
CPP/Bel	Columbia Pictures Publications/Belwin, Inc., Miami
Cra	A. Cranz Editions, Brussels; London
Cur	Curtis Institute of Music, Philadelphia
Curw	Curwin Edition

d	died
Dia	Anton Diabelli & Co., Vienna (no longer in business)
Dit	Oliver Ditson Co., Boston
Dona	E. Donajowski, London
Done	Donemus Publishing House, Amsterdam
Dor	Dorn Publications, Needham, MA
Dur	Durand S.A. Editions Musicales, Paris
EAMD	European American Music Distributors Corp., Valley Forge, PA
ed.	edited
ED	Edizioni Musicali Via M. Ortigara
Edi	Editio Musica, Budapest
Elk	William Elkin Music Services, Norwich, England
Ell	John F. Ellis & Co., Washington, D.C.
EM	Edition Modern, München
EMS	Eulenberg Miniature Score
En	Enoch & Cie., Paris
Esc	Editions Max Eschig
E/V	Henri Elkan Music Pub. Co., Inc./Vogel, Inc., New York; Bryn Mawr, PA (Theodore Presser affiliation)
Fab	Faber Music Ltd., London
Fau	J.H. Faunce Co., Philadelphia
F,C	Carl Fischer, Inc., New York
F,J	J. Fischer & Bro. (no longer in business)
Fee	Feedback Studio Verlag
Fle	Edwin A. Fleisher Music Collection, Free Library, Philadelphia
FMD	Foreign Music Distributors, Chester, NY
Fr/En	Fraser/Enoch Publications
Free	H. Freeman & Co., Brighton, England
Fri	Johannes Fritsch, Rolf Gerhlhaar & Co., Cologne
Forb	Robert Forberg, Leipzig
Fors	Forsyth Bros., Ltd. (no longer in business)
FPQC	*First Piano Quartet Collection*, Special Collections (JOB 76-14), New York Public Library at Lincoln Center
Fur	Adolf Fürstner, Berlin (no longer in business)
G&C	G & C Music Corp., c/o Chappell
G&W	Gebethner & Wolff Publishing, Warsaw

Ger	Musikverlag Hans Gerig, Cologne
Gla	Conrad Glaser, Leipzig
GM	Gesellschaft de Musikfreunde, Vienna
GMC	Galaxy Music Corp., Boston
GME	Galliard Music Editions, Ltd., London
GMP	General Words and Music Publishing Co., Inc., Hastings-on-Hudson, NY
Gou	Goulding, D'Almaine/Potter & Co., Dublin
Gr	Léon Grus, Paris
Gut	A. Gutheil, Moscow
H	hand(s)
Hal	William Hall & Son, New York (no longer in business)
Ham	J. Hamelle et Cie., Paris
HanG	William Hansen Group, Copenhagen, Stockholm, Frankfurt, Oslo, London, New York/Chester Music, Inc., New York
HanM	Charles H. Hansen Music Corp., New York
Har	Harper Music, Inc., New York
Has	Tobias Haslinger, Vienna (no longer in business)
Hen	Henmar Press, Inc., New York
Heu	Au Ménestrel; Heugel et Cie., Paris
H,F	Fredrick Harris Music Co., Ltd.., Oakville, Ontario
H,G	G. Heinze, Leipzig
HinE	Hinrichsen Edition, London
Hin-*MMP*	Maurice Hinson, *Music for More Than One Piano* (1983)
Hin-*MPO*	Maurice Hinson, *Music for Piano and Orchestra* (1981)
Hin-*PCE*	Maurice Hinson, *The Piano in Chamber Ensemble* (1978)
Hin-*PGTAP*	Maurice Hinson, *Pianist's Guide to Arrangements, Transcriptions, and Paraphrases* (1990)
Hins	Hinshaw Music, Inc., Chapel Hill, NC
HM&T	Hammerstein Music & Theatre Co., Inc.
Hoff	L. Hoffarth, Dresden
Hofm	Friedrich Hofmeister, Leipzig (no longer in business)
HU	Harvard University, Eda Kuhn Loeb Music Library, Cambridge, MA

IMC	International Music Co., New York
IU	Indiana University Music Library, Bloomington, IN
IV	Irmaos Vitale
Jui	Juilliard School, Lila Acheson Wallace Library, New York
Jun	Otto Junne, Leipzig
Jur	P. Jürgenson, Moscow; Leipzig
Kal	Edwin F. Kalmus & Co., Ltd., Boca Bouge, FL (formerly Alfred A. Kalmus, Ltd.)
Kálm	Nádor Kálmán, Budapest; Leipzig
Kis	Friedrich Kistner & Siegel Organum, Leipzig
Kj	Neil A. Kjos Music Co., San Diego, CA
Kle	C.A. Klemm, Leipzig (no longer in business)
KMS	Kalmus Miniature Score
Kuh	A. Kühnel, Leipzig
Kzd	*Klavierspiel zu dritt*, 2 vols., Mainz; London: Schott
L&W	Lee & Walker, Philadelphia
LaF	J.R. La Fleur & Son, London
Lam	P.J. Lammers, Baltimore
Lan	E.L. Lancaster, "Ensemble Repertoire for Class Piano," *Clavier* (Nov. 1976):42-44.
LAPL	Los Angeles Public Library
LC	Library of Congress, Music Division, Washington, D.C.
Led	Alphonse Leduc Editions, Paris; P. Bertrand et Cie
Lee	Leeds Music Corp., New York
Lem	Antoine Henry Lémoine et Cie., Paris; Brussels
Leo	Hal Leonard Pub. Corp., Milwaukee, WI
Lew	Lewis Music Pub., Inc., Carlstadt, NJ
Lit	*Collection Henry Litolff*, Braunschweig; Leipzig (Arthur P. Schmidt Co.); London (Enoch & Sons); Paris (Enoch et Cie.); Milan (Carisch and Janichen); St. Petersburg, Moscow (P. Jürgenson), Leipzig, Frankfurt (C.F. Peters)
L'OL	L'Oiseaux Lyre, Editions des Ramperts, Monaco
Lot	*A Series of Overtures*, E.M. Lott, arr., 1877
LPS	Lea Pocket Scores, New York
Luc	F. Lucca, Milan
m/mm.	measure/measures

MA	*Musical America*, New York
Mag	Magnamusic-Baton, Inc., Music Distributors
Manh	Manhattan School of Music, New York
Mann	Mannes College of Music, Clara Damrosch Mannes Memorial Library, New York
Mark	Edward B. Marks Music Corp.
Marx	Josef Marx Music Co.
Mas	Master's Music
MAU	Mount Allison University, Ralph Pickard Bell Music Library, Sackville, NB
May	Mayence
MCA	Russian Music Dept., MCA Music, New York
Mc&Mar	McGinnis & Marx Music Pub., New York
Men	Au Menestrel, Paris
Mes	C.F. Meser, Berlin; Dresden
MIC	Danish Music Information Center, Copenhagen
Mid	Midbar Music Press, New York
Mil	Mills Music, Inc., St. Louis
MMB	MMB Music, Inc., St. Louis
Moe	Hermann Moeck Verlag, Celle, Germany
Mol	George Molineaux, New York (no longer in business)
MW	W.A. Mozart, *W.A. Mozarts Werke*, ed. by L. von Köchel and others (Leipzig, 1877-1888, suppls. 1877-1910, rev. with changes) XVI/i, 165.
Myk	Myklas Music Press, Boulder, CO
Nau	G. Näumann, Dresden
NBA	J.S. Bach, *Neue Bach-Ausgabe*
New	Newberry Library, Chicago
NKAA	National Keyboard Arts Associates, Los Angeles
NMA	W.A. Mozart, *Neue Ausgabe sämtlicher Werke*, ed. by E.F. Schmid, W. Plath and W. Rehm, Internationale Stiftung Mozarteum, Salzburg (Kassel, 1955-), V:15/i, 155.
Nor	F.A. North & Co., Philadelphia (no longer in business)
Nors	Norsk Musikforlag, Oslo
Nov	Novello & Co., London; Dobbs Ferry, NY
NU	Northwestern University, Music Library, Evanston, IL

NYPL	New York Public Library at Lincoln Center, Music Division, Performing Arts Research Center
NYWC	New York Women Composers, Inc., North Tarrytown, NY
OC	Oberlin College, Conservatory Library, OH
OdB	OdB Editions, London
OS	*L'orchestre au salon*, Paris, ©1874
Ox	Oxford University Press, London
P	piano(s)
P,AC	A.C. Peters & Bro., Cincinnati
P-AP	Pro-Art Publications, Inc., Westbury, NY
Pat	Paterson's Pub. House, London
P,CF	C.F. Peters Corp.
PCM	Peabody Conservatory of Music, Friedheim Library, Baltimore
Per	A.W. Perry's Sons, Sedalia, MO
Pic	E. Julius Pickenhahn, Leipzig
Pied	Piedmont Music Co., Inc., New York
Pla	L. Plattner, Rotterdam
Pol	Polskie Wydawnictwo Muzyczne ("Polish Music Publications"), Krakow
Pon	William A. Pond & Co., New York (no longer in business)
PRG	*The Pianist's Resource Guide, 1978-1979: Piano Music in Print and Literature on the Pianistic Art [by] Joseph Rezits and Gerald Deatsman*
PSCM	Peer-Southern Concert Music
P,T	Theodore Presser Co.
Raa	Raabe & Plothow, Berlin (no longer in business)
Rah	D. Rahter, Hamburg
RCM	Royal Conservatory of Music, Toronto
rev.	revised
Ric	Edizioni G. Ricordi & Co., Milan
Rich	Richault et Cie., Paris (no longer in business)
Rie	Ries & Erler, Berlin (no longer in business)
Riet	J. Rieter-Biedermann, Leipzig
Rob	Lee Roberts Music Pub., Inc., Katonah, New York
Robt	Roberton Pub., London
Rod	C.G. Röder, Leipzig

Roh	William Rohlfing Sons Music Co., Chicago, Milwaukee (no longer in business)
S&G	Schoeder & Gunther, New York
Sal	Editions Salabert, Paris, New York
SBTS	Southern Baptist Theological Seminary, James P. Boyce Centennial Library, Louisville, KY
Schl	Schlesinger, Schemusikhandlung, Berlin
Schm	Arthur P. Schmidt Co., Boston, Leipzig, New York
Scho	Schott Music Corp.
Schoe	Schoenwerk & Co., Paris
Schu	Edward Schuberth & Co., Inc., Leipzig
S,EC	E.C. Schirmer Music Co., Inc., Boston
Seca	Edition Seca
Senf	Bartholf Senff, Leipzig (no longer in business)
Seng	Sengstack Group, Ltd., Princeton, NJ
S,G	G. Schirmer, Inc.
Shaw	Shawnee Press, Inc., Delaware Water Gap, PA
S,H,M	Schmitt, Hall, and McCreary Co., Minneapolis
Sie	C.F.W. Siegel's Musikalienhandlung, Leipzig
Sik	Musikverlag H. Sikovski, Hamburg
Sim	Carl Simon, Musikverlag, Berlin (no longer in business)
Simr	N. Simrock, Bonn (no longer in business)
SMC	Seesaw Music Corp., New York
Smi(or W-S)	White Smith Music Pub. Co., Boston, New York
SP/SA	Smith Publications (ASCAP)/Sonic Art Editions (BMI), Baltimore
St&Ho	Stecher & Horowitz Pub.
Sta	State Music Publishers Edition, Moscow
SteV	Steingräber Verlag, Wiesbaden, Germany
Sti	Stipes Pub. Co., Champaign, Illinois
Su-B	Summy-Birchard, Co., Secaucus, NJ (no longer in business; see Sengstack Group)
SZ	Edizioni Suvini Zerboni, Milan
Tal	Tallapoosa Music, New York
Tem	Templeton Pub. Co.
TPR	Chang and Faurot, *Team Piano Repertoire: A Manual of Music for Multiple Players at One or More Pianos* (1976)

trans.	transcription(s) or transcriber(s)
UA	University of Alberta, Music Resources Centre, Edmonton
UB	Uměleckě Besedy
UBC	University of British Columbia
UC	University of Calgary, Music Library
UCLA	University of California, Music Library, Los Angeles, CA
UCol	University of Colorado, Music Library, Boulder, CO
UE	Universal Edition Pub., Inc.
UME	Unión Musical Española, Madrid
UMic	University of Michigan, Earl V. Moore School of Music Building, Ann Arbor
UMon	Université de Montréal, Bibliothèque de musique, Québec
UR	University of Rochester, Eastman School of Music, Sibley Music Library, Rochester, NY
USC	University of Southern California, University Library
UWO	University of Western Ontario, Music Library, London, Ontario
Vit	Editores Vitale, Sao Paulo, Brazil
Vol	Volkwein Brothers
vol(s).	volume(s)
W/C	Warner/Chappell Music, Inc., Los Angeles, CA
Wei	Joseph Weinberger, Ltd., London
Wil	Joseph Williams Editions, London
Wilk	Frank O. Wilking, Indianapolis, IN
Will	Willig & Co., Pub., Baltimore
Win	E. Winterberg, Jr., Bergedorf
Witz	E. Witzmann & Co., Memphis, IN
WM	Willis Music Co., Florence, KY
Wood	B.F. Wood Music Co., Boston
WSU	Wright State University, Music Library, Dayton, OH
YorU	York University, Scott Library, North York, Ontario
YU	Yale University, Music Library, New Haven, Conn.
Zim	Julius Heinrich Zimmerman, Leipzig

1. NINETEENTH-CENTURY WORKS

ARNOLD, Maurice (1865-1937), American
    [4] Valses élégantes, Op. 30, 2P8H
- Br&H (©1893)
  LC-M216.A75
  Hin-*MMP*:4

BERTINI, Henri (Jérôme) (1798-1876), "Bertini le jeune," English;
    and **HENSELT**, Adolph (1814-1889), German
    *Etudes doigtées pour piano (ou Introduction à celles de J.B.
    Cramer), Op. 100, L'accompaniment d'un deuxième piano
    composé par Adolf Henselt*, 2P8H
- Scho (©1879)
  NYPL

BOEKELMANN, Bernardus (1838-1930), Netherlander
    Marche d'inauguration, 2P8H
- Schu (©1885) (*22)
  LC-M216.B68.M3

CZERNY, Carl (1791-1857), Austrian
1)   *Op. 18: Grande polonaise brillante*, 4P8H
- Coc   c.1820
  LC
- Manuscript: GM
- Hin-*MMP*:45
2)   *Op. 38: Premier grand potpourri concertant*, 2P6H
- Coc
  LC
- Manuscript: GM
- Hin - *MMP*:45
3)   *Op. 84: Deuxième grand potpourri concertante*, 2P6H
- Coc
- Manuscript: GM
- Hin - *MMP*:45
4)   *Op. 212, No.?: Grand potpourri brillant et concertant*,
    NB--only one piece of the six is for 2P6H
- Coc (©1851)

- Manuscript: GM
- Hin-*MMP*:46
5)   *Les pianistes associés, ou Compositions brill antes et concertantes pour un pianoforte à six mains*
         Op. 227: Book 1--Rondeaux brillants, 1P6H
- Pla   c.1831
   LC-M213.C99.R5
   (Refer to *Opp. 295, 296* and *297*.)
         Op. 228: Book 2--Variations brill antes sur le thème tyrolien, de l'opéra La fiancée, 1P6H
         Op. 229: Book 3--Divertissement militaire, 1P6H
- New
6)   *Op. 230: [Premier] quatuor concertant*, 4P8H or 4P8H and orchestra/string quartet
                 c.1825
- Cra
- Dia (©1830?)
   LC-M216.C97.Op.230 (Piano II is missing pages 3 and 4)
   UR-M216.C99
- Hin-*MMP*:46
7)   [*Op. 227, No. 1* or] *Op. 295: Variations brill antes sur un thème de l'opéra, I Montechi e Capuletti [par Bellini]*, 1P6H
- New
8)   [*Op. 227, No. 2* or] *Op. 296: Polonaise*, 1P6H
9)   [*Op. 227, No. 3* or] *Op. 297: Variations brill antes sur un thème de l'opéra, Norma [par Bellini]*, 1P6H
- New
   (NB--*Opp. 295, 296* and *297* combine to form *Op. 227, Nos. 1,2* and *3*.)
10)   *Op. 298: Troisième grand potpourri*, 1P6H
11)   From *Op. 609, Nos. 1-24: The Pianist's Library, 24 Easy Pieces for Solo, Duet and Six Hands--Les trois soeurs, Rondinos*, 1P6H
       1.   *Air suisse: The Shepherds Lay*
       2.   *See the Conquering Hero Comes*
       3.   **ARNE**, *Rule Britannia*
       4.   *Paddy Carey*
       5.   *Air suisse: Lullaby*
       6.   **HÄNDEL**, *Hallelujah Chorus* from the *Messiah*

    7.   *Air suisse: Air de chasse*
    8.   *Last Rose of Summer*
    9.   *Paddy O'Carrol*
- Dit (©188-?) (*7)
BPL (*No. 15, See the Conquering Hero Comes, Rondino*)
- Sim   c.1840
NYPL

12)   *Op. 689: Deux grandes fantaisies sur l'airs de l'opéra* **Norma**
       [par Bellini], 1P6H
13)   *Op. 741: Six fantaisies*, 1P6H
        1. *Fantaisie sur des thèmes d'opéras de Mozart*
        2. *Fantaisie sur des airs écossais*
- Scho (©189-?)
LC-M213.C99.Op.741
        3. *Fantaisie sur des airs irlandais*
- Scho (©184?)
LC-M213.C99.Op.741
        4. *Fantaisie sur des airs anglais*
        5. *Fantaisie sur des airs d'opéras de Donizetti*
        6. *Fantaisie sur des airs d'oratories d'Händel*
14)   *Op. 816: [Deuxième] grand quatuor concertant,* 4P8H
                    c.1851
- Cra (© 1851)
- Manuscript: GM
- Hin-*MMP*:46

DUROE, J.B., French
      Hommage à Verdi: Grande fantaisie sur **Il Travatore, La**
      Traviata *et* **Vêpres siciliennes**, 2P8H
- And (©1924)

FODOR, Antoine (1759-1849), French
      Sonate pour le clavecin ou pianoforte, Oeuvre X, 1P6H
- LC-M213.F65

GLAZUNOV, Aleksandr Konstantinovich (1865-1936), arr., Russian
      La mer (Morye; The Sea), Fantaisie pour grand orchestre,
      Op. 28, 2P8H
- Bel (©1890)   1889

BrM-g.724.d.(14.)
UR-M216.G553m
- Hin-*MMP:*72

GLINKA, Mikhail Ivanovitch (1804-1857), Russian
  Divertimento brilliante on thèmes from Bellini's La
  Sonnambula, 2P6H (solo and duet accompaniment)
- BBC

GOTTSCHALK, Louis Moreau (1829-1869), American
a) 1st version: *El Sitio Zaragoza (The Siege of Saragossa)*, 10P
       c.1851-1853
b) 2nd version: *Bunker's Hill Grand National Symphony for Ten*
       Pianos (rev. of *El Sitio Zaragoza*)

GURLITT, Cornelius (1820-1901), German
1)   *Fantaisie sur un air original, Op. 176*, 2P8H
- Aug (©1891)   1890
  BrM-h.559.d.(3.)
2)   *Husarenmarsch*, 1P6H
- F,C (©1908)
  LC-M213.G975
3)   *Jagd-Ouverture, Op. 191*, 2P8H
- Aug (©1893)
  BrM-e.379.f.(4.)
  LC-M216.G87
4)   *Ländliche Bilder (Rustic Pictures): 8 Melodische Tonstücke,*
       Op. 190, 2P8H
       1. *Abmarsch*
       2. *Ankunft auf dem Sande*
       3. *Uber Berg und That*
       4. *Abends in der Waldschenke*
       5. *Ringreiten der Sandleute*
       6. *Die Jagd*
       7. *Unter der Dorflinde*
       8. *Rückkehr zur Stadt*
- Aug (©1893; ©1895)
  BrM-f.459.(1.)

LC-M216.G872
- Hin-*MMP*:80
5)   *Maypole Dance*, 1P6H (Easy)
- Schm
6)   *Ouverture des Marionettes, Op. 105*, 2P8H
- Aug (©1894)
  BrM-e.378.(1.)
7)   *6 Tonstücke, Op. 192*, 1P6H
      1. *Valse noble*
      2. *Gavotta*
      3. *Capriccietta*
      4. *Ballata*
      5. *Serenata*
      6. *Impromptu*
- Aug (©1893)
  BBC-12005;12006
  BrM-g.1169.a.(3.)
  LC-M213.G
- Scho

HÜNTEN, Franz (1793-1878), German
      Rondo agréable sur le thème **Le petit tambour**, 1P6H
- Cra
  LC-M213.H89.R5

KALKBRENNER, Friedrich Wilhelm Michael (1785-1849), German
      Introduction, Marche et Grande Polonaise, 6P10H
- composed for Chopin's première in Paris: February 26, 1932, at the
Salon de Pleyel.

KOCH, Carl [or Charles] (1793-?)
      Trois rondeaux brillantes sur des thèmes favoris du ballet **Dieu**
      et la bayadère *d'Auber, Op. 131*, 2P8H
- NYPL

LIAPUNOV, Sergei Mikhaylovich (1859-1924), Russian
      Polonaise, 2P8H
- Zim; c/o B&H
  LC-M216.L981.P

LISZT, Franz (1811-1886), trans./arr., Hungarian
1)   *Bülow-Marsch, G.230(G657b* in Humphrey Searle's catalogue, *NGG*), 1P8H
- unpublished 1884
- *Liszt:NE* xiv; *BH* ii/10
2)   *Tscherkessenmarsch (March of Chernomor)* from Glinka's *Ruslan und Ludmila*, 1P8H (also for 1P4H, G.406, and full orchestra)
            1843 (6½*)
- Hin-*PGTAP*:58

MARSCHNER, Heinrich (August) (1795-1861), German
        Grande Ouvertüre solenne [on God Save the King], Op. 78, 2P8H (originally for 1P4H)
- Hofm (©186-?) (*25)
PCM-Rare book. M216.A3.18--(*Achthändig Ouvertüre, No. 12)*

MAZZINGHI, Joseph (1765-1844)
        Three Airs, Op.55, 1P4H or 1P6H
        1. *Andantino*
        2. *Grazioso*
        3. *Marchi Pomposo*
- Gou (©181-?)
LC-M213.M

MOSCHELES, Ignaz (1794-1870), German, of Bohemian origin
        Les contrastes, Grand duo, Op. 115, 2P8H
        1. *Andante con moto, ma ben accentuato*
        2. *Fuga: Allegro maestoso*
        3. *Andante Religioso*
        4. *Allegretto Siciliano*
- Art   c.1845 (*27)
- K&S
- Kis [©1847]
LC-M216.M73.Op.115
NYPL
- *TPR*:155

RACHMANINOV, Sergei Vasilevich (1873-1943), Russian

1)   *Valse*, 1P6H
- CPP/Bel (©1988)   1890
  LC-M213.R
  YU
- Sta (©1948)
2)   *Romance*, 1P6H
- CPP/Bel (©1988)   1891
  LC-M213.R
  YU
- Leo (©1960)
  LC-M213.R
- Sta (©1948)

SAINT-SAËNS, (Charles) Camille (1835-1921), arr., French
        Marche héroïque, Op. 34, 2P8H
- Dur (©1871)   1871 (*18)
  Hin-*MMP*:172

SMETANA, Bedřich [or Friedrich] (1824-1884), Bohemian
1)   *Rondo in C Major (*Subtitled *Youth* or *Mozart Rondo), B.73,
        T.57*, 2P8H
                1850
- Bar
- HinE
- P,CF (©1940) (*13)
  UCol-M216.S63.H4
  UR-M216.S638.R
  UWO-MUS 4200 0157
- UB (©1906)
  BBC-11344
  NYPL
- Hin-*MMP*:186
- *PRG*:442
2)   *Skdadba bez nadpisu [Untitled work] in G Minor, B. 47, T.
        26*, 2P8H
                1845
3)   *Sonata in One Movement in E Minor, B.70, T. 47*, 2P8H
                1849 (*27)
- Art;c/o Bo & H

- Bar
- Hin E (©1938)
  BrM-f.690.a.
  PCM-M216.S638
  UA
  UR-M216.S638.sk
  UWO-M216.S547
- P,CF (©1938)
  BBC-5123
  Cur-M216.S638.S6.1938
  UCol-M216.S63.K8
- UB (©1906)
  BBC-12128
  NYPL
- Hin-*MMP*:186
- *PRG*:442
- *TPR*
4)   *Well of Melody*, 2P8H
        1. *Prelude*
        2. *Capriccio*
        3. *Finale*
                1850
- Brian Large, *Smetana* (London: Duckworth, 1970):50.

SZMANOWSKA (*née* **WOLOWSKA**), Maria Agata (1789-1831),
        Polish
        Valse à trois mains, 1P6H
- LC

2. TWENTIETH-CENTURY WORKS

BAGIŃSKI, Zbigniew (*b* 1949), Polish
Ricercar, 2P8H
Andantino Amabile
- AgAu (©1983)   1982 (4½*11)
NYPL-JMF 87-804

BALLOU, Esther Williamson (1915-1973), American
Forty-Finger Beguine, 4P8H
- ACA   1950
UR-M216.B193f

BANK, Jacques (*b* 1943), Netherlander
Two For Four, 2P8H
1. *First*
2. *Second*
3. *Third*
- Done (©1979)   1979   (13*55) LC-M216.B24.T9
NYPL-JMG 81-646
UR-M216.B218.T974.1979

BATTISTONI, Enrico, Italian
Suonatina in due tempi per pianoforte a sei mani, 1P6H
Molto tranquillo
Moderatamente mosso
ED (©1989, ISBN 88-7736-179-4)

BEHRENS, Jack (*b* 1935), Canadian, of American origin
Aspects in 1/6 tones, 3P6H (1P tuned 1/6-tone above normal
concert pitch, A=440; 1P tuned 1/6-tone below A=440).
1. *Prologue*
2. *Six Episodes*
3. *Epilogue*
CMC-BC (manuscript) 1983 (c.6*18)
- Letter from Behrens, January 21, 1991

BENTZON, Niels Viggo (*b* 1919), Danish
1)   *Pezzo, Op. 99a*, 12P

1954   (7*)
2)   *Pièce héroïque, Op. 224*, 3P6H
- HanG; c/o Mag 1967 (4*)

BIEL, Michael von (*b* 1937), German
    Book For Three, 3P6H
- Fee   1961
  NU-M385.B52.B6

BOIS, Rob du (*b* 1934), Dutch
    Allegro, 4P8H
- Done (©1978) 1952, rev. 1978 (6½*12)
  NU-M216.B65.A6
- Hin-*MMP*:19

BOUTRY, Roger, French
    Le voleur d'étincelles, 1P6H
- Sal

BRYERS, Gavin (*b* 1943), English
    Out of Zaleski's Gazebo, 2P8H
          1977

CANINO, Bruno, Italian
    Piano Rage Music, 1P6H
- SZ (©1967)   1962-1964 (10*28)
  NYPL
  UR-M213.C223

CASTILLO, Javier
    The House of 2, 6 "prepared" upright P and 2 grand P
          1971
  IU-M885.C491.H6

CHAPPLE, Brian (*b* 1945), English
    Scherzos, 4P8H
- CM (©1975);HanM(London) 1970
  (17*60)
  HU-Mus637.152.430

- Hin-*MMP*:36
- Letter from Chapple, November 18, 1990

COTEL, Morris Moshe (*b.* 1943), American
     Tehom, 3P6H
- Mid   1974
- Hin: *MMP*:41

DAHL, Ingolf (1912-1970), American, of German/Swiss origin
     Quodlibet on American Folk Tunes (The Fancy Blue Devil's
     Breakdown), 2P8H
- P,CF (©1957) 1953 (5½*22)
   AMC-M216.D131.Q9(NYPL)
   ASU-M216.D22.Q6.P
   BPL-M216.D33.Q6
   IU-M216.D1Z.Q6
   LC-M216.D22.Q6
   UCol-M216.D22.Q6
   UR-M216.D131.Q
   UWO-M216.D334.Q6.1957
- Hin-*MMP*:47
- *PRG*:439
- Review: *Notes*, 15 (Dec., 1957):152.

DALLAPICCOLA, Luigi (1904-1975), Italian
     Musica per Tre Pianoforti (Inni), 3P6H
      1. *Allegro molto sostenuto*
      2. *Un poco adagio; funebre*
      3. *Allegramente, ma solenne*
- Car (©1936)   1935 (15*43)
   AMC-M216.D131.Q9
   BBC-10232
   BPL-M216.D35.M8.1935
   HU-Mus644.21.410
   IU-M216.D144.M9
   LC-M216.D223.M8
   Manh-786.492.D144.M9
   NYPL-JMG 74-798
   PCM-M216.D2

SBTS
UA-M216.D14.M98.1936
UC-M216.D34.M86
UCol-M216.D24.M8
UMic-M216.D14.M9.1954
UMon-M216.D2.M87
UR-M216-D144.M
UWO-M216.D34.M8.C3
YU-M216.D144.M9+
- Hin-*MMP*:47
- *TPR*:117

FELDMAN, Morton (1926-1987), American
1)   *Extensions IV*, 3P6H
- P,CF (©1962) 1952-1953 (*21)
  ASU-M216.F3.E9.1962
  BPL-M216.F3.E9.1962(folio)
  HU-Mus677.513.420
  IU-M216.F3123.E9
  Manh-M216.F3.E9.1962;786.493.F312.E96
  NU-M216.F46.E9.1962
  UA-M216.F32.E964.1962.folio
  UMich-M216.F32.E94.1962
  UMon-M216.F44.E97
  YU
- Hin-*MMP*:63
- *TPR*:117
2)   *Five Pianos*, 5P10H
- UE (©1972)   1972 (35-55*)
  NYPL-JPB 86-2.R.S.186
3)   *Piano*, 3P3H
- P,CF (©1962)
  BPL-M205.F35
4)   *Piece For Four Pianos*, 4P8H
- P,CF (©1962)   1957
  ASU-M216.F3.P5.1962
  HU-Mus677.513.422
  IU-M216.F3123.P64
  LC-M216.F3.P5 (Trio Music Co., Inc., NY, 1960)

Manh-786.492.F312.P6
PCM-M216.F4
UCol-M216.F3.P5.1962
UMon-M216.F3.P5.1962
UMic-M216.F32.P7
UWO-M216.F44.P5.P4
YU-M216.F312.P6+
- Hin-*MMP*:63
- *TPR*:117

5)   *Trio For Three Pianos*, 3P6H
             1959

6)   *Two Pieces For Three Pianos*, 3P6H
- P,CF   1966 (*5)
ASU-M216.F3.F53
BPL-M216.F3.F53.folio
HU-M216.F3.F53;Mus677.513.419
IU-M216.F3123.P63
LC-M216.F3.F53
Manh-786.493.F312.P613.3P
UBC-m216.F44.P54.1966
UBC-M216.F44.P54.1966
UMic-M216.F32.P6
UMon-M216.F44.P54
YorU
- Hin-*MMP*:64

FRITSCH, Johannes (Georg) (*b* 1941), German
        Ikonen, 3P6H
- Fee   1964
- Hin-*MMP*:68

FUJIEDA, Mamoru, Japanese
        Contemporary Japanese Music Series: *Planetary Folklore: Nine Processes of Archetype in [a] Retrograde Canon of [J.S.] Bach*, 3P6H
- Facsimile edition of autograph (©1980)
LC-M216.F

GIBSON, David (*b* 1943), American

Three Pianos, 3P6H
- SMC (1990 catalogue listing) (©1975) (22½*15)
  AMC-M216.G448.P5
  NU-oversize. M216.G52.T4
  NYPL-JNG 75-159
- Hin-*MMP*:72

GODOWSKY, Leopold (1870-1938), Polish
  *Contrapuntal Paraphrase on Weber's **Invitation to the Dance**,*
  3P6H (P3 is an optional accompaniment)
- F,C (©1922) (*74)
  HU
  NYPL
- Hin-*MMP*:73
- *TPR*:117

GOODENOUGH, Forrest (*b* 1918), American
  Dance of the Apes, 4P8H
- ACA (©1953)
  UR-M216.G649d
- *FPQC*-No.408
- Hin-*MMP*:75

GRAHN, Ulf (*b* 1942), Swedish
  Scherzo, 1P6H
              c.1986 (8*)
  AMC-M213.G742.S3

GRAINGER, Percy Alderidge (1882-1961), American, of Australian
          origin
1)   *Bridge on the River Kwai Marches* (an amalgamation of the
      Colonel Bogey March by Kenneth J. Alford with a counter-
      theme by Malcolm Arnold entitled *River Kwai March*), 1P6H
- manuscript
2)   *British Folk-Music Settings*
  a)   *No. 22: Country Gardens*, 2P8H
              1918 (roughly sketched for 2 whistlers and a few
      instruments c.1906-1908); arr. in 1936 for 2P8H
              (2*7)

- S,G (©1938;©1965)
  LC-M216.G7.C6
  UMic-M216.G74.A82
  UR-M216.G743.C
- Scho
- Hin-*MMP*:77
- *PRG*:440
  b)   *No. 25: Green Bushes (Passacaglia)*, 2P6H
- S,G (©1937) 1905-1906 (*15)
- LC-M216.G7
  NYPL
3)   *British Folk Song*, arr.: *In Bristol Town (The Easy Grainger)*,
         1P6H
                  1906, arr. 1951 for 1P6H
- manuscript, LC
4)   *Danish Folk-Music Settings*
         No.9: Jutish Medley (Jysk Sammenpluk), 2P6H
                  1. *Choosing the Bride (Ungersvendens Brudevalg)*
                  2. *The Dragoon's Farewell (Dragonens Hjaertesorg)*
                  3. *The Shoemaker from Jerusalem (Jerusalems*
                       Skomager)
                  4. *Husband and Wife (Manden og Konen)*
                       (©1928;©1930) 1923-1929
5)   *English Dance*, 2P6H
                  1899-1909; arr. 1921 for 2P6H
- Scho (©1921;©1951)
  BPL
  LC-M216.G7.E5
- S,G (©1924;©1951)
  NYPL
  UR-M216.G743.E
  UWO-M216.G743.E6
- *PRG*:440
- *TPR*:154
6)   *English Morris (Dance Tune)*, 2P8H
- S,G
- *PRG*:440
7)   *Faeroe Island Dance Folk-Song: Let's Dance Gay in Green*
         Meadow, 1P6H

1905 (sketched for chorus); arr. 1932 for 1P6H
- manuscript, LC
8)   *Harvest Hymn*, 2P8H
1905 (sketched); completed 1932 for 2P8H
- manuscript, LC (©1940)
9)   *The Lads of Wamphray*, 2P6H (incomplete) 1904
10)   *Room-Music Tit-Bits*
  a)   *No. 6: Zanzibar Boat Song* (inspired by *Salsette Boat-Song*
        from *Plain Tales from the Hills* by Rudyard Kipling), 1P6H
- Scho (©1923;©1990)   1902
  BBC-12225
  LC-M213.G
  NYPL
- S,G
  b)   *No. 8: Random Round*, 2P10H or 2P12H (a "join-in-when-
        you-like" Round) 1912-1914; 1943 (two-piano version);©1943
- manuscript, White Plains, New Jersey
11)   *The Warriors (Music to an Imaginary Ballet)*, 3P6H
- Scho (©1923) 1913-1916; arr. 1922 for 2P6H
  UR-M216.G743.W
- S,G
- See   3. Works with Orchestra/Orchestral Reductions: Grainger
12) See   8. Transcriptions/Arrangements: Arnold/Alford, J.S. Bach,
            Gershwin and Grainger

GRETCHANINOV, Alexander (1864-1956), Russian
1)   *In modo antico, Op. 81*, 2P8H
        2. *Sarabande. Allegro moderato*
        3. *Gavotte. Allegro non troppo*
- (©1924)
  LC-M216.G735.Op.81
  UR-M216.G789p
2)   *Suite Bachkirienne, Op. 28a*, 2P8H

HAAS, Polo De (*b* 1933), Dutch
Orgella, 2P8H
- Done (©1975)(*14)
  NYPL-JMH 76-38
- Hin-*MMP*:82

HAMPTON, Calvin (1938-1984), American
Catch-Up, 4P8H (or 2P4H and tape)
- P,CF (©1970) 1970 (*4)
  AMC-M216.H232.C3(NYPL)
  ASU-M216.H2.C3
  BU
  LC-M216.H2.C3
  NYPL-Music-Am (sheet)71-34.1
  SBTS
  UR-M216.H232.C
- Hin-*MMP*:83
- *PRG*:440
- *TPR*:118-119

HANSEN, Johannes, Danish
Papita Ninononina, Op. 151, 3P6H
1977 (4½*)
- MIC; c/o Bendt Viinholt Nielsen

HIDALGO, Juan (*b* 1927), Spanish
Tamaran (Gocce di Sperma), 12P (avant garde)
1974 (40*)
- See Discography

HILLER, Lejaren (Arthur), Jr. (*b* 1924), American
Fantasy for Three Pianos, 3P6H
1951 (16½*71)
- SBTS
- Hin-*MMP*:89

HOBBS, Christopher, American
Three For Redlands, 3P6H
- Dor (©1981)

NYPL-JNH 85-15

HOLT, Simeon ten, Netherlander
   Horizon: 1983-85, 4P8H
- Done (©1986) (*87)
   NYPL-JMF 88-179

ICHIYANAGI, Toshiro (*b* 1933), Japanese
   Prana, 5P10H
- Scho

KAGEL, Mauricio (Raúl) (*b* 1931), Argentinian, active in Germany
   Der Eid des Hippokrates, 1P6H (one line each)
- P,CF; Lit (©1984) (2½*4)
   IU-M205.K34.E5
   UA-M205.K12.E34.1984.folio

KENINS, Talivaldis (*b* 1919), Canadian, born in Latvia
   Folk Dance, Variations, and Fugue, 2P8H
- CMC-Nat 1962-1963 (c.10*16)
- Letter from Kenins, November 14, 1990

KORNGOLD, Erich Wolfgang (1897-1957), American, of Austro-
   Hungarian origin
   Pianoforte Trio in D Major, Op. 1, 3P6H
- Mas   1909
   RCM

KUPKOVIČ, Ladislav (*b* 1936), Czechoslovakian, active in Germany
      1)   *Präludium und Fuga in Form einer Klavierübung*, 4P8H
- Available from composer 1977 (8*64)
   Rühmkorffstrasse 17
   3000 Hannover 1
- Hin-*MMP*:110
      2)   *Happy-End*, 4P8H
- Available from composer 1975-1976
   (45*262)
- Hin-*MMP*:110

- Letter from Kupkovič, November 17, 1990

LACHERT, Piotr, Netherlander
    1) *Friedrich Rzewski's Spiel 2-*
       1973, 1P6H
- CeBeDeM   1973
    2) *Kauffolie-1987*, 36 pianists
- CeBeDeM   1987

LANZA, Alcides Emigdio (*b* 1929), Canadian, of Argentinian origin
1)   *Penetrations II*, "open instrumentation and which could perhaps be done with three pianos." (Lanza)
- Letter from Lanza, December 5, 1990
2)   *Trio Concertante*, "open instrumentation and which could perhaps be done with three pianos." (Lanza)
- Letter from Lanza, December 5, 1990
- Hin-*MMP*:163

LENK, Thomas Timothy (*b* 1952), American
    Three Pianos, 3P6H
- AMC-M1216.L566.T5 1989

LOEVENDIE, Theo (*b* 1930), Netherlander
    Voor Jan, Piet, en Klaas, 2P8H
- Done (facsimile of autograph)
  1979
  LC-M216.L85.V6
  NYPL-JMG 80-422

MARIÉTAN, Pierre (*b* 1935), Swiss
1)   *Circulaires*, 1P-3P, 1H-12H
          1966
2)   *Un âge va, un âge vient: pour récitant, soli, choeur et orchestre*, 5P10H
          1983

MATHER, Bruce (*b* 1939), Canadian
    Poème du délire: musique pour trois pianos en sixièmes de ton, 3P6H (1P tuned 1/6-tone above normal concert pitch, A=440;1P is tuned 1/6-tone below A=440)
  CMC-BC-MI2140.M427po 1982 (c.17½*19)
  CMC-Nat-MI2140.M427po
  CMC-P-MI.2140.M427po
  CMC-Q-MI2140.M427po (original manuscript located here)
- Letters from Mather, November 13, 1990; February 15, 1991

McQUIRE, John (*b* 1942)
    Frieze For Four Pianos, 4P8H
- Fee (1987 catalogue listing) (©1975) 1969-1974 (c.22*)
- UE (Paris)

MELNYK, Lubomyr (*b* 1948), Canadian, of German/Ukrainian origin
1)   *During*, 3P6H
- Facsimile of manuscript 1975, rev. 1977
  (c.50*4)
  CMC-BC-MI2140.M527.du
  CMC-Nat-MI2140.M527.du
  CMC-P-MI2140.M527.du
  CMC-Q-MI2140.M527.du
- Letter from Melnyk, January 3, 1991
2)   *The Fountain*, 2P4H or 3P6H
      1985 (c.22*)
- Letter from Melnyk, January 3, 1991
3)   *Lund-St. Petri Symphony for Pianos*, 1P or 2P or 3P (or organs)
      1979 (99*)
- Letter from Melnyk, January 3, 1991
4)   *Macrovision*, 3 or more P (up to 6 players)
      1988 (c.70*)
- Letter from Melnyk, January 3, 1991
5)   *Page Music (Attenay Attenarro)*, 2P4H "plus a third piano that enters sporadically"
      1983 or 1982 (65*)
- Letter from Melnyk, January 3, 1991

6)   *This*, 3P6H
- Facsimile of manuscript 1976 (c.30*4)
  CMC-BC-MI2140.M527.th/thl ("lesser version," c.20*)
  CMC-Nat-MI2140.M527.th/thl
  CMC-P-MI2140.M527.th/thl
  CMC-Q-MI2140.M527.th/thl
- Letter from Melnyk, January 3, 1991

MICHEL, Paul Baudouin, Belgian
    Un drôle de bonhomme à 6 mains, 1P6H
- CeBeDeM   1985

MILHAUD, Darius (1892-1974), French
1)   *Paris, suite pour quatre pianos, Op. 284a*, 4P8H
    1. *Montmartre*
    2. *L'île Saint-Louis*
    3. *Montparnasse*
    4. *Bateaux-mouches*
    5. *Longchamp*
    6. *La tour Eiffel*
- Esc; c/o AMP (©1959) 1948 (10*36)
  BBC-13286
  HU
  NYPL
  UMic-M216.M64.P3
  UMon-M216.M55.P37
  UR-M216.M644.Pa
  UWO-M216.M56.P4
- *FPQC*-Nos.341-346
- S,G (1990 catalogue listing)
- Hin-*MMP*:135

MULLINS, Hugh E. (*b* 1922), American
    Statistics, 3P6H
    1. *Adagio*
    2. *Allegro*
- Available from composer

1977 (6*)
- Hin-*MMP*:140-141

NAKADA, Yoshinao (*b* 1923), Japanese
   Theme and Variations Based on a Japanese Melody, 2P8H
- Ongaku-no-Tomo; c/o P,T 1966
- Hin-*MMP*:142

NASVELD, Robert (*b* 1955), Netherlander
   Drei Stücke, 2P8H
- Done (©1983) 1982 (*47)
- NYPL-JMG 86-1055

OLIVEROS, Pauline (*b* 1932), American
1) *Gathering Together*, 1P8H
- AMC-M213.0488.G2 1983
2) *More*, 1P8H

OSIECK, (Hendrik Willem) Hans (*b* 1910), Dutch
   Le petit rêve, 3P6H
   Andantino semplice con moto
- Done 1956 (*3)
- Hin-*MMP*:145

PAGANINI, Nicolò (1782-1840), Italian;
 and
FIRST PIANO QUARTET
   Variations on a Theme of Paganini [by the First Piano
   Quartet], 4P8H
- *FPQC*-No.226

PHILIPP, Isidore (Edmond) (1863-1958), French, of Hungarian origin
   Concertino sans orchestre, pour trois pianos, Op. 82, 3P6H
    1. *Prélude: Andante*
    2. *Barcarole: Allegretto maliconico*
    3. *Scherzo et intermezzo: Vivacissimo*
    4. *Toccata: Allegro vivo*
- Col; c/o Sal (©1931)
 LC-M216.P53.Op.32

PCM-M216.P51
- Col; c/o Belw
HU
NYPL
PCM-M216.P551
SBTS
- S,G (1988 catalogue listing)
- Seca
- Cur

POUSSEUR, Henri (Léon Marie Thérèse) (*b* 1929), Belgian
Prospectives in 1/6 tones, 3P6H 1952

POWELL, John (1882-1963), American
1)   *Dirge, Op. 26,* 2P12H
- S,G   1932
BrM-a.1122.a.(6.)
LC-M216.P88.D4
- Hin-*MMP*:154-155
- *PRG*:441
2)   *In a Hammock (Scène sentimentale), Op. 19,* 2P8H
- S,G   1920 (*9)
NYPL
- Hin-*MMP*:154
- *TPR*

RASMUSSEN, Karl Aage (*b* 1947), Danish
Genklang (Echo), 3P (1 grand, 1 "prepared," 1 mistuned) 8H
and celesta 1972 (22*)
- HanG;c/o Mag
- CM
- Nors

REICH, Steve [or Stephen] (Michael) (*b* 1936), American
1)   *Music,* 3P or more P (also for piano and tape) 1964
2)   *Six Pianos,* 6P12H 1973
- Letter from Reich, November 26, 1990

ROY, Klaus George (*b* 1924), American, of Austrian origin
　　　Forty Bars for Forty Fingers, 2P8H
- Rob
- *PRG*:442

SACKS, Jonathan, American
　　　Incantations, 3P6H (based on text and paintings by Heidi
　　　Hardin) c.1981
- AMC-M214.S122.I3

SCHICKELE, Peter [pseud. P.D.Q. BACH] (*b* 1935), American
　　　Monochrome VI, 10P20H
- E/V (rental) 1989
- Letter from Schickele, December 5, 1990

SCHMIDT, Yves R. (*b* 1933), Brazilian
　　　*"As aulas do Visconde de Sabuyosa" da série Minioturas
　　　Lobateanas*, 2P8H
- IV (©1976)　　1964 (2*)
　WSU

SCHWARTZ, Elliot (*b* 1936), American
　　　Mirrors, 3P6H 1973
- Letter from Elliot Schwartz, November 20, 1990

SENN, Dan (*b* 1951), American
　　　Might nots, 2P8H
　　　c.1984 (*40)
　AMC-M216.S478.M6

TENNER, James (*b* 1934), American
　　　Bridge, 2P8H (in a microtonal tuning system)
-SP/SA (1992 listing)

TITTLE, Steve (*b* 1935), Canadian, of American origin
1)　　*Find Your Own Way Out*, 2P8H
- CMC-Nat 1977 (*4)

2)   *Harmony One*, 2P8H
- CMC-Nat 1980 (*17)

TOEBOSCH, Louis (*b* 1916), Dutch
        Zes speelstukken, Op. 126, 3P6H
- Done (©1983) 1983 (*23)
  NYPL-JMG 86-1020

VAN DE VATE, Nancy (*b* 1930), American
        Contrasts, 2P6H
- ACA (©1984) 1984 (*18)
  AMC-M216.V244.C7
- Letter from Van de Vate, November 25, 1990

WAGEMANS, Peter-Jan, Netherlander
        Ira, Op. 20a, 2P8H
- Done 1983; rev. 1984 (*28)
  NYPL-JMG 86-1017

WANEK, Friedrich K. (*b* 1929), German
        Drei Etüden, 1P or 2P or 3P, 6H
        1. *Fliessand und keck*
        2. *Getragen, mit grossen Ausdruck*
        3. *Sehr präzis und mechanisch, marsch-mässig, trocken*
- Scho (Pub. No. ED 7611)

WEHNER, G.
1)   *Allegro* and *Andante* from the *Four Piano Suite*, 4P8H
- *FPQC*-Nos.86,85
2)   *Piano Quartet No. 1*, 4P8H
- *FPQC*-No.71
3)   *Song of the Brook*, 4P8H
- *FPQC*-No.73

WILSON, Dorothy (*b* 1904), American
1)   *Dance Diversion No. 1*, 2P8H
        (*7)
- AMC-M216.W7472.D2.No.1
- Hin-*MMP*:208

2)   *Dance Diversion No. 2*, 2P8H
        (*8)
- AMC-M216.W7472.D2.No.2
- Hin-*MMP*:208

WINIARZ, John [or Jack] Jullien (*b* 1952), Canadian
        Le parcours du jour, 3P6H (1P tuned 1/6-tone above normal
        concert pitch A=440; 1P tuned 1/6-tone below A=440)
        1983 (16*17)
- CMC-BC-MI2140.W772
- CMC-P-MI2140.W772
- CMC-Q-photocopies of autograph manuscript available here
- Letter from Winiarz, December 20, 1990

WOLPE, Stefan (1902-1972), American, of German origin
1)   *Enactments*, 3P6H
        1. *Chant*
        2. *In a State of Flight*
        2. *Held In*
        4. *Inception*
        5. *Fugal Motions*
        Autograph manuscript, 1950-1953, NYPL (Special Collections,
        No.59):Nos. 1,2,3,5
- Marx (©1970)
  HU-Mus868.10.420
- PSCM (©1977)(*68)
  LC-M216.W77.E5
2)   *Seven Pieces for Three Pianos*, 3P6H
        1. *Calm*
        2. *Aggressive*
        3. *Precipitately*
        4. *Not too much motion, stiff throughout*
        5. *Tired*
        6. *Taut like a high voltage wire, rather slow*
        7. *Moving moderately*
- Autograph manuscript, 1950-1957, NYPL (Special Collections,
  Nos.56 and 57)(3 scores *23 ea.)
- SMP, Ed. Austin Clarkson (©1977; ©1981)
  ASU-M216.W6.P5x.1981p

LC-M216.W77.P5
NYPL-JMG84-267
UA-M216.W86.P6.1977.folio
- PSCM (©1981)
- Hin-*MMP*:209

WYSCHNEGRADSKY [or Vïshnegradsky], Ivan (1893-1979),
Russian, active in Paris
1)   *Ainsi parlait Zarathoustra. Symphonie en système de quarts
tons, Op. 17, in 1/4 tones*, 4P8H (2P tuned to normal concert
pitch, A=440; 2P 1/4-tone above A=440)
     1. *Tempo giusto*
     2. *Scherzando; Lento*
     3. *Allegro con fuoco*
       1929-1930; rev. 1936(24*84)
- L,OL (©1938)
   BBC-8272
   UR-M216.V998A
- Bel (©1948)
   HU-Mus871.774.420
   NYPL
- Hin-*MMP*:209-210
2)   *Premier fragment symphonique, Op. 23, in 1/4 tones*, 4P8H
     (2P tuned to A=440, 2P 1/4-tone below A=440)
- Bel   1934; rev. 1936; orchestrated 1967
- Bo&H
3)   *Deuxième fragment symphonique, Op. 24, in 1/4 tones*, 4P8H
     (2P tuned to A=440; 2P 1/4-tone below A=440) 1937
4)   *Cosmos, Op. 28, in 1/4 tones*, 4P8H (2P tuned to A=440; 2P
     1/4-tone below A=440) 1939-1940
- Editions du Mordant, 106 Blvd. Lefèvre, 93600 Aulnay sous Bois,
France
5)   *Prélude et fugue, Op. 30, in 1/6 tones*, 3P6H 1945
6)   *Troisième fragment symphonique, Op. 32 in 1/4 tones*, 4P8H
     (2P tuned to A=440; 2P 1/4-tone below A=440) 1946
7)   *Quatrième fragment symphonique, Op. 37 in 1/4 tones*, 4P8H
     (2P tuned to A=440; 2P 1/4-tone below A=440) and *ondes
martenots* 1956
8)   *Arc-en-ciel, Op. 38, in 1/12 tones*, 6P12H 1956

9) *Etude sur les mouvements rotatoires, Op. 45 in 1/4 tones*,
    2P8H 1961; orchestrated in 1964
10) *Composition, Op. 46, No. 1, in 1/6 tones*, 3P6H (1P tuned
    1/6-tone above A=440; 1P tuned 1/6-tone below A=440)
    1961
11) *Dialogue à trois, Op. 51, in 1/6 tones*, 3P6H 1973-1974
    (c.12½*)
12) *Four Pianos, Op. Posth.*, P1 (tuned to A=440) P2 (1/6- tone
    higher), P3 (1/4-tone higher), P4 (1/6-tone lower)

- NB--Except for *Cosmos*, scores of the above may be obtained from
    the composer's son: M. Dimitri Vicheney
                             6 rue Plumet
                             75015 Paris, France

- Letter from Bruce Mather, February 15, 1991

3. WORKS WITH ORCHESTRA/ORCHESTRAL REDUCTIONS

ANSON, Hugo Vernon (1894-1958), English
Concerto for Two Pianos and Strings (reduced), 3P6H
- Nov (©1941)(*59)
  BBC-5982
  LC-M111.A58
- Hin-*MPO*:6

BABIN, Victor (1908-1972), American, of Russian origin
Concerto No. 2 [for Two Pianos and Orchestra] (reduced), 3P6H
  1. *Moderato*
  2. *Molto vivo e ben ritmico*
  3. *Molto sostenuto, intimo e calmo*
  4. *Finale alla fuga: Allegro con spirito*
- Bel; c/o Bo&H (©1961) 1956 (23*)
  LC-M1011.B113.No.2
  UR
- Hin-*MPO*:11
- *PRG*:426

BACEWICZ, Grażyna (1913-1969), Polish
Concerto for Two Pianos and Orchestra (reduced), 3P6H
  1. *Tempo mutabile*
  2. *Larghetto*
  3. *Vivace*
- Pol; c/o Mark (© 1968) 1966 (17*63)
  LC-M1011.B116.C6.1968
  NYPL
- Hin-*MPO*:11

BACH, Carl Philipp Emanuel (1714-1788), German
1)   DARVAS, Gábor, arr.
      Concerto doppio in E-Flat Major, H. 479, W. 47 (1788), 3P6H (3rd piano, orchestral reduction)
      1. *Allegro molto*
      2. *Larghetto*
      3. *Presto*

- EMS (©1969) (18*67)
  LC-M1011.B12.W47.G3
  NYPL
- Hin-*MPO*:13
2) SWARTZ, H., arr.
  Concerto doppio in F Major, H. 408, W. 46 (1740), 3P6H
  (3rd piano, orchestral reduction)
  1. *Allegro*
  2. *Largo*
  3. *Allegro assai*
- Sik (©1988) (25*)
  UA-M1010.B115.H408.1988.folio
- StriV
- Hin-*MPO*:13

BACH, Johann Sebastian (1685-1750), German
1) *Concerto for Three Harpsichords in D Minor, BWV 1063*,
  3P6H, 1st and 2nd violins, violas and basso continuo (cello
  and violone)
  1. *[Allegro: ritornello, rondo]*
  2. *Alla Siciliana*
  3. *Allegro*
    c.1730-1733 (15*)
- *B-W*, ed. *Bach-Gesellschaft* (Leipzig, xxxi/3,3)
  LAPL
  UA
- Bar (*NBA* vii/6,3) (©1975)
  UA-M3.B11.Ser.4-8.1954.folio.Ser.vii:6
- Br&H; c/o AMP
  Manh-786.493.B118.C744(3H).S.1063
  UR
- EMS (©1923)
- Fle
- Kal
  BC-MI2140.B118.6.05339 (3 solo parts only)
- KMS
  WSU
- LPS; c/o EAMD
- P,CF

- Hin-*MPO*:17
- *PRG*:427;439
- *TPR*:116
2)   *Concerto for Three Harpsichords in C Major, BWV 1064*,
        3P6H, 1st and 2nd violins, violas and basso continuo (cello
        and violone)
        1. *[Allegro]*
        2. *Adagio*
        3. *Allegro*
                c.1730-1733 (11*)
- *B-W*, ed. *Bach-Geselschaft* (Leipzig, xxxi/3,53)
- Bar (*NBA*, vii/6,57) (©1975)
  UA-M3.B11.Ser.4-8.1954.folio.Ser.vii:6
- Br&H; c/o AMP
- EMS (©192-?)
  BPL-M8677
- F,C
- Fle
- IMC
- Kal
  BC-MI2140.B118.6.05335 (3 solo parts only)
- KMS
- LPS; c/o EAMD
- P,CF (©1923)
  BPL-M.353.17
  UR
- S,G (©1929) [BAUER, Harold (1873-1951), arr. for 3P6H, without
  orchestra]
  ASU-M216.B12.S.1064.1929
  BBC-37
  IU-M1011.B118.C73.S.1064
  LAPL-78.6484.B118
  LC-M216.B13.B2
  Manh-786.493.B118.C744(3H).S.1064
  Mann
  PCM-M216.B118.S.1064
  UR-M216.B11.B340;M216.B11.B34.C
  - Hin-*MPO*:17
  - *PRG*:426;439

- *TPR*:116
3)   *Concerto for Four Harpsichords in A Minor, BWV 1065*,
       4P8H, 1st and 2nd violins, violas and basso continuo (cello
       and violone)
       1. *[Allegro]*
       2. *Largo*
       3. *Allegro*
                c.1730-1733 (11*)
- *B-W*, ed. *Bach-Gesellschaft* (Leipzig, x/iii/1,71)
  LAPL
  UA
- Bar (*NBA*, vii/6, 117) (©1975)
  UA-M3.B11.Ser.4-8.1954.folio.Ser.vii:6
- Br&H; c/o AMP
  UR
- EMS (©1923)
- Fle
- Kal
  BC-MI2140.B118.6.03754 (4 solo parts only)
- S,G
- Ste V
- Hin-*MPO*:17
- *PRG*-426;439
- *TPR*:116

BERIO, Luciano (*b* 1925), Italian
         Concerto: per due pianoforti e orchestra (reduced) Berio:
         edizione per due pianoforti soli, con parte del pianoforte in
         orchestra, 3P6H
- UE (©1973) 1972-1973 (25*48)
  YU-M1010.B511++

BERKELEY, Sir Lennox (Randall Francis) (1903-1989), English
         Concerto for Two Pianos and Orchestra (reduced), *Op. 30*,
         3P6H
         1. *Molto moderato*
         2. *Theme and Variations*
- CM (©1953)1948 (30*83)
  BBC-9913

LC-M1011.B497.C64
UR-M216.B512c

BETTINELLI, Bruno (*b* 1913), Italian
    Concerto per due pianoforti e orchestra da camera (reduced),
    3P6H
- Col; c/o Bel
- Ric; c/o S,G (©1922)   1962
  LC-M1022.B513.C8
- *PRG*:428;439

BLISS, Sir Arthur (Edward Drummond) (1891-1975), English
    Concerto For Two Pianos and Orchestra (reduced), 3P6H
- Ox 1968 (12*)
  BBC-1861
- *PRG*:428

BOUTRY, Roger
    Concerto-fantaisie, 3P6H (3rd P, orchestral reduction)
- Sal (©1966) (*143)
  LC-M1111.B69.C72

BRUCH, Max (Karl August) (1838-1920), German
    BRÜCKNER-RUGGEBERG, Wilhelm, arr.
    Concerto for Two Pianos and Orchestra (reduced), *Op. 88a*,
    3P6H
- Sim (©1977) 1916 (22*80)
  NYPL-JMG 81-272
  YU-M1011.B887+

CASADESUS, Robert (Marcel) (1899-1972), French
    Concerto pour trois pianos et orchestre à cordes (reduced),
    Op. 65, 3P6H and string orchestra
      1. *Allegro marziale*
      2. *Andante sicilano*
      3. *Presto spagnuolo*
- Dur; E/V (©1966; ©1968)1964 (15*69)
  LC-M110.C32.Op.65
  UCLA-A.000.157.236.1

UR
- Hin-*MPO*:59-60
- *PRG*:429;439

CESANA, Otto (1899-1980), American
    Concerto for Three Pianos and Orchestra, 3P6H and orchestra
- Manuscript

CLAFIN, Avery (1898-?), American
    Pop Concert Concerto for Piano and Orchestra (reduced),
    2P6H
- ACA (©1958) (*58)
  LC-M1011.C65.P7.1958

CRAS, Jean (Emile Paul) (1879-1932), French
    Ames d'enfants pour orchestre (reduced), multiple pianos
- Col; c/o Sal   1918
- *PRG*:439

CZERNY, Carl (1791-1857), Austrian
    [Première] Quatuor concertante in C Major, Op. 230, 4P8H
    and orchestra (also for 4P8H; and 4P8H and string quartet)
- Dia
- Manuscript: GM
- Hin:*MPO*:75

DÖHL, Friedhelm (*b* 1936), German
    Cadenza from *Sound-Scene III: Zorch*, 3P6H and orchestra
- EAMD (©1981) 1972 (*4)
  UWO-M216.D64.C3.1981

DUBOIS, Pierre Max (*b* 1930), French
    Concerto italien, pour deux pianos et orchestre (reduced),
    3P6H
- Led (©1963) (21*85)
  LC-M1011.D83.C7
  NYPL

FALLA (Y MATHEU), Manuel de (1876-1946), Spanish
     SAMAZEWITH, Gustave (1877-?), arr.
     Noches en los jardines de España, 2P6H (2nd P, orchestral
     reduction)
       1. *En el Generalife*
       2. *Danza lejana*
       3. *En los jardines de la Sierra de Cordoba*
- Esc ([©]1922) 1911-1915 (*56)
  BBC
  BPL-M216.F35.N6.1922
  UBC
  UMic-M1011.F19.N8
  UR-M216.F19n

FORTNER, Wolfgang (*b* 1907), German
     Triplum, 3P6H and orchestra
       1. *Giuoco*
       2. *Intermezzo*
       3. *4 Variazioni*
- Scho 1965-1966 (25*87)
  NYPL
  UCLA-D.000.035.903.4
- Hin-*MPO*:99

FRANÇAIX, Jean (*b* 1912), French
     Double Pianoforte Concerto, 3P6H (3rd P, orchestral
     reduction)
- Scho ([©]1977)   1965 (25*143)
  NYPL-JMG 86-179
  YU-M1011.F814.C8+

FRICKER, Peter Racine (*b* 1920), English
     Concertante No. 2, Op. 15, 3P6H, strings and timpani
- Scho   1951
- Hin-*MPO*:102

GHEDINI, Giorgio Federico (1892-1965), Italian
     Primo concerto, per due pianoforti e orchestra (reduced),
     3P6H

- SZ (©1947)   1947 (19*72)
  BBC-Misc.Sec.3954
  Manh-786.493.G411.C744(2P).#1

GOULD, Morton (*b* 1913), American
Inventions, 4P8H, piccolo, 2 flutes, 2 oboes, English horn, 2 clarinets, bass clarinet, 2 bassoons, contra bassoon, 4 horns, 3 trumpets, 3 trombones, tuba and percussion
1. *Warm-Up*
2. *Ballad*
3. *Schottische*
4. *Toccata*
        1953 (17½*)
- G & C Music Corp.; c/o Cha
- S,G
  LC-M1045.G715
- *FPQC*-Nos.388-391
- Hin-*MPO*:115
- Letter from Gould, August 30, 1990

GRAINGER, Percy Alderidge (1882-1961), American of Australian origin
The Warriors (Music to an Imaginary Ballet), 3P6H and orchestra (also arr. for 2P6H, 1922)
- Scho (©1923)   1913-1916

GREEN, John
Night Club, 3P6H and orchestra
1933

d'INDY, (Paul Marie Théodore) Vincent (1851-1931), French
Symphony on a French Mountain Air, Op. 25, 2P6H (2nd P, orchestral reduction)
- Ham   1886
  UR-M216.I42x

KLEPPER, Leon
Concertino, pour piano à 4 mains et orchestre, 2P6H (2nd P, orchestral reduction) (17*33)

LC-M1011.K67.C6

LACHERMANN, Helmut (*b* 1935), German, active in Canada
    Klangschatten--Mein Saitenspiel, 3P6H and 48 strings
- Ger (©1978)   1972 (*54)
- Hin-*MPO*:161

LOPATNIKOFF, Nikolai (*b* 1903)
    Concerto for Two Pianos and Orchestra (reduced), *Op. 33*,
    3P6H
- Lee (©1953)   1949-1950
  LC-ML96.L69.No.1.Case

MILHAUD, Darius (1892-1974), French
1)   *Concerto For Two Pianos and Orchestra* (reduced), 3P6H
- E/V (©1950)   1950
  BBC-10004
  LC-M1011.M;M1011.M7.C63;ML96.
  M77
  NYPL-JMG 81-53
2)   *Suite for Two Pianos and Orchestra* (reduced), *Op. 300*, 3P6H
      1. *Entrée*
      2. *Nocturne*
      3. *Java fuguée*
      4. *Mouvement perpétual*
      5. *Finale*
- Heu (©1951) 1950 (18¼*74)
  LC-M1041.M;M1011.M7.Op.300
  YU-M1011.M6445+ Op.300 (also E/V)
- Hin-*MMP*:135

MOZART, Wolfgang Amadeus (1756-1791), Austrian
    Concerto No. for Three Fortepianos 7 in F Major, K. 242a
    (Lodron), 3P6H, 2 oboes, 2 horns and strings (bassoon ad.
    lib.)
      1. *Allegro*
      2. *Adagio*
      3. *Rondo: Tempo di Minuetto*
         1776 (23*)

- *AMA*, XVI, 1 (*Piano Concerto No. 7*)
- Bar (©1972)
  LAPL-78.12.M939a (*New Edition of Collected Works*)
- Br&H
- EMS (ed. Badura-Skoda) (©1973)
  BC-MI2140.M939.6.04589 (piano solo parts only)
  NYPL-JMF 83-149
  UMic-M1010.M94.C67.1973
  UR
- Kal
- *MW*, XVI/i, 165
- *NMA*, V:15/i, 155
- S,G
- *PRG*:434

PISTON, Walter (Hamor) (1894-1976), American
     Concerto for Two Pianos and Orchestra (reduced), 3P6H
- AMP (©1966) 1959 (19*57)
  LC-M1011.P66
  UR
  YU-M1011.P679.C72+

QUINET, Marcel, French
     Dialogues pour deux pianos et orchestre de chambre (reduced), 3P6H
- CeBeDeM; E/V (©1976) (9*43)
  LC-M1011.Q55.D5
  NYPL-JMG 76-1170

RAWSTHORNE, Alan (1905-1971), English
     Concerto for Two Pianos and Orchestra (reduced), 3P6H
- Ox (©1970)   1968 (18*48)
  NYPL-JMG 72-109
  LC-M1011.R27.C61

SCHÄFFER, Boguslav (Julien) (*b* 1929), Polish
     Concerto for Three Pianos and Orchestra (reduced), 4P8H
- AA (©1972)   1972 (c.4½*)

SKALKOTTAS, Nikos (1904-1949), Greek
> *Concertino for Two Pianos and Orchestra* (reduced), 3P6H
- UE (©1969)   1935 (14*48)
  LC-M1011.S647.C7
  YU-M1011.S626+

TANSMAN, Alexandre (1897-1986), French, of Polish origin
> *Suite*, 3P6H (3rd P, orchestral reduction)
>   1. *Introduction et allegro*
>   2. *Intermezzo*
>   3. *Perpetuum mobile*
>   4. *Variations, double fugue et finale sur un thème slave*
- Esc (©1935)   1930 (*72)
  UR-M216.T168s
  YaU-M1011.T168.S9+

WOLMAN, Amnon, Canadian
> *Concerto for Piano, Pianos, and Orchestra*, 1P2H (MIDI
> grand P, 6 upright diskclavier P (MIDI controlled) and
> chamber orchestra. Everything is connected to a computer in
> front of the stage and controlled by the conductor.
>   1990
- Banff Centre newsletter, *Music at Banff* (1990-1991):4.
- Debbie Rosen, Music Librarian, Banff Centre Library, August 17,
  1990
NB--Antheil's *Ballet mécanique, No. 156a* (first version, 1924) was
scored for sixteen player pianos operated from a master switchboard.

ZAFRED, Mario (1922-1987), Italian
> *Concerto for Two Pianos and Orchestra* (reduced), 3P6H
- Col
- Ric (©1961)
- S,G (1988 catalogue listing)
- *PRG*:438;442

4. WORKS WITH OTHER INSTRUMENTALISTS/SINGERS

ANTHEIL, George (Carl Johann) (1900-1959), American
1) First version: *Ballet mécanique, No 156a*, 16 pianolas (premiered with 1)
    Allegro (féroce)
- title pages stamped 1924; "Paris, 1925" on 2nd page
- composed to accompany film of same name by Fernand Léger (not synchronized until Oct. 18, 1935--*No. 156c*).
- 4 xylophones, 4 bass drums, siren, wood airplane propeller sound, steel airplane propeller sound, 2 electric bells and tam-tam
2) Autograph score: *Ballet pour instruments mécaniques et percussion, No. 156b*, 1 pianola with amplifier, 2P4H.
- c.1926; premiere June 19, 1926
- 3 xylophones, electric bells, small wood propeller sound, large wood propeller sound, metal propeller sound, tam-tam, 4 bass drums and siren
3) Published final version: *Ballet mécanique*, 4P8H
- Tem (photoreproduced holograph)(©1959) "March 25, 1953" (18*121)
- Glockenspiel, small airplane propeller sound, large airplane propeller sound, gong, cymbal, woodblock, triangle, military drum, tambourine, small electric bell, large electric bell, tenor drum, bass drum and 2 xylophones
  LC-M985.A
  UA-M985.A62.B19.1954
4) Other performances: scoring
- July 16, 1926 (Paris):8P, unspecified number of xylophones and percussion
- July 17, 1926 (Paris):3P with percussion instruments used for the June 19, 1926 première
- April 10, 1927 (Carnegie Hall): 10P, 1 mechanical P (Antheil), 6 xylophones, 2 bass drums, a wind machine with a regulation airplane propeller, siren, anvils, automobile horns and buzzsaws
- October 18, 1935 (NY, Museum of Modern Art): performed first version for 1 pianola with Léger's film; *No. 156c*.

BECKWITH, John (*b* 1927), Canadian
1)   Theater Piece: *Avowels*, 3 keyboards, 2H, and a tenor voice
- CMC [Nat]   1985
- Letter from Beckwith, November 15, 1990
2)   Incidental Music: *The Journals of Susannah Moodie*, 6
        keyboards, 4H (text by Margaret Atwood, 1973)
- CMC-[Nat]
- Letter from Beckwith, November 15, 1990
3)   *Keyboard Practice*, 10 different keyboards, 8H: regal or
        chamber organ, harmonium (8' only), two-manual
        harpsichord, clavichord, celeste, grand piano, upright piano,
        electronic piano, electronic practice keyboard and dummy
        keyboard
                1979 (16*48)
- CMC-P
  CMC-Q
- Letter from Beckwith, November 15, 1990

BENTZON, Niels Viggo (*b* 1919), Danish
        Chamber Concert, Op. 52, 3P6H, clarinet, bassoon, 2
        trumpets, double bass and percussion
- HanG; c/o Mag (©1950) 1948 (18*51)
  LC-M947.B4.Op.54
- Hin-*MPO*:34

BOIS, Rob du (*b* 1934), Dutch
        Pour faire chanter la polonaise, 3P6H, flute, and soprano
- Done (©1966)1965 (*19)

BON, Maarten (*b* 1933), Dutch
1)   *Display IV*, 6P and piano tuner
- Done (©1982) 1980, rev. 1982 (*62)
  NYPL-JMG 87-407
2)   *Let's Go Out for a Drive (and Pollute the Air)*, 3P, trombone
        and conductor
- Done 1970; rev. 1974 (20*)

DODGE, Charles (*b* 1942), American
        Piece, 3P6H, trombones and percussion

- ACA (©1966) 1966
NYPL-JNG 75-147

FELDMAN, Morton (1926-1987), American
1)   *False Relationships and the Extended Ending*, 3P6H, violin,
        cello, trombone and chimes
- P,CF (©1968) 1968 (16*15)
UCLA-M747.F44.F3.1968
UMic-M747.F32.F2
YorU
- Hin-*MMP*:64
2)   *First Principles*, 4P8H, 2 violins, 3 cellos, 2 contrabassoons,
        harp and 2 percussion instruments
- P,CF 1966-1967 (17*20)
3)   *Pianos and Voices I*, 5P10H (pianists required to hum)
- UE (©1972)   1971-1972 (*11)
UMon-M216.F44.P53
4)   *Pianos and Voices II*, 5P10H and 5 sopranos 1972

GILBERT, Pia S. (*b* 1921), American
        Interrupted Suite, 3P (one prepared) and clarinet
- P,CF (©1976) (10*17)
UCLA-M447.G54157.1976

IVES, Charles (Edward) (1874-1954), American
        Vote For Names (Song No. 87), 3P6H and high voice (tenor
        or soprano or both or with chorus); text by Ives
- Autograph manuscript: NYPL (Music Division Archival
        Collections, Reel #6, #6792) Nov. 1912
- PSCM (1990 catalogue listing) UA-M1621.I95.V972.1968.folio

KOPPEL, Thomas (*b* 1944), Danish
        Concert héroïque, Op. 22, 3P6H, chorus and wind machine
- MIC

MELNYK, Lubomyr (*b* 1948), Canadian, of German/Ukrainian
        origin
        Contra, 3P6H and 3 violins
        c.1981 (c.45*)

- Letter from Melnyk, January 3, 1991

ORFF, Carl (1895-1982), German
1)   Cantata: *Der gute Mensch ("The Noble Man"): Partitur, zu gleich*, 3P6H, SATB chorus and percussion (6 performers); text by Franz Werfel (1890-1945)
      1. *Lächeln, atmen, schreiten*
      2. *Liebeslied*
      3. *Der gute Mensch*
- Scho (©1968)   1931
  LC-M2021.07.G9
  YU
2)   Cantata: *Veni Creator Spiritus*, 3P6H, SATB chorus, and percussion (5 performers); text by Franz Werfel (1890-1945)
      1. *Litanei*
      2. *Nacht*
      3. *Veni Creator Spiritus*
- Scho (©1968) 1931 (20*83)
  LC-M2021.07.V5
  YU
3)   Cantata: *Vom Fruhjahr, Öltank und vom Fliegen ("On Spring," "an Oil Tank" and "On Flying")*, 3P6H, SATB chorus and percussion; text by Berthold Brecht (1898-1956)
      1. *On Spring*
      2. *Seven Hundred Intellectuals Pray to an Oil Tank*
      3. *Report on Flying*
- Scho (©1968)   1931 (15*40)
  LC-M1531.07.V6b
  YU

REICH, Steve [or Stephen] (Michael) (*b* 1936), American
1)   *Music for 18 Musicians*, 4P8H, violin, cello, 2 clarinets, 4 female voices, 3 marimbas, 2 xylophones and metalophone
        1975
2)   *Variations for Winds, Strings, and Keyboards*
        1979; 1980 (full orchestral version)

SCHÄFFER, Boguslav (Julien) (*b* 1929), Polish
    Montaggio No. 53, 4P8H and percussion instruments (2

players)
- Pol (©1967)   1960 (5*)
  BPL-M1040.S43.M6
  IU-M635.S28
  NYPL

SCHICKELE, Peter [pseud. "P.D.Q. BACH"] (*b* 1935), American
Liebeslieder Polkas, S. 2/44, 1P5H and chorus
  1. *To His Coy Mistress*
  2. *To the Virgins, to Make Much of Time*
  3. *The Passionate Shepherd to His Love*
  4. *Why So Pale and Wan, Fond Lover?*
  5. *It was a Lover and His Lass*
  6. *The Constant Lover*
  7. *Song to Celia*
  8. *Interlude* (1P5H)
  9. *Farewell, Ungrateful Traitor*
  10. *Who is Sylvia?*
- P,T (Commissioned by U. of Cal. at Hayward)
- Letter from Schickele, December 5, 1990

STRAVINSKY, Igor (Fyodorovich) (1882-1971), Russian
  Ballet-cantata: *Les noces* (*Svadebka; The Wedding*), [4]
  "Russian choreographic scenes with song and music"
Part One: First Scene. *The Bride's Chamber*
                   Second Scene. *At the Bridegroom's House*
                   Third Scene. *The Bride's Departure*
Part Two: Fourth Scene. *The Wedding Feast*
- text by Piotr Kireievsky, *Sobranniye Piesni* (10 Vols. Moscow,
  1868-1871)
- *First Version* (1914-1917): SATB chorus, 4 vocal soloists (soprano,
  mezzo soprano, tenor, bass), 3 flutes (including piccolo), 3
  oboes (including English horn), 3 clarinets (including E-flat
  and bass), 2 bassoons, 4 horns, 4 trumpets, 2 keyed bugles
  (Flügelhorns), 3 trombones, 1 baritone horn in B-flat, bass
  tuba, 3 solo violins, 2 solo violas, 2 solo cellos, solo bass,
  harp, harpsichord, piano, cimbalom, timpani, bass drum,
  tambourine, triangle and drum (without snare)
- *Second Version* (1919), *Scenes I* and *II* only: SATB chorus, 4 vocal

soloists (Soprano, mezzo soprano, tenor, bass), 2 cimbaloms, harmonium, pianola, 3 side drums (large, middle and small, all without snare), tambourine, bass drum, triangle and 2 small suspended cymbals (5 performers)

NB - *Third/Final Version* (1921-1923): 1922--vocal score; 1923--full score: 4P8H, SATB chorus, 4 vocal soloists (soprano, mezzo soprano, tenor, bass), xylophone, timpani, 2 crotales (B-natural and C-sharp), 2 side drums (with and without snare), 2 drums (with and without snare), tambourine, bass drum, cymbals and triangle

- CM (©1922)
  BU
- English/German vocal score
  UA-ML1523.S92.N75.1922A.folio
- French/Russian vocal score
  UA-M1523.S92.N75.1922
- See Discography

WILLIAMSON, Sir Malcolm (Benjamin Graham Christopher) (*b*1931)
  English, of Australian origin
  Concerto for Two Pianos/Eight Hands and Wind Quintet,
  2P8H, flute, oboe, clarinet, bassoon and horn
- Wei (©1965)   1965
  BU
  NYPL-JMF 78-520

WYSCHNEGRADSKY [or Vïshnegradsky], Ivan (1893-1979),
  Russian
1) *Deux choeurs, Op. 14 in 1/4 tones*, 4P8H and chorus (on texts
    by A. Pomorsky)
2) *Linnita, Op. 25, in 1/4 tones*, 4P8H (2P tuned to A=440; 2
    P 1/4-tone below) and 3 female singers; one-act pantomime on
    a text by S. Wyschnegradsky, the composer's mother
    1937
3) *Acte choréographique, Op. 27, in 1/4 tones*, 4P8H, bass
    baritone, chorus and percussion (on a text by the composer)
    1938-1940; revised 1958-1959
4) *L'éternel étranger, Op. 51, in 1/4 tones*, 4P8H, solo singers,
    chorus and percussion (*action musico-scénique* on a text by the
    composer)

1950s - 1960s
- NB--The scores of the above may be obtained from the composer's
son: M. Dimitri Vicheney
        6 rue Plumet
        75015 Paris, France
- Letter from Bruce Mather, February 15, 1991

5. WORKS WITH VARIABLE INSTRUMENTATION

BEURLE, Jürgen (*b* 1943), German
      Kontra, 3P, 4P, 5P, . . .
- Moe (facsimile edition)

BOUCHARD, Linda (*b* 1957), American
      Pulsing Flighty, 2P or 4P
          1985 (*31)
  NYPL-AMC.M214.B7525.P4

BROWN, Earle (*b* 1926), American
1)   *Corroboree*, 3P6H
- UE (©1970)   1963-1964 (12*12)
  AMC-M216.B877.C8
  ASU-M216.B78.CPP
  HU-Mus632.664.415
  IN-M216.B877.C7
  NYPL-AMCM.216.B77m
  PCM-M342.B8.C82.1970
  UCLA-M216.B938.C7
  UCol-M216.B938.C7
  UMon-M216.B7.C6
  UR-M216.B877.C
  UWO-M116.B938.C7.U5
- Hin-*MMP*:26
- *TPR*:116-117
2)   *Folio*, 2P, 3P, 4P, . . . or various other instruments
        1. October (1952)
        2. November (1952) (Synergy)
        3. December (1952)
        4. MM87 and MM135
- AMP (©1961) (*8)
  LC-M22.B834.F6
- Hin-*MMP*:25-26
3)   *Four Systems*, 2P, 3P, 4P, . . . or various other instruments
- AMP (©1961) 1954
- Hin-*MMP*:25-26
4)   *Twenty-Five Pages*, 1P-25P

- UE (©1975)   1953 (8-25*6)
  AMC-M256.B877.T9
  BU
  HU-Mus632.664.407
  LC-M25.B
  NYPL-JNG76-303
  NU-M25.B76.T8
  UA-M25.B87.T97.1975.folio
  USC
  UWOP-M25.B769.T8
- Hin-*MMP*:26

CAGE, John (1912-1992), American
1)   16 Pieces: *Music for Piano 4-19*, "for any number of
        pianists." The sixteen pages "may be played as separate pieces
        or continuously as one piece." (Cage)
- P,CF(©1960)   1953 (*16)
  LC-M25.C
- Letter from Cage, October 20, 1990
2)   2 Groups of 16 Pieces: *Music for Piano 21-36, 37-52*, "for
        any number of pianists. May be played alone or together and
        with or without *Music For Piano 4-19*." (Cage)
- P,CF(©1960)   1955 (*32)
  UA-M22.C13.M98.1960
- Letter from Cage, October 20, 1990
3)   16 Pieces: *Music for Piano 53-68*, "for any number of
        pianists. May be played alone or together and with or without
        Music For Piano 4-19, 21-36, 37-52." (Cage)
                                    1956 (*16)
- P,CF(©1960)
  UA-M25.C13.M986.1960
- Letter from Cage, October 20, 1990
4)   16 Pieces: *Music for Piano 69-84*, "for any number of
        pianists. The sixteen pieces in this series . . . may be
        performed in whole or part . . . " (Cage)
- P,CF(©1960)   1956 (*16)
  UA-M25.C13.M987.1960
- Letter from Cage, October 20, 1990
- Realizations:

1. 4P8H--Maro Ajemian, John Cage, Grete Sultan, and David Tudor; Carl Fischer Concert Hall, New York, May 30, 1956 ("Music for 4 Pianos").
2. 4P8H--John Cage, William Masselos, Grete Sultan, and David Tudor; Carl Fischer Concert Hall, New York, April 30, 1957 ("Music for 4 Pianos").
3. 3P6H--John Cage, Marcelle Mercenier, and David Tudor; International World's Fair, Brussels, Belgium, Oct. 8, 1958 ("Music for 3 Pianos").

5) *Winter Music*, "to be performed in whole or part by a pianist or shared by two to twenty to provide a program of an agreed upon length. Can also be performed with *Atlas Edipticalis* (1961), a work for orchestra."
- Hen; c/o P,CF (©1960) 1957 (*20)
  BC-MI2140.C131.1.01517
  HU-635.419.430.PF
  LC-M25.C.fol.
- Hin-*MMP*:31
- Letter from Cage, October 20, 1990
- Realizations:
  1. 4P8H--John Cage, William Masselos, Grete Sultan, and David Tudor, Carl Fischer Concert Hall, New York, April 30, 1957 ("Music for 4 Pianos").
  2. 3P6H--John Cage, Marcelle Mercenier, and David Tudor, International World's Fair, Brussels, Belgium, Oct. 8, 1958 ("Music for 3 Pianos").
  3. 13P26H--Luciano Berio, Robert L. Moran, Lillian T'Sang, Patricia Caballero, Ann Uran, Robert Kuykendall, Irene Lathrop, Jane Hill, Philip Lesh, Tom Constanten, Nancy Thallhammer, Ronald Hotek, and Maxine Goldberg; California Composers Forum, Mills Concert Hall, Mills College, Oakland California, May 1, 1962.

CAZABAN, C., French
Naturalia 1, 7 keyboard instruments
- Sal   1982

COLEMAN, Randolf (*b* 1937), American
1)   *Format 1*, 3 or more instrumentalists
- SP
- Letter from publisher
2)   *Format 2*, 3 or more instrumentalists
- SP
- Letter from publisher
3)   *Format 8*, 3 or more instrumentalists
- SP
- Letter from publisher

DECOUST, Michel (*b* 1936), French
1)   *8 000 000 000*, for any instruments
                1972
2)   *Et/ou*, for 1-44P or pianists
- Sal   1972;©1982 (*5)
3)   *Polymorphie*, 105 instruments in small groups
                1967
FRID, Géza (*b* 1904), Dutch, of Hungarian origin
        Dimensies (Dimensions), Op. 74, 3P or 2P or 1P
- Done   1967 (10*)

GOLDSTEIN, Malcolm (*b* 1936), American
        On the First Day of Spring There Were Forty Pianos, 2P, 3P,
        4P, . . .
    (©1981) (*1)
    AMC-M214.G624105

ICHIYANAGI, Toshiro (*b* 1933), Japanese
        Music for Piano No. 4 for David Tudor, for any number of
        pianos/pianists ("use sustaining sound(s) and silence(s) only;
        no attack should be made")
- P,CF(©1963) December 1960 (*1)
- IU-M215.I25.M8.No4

KAMEL, Trisutji, Indonesian
        ?, 2P6H and woman's chorus
                1984

- Letter from Nancy Van de Vate, November 25, 1990

LENOT, Jacques, French
 Sphinx. Belvédères 4, 2P or 3P or 4P
- Sal 1982

LIBERDA, Bruno (*b* 1953), German
 Turn Slowly: Blues, 2P or 3P, 4H or 6H
- Ari (©1979) (*3)
 NYPL-Music(sheet)83-807

LOUVIER, Alain (*b* 1945), French
1) *Études pour agresseurs, Book 4, No. 21*, 2P or 3P, 4H or 6H
- Led (©1977)
 LC-M25.L
- Hin-*MMP*:119-120
2) *Quatre préludes pour cordes, pour les cordes du piano*, for
 many pianos
- Led (©1971) 1970 (9 3/4*9)

LUENING, Otto (*b* 1900), American
 The Bells of Bellagio, 2P or 3P, 4H or 6H
 1. *Hail!*
 2. *Farewell*
- P,CF (©1973) 1973 (*11)
 AMC
 HU-Mus740.6.403
 LC-M204.L
 Manh-789.49.L948.B448
 NYPL-JNF73-106
 UA
 UCLA-M214.L83.B4
 UMic-M204.L95.B4
 UR
 YU-M204.L95.B4
- Hin-*MMP*:120
- *TPR*:117-118

- Letter from Luening, December 11, 1990.

MENDES, Gilberto (Ambrósio García) (*b* 1922), Brazilian
      blirium c-9, 1 or 2 or 3 keyboard instruments; or for 3 or 4
      or 5 different instruments of the same family
- Ric Braziliara S.A. (©1969)
  SBTS
- Hin-*MMP*:129

MOZETICH, Marjan (*b* 1949), Canadian, of Italian origin
      Apparition, 3P6H; or P, harp and harpsichord; or 2P4H and
      harp; 1 P 2 harps; or 2 harps and harpsichord.
      1979, rec. 1988
- Letter from Mozetich, November 18, 1990

MUMMA, Gordon (*b* 1935), American
1)   *Medium Size Mograph*, for any number of P & H (chance
       composition)
  (©1967)   1962
  UC-M216-M84.M42.B53
  LC-M25.M
2)   *Very Small Size Mograph*, for any number of P & H (chance
       composition)
           1962

NUNES, Emmanuel (*b* 1941), Portuguese, of French origin
      Litanies du feu et de la Mer, 1P or 2P or 3P or 4P or 5P
  Sal (©1969) (25*4)

POUSSEUR, Henri (Léon Marie Thérèse) (*b* 1929), Belgian
      Mnemosyne II (systems of improvisation), for one or more
      performers
- SZ (©1977)   1969

REICH, Steve [or Stephen] (Michael) (*b* 1936), American
      Music for Mallet Instruments, Voices, and Organ, version for
      6 pianos 12 H (originally for 4 marimbas, 2 glockenspiels,
      metallophone, 3 female voices, and electronic organ
      1973

- Letter from Reich, November 26, 1990

RILEY, Terry (*b* 1935), American
In C, for "any number of melodic instruments." première:
May 21, 1965
- liner notes for *Piano Circus, Steve Reich's Six Pianos; Terry Riley's In C* (Argo, 430 380-2, 1990). This recording uses a concert grand, upright piano, Rhodes piano, two harpsichords and vibraphone.

SCHWARTZ, Elliot S. (*b* 1936), American
Pentagonal Mobile, 5P10H or pianos and tape
- ACA c. 1978 (13*)
- Hin-*MMP*:180
- Letter from Schwartz, November 20, 1990

TAKEMITSU, Tōru (*b* 1930), Japanese
1) *Corono for Pianist(s)*, for any number
- Sal 1962 (15*)
2) *Rain Tree*, 3P6H (or 3 percussion players)
- Scho (© 1981) (*15)
  UBC-M385 T34 R34 1981

VIVIER, Claude (1948-1983), Canadian
Pulau Dewata, for keyboard ensemble or any other combination of instruments 1977 (c.12 3/4*7)
- Reproduced from holograph
  ASU-M216.V58.P8x

WILSON, Dorothy (*b* 1904), American
The Grapevine (Tone Clusters), 2P4H or 7H or 8H (*1)
- AMC

WISE, Mathew W. (*b* 1961), American
Kranko: a Game For Two or More Players ("Ages 21 and Up") and Grand Piano, 1P4H, 6H, 8H, . . .
  (©1986) 1986 (*3)
- AMC-M213.W813.K8

6. WORKS WITH OTHER ACOUSTIC AND ELECTRONIC INSTRUMENTS/TAPE—MISCELLANEA

BENTZON, Niels Viggo (*b* 1919), Danish
  Studie, Op. 398, 7 electronic keyboards
                        1977
- CM
- HanG; c/o Mag

CAGE, John (1912-1992) and Lejaren **HILLER**, Jr. (*b* 1924),
       Americans
       HPSCHD, multi-media/mixed-media event "for tapes and
       harpsichords. There are solos for 1-7 amplified harpsichords,
       and tapes for 1-51 amplified monaural machines to be used in
       whole or in part with or without interruptions, etc., to make
       an indeterminate concert of any agreed upon length having 2-
       58 separate channels with loudspeakers around the audience."
       (Cage)
- Hen; c/o P,CF (©1969)   1967-1969
  LC-M216.C24.H7 (*Solo VII* only)
- Letter from Cage, October 20, 1990
- Realization and premiere: 16,000-seat assembly hall at the
  University of Illinois in Urbana, May 16, 1969

CRUMB, George (Henry), Jr. (*b* 1929), American
       Celestial Mechanics from ***Makrokosmos IV: Cosmic Dances
       for Amplified Piano, four hands***, 1P4H; 1P6H at "two short
       passages" (Crumb)
       3. *Gamma Draconis*
       4. *Delta Orionis*
- P,CF (©1979)   1979
  IU
  LC
  PCM-M204.C79.C4.oversize
  UA-M204.C956.C392.1979.folio
  UCLA-M204.C78.M3.No.4.1979. oversize area
  UMic-M204.C96.M2
  YU-M204.C956.M23++v.4
- Letter from Crumb, November 19, 1990

DIEMER, Emma Lou (*b* 1942), American
Pianoharpsichordorgan, for piano, harpsichord and organ, 2H to 6H; "live or may be taped separately on multi-track." (Diemer)
- SMC (1990 catalogue listing)
1974 (7*)
- Letter from Diemer, December 4, 1990

HAYS, Doris (*b* 1941), American
Music Only Music, Piano Only Piano, 3P6H, tape and film
1. *Na-Na Practice I*
2. *Descales I*
3. *Windy Gestures*
4. *Descales II*
5. *Music Box Practice*
6. *Cadence Practice*
7. *Noise Practice*
8. *Na-Na Practice II*
9. *Glissando Practice*
- Tal (©1984)
LC-M216.H(Nos.1,4,5,6,7,8 and 9)

HORWOOD, Michael S. (*b* 1947), Canadian of American origin
Durations, 1 to 4 different keyboards
- Available from composer   1965 (11*)
8 Grovetree Place
Bramalea, Ontario
L6S 1S8
- Letter from Horwood, November 20, 1990

MIEREANU, Costin, French
Musique tétanique, for acoustic or electronic keyboards
- Sal   1979

MITREA-CELARIANU, Mihai, French
Recoins, P, synthesizer, electric P, organ and *dispositif électroacoustique*
- Sal   1982

MONTAGUE, Stephan (Rowley) (*b* 1943), American
1)   *Inundations I*, 3P12H and tape
- EM   1975 (21*)
2)   *Quiet Washes*, 3P6H and trombones
- EM   1974

POUSSEUR, Henri (Léon Marie Thérèse) (*b* 1929), Belgian
        Crosses of Crossed Colors, 2P-5P 4H-10H, amplified female
        voices, 2 radios, tape recorders and 2 disc players
        1970

RAVEL, Maurice (1875-1937), French
        Frontispice, 2P5H
- Sal; c/o S,G (©1975)   1918
  UA-M214.R25.F93.1975.folio
  UCLA-M214.R196.fr
  UR-M216.R252.F9.1975
  UWO-M216.R27.F7.1975
  WSU

REICH, Steve [or Stephen](Michael)(*b* 1936), American
1)   *Four Organs*, 4 electronic organs and maracas
        1970
2)   *Phase Patterns*, 4 electronic organs
        1970
- Letter from Reich, November 26, 1990

RUSH, Loren
        Soft Music, Hard Music, 3 amplified P
- See Discography   1971

SATIE, Erik (Alfred Leslie)(1866-1952), French
        Vexations, performed 840 times in succession. This work was
        realized (literally) in New York on September 9, 1963, by a
        group of 5 pianists (1P10H) working in relays--thus setting a
        world's record for duration of any musical composition.

SOUSTER, Timothy (Andrew James)(*b* 1943), English
> *Afghan Amplitudes*, 3 electronic keyboards 6H and percussion
> (one must double on a rock drum kit as well as conventional
> percussion)
- OdB   1976 (8½*)
- Hin-*MMP*:187

7. SALON WORKS

ALFÖLDY, Imre, Hungarian
Hungarian Concert Polka, 2P8H
- Rie (Op.80,No.55)
- P,T (©1923) (*7)
  LC-M216.A45.H7

ANDRÉ, Julius [or Jules](1808-1880), German
Amusement en forme d'un rondeau, Op. 41, 1P6H
- And (©1866) (*19)
  Parts for 2 violins, cello, tambourine, cymbals and triangle--ad. lib.
  BPL-M1001.A623.Op.41
  NYPL

d'ANTALFFY, Dezsö (1885-?), American
Variations on a Theme--Dixie, 12P24H
- Facsimile of manuscript (©1934) 1934
  LC-M216.A57.D4

ANTHONY, Bert R. (*d* 1923), American
Salute to the Colors March, 2P8H
- P,T (©1922)
  LC-M216.A62.S3

ASCHER, J., French
Fanfare militaire, Op. 40, 2P8H
- Rie
- Lem

ATHERTON, Frank P., American
Crown of Triumph, Military March, Op. 221, 2P8H
- P,T (©1911)   (*7)
  LC-M216.A83

B., S.M.
Loretto Entrance, an Operatic Medley, 1P6H
- B&W (©1874)
  LC-M213.B115

BACH, N.G.
>   *Divertissement, Op. 10*, 1P6H
- *OS*, No.18
  BrM-h.1427

BEHR, Franz
a)   *Birthday March*, 1P6H
- Lam (©1902)
b)   *Festive March*, 1P6H
- S,G (©1923)
c)   *Spring Flowers, a Polka in Thirds, Op. 295, No.2*, 1P6H
- P,T (©1905)
  LC-M213.B

BERINGER, Robert
>   *Danse persane, Impromptu fantastique*, 1P6H
- (©1881)
  BrM-h.3275.a.(44.)

BEYER, Ferdinand (1803-1863)
>   *L'alliance, Fantaisies brillantes, Op. 149*, 1P6H
- Scho (©1864)
  BrM-h.814.d.(3.)

BICQUET, L.
>   *Jolly Fellows, Polka-march*, 1P6H;2P8H
- F,J

BISHOP, Mabel M., American
>   *A Day in June*, 2P8H
- Manuscript (©1926)
  LC-M216.B52.D2

BLANC, Adolphe (1828-1885)
1)   *Ah! vous dirai-je maman, Air varié*, 1P6H
- *OS*, No.25 (©1874)
  BrM-h.1427
2)   *Au clair de la lune, Caprice*, 1P6H
- *OS*, No.34 (©1874)

BrM-h.1427
3)   *Chantons victoire, Choeur d'Händel*, 1P6H
- *OS*, No.42 (©1874)
   BrM-h.1427
4)   *God Save the Queen*, 1P6H
- *OS*, No.40 (©1874)
   BrM-h.1427
5)   *Marlbrough s'en va-t-en guerre, Caprice facile*, 1P6H
- *OS*, No.39 (©1874)
   BrM-h.1427

BOLLMAN
      Lily Polka, 4P8H
- Nor

BRANT, A., American
      Four Square March, 4P8H
- AME
- *PRG*:439

BRATTON, John Lilley
1)   *Hebe (Petite valse gracieuse)*, 1P6H
- WM (©1915) (*7)
   LC-M213.B83.H3
- *PRG*:439
2)   *Iolas*, 1P6H
- WM (©1918)
   LC-M213.B83.I5

BROCKENSHIRE, J.O.
      The Elation of Triumph, 2P8H
- Chu (©1922)
   LC-M216.B93.E4

BROUTIN
      Ouverture triomphale, 2P8H
- Lem

BRYANT, Gilmore Ward, American
   Marche Militante, 1P6H
- Ell (©1904)

CALT, Gabriel van
   Boléro-fanfare, 1P8H
- Lem (©1885;©1917) (*21)
LC-M213.V
NYPL

de CHANCET
   Hungarian Dance, 1P6H
- A

CHAVARRI, Eduardo L.
   El Viejo Castillo Moro (The Old Moorish Castle), arr. 4P8H
- *FPQC*-No.232

CHELARD
   Marche hongroise, 2P8H
- Lem

"CINQ MARS"
   Chasse et marche, 1P6H
- Dit

CLARK, C.B.
   A Sleigh Ride, 1P6H
- P,T (©1918)
LC-M213.C58.S5

COWLES, Cecil, American
1)   *In a Ricksha*, 4P8H
- *FPQC*-No.214
2)   *Mandarin*, 4P8H
- *FPQC*-No.213

CRAMMOND, C.C.
   Commencement Day, Op. 190, 1P6H

- P,T
- *PRG*:439

CROISEZ, A.
   Voyage d'une hirondelle, multiple pianos
- Col; c/o Sal
- *PRG*:439

CURTI, Carlos
   La Tipica, Polka, 1P6H; 2P8H
- P,T
- Witz (©1902)   (*9)
   LCM-213.C;M216.C95.T4

CZIBULKA
   Stephanie Gavotte, 2P8H
- Nor

DALE, Agnes
   The Racing Sleighs, 1P6H
- S,G (©1960) (*5)
- Cha
- *PRG*:439

DAVID, French
   Boléro-fanfare, 2P8H
- Lem

DRUMHELLER, Charles, American
1)   *Circus Galop*, 1P6H
- B&W (©1885)
   LC-M213.D
2)   *Drifting Clouds, Caprice élégant*, 1P6H
- B&W
3)   *Golden Spray, Morceau de salon*, 1P6H
- B&W
   LC-M213.D
4)   *Grand Imperial March*, 1P6H
- B&W

5)   *No You Don't, Galop burlesque*, 1P6H
- B&W
6)   *Ocean Pearl*, 1P6H
- B&W
7)   *Pandora March*, 1P6H
- B&W (©1909)
  LC-M213.D
8)   *Silver Spray, Caprice de salon*, 1P6H
- B&W
9)   *Sunshine on the Lea, Valse élégante*, 1P6H
- B&W
  LC-M213.D

DUCELLE, Paul, American
        Musical Memories, Op. 16, 1P6H
        1. *Dancing Stars, Waltz*
        2. *Lilliputian Parade*
        4. *Dance of the Dewdrops*
        7. *Nita, Spanish Dance*
        11. *Alpine Song*
- S,G
- *PRG*:440

DURAND, Charles, American
1)   *Bride's Welcome March*, 1P6H; 2P8H
- Witz (©1902) (*7)
  LC-M213.D;M216.D89
2)   *Charge of the Uhlans, Galop*, 1P6H
- Witz (©1902)
  LC-M213.D
3)   *Famous, Two-step*, 2P8H
- P,T
- Witz (©1904)   (*5)
  LC-M216.D892
4)   *Love By Moonlight Waltz, Op. 90, No. [11]*, 1P6H; 2P8H
- P,T
- Witz (©1897)
  LC-M213.D;M216.D894

5)   *Peerless Waltz*, 1P6H; 2P8H
- P,T (©1901)

ECKSTEIN, Maxwell (*b* 1924)
        Cornish May Dance, 2P8H
- F,C
- *PRG*:440

EDGINTON, Mary Joyce
        A Gay March, 2P12H
- HinE (©1964) (1 3/4*)
  UR-M216.E23g
- P,CF
- *PRG*:440

EILENBERG, Robert Braun
        Air de ballet, 2P8H
- Wood (©1914)
  BrM-g.545.t.(7.)

EMERY, Dorothy Raddle (*b* 1901), American
        Fairy Lullaby, 1P6H
- S,G (©1951)
  LC-M213.E
- *PRG*:440

ENGELMANN, Hans, American
1)   *Concert Polonaise*, 2P8H
- P,T (©1908)
  LC-M216.E54
2)   *Grand American Festival March*, 2P8H
- P,T (©1912)
  LC-M216.E542
3)   *Grande Valse Caprice*, 2P8H
- P,T (©1920)
  LC-M216.E545
4)   *In Jolly Mood, Polonaise, Op. 482*, 2P8H
- W-S (©1905)
  LC-M216.E546

5)   *In the Arena, Op. 608*, 1P6H; 2P8H
- P,T (©1907)
  LC-M216.E548
  MAU
6)   *Parade Review, Op. 307*, 2P8H
-P,T (©1900)
  LC-M216.E562

FAX, Mark, American
        Waltz Specialty, 4P8H
- *FPQC*-No.184

FERBER, Richard, American
        On to Prosperity, March, 2P8H
- P,T (©1911)
  LC-M216.F34.Q5

FOWLER, J.A., American
        Rosemary Waltzes, 2P8H
- Pon (©1888)
  LC-M216.F684

FRANKLIN, Fred A., American
        Summer Night, Waltz, 1P6H
- P,T (©1915)
  LC-M213.F

FRIML, Rudolf (1879-1972), American
1)   *Butterfly Waltz, Op. 85, No. 2*, 2P8H (Moderately difficult)
- Schm (©1910)
2)   *Oberck, Danse Polonaise, Op. 55, No. 3*, 2P8H (Moderately
        difficult)
- Schm (©1910)
  LC-M216.F75

FRYSINGER, J. Frank (1878-?), American
        Inauguration March, Op. 88, No.1, 2P8H
- P,T (©1915)

GAEL, Henri van, French
  Morceaux choisis, 1P6H
  1. *Parfums de roses, Valse (Mouvement de valse), Op. 120*
  2. *En chasse, Op. 46 (Allegretto)*
  3. *Les glissandos, Mazurka, Op. 55 (Tempo di mazurka)*
  4. *Fantaisie, Op. 59 (Allegro)*
  5. *Dans les champs, Op. 104 (Moderato)*
  6. *Comme autrefois, Op. 112 (Tempo di gavotta)*
  7. *Valse-Berceuse, Op. 89 (Mouvement de valse)*
  8. *Echos des montagnes, Op. 61 (Allegretto)*
  9. *Chanson portugaise, Op. 96 (Allegretto)*
  10. *Chanson tyrolienne, Op. 66 (Moderato)*
  11. *A la fontaine,Idylée, Op. 88 (Allegretto vivo)*
  12. *Marche guerrière, Op. 83 (Tempo di marcia)*
- Jun (©1910)
- Scho (©1910)
  LC-M213.G13

GÁL, Hans (1890-1987), Austrian
        Pastorale Tune, 1P6H
- Cur; S,G (©1954) (3*7)
  BBC-17995
  BrM-h.3292.b.(2.)
  RCM

GARNER, Adam, American
        Hawaiian Melody, 4P8H
- *FPQC*-No.2

GOERDELER, Richard, American
1)   *Bugle Call, March*, 1P6H (Easy)
- Schm (©1913)
  LC-M213.G
2)   *Darkies' Moonlight Dance, Morceau caractéristique*, 1P6H
        (Grade 3)
- W-S (©1898)
  LC-M213.G

GRASS, J.B.
Ad Astra, 2P8H
- Chu (©1886)
LC-M216.G72

HAHN, Reynaldo (1874-1947)
Pour bercer un convalescent, trois pièces, 2P8H
- Heu (©1916)
LC-M216.H15

HAMMEREL, Victor
1)   *Recreation March*, 1P6H
  F,J
2)   *Stampede, Grand Galop*, 1P6H
  F,J
3)   *Steinert's March*, 1P6H
  F,J

HAYS, F. Clifton, American
Comrades in Arms, March-galop and Two-step, 2P8H
- P,T (©1907)
LC-M216.H28

HEARTZ [or Hart], Harry Lawson (1869-?), American
From an Ocean Garden, Barcarole, 1P6H
- W-S (©1918)
LC-M213.H57.F6

HETÉNYI-HEIDLBERG, Albert (1875-?)
[12]*Klavierstücke*, 1P6H
- Kálm (©1912)
LC-M213.H(vol.3 only)

HOFFMANN, Heinrich (1842-1902), German
March, Novelette, and Waltz, Op. 103, 2P8H
- Br&H (©1890)
- Hin-*MMP*:91

HOLLAENDER, Alexis (1840-?)

   March, Op. 39, No. 1, 1P6H
- P,T (©1905)
 LC-M213.H

HOLMÉS, G. Augusta (Mary Anne) [pen name: Hemann
  Zenta](1847-1903), French
1) *Fantasia sur Les cloches de Corneville [par R. Planquette]*,
  2P8H
- Wil (©1893)
 BrM-h.3544.(4.)
2) *The Sentinel's Night March*, 2P8H
- Wil (©1893)
 LC-M216.H64

HOLST, Edward (1843-1899), American
1) *Bloom and Blossom Waltz*, 1P6H (Grade 2)
- W-S (©1894)
 LC-M213.1P.6H
2) *Camp of Glory, Grand March*, 1P6H; 2P8H
- P,T
- Witz (©1895)
 LC-M213.H;M216.H68.C2
3) *Dance of the Demon, Grand galop de concert*, 1P6H; 2P8H
- Roh (©1887;©1888;©1890)
 LC-M213.H75.D3;M216.H68.D3
4) *Dixie Doodle, A Medley*, 1P6H; 2P8H
- P,T (©1905)
- Witz
 LC-M213.H;M216.H68.D6
5) *Elaine, Grande valse de concert*, 2P8H
- W-S (©1888)
 LC-M216.H68.E5
6) *Flag of Honor, Grande marche triomphale*, 1P6H
- Roh (©1888)
 LC-M213.H
7) *Imps and Sprites at Work, Grande marche héroïque*, 1P6H;
  2P8H
- Roh (©1892)
 LC-M213.H;M216.H68.I5

8)   *The June-bug's Dance, Polka-rondo*, 1P6H; 2P8H
- Roh (©1888)
   LC-M213.H75.T3;M216.H68.J7
9)   *March of the Phantoms, Grande marche de concert*, 2P8H
- Roh (©1888)
   LC-M216.H68.M3
10)   *On to the Battle, Marche triomphale*, 1P6H; 2P8H
- Roh (©1890)
   LC-M213.H;M216.H68.05
11)   *Revel of the Witches, Morceau fantasque*, 2P8H
- W-S (©1890)
   LC-M216.H68.R3
12)   *Seguidilla, Danse espagnole*, 1P6H; 2P8H (with castanets,
        triangle and tambourine)
- Roh (©1892; ©1893)
   LC-M213.H;M213.H6852
13)   *Shooting Stars, Grand galop*, 1P6H; 2P8H
- P,T (©1893)
- Witz
   LC-M216.H68.S4
14)   *The Sleigh Race, Grand galop de concert*, 1P6H; 2P8H
- Roh (©1890) (11*)
   LC-M213.H75.H3;M216.H68.S6[8h.]
15)   *Summer Zephyr, Idyll*, 1P6H (Grade 3)
- W-S
   LC-M213.H
16)   *Tripping Thro' the Heather*, 1P6H; 2P8H
- Witz (©1895)
   LC-M213.H;M216.H68.T7
17)   *Under the American Flag, March of the Mariners*, 1P6H;
        2P8H
- Roh (©1893)
   LC-M213.H75.M3;M216.H68.U5
18)   *World's Columbian Exposition March*, 1P6H
- Roh (©1892)
   LC-M213.H

JOHANNING, Paul F., American
        Yellow Jonquils, Danse à la gavotte, 1P6H (Grade 3)

- W-S (©1901)
  LC-M213.J

JOHNSON, Thomas Arnold (*b* 1908), American
       Scherzo, 1P6H
- Curw (©1952)
  LC-M213.J
- Robt; c/o P,T
- S,G
- *PRG*:440

JUHÁSZ, Aladár
SEIFERT, Hans T., rev. & fing.
       Trio of Hungarian Folk Songs, 1P6H
- F,C (©1908)
  LC-M213.J93

JULLIEN, P., American
       Posthaste, 1P6H; 2P8H
- F,J

KEATS, F., American
       Dance of the Rosebuds, [1P6H]
- P,T
- *PRG*:440

KEENAN, Thomas P. (1861-1947), Irish
       The Kilties are Coming, 1P6H
- F,C
- *PRG*:440

KÉLER-BÉLA, German
       Lustspiel Overture, 1P6H
- F,J

KELLER, Wilhelm (*b* 1920)
       Christmas Holidays, Fantasia, 1P6H
- Bea (©1892)
  BrM-h.3292.(4.)

KENNEDY, A., American
  Star of Hope, 1P6H
- CMP
- *PRG*:440

KERN, Carl Wilhelm, American
  Assembly Grand March, Op. 475, 1P6H
- Dit (©1923)
  LC-M213.K4.A6

KIENZL, Wilhelm
  Steirischer Tanz, Op. 50, No. 60, 2P8H
- Rie

KOELLING, Carl (1831-1914)
1) *Commencement March, Op. 401*, 2P8H
- P,T (©1915)
  LC-M216.K63
2) *Hungary, Rapsodie mignonne, Op. 410*, 2P8H
- P,T (©1908)
  LC-M216.K632
- *PRG*:440
3) *Marche lyrique, Op. 414*, 1P6H; 2P8H
- P,T (©1909)
  LC-M213.K77;M216.K
4) *Marche militaire, Op. 413*, 1P6H
- P,T (©1909)
  LC-M213.K;M213.K77
5) *Sailor's Song and Hornpipe, Op. 392*, 2P8H
- P,T (©1908)
  LC-M216.K634
6) *Zwei Blumen, Op. 364*, 1P6H
- P,T (©1913)
  LC-M213.K

KONTSKI, Anton [or Antoinede] (1817-1899)
  Persian March, Op. 369, 2P8H
- P,T

LC-M216.K67

KORTHEUER, A.W.
>	*Marche Arabesque*, 1P6H;2P8H
- F,J

KOWALSKI, Henri (1841-1916), French
>	*Marche hongroise, Op. 13*, 2P8H
- Scho 1864
  UCLA-C.000.001.003.3

KRAMER, Wilhelm, German
1)	*Glockenspiel Polka, Op. 19*, 1P6H
- And (©1892)
  LC-M213.K89.G5
2)	*Im Flügelkleide, Mazurka, Op. 9*, 1P6H
- And (©1884)
  BrM-h.3285.b.(33.)
3)	*Jubelfeier, Polonaise, Op. 7*, 1P6H; 2P8H (Grade 3)
- And (©1924)
- FsC
  LC-M13.K89.P5
- W-S
- *PRG*:440
4)	*Pensionat streuden, Waltzer, Op. 18*, 1P6H
- And (©1892)
  LC-M213.K

LACK, Théodore (1846-?), French
1)	*Cabaletta, Op. 83*, 2P8H
- Dur (©1909)
  LC-216.L13
2)	*Le départ des chasseurs, Marche, Op. 265*, 1P8H
- Lem (©1907)
  LC-M213.L14

LACOME [or LACOME D'ESTALINX], Paul Jean Jacques (1838-
	1920)
>	*Impromptu à la hongroise*, 2P8H

- P,T (©1906)
  LC-M216.L17

LANDRY, Albert
1)   *Faneuses et faucheurs, Deux chansons rustiques, Op. 254,*
        1P8H
- Lem
2)   *Hidalgo, Danse andalouse, Op. 214,* 1P6H
- Led (©1903)
  LC-M213.L
3)   *Mariée de village, Fête paysanne, Op. 216,* 1P6H
- Led (©1904)
  LC-M213.L
4)   *Le petit moulin,* 2P8H
- Led
5)   *Pierrette et Arlequine,* 2P8H
- Led
6)   *Tarantelle et napolitaine,* 2P8H
- Led

LANGDON, C., American
1)   *Grace and Favor,* 2P8H
- WM
- *PRG*:441
2)   *Hall of Mirrors,* 1P6H
- WM
- *PRG*:441

LANGE, Gustav, German
        Zu Weihnachten, Fantasie, Op. 172, No. 5, 1P6H
- Forb (©1910)
  LC-M213.L

LANGE, Otto, American
1)   *Awakening of the Birds,* 1P6H; 2P8H
- P,T
- Witz (©1901)
  LC-M213.L;M216.L25
2)   *Flight of the Swallows,* 1P6H; 2P8H

- P,T
- Witz (©1901)
 LC-M213.L;M216.L252
3)   *Joyous Shepherd*, 1P6H; 2P8H
- P,T
- Witz (©1901)
 LC-M213.L;M216.L256
4)   *Happy Gondolier*, 1P6H; 2P8H
- P,T
- Witz (©1901)
 LC-M213.L;M216.L254
5)   *Medley on Popular Airs*, 1P6H
- B&W (©1889)
 LC-M213.L
6)   *Moonlight Serenade*, 1P6H; 2P8H
- P,T
- Witz (©1901)
 LC-M213.L

LANSING, A.W., American
        Concert Polka, 1P6H; 2P8H
- P,T (©1915)
 LC-M213.L;M216.L3

LAVIGNAC, Albert (1846-1916)
        Galop-marche, 1P8H
- P,T   (*23)
 LC-M213.L

LE PRE, Pierre, French
        Marche des aviateurs, 1P6H
- WM
- *PRG*:441

LICHNER, P.
        Idle Moments March, 1P6H
- CMP
- *PRG*:441

LIFTL, Franz J.
1)   *En garde! Polka de salon, Op. 116,* 1P6H
- Bos (©1911)
2)   *Fest-Marsch, Op. 112,* 2P8H
- Bos (©1911)
3)   *Kleine konzert, Mazurka, Op. 113,* 2P8H
- Bos (©1911)
   LC-M213.L
4)   *Maguets, Gavotte, Op. 115,* 1P6H
- Bos (©1911)
   LC-M213.L
5)   *Très-jolie, Waltzer, Op. 114,* 1P6H
- Bos (©1911)
   LC-M213.L

LINDSAY, Charles, American
1)   *Autumn Days March,* 1P6H
- P,T (©1916)
   LC-M213.L
2)   *Homeward March,* 1P6H
- P,T [©1916]

LUIGINI, A.
        Ballet égyptien, 2P8H
- Gr
   UR-M216.L952

LVOFF [or L'VOV], Alexis Fedorovich (1798-1870), Russian
        Russian Hymn, 1P6H
- P,T (©1905)
   LC-M213.L

MACFADYEN, Alexander (1879-1936), American
        Country Dance, 2P8H
- Chu (©1922) (*9)
- P,T
- WM
- *TPR*

MAGNUS, Désiré (pseud. Georges MICHEUZ)
    Marche russe, Op. 101, 2P8H
- Led (©1868)
  LC-M216.M18.M4

MANGDON, C.
    Grace and Favor, 1P6H
- WM
- *PRG*:441

MANGER, Edward
    Amusement, Deuxième rondo, 1P6H
- Rich   c.1850 (*19)
  NYPL

MANOUVRIER
    Imperial, Schottische, 1P6H
- B&W

MARIE, Gabriel (1852-1926), French
    La cinquantaine, Air dans le style ancien (The Golden
    Wedding), 1P6H
- F,J
- P,T (©1906)
  LC-M213.G

MARSDEN, Ernest
    Waltz of the Snowflakes, 1P6H
- H,F

MARTIN, G.
1)   *Betty's Waltz*, 1P6H
- CMP; c/o Ash
- *PRG*:440
2)   *Cuckoo Song*, 1P6H
- CMP; c/o Ash
- *PRG*:441
3)   *The Floral Parade, Valse*, 1P6H
- CMP; c/o Ash

- *PRG*:441

MASON, William (1829-1908), American
1)   *[4] Quartettes*, 2P8H
- Dona (©1890)
   BrM-h.3291.b.(2.)
        [6] Sextettes, 2P12H
- Dona (©1889-1890)
   BrM-h.3129.(9.)

MATHIAS, L.
        Christmas Polonaise, 1P6H; 2P8H
- F,J

MAY, Dominic M.H., American
        Southern Medley, 1P6H (with ad. lib. part for mandolin)
- Will (©1902)
   LC-M213.M

MAYER, Charles (1799-1862)
        Galop militaire, Op. 117, 1P6H; 2P8H
- F,C (©1908)
   LC-M213.M468
- Sie
   NYPL

McDOWALL, American
1)   *The Flatterer*, 1P6H; 2P8H
- Witz
2)   *Forest Scenes, Musical Sketch*, 1P6H; 2P8H
- Witz
3)   *In the Gondola*, 1P6H; 2P8H
- Witz
4)   *Valse Arabesque*, 1P6H; 2P8H
- Witz

MELLICHAMP, Nell V.
        Three Clocks, 1P6H
- CMP; c/o Ash (©1952)

- *PRG*:441

MENOZZI, Giovanni, Italian
1)   *Capriccio élégante per due pianoforti a quattro mani ciasurro,*
       Op. 214, Postuma, 2P8H
- Ric (©1885)
  BrM-h.3607.(21.)
2)   *Mattinata in famiglia, Pezzi per pianoforte a sei mani, 3 Nos.,*
       1P6H
- Ric (©1884)
  BrM-h.3607.(25.)

MERKUR, Jacob Louis
       New Horizons, 2P8H
- CCP/Bel (©1963)
- *PRG*:441

MERZ, Karl (1836-1890)
1)   *Pearl of the Sea,* 2P8H
- Brai (©1869;©1878) (*13)
  LC-M216.M45.P3
2)   *Sounds From the Ohio, Valse élégante,* 2P8H
- Brai (©1867)
  LC-M216.M4.S55

MICHAELIS, L., American
       Blacksmith in the Woods, Idyll, 1P6H
- Dit (©1885)
  LC-M213.M62.B5

MILDE, Louis
       Grande marche triomphale, Op. 16, 2P8H
- Schl (©1892)
  LC-M216.M55

MISSA, Edmond Jean Louis (1861-1910), French
1)   *Cloches et carillons,* 1P6H
- P,T [©1910]
2)   *Fête des vendanges,* 1P6H

- P,T [©1910]
3)   *Gavotte puccinella*, 1P6H
- P,T [©1910]
4)   *Matinée de printemps*, 1P6H
- P,T [©1910]
5)   *Noël enfantin*, 1P6H
- P,T [©1910]
6)   *Valse Lorraine*, 1P6H
- P,T (©1910)
   LC-M213.M

MONTANI, Pietro (1895-?), Italian
        Trivalzer (Three Waltzes), 1P6H
- Col
- Ric (©1956) (*7)
   NYPL
- *PRG*:441

MOREL, Gabriel, arr.
1)   *Danse espagnole*, 1P6H
- A
2)   *Norwegian Cradle Song, No. 7*, 1P6H
- A (©1916)
   LC-M213.T83

MORLEY, Charles
        Napolitana, Saltarello, 1P6H (Moderately difficult)
- Schm

MORRISON, R.S.
        Musical Motion Pictures: Five Characteristic Pieces, 2P8H
        1. *No Surrender, March*
        2. *Undulation, Valse lente*
        3. *Nip and Tuck, Polka caprice*
        4. *Coryphees, Air de ballet*
        5. *African Antics, Characteristic March and Two-step*
- P,T (©1915)
   LC-M216.M67

MÜLLER, Edward A., American
1)   *A Balcony in Venice*, 1P6H
- Chu (©1926)
  LC-M213.M955.B2
2)   *A Festival in San Remo*, 1P6H
- Chu (©1926)
  LC-M213.M955.F3

MÜLLER, Julius E., American
        May Festival March, Op. 216, 1P6H
- Will (©1894)
  LC-M213.M

NICHOLLS, Heller (1874-?), arr.
        Neopolitan Popular Air, 1P6H
- Pat (©1976)
  LC-M213.N

NINI, Corrado, Italian
        Pagina d'Album, 1P6H
- Car (©1925)
  LC-M213.N7.P3

NOPS, Marjory
        Elm Glade, 1P6H
- Aug (©1959)   (*3)
  BrM-h.3292.b.(5.)

OESTEN, Theodor
        The Coming of Spring, Op. 319, 1P6H
- Chu

OLDENBURG, Elizabeth (*b* 1910), American
        Forward March, 1P6H
- S,G
- *PRG*:441

PACE, Robert Lee, American
1)   *Jig* from the ***Western Suite***, 2P8H

- Mil (©1961)
  ASU-M216.P3.J5
  LC-M216.P22.W5
2)   *Rhumba*, 2P8H
- F,C (©1954)
  LC-M216.P22.R5
  WSU
- *PRG*:441

PAGNONCELLI, G.B., Italian
        Ballata e Bizzaria, unite in facile divertimento, 2P8H
- Luc (©1887; ©1907)
  BrM-h.3291.a.(13.)
- P,T
  LC-M216.P15

PARLOW, Edmund (1855-?), American
1)   *The Dancing Master, Gavotte*, 1P6H
- P,T (©1921)
  LC-M213.P25.D3
2)   *On and On, March*, 1P6H
- P,T (©1921)
  LC-M213.P25.05
3)   *Tarantella in A Minor, Op. 78*, 2P8H
- Sim (©1904)
  LC-M216.P274

PASQUOTTI, Corrado (*b* 1954), Italian
        Racconti, 2P6H
- SZ   1974 (14½*9)

PEABODY, A. Jackson, Jr., American
        Dance of the Winds, Galop de concert, 2P8H
- P,T (©1915)
  LC-M216.P32

PESSARD, French
        Retraite aux flambeaux, 2P8H
- Lem

PESSE, Maurice, French
>*Deux pièces originales*, 2P8H
>>1. *Sous le brillant soleil de mai*
>>2. *Marche triomphale*

- Dur (©1914)
  LC-M216.P38
- *PRG*:441

POPP, American
>*Forget-me-not, Gavotte*, 2P8H

- Nor

POTTER, Bert
>*Dance of the Cossacks, Galop-caprice*, 1P6H (Grade 3)
- W-S

PRESTON, M.L.
>*Here Comes the Parade*, 1P6H
- P,T

RAFF, Joseph Joachim (1822-1882), American
>*Suite, Op. 200*, 2P8H
>>1. *Introduction and Fugue*
>>2. *Menuett*
>>3. *Gavotte and Musette*
>>4. *Gavatine*
>>5. *Finale*

- Sie
  UR-M216.R135

RAMÓN GÓMIS, José (*d* 1936)
>*Jota*, 1P6H
- UME (©1956)
  LC-M213.R

RAND, Josie, American
>*Nodding Roses, Morceau de salon*, 1P6H
- W-S (©1909)
  LC-M213.R18

RATHBURN, Frederic G., American
1)   *Marche triomphale*, 2P8H
- P,T (©1907)
  LC-M216.R23.M3
2)   *A May Day*, 1P6H
- P,T (©1905)
  LC-M213.R
3)   *The Young Recruit*, 1P6H
- P,T

RAVINA
        Tyrolienne, Op. 696, 3P12H
- P,T

RENARD, Pierre
        Iris, Intermezzo, 1P6H
- P,T (©1913)
  LC-M213.R

RIEDEL, August
        *Variationen über R. Schumann's **Fröhlicher Landmann**, Op.
        13*, 2P8H
- Riet (©1887)
  BrM-h.3291.a.(18.)

RITTER
1)   *Cavalier's Farewell March*, 2P8H
- Nor
2)   *Cavalier's Farewell Polka*, 2P8H
- Nor
3)   *Light Cavalry March*, 2P8H
- Nor

RÖCKEL, Joseph Leopold (1838-1923), English, of German
        origin
        Air du Dauphin, Ancienne danse de la cour, 2P8H
- Aug (©1890)
  BrM-g.142.i.(4.)

ROCKWELL, George Noyes, American
    Instillation March, 1P6H; 2P8H
- P,T (©1915; ©1916)
    LC-M213.R65.I5;M216.R65.I5

ROSENAUER, Alois
1)   *Jubel-Ouverture, Die Primopartie in Umfange einer Quinte,*
       Op. 34, 1P6H
- Frob (©1913)
    LC-M213.R78.Op.34
2)   *Tableaux russes, Suite petite, Op. 29*, 1P6H
          1. *Introduction et chant ancien russe*
          2. *Arrivée des cosques; Hymne; Danse des femmes et filles*
          3. *Camanrinsca (Danse nationale)*
- Frob (©1911)
    LC-M213.R78

RUCKGABER
    Mazurka, 1P6H
- Dit

RUMMEL
    Rondeau en forme de valse, Op. 66, 2P6H
- P,T

SABATIER, French
    Marche aux flambeaux, 2P8H
- Nor

SALVAYRE
    Ouverture du bravo, 2P8H
- Lem

SAMPSON, Godfrey, English
1)   *A Jig*, 1P6H
- Aug
2)   *Old Round*, 1P6H
- Aug

SARESKI, Polish
> *Polish Dance*, 1P6H
- A

SARTORIO, Arnoldo (1853-1936), American
1)   *Carnival of Roses*, 1P6H; 2P8H (Moderately difficult)
- Schm (©1905;©1925)
  LC-M213.S3.C3;M216.S19.C3
2)   *Coquetterie*, 1P6H
- P,T (©1924)
  LC-M213.S3.C5
3)   *Country Dance Scene*, 1P6H
- Schm (©1928)
4)   *Dancing and Singing, Danse espagnole*, 1P6H
- P,T (©1924)
  LC-M213.S3.D3
5)   *Early Spring*, 1P6H
- P,T (©1924)
  LC-M213.S3.E3
6)   *Fairy Bells, Waltz*, 1P6H (Easy)
- Schm (©1925)
  LC-M213.S3.F3
7)   *La Jota Aragonesa*, 1P6H
- P,T (©1924)
  LC-M213.S3.S5
8)   *March of the Dragons*, 1P6H
- P,T (©1924)
  LC-M213.S3.M3
9)   *The Masked Ball, Polonaise*, 2P8H (Moderately difficult)
- P,T
10)   *Smiling Springtime*, 1P6H
- P,T (©1924)
  LC-M213.S3.S5
11)   *Souvenir de Beethoven*, 1P6H
- P,T (©1924)
  LC-M213.S3.S7

12)   *Steeple Chase*, 1P6H
- Schm (©1928)
13)   *Triumphal March*, 2P8H
- P,T (©1920)
  LC-M216.S19.T6
14)   *Turkish Impromptu*, 1P6H
- P,T (©1924)
  LC-M213.S3.T7

SCARMOLIN, A. Louis, American
       Chimes, 1P6H
- Schm (©1928)

SCHER, William (*b* 1900), American
       Dancing Puppets, 1P6H
- P,T
- *PRG*:442

SCHILLER, (Johann Christoph) Friedrich von (1759-1805)
       Humming-bird Waltz, 1P6H
- P,T
- *PRG*:442

SCHNECKER, Peter August (1850-1903), American
       Twilight Idyll, 1P6H
- P,T (©1913)
  M213.S

SCHNEIDER, Erwin
1)   *Bridal March, Two-step*, 1P6H
- P,T (©1903)
- Witz
  LC-M213.S
2)   *Cavalry Advance Galop*, 1P6H; 2P8H
- P,T (©1895)
- Witz
  LC-M213.S37.C3

3)   *Southern Beauty, March and Two-step*, 1P6H
- P,T (©1904)
  LC-M13.S

SCHUBERT, F.L.
      Mardi gras aux enfers-quadrilles, 2P8H
- Nor

SCHULTZ, Edwin (1827-1907), German
1)   *Lustige Musikanten in D Major, Op. 198, No. 2*, 2P8H
- Sim (©1896)
  LC-M216.S34.L7
2)   *Kleiner Festmarsch in C Major, Op. 182, No. 1*, 2P8H
- Sim (©1894)
  LC-M216.S37.K5
3)   *Menuett in G Major, Op. 182, No. 2*, 2P8H
- Sim (©1894)
  LC-M216.S34.M4
4)   *Matrosentanz in C Major, Op. 198, No. 1*, 2P8H
- Sim (©1896)
  LC-M216.S34.M3
5)   *Rondino, Op. 84, No. 1*, 2P8H
- Sim (©1883)
  BrM-h.3291.a.(23.)
6)   *Serenade in F Major, Op. 157*, 2P8H
- Sim
  BBC-4571

SELLENICK, Sid
      Marche indienne, 1P6H; 2P8H
- Led (©1911)
  UR-M213.S477;M216.S467

SILVER, Alfred J. (1870-?)
      Our Festal Day, 1P6H
- F,J (©1912)
  LC-M213.S54

SINNHOLD, Rudolf
Under the Palm Trees, Waltz, 1P6H
- F,J (©1905)
LC-M213.S

SISSON, C.T.
Tourist's March, 1P6H; 2P8H
- F,J

SMITH, William Seymour
Six Trios, 1P6H
- Ash (©1897)
BrM-h.3679.d.(39.)

SOURILAS, Theodore
Hip! Hip! Hip!, 1P6H
- F,J (©1902)
LC-M213.S

SPAULDING, George L., American
1)   *The Contented Fairy*, 1P6H
- P,T
2)   *Little Camp-fire Girls*, 1P6H
- P,T (©1918)
LC-M213.S72.L4
3)   *Marche héroïque*, 1P6H
- P,T (©1915)
LC-M213.S72.L4
- *PRG*:442
4)   *Three Little Children*, 1P6H
- P,T
5)   *Through the Meadow*, 1P6H
- P,T (©1919)
LC-M213.S72.73 and T4
6)   *Ting-a-ling*, 1P6H
- P,T (©1918)
LC-M213.S72.T5
7)   *Waltzing Merry-makers*, 1P6H
- F,C (©1919)

LC-M213.S72.W3

STEPHENSON
1)   *Forest Home March*, 1P6H
- B&W
2)   *Forest Oak*, 1P6H
- B&W

STONE, Alonzo, American
1)   *Dancing Butterflies, Valse*, 1P6H
- W-S (©1899)
    LC-M213.S
2)   *Dancing Cupids, à la mazurka in D Major*, 1P6H (Grade 4)
- W-S (©1909)
3)   *Les papillons dansant in A-Flat Major*, 1P6H (Grade 4)
- W-S

STREABBOG, (Jéan) Louis (pseud. Jéan Louis GOBBAERTS)
      (1835-1886)
1)   *Aux pensionnats, [3] Morceaux brillants*, 1P6H
- May (©1881)
    BrM-h.3197.b.(30.)
2)   *Fast Mail Galop*, 2P8H
- P,T (©1891)
- *PRG*:442
3)   *Op. 75: March*, 1P6H
- Dit
- S,G
4)   *Op. 83: Triumphal March*, 1P6H
- S,G
5)   *Op. 100*, 1P6H (Grade 2)
      1. *Pas redoublé*
      2. *Valse*
      3. *Galop*
      4. *Rondo*
      5. *Polonaise*
      6. *Boléro*
      7. *Le départ, Marche militaire*
      8. *Les amazones*

     9. *La fileuse*
    10. *Rondino*
    11. *Chanson napolitaine*
    12. *Echo des montagnes, Tyrolienne*
- F,J (Nos.1-6) (©1904)
  LC-M213.S
- W-S
6)   *Op. 183: Morceaux brillants*, 1P6H
- F,C (©1908)
  LC-M213.S925

STULTS, Robert M. (1861-1923), American
     Stand By the Flag, 2P8H
- P,T (©1917)
  LC-M216.S97

SUDDS, William F. (1843-1920), American
1)   *From Ocean to Ocean, Overture, Op. 162*, 1P6H
- Chu (©1890)
  LC-M213.S
2)   *The Merry Chanter, Overture*, 1P6H
- Chu (©1892)
  LC-M213.S
3)   *A Night in June, Overture*, 1P6H
- Chu (©1889)
  LC-M213.S
4)   *The Pompous Soldier, March, Op. 170*, 1P6H
- Chu (©1889)
  LC-M213.S95.P5

THIMEN, Eric (Harding) (1900-1975), English
     Pastorale, 1P6H
- RCM

THUILLIER, Edward, American
     Feast of the Rose, March, 1P6H
- S,G

TORRA-PORTULAS, Enrique
   Vidalita, 1P6H
- Col
- *PRG*:442

WACHS, Paul, American
   Golden Rays, Valse brilliante, 1P6H (Grade 4)
- W-S (©1903)
   LC-M213.W

WALDMAN, American
   Wedding Day March, 2P8H
- Nor

WATSON, Leslie, American
   Picnic March, 1P6H
- Chu (©1889)
   LC-M213.W

WEBB, F.R., American
1)   *Inspiration Waltzes*, 1P6H; 2P8H
- F,J
2)   *Modern Chivalry March, Op. 108*, 2P8H
- P,T (©1909)
   LC-M216.W32.M6
3)   *Shenandoah, Caprice militaire, Op. 64, No. 3*, 2P8H
- Chu (©1892)
   LC-M216.W32.S4

WECKERLIN, Jean Baptiste (Théodore) (1821-1910), French
1)   *Marche*, 1P6H
- Dit
2)   *Menuet de la reine*, 1P6H
- Gr (©1886)
   BrM-h.458.a.(46.)
3)   *Panama* from *Les portraits de famille*, 1P6H
- Gr (©1882)
   BrM-h.458.a.(25a.) *Morceaux concertantes à six mains, No. 11*

WIEGAND, John, American
1)   *G.A.R. March*, 1P6H; 2P8H
- F,J
2)   *Morning Prayer, Meditation*, 1P6H; 2P8H
- F,J
3)   *Sans souci, Gavotte*, 1P6H; 2P8H
- F,J
4)   *To the Front, March*, 1P6H; 2P8H
- F,J

WILLING, W.
        Forget Me Not, Waltz, 1P6H; 2P8H
- F,J

WINTERBERG, E., German
        Ein Clavier-Quartett: *Scherzo, Piece in Polka Form, Op. 49*,
        [2P8H]
- Win (*4)
  NYPL

WON(Sp.?), S. Constantino
        Knickerbocker, Intermezzo, 1P6H
        Gavotte
- F,J

WOODROW, Roger H.
        Off to the Fox Hunt, 1P6H
- WM (©1978)

WYMAN, Addison P. (1832-1872), American
        Silvery Wave, Original Theme With Variations, 2P8H
- Brai (©1863)
  LC-M216.W95.S4

8. TRANSCRIPTIONS/ARRANGEMENTS

ADDINSELL, Richard (1904-1977), English
FPQC, arr.
   Warsaw Concerto, 4P8H
- *FPQC*-No.335

AKOULENKO, Russian
FPQC, arr.
   Step Lively (Red Army Marching Song), 4P8H
- *FPQC*-No.229

ALBÉNIZ, Isaac (1860-1909), Spanish
FPQC, arr.
1)   *Tango in D Major*, 4P8H
- *FPQC*-No.195
2)   *Triana*, 4P8H
- *FPQC*-No.245

ALETTER, W., American
PARLOW, Edmund (1855-?), arr.
   In Stately Measure, 2P8H
   Menuetto piccolo
- Schm (©1906)
  LC-M216.A4

AMADEI, Albert, German
BOCKLET, Heinrich von, arr.
   Trauermarsch, Op. 16, 2P8H
- Senf (©1912) (*7)
  LC-M216.A52

ANDERSON, Leroy (1908-1975), American
FPQC, arr.
1)   *Bugler's Holiday*, 4P8H
- *FPQC*-No.405
2)   *Fiddle-Faddle*, 4P8H
- *FPQC*-No.354
3)   *Syncopated Clock*, 4P8H
- *FPQC*-No.360

ANDRÉ, Ludwig, German
KRAMER, Wilhelm, arr.
1)   *Christkindl, Gavotte, Op. 142*, 1P6H
- And (©1900)
  LC-M213.A
2)   *Krausköpfchen, Polka-mazurka, Op. 119*, 1P6H
- And (©1894)
  LC-M213.A

ANONYMOUS
FPQC, arr.
       Yankee Doodle, Humoresque, 4P8H
- *FPQC*-No.93

ARENSKY, Anton (1861-1906), Russian
FPQC, arr.
       Waltz, 4P8H
- *FPQC*-No.336

ARNE, Thomas Augustine (1710-1778), English
CZERNY, Carl (1791-1857), arr.
       Rule Britannia, 1P6H
- *OS, No.7* (©1874)
  BrM-h.1427

ARNOLD, Maurice (1865-1937), American
WIRTH, Ernest, arr.
       La Zingara (The Fortune Teller), 1P6H
       Allegro moderato
-Chu (©1902) (*5)
  LC-M213.A

ARNSTEIN, A., American
PAUL, Oscar, arr.
       The Clock, Polka française, 1P6H
- Lam (©1914)
  LC-M213.A

ARTHUR, C.M., American
MOELLING, Theodore, arr.
1)   *Assembly March*, 1P6H
- Ell (©1893)
  LC-M213.C
2)   *My Heart's Darling, Gavotte*, 1P6H
- Ell (©1893)
  LC-M213.C

ASHLEY, Glenn W., American
ZILCHER, Paul (1855-1943), arr.
        Heather Blossom, Waltz, 1P6H
- P,T (©1931)
  LC-M213.A6.H3

AUBER, Daniel François Espirit (1782-1871), French
1) BURCHARD, Carl (1820-1896), arr.
   a)   *Overture* to *Der Mauerer und der Schlosser*, 2P8H
- Hofm (©187-?) (*15)
  PCM-M216.A3.18--(Rare book)
   b)   *Overture* to *Stumme von Portici*, 2P8H
- And (©1924)
2) DECOURCELLE, Marcelle, arr.
        Overture to *Le cheval de bronze*, 2P8H
- Scho (©1885)
  NYPL-JM G73-1
3) LOTT, E.M., arr.
        Overture to *Fra Diavolo (L'hôtellerie de terracine)*, 1P6H
- Lot, No. 12 (©1877)
  BrM-h.848.c.
4) PARLOW, Edmund (1855-?), arr.
        Tarantella from *Masaniello*, 2P8H
- P,T (©1911) (*11)
  LC-M216.A9

BACH, Carl Philipp Emanuel (1714-1788), Germany
C.F.W. Siegels Musikalienhandlung, arr.
        Frühlings Erwachen, Romance, 2P8H
  UR-M216.B119.F14

BACH, Johann Sebastian (1685-1750), Germany
1) BADER, Franz, arr.

> *Orchestral Suite No. 3 in D Major, BWV 1068,*(c.1729-1731),
> 2P8H
> 1. *Ouverture*
> 2. *Air*
> 3. *Gavotte*
> 4. *Bourrée*
> 5. *Gigue*

- Br&H (©1910)
  ASU-M216.B12.S.1068.B3.v.2
  UR-M216.B11.Su.3
2) BRAGDON, Sarah Coleman (1880-?), arr.

> *Fughettas* from *18 Little Preludes and Fugues (Nos. 1, 12,*
> *15, 18); Prelude and Fugue in B-Flat Major,* 2P8H

- Bel (©1959) (*23)
  LC-M216.B13.B7
3) BURCHARD, Carl (1820-1896), arr.

> *Passacaglia,* 2P8H

- H,G (©186-?)
  NYPL
- *TPR*:154
4) CONNOR, Dorothy, arr.

> *Five Chorales,* 2P8H
> 1. *Ach, was soll ich Sünder machen? (Ah, what shall I,*
>   *a Sinner, do?)*
> 2. *O Gott, du frommer Gott (O God, Thou pious God)*
> 3. *Aus meines Herzens Grunde (From the depths of my*
>   *Heart)*
> 4. *Aus tiefer Noth schrei ich zu dir (Out of deep need I*
>   *cry to Thee)*
> 5. *Freuet euch, ihr Christen alle (Rejoice, all ye*
>   *Christians)*

- S,G (©1951)   c. 1944
  BrM-g.548.yy.(3)
- *PRG*:439
- *TPR*:154

5) GRAINGER, Percy Alderidge (1882-1961), arr.
- a) *Bach for Team-Work: Fugue in A Minor, Well-Tempered Clavier, Bk. I, No. 20, BWV 865* (1722), 2P (or any multiple of 2),8H (or any multiple of 4 pianists)
- Scho (©1931, ©1958) arr. 1922 (*13)
- S,G (©1930)
  ASU-M216.B4.K5x.1900.v.5:2;M216.
  B12.W63x.T.1.Nr.10.F8
  PCM-M216.B118.F
  UR-M216.B11.fG
- *PRG*:439
- *TPR*:154
- b) *Bach for Team-Work: Fugue in E Major, Well-Tempered Clavier, Bk. II, No. 9, BWV 878* (1744), 2P8H; 4P8H arr. 1928 for 4P8H (octave study); arr. 1950 for 2P8H
- manuscript, UR (2P8H, ©1950)[*organ*]
- c) *Bach for Team-Work: Toccata in F Major, BWV 540*, 3P(or any multiple of 3), 6H (or any multiple of 3 pianists)
- S,G (©1940) (*19)
  LC-M216.B
  PCM-M216.B118.T
  UR
6) HART, Jane Smith, arr.
- a) *Jesus, bleibet meine Freude (Jesu, Joy of Man's Desiring) in G Major,* from *Cantata No. 147* (1723), 1P6H
- Available from arranger
  120 Pelham Road
  North Rochelle, NY 10805
- Letter from Hart, November 17, 1990
- b) *Schafe können sicher weiden (Sheep May Safely Graze)* from *Birthday Cantata No. 208* (1713), 1P6H
- Available from arranger (©1983)
- Letter from Hart, November 17, 1990
7) KASSCHAU, Howard, arr.
  Three Compositions [of J.S. Bach] In the Form of a Suite, 2P8H
  1. *Intrada*
  2. *Aria (*from *Clavierbüchlein für Anna Magdalena, 1725)*
  3. *Minuet in G Major*

- S&G (©1942)
  UR-M216.B11 com
8) LISZT, F./*FPQC*, arrs.
        Organ Prelude and Fugue No. 3 in C-Flat Minor, 4P8H
- *FPQC*-Nos.383,384
9) OHLEY, Henry Maxwell (1912-1944) and Harry WATTS (*b* 1901), arrs.
   a)   *Bourrée in D Major* from *Suite For Trumpet*, 2P8H
- S,G (©1942)
  LC-M216.B
  UR-M216.B119.F14
   b)   *Jesus, bleibet meine Freude (Jesu, Joy of Man's Desiring) in G Major* from *Cantata No. 147*, 2P8H
- S&G (©1942)   1723
  ASU-M216.B12.H4x.1942
  LC-M216.B
  UR-M216.B11.ca.147J
   c)   *Ten Bach Chorales*, 2P8H
         1. *Adorn Thyself, O My Soul*
         2. *A Child Is Born in Bethlehem*
         3. *Entrust Thy Ways*
         4. *From Heaven High*
         5. *Jesus, My Joy*
         6. *A Mighty Fortress Is Our God*
         7. *Rejoice Greatly, O My Soul*
         8. *We All Believe in One God*
         9. *When We Are in Deepest Need*
        10. *Whither May I Flee*
- S&G
  PCM-M216.B118
  UR-M216.B11.CHO
  WSU
- *TPR*:154
10) WAGNER, E.D. and F.BRISSLER, arrs., Op. 80, No. 42
        Bourrée in A Minor, 2P8H
- Rie
11) WILBERG, Mack, arr.
        Sicilienne from *Sonata in E-flat for Flute and Klavier, BWV 1031*, 2P8H

- Kj (© 1991), WP 323, American Piano
Quartet Series
12) *First Piano Quartet Collection*, arrs.:
　　a)　　*Air on the G String*, 4P8H
- *FPQC*-No.348
　　b)　　*Concerto in D Minor, BWV 1063*, transcribed for
　　　　4P8H without orchestra
- *FPQC*-Nos.118,311,312
　　c)　　*Concerto in A Minor, BWV 1065*, transcribed for
　　　　4P8H without orchestra
- *FPQC*-No.315
　　d)　　*Jesu, Joy of Man's Desiring*, 4P8H
- *FPQC*-No.248
　　e)　　*Organ Prelude in D Major*, 4P8H
- *FPQC*-No.114
　　f)　　*Praeludium in C Minor*, 4P8H
- *FPQC*-No.58
　　g)　　*Praeludium* (from *Partita No.6* for solo violin), 4P8H
- *FPQC*-No.325
　　h)　　*Prelude and Fugue in C Minor, WTC I*, 4P8H
- *FPQC*-Nos.158,159
　　i)　　*Prelude and Fugue in C-Sharp Major, WTC I*, 4P8H
- *FPQC*-Nos.235,292
　　j)　　*Prelude and Fugue in C-Sharp Minor, WTC I*, 4P8H
- *FPQC*-Nos.242,243
　　k)　　*Prelude in D Major, WTC I*, 4P8H
- *FPQC*-No.323
　　l)　　*Prelude and Fugue in D Minor, WTC I*, 4P8H
- *FPQC*-Nos.284,285
　　m)　　*Fugue in F Major, WTC I*, 4P8H
- *FPQC*-No.324
　　n)　　*Prelude in G Major, WTC I*, 4P8H
- *FPQC*-No.352
　　o)　　*Prelude in A Minor, WTC I*, 4P8H
- *FPQC*-No.353
　　p)　　*Prelude in D Minor, WTCI I*, 4P8H
- *FPQC*-No.189
　　q)　　*Fugue in A Minor, WTC I*, 4P8H
- *FPQC*-No.256

    r)   *Rejoice, Beloved Christians*, 4P8H
- *FPQC*-No.279
    s)   *Sheep May Safely Graze*, 4P8H
- *FPQC*-No.339
    t)   *Sinfonia*, 4P8H
- *FPQC*-No.244
    u)   **Orchestral Suite No. 2 in B Minor: Rondeau, Sarabande, Bourrée, Polonaise, Minuet and Badinerie**, 4P8H
- *FPQC*-Nos.216,217,223,224,228 and 218.

BACHMANN, G.V., arr.
1) BEYER, V. arr., rev. and fingered by Hans T. SEIFERT
    Sorrento, Mazurka élégante, 1P6H
- F,C (©1908)
  LG-M213.B124
2) BROWNOLD, Max, arr.
    Les sylphes, Valse, Op. 10, No.2, 2P12H
- Ell (©1890) (*13)
  LC-M216.B15.S8

BAKER, Fred T., American
1) FENIMORE, W.P., arr.
  a)   *Empire State March*, 2P8H
- Nor (©1887)
  LC-M216.093
  b)   *Sous les magnolias, Danse américaine*, 2P8H
- Nor (©1887)
  LC-M216.B21
2) LOSSE, F., arr.
  a)   *American Line March*, 1P6H; 2P8H
- Nor (©1885; ©1886)
  LC-M216.093
  b)   *Danse écossaise*, 2P6H
- Nor (©1885)
  LC-M216.093
  c)   *Queen of the North, Waltzes*, 1P6H
- Nor (©1885)
  LC-M213.B

3) MAYSEDER, arr.
  Danse écossaise, 1P6H
- Dit (©1890)
  LC-M213.B17.D3

BALAKIREV, Mily (1837-1910), Russian
PETROW, A., arr.
1) *Ouverture sur trois thémes russes*, 2P8H
- Br&H
  UR-M216.B1710
2) *Tamara* [or *Thamar*], 2P8H
- Jur (©1908)
  LC-M216.B23.T3.1908
  UR-M216.B17.1T

BARRON, W. Caven, American
SPROSS, Charles Gilbert (1874-?), arr.
  Lullalo (Irish Lullaby), 1P6H
- Chu (©1922)
  LC-M213.B

BAZIN, François Emmanuel Joseph (1816-1878), French
LÉMOINE, Léon (1855-1916), arr.
  Overture to *Le voyage en Chine* (1865), 1P6H
- *OS*, No. 29
  BrM-h.1427

BEAUMONT, American
ROEDER, Carl, arr.
  Slumber Sweetly, Gavotte, 1P6H; 2P8H
- Witz (©1901)
  LC-M213.B; M216.B28

BECHT, Julius, American
DRESSLER, William (1826-1914), arr.
1) *Canary Schottische*, 1P6H
- Dit (©1887)
  LC-M213.B
2) *Honeysuckle March*, 1P6H

- Dit (©1859)
  LC-M213.B
3)   *Reception March*
- Dit (©1859)
  LC-M213.B

BEETHOVEN, Ludwig van (1770-1827), German
1) BRISSLER, F., arr.
        Overture to *König Stephan, Op. 117*, 2P8H
- Br&H
  UR-M216.B41.K
2) BURCHARD, Carl (1820-1896), arr.
   a)   *Fideleo Overture, Op. 72b (1804-1805)*, 2P8H
- P,CF (Lit)
  PCM-M216.B415
- *PRG*:439
   b)   *Grande Polonaise, Op. 56 (1803-1804)*, 2P8H
- H,G (©1868)
  PCM-M216.B415.A
  UR-M216.B41p
   c)   *Grand Septett, Op. 20 in E-Flat Major, (1777-1800)*, 2P8H
- And (©1924)
   d)   *III. Marche funèbre* from *Symphony No. 3 (1803) in E-Flat
        Major, Op. 55 (Eroica)*, 2P8H
- And (©1924)
   e)   *Marsch* from *Fideleo, Op. 72b, (1804-1805)*, 2P8H
- Br&H
  UR-M216.B41.M
   f)   *Marsch und Chor* from *Die Ruinen von Athen, Op. 113*,
        2P8H
- Br&H
  UR-M216.B41.M
   g)   *Marsch (Zapfenstreich)* for *Militärmusik*, 2P8H
- Br&H
  UR-M216.B41.M
   h)   *Militärmarsch* in *D Major*, 2P8H
- Br&H
  UR-M216.B41.M
   i)   *Overture* to *Leonore, Op. 72c (1805-1806)*, 2P8H

- And (©1924)
  UR-M216.B41.L3.B
  j)   *Polonaise* from *[String Trio:] Serenade in D Major, Op. 8,*
         2P8H
         Allegretto alla Polacca
- And (©1724)
  k)   *Triumphmarsch* from Kuffner's *Trauerspiel: Tarpeja,* 2P8H
- Br&H
  UR-M216.B41.M
3) CHEWATAL, F.X., arr.
  a)   *Fideleo Overture, Op. 72b,* 2P8H
- P,CF (Lit)
  UR-M216.B41.F.C.
  b)   *[Incidental Music* to] Goethe's *Egmont: Overture, Op. 84,*
         2P8H
- P,CF (Lit)
  PCM-M216.B415.E35
  UR-M216.B41.eC
- *PRG*:439
4) DIETER, Bernard, arr.
         Three Bagatelles from *Op. 119,* 2P8H
         No. 1.--*Bagatelle in G Minor*
         No. 2.--*Bagatelle in C Major* (sketched 1794-1795)
         No. 22.--*Bagatelle in B-Flat Major*
- Su (©1938)
  LC-M216.B
  PCM-M216.B415.T
5) HERMANN, Friedrich, arr.
         Symphony No. 9 in D Minor, Op. 125 (Choral), 2P8H
- Br&H
  LC-M216.B4.Op.125.H5
6) HOLLINGSWORTH, Louis (*b* 1920), arr.
         Contra Dance No. 1 in C Major, K.14, WoO 4, 4P8H
- HanM (©1958)
  LC-M216.B33.K14
7) HORN, August (1825-1893), arr.
  a)   *Marsch* from Goethe's *Egmont, Op. 84,* 2P8H
- Br&H
  UR-M216.B41.M

b)   *Ouvertüre* to the Ballet *Die Geschöpfe des Prometheus, Op.*
       43, 2P8H
- Br&H
  UR-M216.B41.P
c)   *Ouvertüre* to *Die Ruinen von Athen, Op. 113*, 2P8H
- Br&H
  UR-M216.B41.R
d)   *Siegesmarch* from *König Stephan, Op. 117*, 2P8H
- Br&H
  UR-M216.B41.M
e)   *Symphonie Eroique [No. 3], Op. 55*, 2P8H
              1. *Allegro con brio*
- Br&H
  UR-M216.B41.3
f)   *III. Trauermarsch* from *Piano Sonata in A-Flat Major, Op.*
       26, 2P8H
- Br&H
  UR-M216.B41.M
8) KIRCHNER, Theodor (1823-1903), arr.
       [9] Symphonien, 2P8H
       Symphony No. 1 in C Major, Op. 21 (1800)
       Symphony No. 2 in D Major, Op. 36 (1801-1802)
       Symphony No. 3 in E-Flat Major, Op. 55 (Eroica) (1803)
       Symphony No. 4 in B-Flat Major, Op. 60 (1806)
       Symphony No. 5 in C Minor, Op. 67 (1807-1808)
       Symphony No. 6 in F Major, Op. 68 (Pastoral) (1808)
       Symphony No. 7 in A Major, Op. 92 (Dance) (1811-1812)
       Symphony No. 8 in F Major, Op. 93 (1812)
       Symphony No. 9 in D Minor, Op. 125 (Choral) (1822-1824)
- Br&H
  UR-M216.B415.S9.P48:vols.1-9;M216.B415.S9.B63 (with *Septett,*
       Op. 20)
- P,CF (©1887)
  ASU-M216.B4.K5x.1900.v.3.1
  Cur-No.2:M216.B415.Op.36.1887
     No.3:M216.B415.Op.55.1887
     No.4:M216.B415.Op.60.1887
     No.5:M216.B415.Op.67.1887
     No.7:M216.B415.Op.92.1887

LC-No.3:M216.B33.Op.55.K6

PCM-No.2:M216.B415.S2

  No.9:M216.B415.Op.125.19--

9) KNORR, Iwan (1853-1916), arr.

    Rondino For Winds in E-Flat Major, WoO 25 (1793), 2P8H

- Br&H

PCM-M216.B415.R

UR-M216.B41.Rok

10) LÉMOINE, Léon (1855-1916), arr.

    Allegretto scherzando de la 8ᵉ Symphonie en fa majeur, Op. 93, (1812), 1P6H

- *OS, No.37*

BrM-h.1427

11) LESSMANN, Otto, arr.

    [Incidental Music to] Goethe's *Egmont: Overture, Op. 84,* 2P8H

- Schl (©1871)

NYPL

 - *TPR*:154

12) MACGREGOR, Helen, arr.

    Themes from *Rondo a Capriccio in G Major, Op. 129 (Rage Over the Lost Penny)* (1795), 2P8H

- S,G   1795

- *PRG*:439

13) MÉTIS, Frank, arr.

    Schiller's *Ode to Joy* from *Symphony No. 9 in D Minor, Op. 125, IV* (1822-1824), 2P-4P (or 1P and tape recorder)

- Mark (©1970)

LC-M216.B4.Op.125.M5

14) NAUMANN, Ernest, arr.

    Symphony No. 7 in A Major, Op. 92, 2P8H

- Br&H

UR-M216.B41.7

15) PARLOW, Edmund (1855-?), arr.

  a)   *[7] Country Dances, K.14*(1795-1802), 2P8H

          Nos. 1,2,3,4,6,7,12

- Schm (©1910) (*7)

Cur-M216.B415.K.14.1910

LC-M216.B33.C5

UR-M216.B415.CoP

  b)   *Menuett in G Major*, 2P8H

- P,T (©1922)

LC-M216.B33.M4

16) PAUER, Ernest (1826-1905), arr.

      Grand Septett in E-Flat Major, Op. 20 (1799-1800), 2P8H

      1. *Adagio; Allegro con brio*

      2. *Adagio cantabile*

      3. *Tempo di Menuetto*

      4. *Tema con Variazioni*

      5. *Scherzo: Allegro molto vivace*

      6. *Andante con moto; Alla marcia; Presto*

- Aug (©1939)

BrM-f.133.ee.(9.)

UR-M216.B415.Op20

17) RITTER, A.G., arr.

  a)   *Ouvertüre* to *Fideleo, Op. 72a*, 2P8H

- Br&H

UR-M216.B41.L1

  b)   *Ouvertüre* to *Fideleo, Op. 72b*, 2P8H

- Br&H

UR-M216.B41.L2

18) RÖSLER, Gustav (1819-1882), arr.

  a)   *Ouvertüre* to *Weihne des Hauses, Op. 124*, 2P8H

- Br&H

UR-M216.B41.W

  b)   *Ouvertüren*, 2P8H

      1. *Egmont, Ouvertüre, Op. 84*

      2. *Coriolan, Ouvertüre, Op. 62*

      3. *Fideleo, Ouvertüre, Op. 72*

      4. *Leonore No. 3, Ouvertüre, Op. 72c*

- P,CF (©1897)

LC-M216.B33.087;M216.B(2nd piano part missing)

UR-M216.B41.OR

19) RUBINSTEIN, Anton (1829-1894), arr. 2P4H; Bernard DIETER, arr. 2P8H

      Marcia alla turca from *Die Ruinen von Athen, Op. 113*, (1811), 2P8H

- Su (©1938)

LC-M216.B
PCM-M216.B415.77
20) RUBINSTEIN, Anton (1829-1894), arr. 2P4H; Alfred J. SILVER
    (1870-?), arr. 1P6H
    Marche à la turque, 1P6H
- F,J (©1915)
LC-M213.B
21) SARTORIO, Arnoldo (1853-1936), arr.
    a)   *Adieu to the Piano*, 2P8H (Elementary)
- WM (©1925)
LC-M213.B453
- *PRG*:439
    b)   *Menuett in G Major*, 2P8H
- Schm (©1927)
UR-M216.B415.sS (1st piano part missing)
    c)   *Menuett* from *Septett, Op. 20, No.3*, 2P8H
- Schm (©1927)
LC-M216.B33.M45
    d)   *Polonaise in D Major* from *[String Trio:] Serenade in D
         Major, Op. 8 (1796-1797)*, 2P8H
         Allegretto alla Polacca
- Schm (©1927) 1796-1797 (*11)
Cur-M216.B415.Op.8.1927
LC-M216.B33.P5
22) SCHMIDT, Gustav Martin, arr.
    a)   *Grand Septett, Op. 20 in E-Flat Major*, 2P8H
- P,CF
ASU-M216.B4.Op.20.M3.P
NYPL
    b)   *Leonore* Overture, *Op. 72*, 2P8H
- Br&H (©1843)
- *TPR*:154
23) THOMPSON, John Sylanus (1889-1963), arr.
         Contra-Dance [No. 1], K.14, WoO 4 (1802), 2P8H
-WM (©1971)
24) WITTMAN, Robert, arr.
         Quintett in E-Flat Major, Op. 16, 2P8H
- Hofm
UR-M216.B41.Q

25) Arr. by ?

a)   *March* from *Die Ruinen von Athen, Op. 113*, 1P6H
- Dit

b)   *Minuet in G Major*, 1P6H
- CMP;c/o Ash
- *PRG*:439

c)   *Phantasie für Pianoforte, Chor und Orchester in C Minor, Op. 80* (1808), 2P8H
- Br&H (©1857)
  NYPL
  UR-M216.B41.F
- *TPR*:154

26) *First Piano Quartet Collection*, arrs.

a)   *Bagatelle*, 4P8H
- *FPQC*-No.175

b)   *Contre Dances, Nos. 1,2,3 and 11*, 4P8H
- *FPQC*-Nos.103,106

c)   *March* from *Fideleo*, 4P8H
- *FPQC*-No.30

d)   *Minuet in G Major*, 4P8H
- *FPQC*-No.329

e)   *Piano Sonata in C-Sharp Minor (Moonlight)*, 4P8H
- *FPQC*-Nos.162,227, 278

f)   *Peasant Dance*, 4P8H
- *FPQC*-No.65

g)   *Piano Concerto No. 5 in E-Flat Major (Emperor), I*, 4P8H
- *FPQC*-No.187

h)   *Piano Sonata in F Major, Op.10, No.2, Presto*, 4P8H
- *FPQC*-No.54

i)   *Rose Waltz*, 4P8H
- *FPQC*-No.53

j)   *Sonata in D Major, Op. 28, III. Scherzo*, 4P8H
- *FPQC*-No.305

k)   *Für Elise*, 4P8H
- *FPQC*-No.298

BEHR, Franz (1837-1898), German
1) LÖW, Josef, arr.
   a)   *Fire-balls, Mazurka (Leuchtkugeln), Op. 375*, 1P6H (Grade 3)
- Smi
   b)   *Shooting-stars, Mazurka, Op. 375*, 1P6H
- F,J (©1902)
  LC-M213.B
   c)   *Spatz am Dach (The Chirping Sparrow), Polka, Op. 377*,
      1P6H
- F,J (©1902)
  LC-M213.B
2) SCHARFENBERG, William, arr.
      Festival March, 1P6H
- Hofm
- LC-M213.B
- S,G (©1889)
- *PRG*:439
3) SEIFERT, Hans. T., ed., rev. and fingered *Geburtstags, Gavotte*,
      1P6H
4) STONE, Alonzo, arr.
      March of Gnomes (Gnomenzug), Op. 590, No. 7, 1P6H
      (Grade 3)
- Smi (©1897)
  LC-M213.B

BELLINI, Vincenzo (1801-1835), Italian
BURCHARD, Carl (1820-1896), arr.
   a)   *Overture* to *I Capuleti ed Montecchi (1830)*, 2P8H
- And (©1924)
   b)   *Overture* to *Norma* (1831), 2P8H
- Hofm (©186-?) (*15)
  PCM-Rare book. M216.A3.186-?

BENJAMIN, Arthur (1893-1960), Australian
FPQC, arr.
      Jamaican Rumba, 4P8H
- *FPQC*-No.254

BERG, Albert W. (1825-1906), arr., American
1)   *Canadian Boat Song (Old English Melody)*, 1P6H
- Pon (©1903)
  LC-M213.B
2)   *Exhibition Pieces*, 2P8H
  LC-M216.B36.E8
3)   *My Old Kentucky Home*, 1P6H
- Pon (©1903)
  LC-M213.B
4)   *Old Black Joe*, 1P6H
- Pon (©1903)
  LC-M213.B

BERLIOZ, Hector (1803-1869), French
1) ADLER, arr.
        Hungarian (Räkóczy) March, 1P6H
- F,J
2) AUZENDE, A.M., arr.
   a)   *Choeur de soldats* and *Chanson d'étudiants* from *La
        damnation de Faust, Op. 24 (1845-1846)*, 2P8H
- Cos
  UR-M216.B515.dc
- Rich (©1886)
  BrM-h.3250.b.(16.)
   b)   *Marche hongroise* from *La damnation de Faust, Op. 24*,
        2P8H
- Cos
  UR-M216.B515.dm,No.1
   c)   *Menuet des follets* from *La damnation de Faust, Op. 24*,
        2P8H
- Cos
  UR-M216.B515.dme,No.4
   d)   *Les Troyens à Carthage:* Fantasy on the Themes from the
        Opera (1856-1858), 2P8H
- P,CF
- *PRG*:439
3) RIHM, Alexander, arr.
   a)   *Drei Stücke aus Faust's ver dammung*, 2P8H
            1. *Ungarischer-marsch*

2. *Sylphen-ballet*
3. *Tanz der Irrlichter*
- Scho (©1910)
  LC-M216.B38.F3 (2nd piano part missing)
  b) *Ouvertüre* to *König Lear, Op. 4*, 2P8H
- Hofm (©1907)
  UR-M216.B515.K0
4) *FPQC*, arr.
  Roman Carnival Overture, 4P8H
- *FPQC*-No.160

BEY, Adolfe, arr., German
  Die ersten Versuche im Ensemble spiel. Acht leichte Stücke aus klassischen Meistern, 2P8H
  1. **HÄNDEL**, G.F., *Trauermarsch aus Saul*
  2. **HÄNDEL**, G.F., *Chor aus Judas Maccabäus: Seht da kommt er*
  3. **MOZART**, W.A., *Priestmarsch aus Der Zauberflöte*
  4. **MOZART**, W.A., *Duett aus Cossì fan tutti*
  5. **WEBER**, C.M.v., *Chor aus Preciosa: Jm. Wald*
  6. **MENDELSSOHN**, F., *Elfenmarsch aus Dem Sommernachtstraum*
  7. **MENDELSSOHN**, F., *Chor aus Der Walpurgisnacht*
  8. **BEETHOVEN**, L.v., *Quartett-Canon aus Fideleo*
- Scho (©1883)
  BrM:h.3276.a.(2.)
  PCM-M216.B573.1884
  UR-M216.B573e.Vol.1 and 2

BILLI, Vincenzo (1869-1938), Italian
TUCCI, Cecilia, arr.
  Sorreto, Petite tarantelle, 1P6H
- Col
- Ric (©1959)
  LC-M213.B
- *PRG:439*

BILLINGS (1746-1800), American
GUNTHER, Phyllis, arr.

        Chester, 2P6H or 8H
- Bel (©1975)
  LC-M216.B46.S523
  SBTS

BISCHOFF, John W. (1850-1909)
PARLOW, Edmund (1855-?), arr.
       Fête napolitaine, Tarantelle, 1P6H
- Schm (©1913)
  LC-M213.B

BIZET, Georges (Alexandre César Léopold) (1838-1875), French
1) KRONKE, Emil (1865-?),arr
       Scherzo aus Roma, 2P8H
- Schu
-SteV
  LC-M216.B594.R6
  UR-M216.B625.rk
2) PARLOW, Edmund (1855-?), arr.
       [Selection from] **Carmen** (1873-1874), 2P8H
- P,T (©1907)   1873-1874 (*11)
  BrM-h.3291.c.(1.)
  LC-M216.B594
3) ROSENAUER, Alois
       Op.33: from **L'opéra moderne** *(Small Transcriptions on the*
       themes of the most celebrated operas), No. 1: **Carmen**, 1P6H
         1. *Lied des Eskamillo*
         2. *Habanera*
         3. *Tanz der Carmen*
         4. *Sequidilla*
         5. *Aufzug der Toreador*
- For (©1911)
  LC-M213.B
4) SARTORIO, Arnoldo (1853-1936), arr.
  a)   *Intermezzo* and *Menuet* from **L'arlésienne**, 2P8H
- P,T (©1926) (*14)
  LC-M216.B58
  b)   *Overture* to **Carmen**, 1P6H
- WM

LC-M213.B52.S2
- *PRG*:439
5) TIMM, Henry Christian (1811-1892), arr.
  a)   *Habañera* from *Carmen*, 2P8H
- S,G (©1892)
LC-M216.B59
- *PRG*:439
  b)   *Toreador's Song* from *Carmen*, 2P8H
- S,G (©1892)
LC-M216.B59
- *PRG*:439
6) *First Piano Quartet Collection*, arr.
  a)   *Carmen* Fantasy, 4P8H
- *FPQC*-No.380
  b)   *Farandole* from *L'arlésienne*, 4P8H
- *FPQC*-No.206
  c)   *Gypsy Song* from *Carmen*, 4P8H
- *FPQC*-No.60
  d)   *La toupie* from *Les jeux d'enfants*, 4P8H
- *FPQC*-No.185
7) Arr. by ?
  a)   *L'arlésienne* Fantasy, 2P8H
- P,CF   1872
- *PRG*:439
  b)   *Carmen* Fantasy, 2P8H
- P,CF
- *PRG*:439
  c)   *First Minuet* from *L'arlésienne*, 2P8H
- P,CF
- *PRG*:439

BLAKE, Charles Dupee (1847-?), American
HARTS [or HEARTZ], Harry Lawson, arr.
1)   *Clayton's Grand March*, 1P6H (Grade 3)
-W-S (©1920)
LC-M213.B6.C6
2)   *On the Race Course*, 1P6H (Grade 3)
-W-S (©1920)
LC-M213.B605

BLANDNER, Charles F., American
O'NEILL, T., arr.
    Cumberland March, 2P8H
- Nor (©1884)
  LC-M216.B61.C+

BLON, Franz von (1861-1945)
HAMMEREL, Victor, arr.
    To Battle and Victory, March, 1P6H
- F,J (©1899)
  LC-M213.B

BOCCHERINI, Luigi (1743-1805), Italian
FPQC, arr.
    III. Minuet from *String Quintet in E Major*, 4P8H
- *FPQC*-No.84

BODENHOFF, H.
PARLOW, Edmund (1855-?), arr.
    Polonaise, Op. 7, No. 9, 2P8H
- (©1910) (*7)
  LC-M216.B63

BOEKELMANN, Bernardus (1838-1930)
NICHOLL, Horace Wadham (1848-1922), arr.
    Polonaise de concert, Op. 4, 2P8H
- Schu (©1889) (*21)
  LC-M216.B72

BOELLMANN, Léon (1862-1897), French
ROQUES, Léon, arr.
    Suite gothique pour grand orgue, Op. 25, 2P8H
- Dur (©1915)
  LC-M216.B67.Op.25
  UR-M216.B671

BÖHM, Carl
1) FENIMORE, W.P., arr.
    La grâce, Op. 302, No.5, 2P8H

- Nor (©1886)
 LC-M216.093
2) PARLOW, Edmund (1855-?), arr.
 a) *Brise printanière, Polka brillante, Op. 357, No. 3*, 2P8H
 (Moderately difficult)
- Schm (©1907)
 LC-M216.B76
 b) *Rosetta, Fantaisie-mazurka, Op. 357, No. 4*, 2P8H
 (Moderately difficult)
- Schm (©1905)
 LC-M216.P
3) RAYMOND, Louis, arr.
 Change of Cavalry, Grand galop militaire, 2P8H
- Pon (©1885)
 LC-M216.R3.E8
4) WEBB, F.R., arr
 Polacca brillante, Op. 93, 2P8H
- Chu (©1900) (*15)
 LC-M216.B764
- P,T

BOIELDIEU, (François) Adrien (1775-1834), French
BURCHARD, Carl (1820-1896), arr.
1) *Overture* to **Le calif de Baghdad**, 2P8H
- And (©1924)   1800
2) *Overture* to **La dame blanche**, 2P8H
- And (©1924)
3) *Overture* to **Jean de Paris**, 2P8H
- And (©1924)

BOREL/CLERC, Charles
1) HAMMEREL, Victor, arr.
 La Mattchiche or *Sorella (Celebrated Spanish March)*, 1P6H
- F,J (©1906)
 LC-M213.B
2) LERMAN, J.W., arr.
 La Sorella (Celebrated Spanish March), 1P6H
- Mol (©1906)
 LC-M213.B

BORODIN, Alexander (1833-1887), Russian
FPQC, arr.
1)   *Polovetsienne Dances* from *Prince Igor*, 4P8H
- *FPQC*-No.96
2)   *Serenade* from the *Little Suite*, 4P8H
- *FPQC*-No.149

BRAHAM, Edmund
BRUESCHWEILER, F., arr.
        Piccolo fantasie, 2P8H
- Roh (©1897) (*11)
  LC-M216.B81

BRAHMS, Johannes (1833-1897), German
1) CARPER, Virginia Speiden, arr.
        St. Anthony Chorale from *Variations on a Theme by Haydn*,
        Op. 56 (1873), 2P8H
- S,G (©1954)
  LC-M216.B82.V33
- *PRG*:439
2) JUON, Paul (1872-1940), arr.
        Piano Concerto No.2 in B-Flat Major, Op. 83 (1878-1881),
        2P8H
- Sim (©1906)
  PCM-Mb216.B813.Op.83.No.2
3) KELLER, Robert, arr.
   a) *Vier symphonien von Johannes Brahms*, 2P8H
       Symphony No. 1 in C Minor, Op. 68 (1855-1876)
       Symphony No. 2 in D Major, Op. 73 (1877)
       Symphony No. 3 in F Major, Op. 90 (1883)
       Symphony No. 4 in E Minor, Op. 98 (1885)
- Sim
  Cur-No.1:M216.B813.Op.68.1878
     No.2:M216.B813.Op.73.1879
  LC-No.2:M216.B82.Op.73.K4
     No.3:M216.B82.Op.90.K4(©1930)
  UR-No.1:M216.B813.S9.No.1(©1878)
     No.2:M216.B813.S2(©1879)
     No.3:M216.B813.S3

No.4:M216.B813.S3

b)   *Tragische Ouvertüre, Op. 81*, 2P8H
- Sim
 UR-M216.B813.T
4) KLENGEL, Paul, arr.
a)   *Serenade in A Major, Op. 16*, 2P8H
- Sim (©1898)
 NYPL-JMG 72-531
 UR-M216.B813.2
b)   *Variationen über ein Thema von Josef Haydn, Op. 56b*, 2P8H
- Sim (©1896)
 UR-M216.B81.vHK
5) OHLEY, Henry Maxwell (1912-1944) and Harry WATTS (*b* 1901), arrs.
a)   *A Rose Breaks Into Bloom*, 2P8H
- S&G (©1942)
 LC-M216.B
 UR-M216.B813.ch.8
b)   *O World, I Now Must Leave Thee*, 2P8H
- S,G (1990 catalogue listing)(©1990)
- S&G (©1942)
 LC-M216.B
 UR-M216.B813.ch.3
6) SARTORIO, Arnoldo (1853-1936), arr.
  Hungarian Dance No. 6, 1P6H; 2P8H
- P,T (©1925)   ©1925
 LC-M216.B82.H7.S3
- *PRG*:439
7) ZILCHER, Paul (1855-1943), arr.
  Hungarian Dances, 1P6H
  No. 1 in F Major
  No. 2 in G Minor
  No. 3 in D Major
  No. 4 in F Major
  No. 5 in G Minor
- Schm (©1928) (*9)
 IU-M213.B81.Z6
 LC-No.4:M213.B (©1939)
   No.5:M213.B (©1939)

MAU-No.5
PCM-M213.B813
8) *First Piano Quartet Collection*, arr.
  a)   *Hungarian Dances, Nos. 2, 4 and 6*, 4P8H
- *FPQC*-Nos.396,397,124
  b)   *Liebeslieder, Op. 52, Nos. 1, 6, 11, 15 and 18*, 4P8H
- *FPQC*-Nos.143,144,152
  c)   *Lullaby*, 4P8H
- *FPQC*-No.91
  d)   *Symphony No. 1, III*, 4P8H
- *FPQC*-No.164
  e)   *Waltzes, Op. 39, Nos. 1, 2, 4 and 15*, 4P8H
- *FPQC*-Nos.364,365,366,109
9) Arr. by ?
  a)   *Serenade in D Major, Op. 11*, 2P8H
- Sim
  UR-M216.B813.C3
  b)   *Ungarische Tänze, Nos. 1-10* (1852-1869), 1P6H
- Sim
  PCM-M213.B813.U5
  UR-M216.B813.V1-U.4
  c)   *Wiegenlied*, 1P6H
- Dit

BRUCKNER, Anton (1824-1896), Austrian
GRUNSKY, Karl, arr.
       Nine Symphonies, 2P8H
- P,CF
- Hin-*PGTAP*:33

BUDIK, B.
LERMAN, J.W., arr.
       Jolly Brothers, Galop, 1P6H
- Mol (©1913)
  LC-M213.B

BÜLOW, Hans Guido von (1830-1894), German
VEGH, Johann von, arr.
       Königsmarsch, Op. 28, 2P8H

- Aib (©188-?)
  NYPL-JMG 72-539

BURCHARD, Carl (1820-1896), arr.
  Räkóczy Marsch, Ungarischer National Marsch, 2P8H
- Br&H (*9)
  NYPL

CALDES, R.A. de
SOURILAS, Theodore arr.; rev. and fingered by Reginald BARRETT
  Pursued by the Hounds, Galop for Piano, 1P6H
- F,J (©1902)
  LC-M213.C

CHABRIER, (Alexis) Emmanuel (1841-1894), French
1) CHEVILLARD, Camille (1859-1923), arr.
  España, Rapsodie pour orchestre, 2P8H
- En;Cos
  UR-M216.C42.C
2) *FPQC*, arr.
  España, Rhapsody, 4P8H
- *FPQC*-No.358

CHAMINADE, Cécile (1857-1944), French
ROQUES, Léon, arr.
  Pièce romantique et gavotte, Op. 9, 2P8H
- Dur (©1910)
  LC-M216.C4.R5

CHASINS, Abram (*b* 1903), American
FPQC, arr.
  Rush Hour in Hong Kong, 4P8H
- *FPQC*-No.177

CHERUBINI, Luigi (1760-1842), Italian
KELLER, Robert, arr.
1)   *Overture* to *Anacréon*, 2P8H
- Kuh
  LC-M216.C425.A5

2) *Overture* to *Wasserträger*, 2P8H
- Kuh
UR-M216.C52.W

CHOPIN, Fryderyk Franciszek (1810-1849), Polish
1) BURCHARD, Carl (1820-1896), arr.
   Polonaise in A Major, Op. 40, No. 1 (Military) (1838), 2P8H
- Br&H
UR-M216.C549p
2) SARTORIO, Arnoldo (1853-1936), arr.
   Polonaise in A Major, Op. 40, No.1 (Military), 2P8H
- Schm
3) WAGNER, E.D., and F. BRISSLER, arrs., Op. 80, No. 41
   Mazurka in B Major, Op. 7, No. 1, 2P8H
- Rie
4) First Piano Quartet Collection, arrs.
   a)   *Ecossaises in D Major, G Major and D-Flat Major*, 4P8H
- *FPQC*-No.195,a,b,c
   b)   *Etudes, Op. 10, Nos. 2, 3, 5, 7 and 12*, 4P8H
- *FPQC*-Nos.116,316,10, 167,386
   c)   *Etudes, Op. 25, Nos. 1, 2, 3, 6, 8, 9 and 11*, 4P8H
- *FPQC*-Nos.161,270,338,23,340,6,350
   d)   *Fantaisie Impromptu*, 4P8H
- *FPQC*-No.288
   e)   *Mazurkas, Op. 6, No. 1; Op. 7, No. 2; Op. 33, No. 2; Op. 56, No. 2; Op. 68, No.3;* and *A Minor*, 4P8H
- *FPQC*-Nos. 398,399,400,401,402,403
   f)   *Nocturne in E-Flat Major, Op. 9, No. 2*, 4P8H
- *FPQC*-No.309
   g)   *Polonaise in A Major, Op. 40, No.1* (Military), 4P8H
- *FPQC*-No.97
   h)   *Polonaise in A-Flat Major, Op. 53*, 4P8H
- *FPQC*-No.296
   i)   *Preludes, Op. 28, Nos. 3, 4, 6, 7, 15, 16, 17, 20, 21* and *23*, 4P8H
- *FPQC*-Nos.293,349,297,276,120,304, 291,302,363,294
   j)   *Tarantelle, Op. 43*, 4P8H

- *FPQC*-No.290
  k) *Waltzes, Op. 18; Op. 34, No.1; Op. 64, Nos. 1* and 2; and *Op. Posth.*, 4P8H
- *FPQC*-Nos.24,381,44,39,201

CLARK, Scotson
HERMANN, F., arr.
       Marche aux flambeaux, Op. 32, 1P6H; 2P8H
- Aug
- P,T
- *PRG*:439

CODINA, Geuaro
ROEDER, C., arr.
       Santiago March, 1P6H; 2P8H
- Witz (©1890)
  LC-M213.C;M216.C63

COHAN, George Michael (1878-1942), American
MÉTIS, Frank, arr.
       You're a Grand Old Flag, multiple pianos
- Mark
  LC-M215.C (erroneously placed in M216 section)

COUPERIN, François (*Le grand*) (1668-1733), French
FPQC, arr.
       Les petits moulins, 4P8H
- *FPQC*-No.247

CROSSE, Mentor
1) HUGO, Carl (1890-?), arr.
       Melody, Op. 23, 1P6H
- Chu (©1922)
  LC-M213.C
2) SPROSS, Charles Gilbert (1874-?), arr.
       Polonaise, Op. 14, No. 6, 2P8H
- Chu (©1922)
  LC-M216.C72.P5

CUI, César (1835-1918), Russian
FPQC, arr.
    Orientale, 4P8H
- *FPQC*-No.280

CZERNY, Carl (1791-1857), arr., Austrian
    Overtures, 1P6H
      1. **ROSSINI**, *Tancredi*
      2. **AUBER**, *Fra Diavolo*
      3. **WEBER**, C.M.v., *Der Freishütz*
      4. **MOZART**, *Don Giovanni*
      5. **ROSSINI**, *Il barbiere di Sevigilia*
      6. **MOZART**, *Il nozze di Figaro*
- Dit (©1876?)
  LC-M213.C99.S4(No.2 only)

DANA, Arthur
PARLOW, Edmund (1855-?), arr.
    *Rückkehr aus den Ferieu (Returning From Vacation) Op. 30,
    No. 9*, 2P8H (Easy)
- Schm (©1906)
  LC-M216.D25

DANKS, Hart Pease (1834-1903), American
LONG, J. Owen (1876-?), arr.
    Silver Threads Among the Gold, 1P6H (or 1 organ, 6H)
- Per (©1919)
  LC-M213.D3.S4

DARGOMYZHSKI, Aleksandr Sergeyevich (1813-1869), Russian
1) HLAVÁČ, V.J.
   a)   *Rogdana, Choeur des fées*, 2P8H
- Bes
  UR-M216.D2-17Rc
   b)   *Overture* to **Rusalka (The Mermaid)**, 2P8H
- Gut
  UR-M216.D217.RouO
2) LANGER, Eduard Leontevich (1835-1905), arr.
    Costachoque, Fantaisie pour orchestre, 2P8H

- Jur (©1893) (*13)
  LC-M216.D27.C7
  NYPL
  UR-M216.D217.C

DEBUSSY, (Achille) Claude (1862-1918), French
1) BÜSSER, Henri-Paul (1872-1973), arr.
           Petite suite (1886-1889), 2P8H
              1. *En bateau*
              2. *Cortège*
              3. *Menuet*
              4. *Ballet*
- Dur (©1910) (*25)
  ASU-M216.D4.P4x.1910
  LC-M216.D344
- *PRG*:439
2) HART, Jane Smith, arr.
           IV. Ballet from *Petite suite* (1886-1889), 1P6H
- Available from arranger (©1983)
  120 Pelham Road
  North Rochelle, NY 10805
3) ROQUES, (Jéan) Léon (1839-?), arr.
    a)   *Première arabesque*, 2P8H
                Andantino con moto
- Dur (©1911) (*7)
  ASU-M216.D4.No.1.A7x
  LC-M216.D34.No.1
- *PRG*:439
    b)   *Deuxième arabesque* (1881-1891), 2P8H
                Allegretto scherzando
- Dur (©1911) (*9)
  ASU-M216.D4.No.2.R6x
  LC-M216.D34.No.2
  UR-M216.D289.A6.No.2
- *PRG*:439
4) *First Piano Quartet Collection*, arrs.
    a)   *Deux arabesques*, 4P8H
- *FPQC*-Nos.207,198
    b)   *Beau soir*, 4P8H

- *FPQC*-No.35
  c)   *III. Clair de lune* from **Suite bergamasque**, 4P8H
- *FPQC*-No.249
  d)   *Fêtes*, 4P8H
- *FPQC*-No.205
  e)   **Prélude**: *La fille aux cheveux de lin, (Bk. I, No. 8)*, 4P8H
- *FPQC*-No.308
  f)   *No.6: Golliwog's Cakewalk* from **Children's Corner Suite**, 4P8H
- *FPQC*-No.307
  g)   *Rêverie*, 4P8H
- *FPQC*-No.334
  h)   **Prélude**: *La Cathédrale engloutie, (Bk. II, No. 10)*, 4P8H
- *FPQC*-No.330

DECEVÉE, Edwin J.
PARLOW, Edmund (1855-?), arr.
1)   *Olga, Mazurka caprice*, 2P8H (Moderately difficult)
- Schm (©1922)
  LC-M216.D37.05
2)   *Polonaise brillante, Op. 35*, 2P8H (Moderately difficult)
- Schm (©1906) (*11)
  LC-M216.D37

DELIBES, (Clément Philibert) Léo (1836-1891), French
1) SARTORIO, Arnoldo (1853-1936), arr.
  a)   *Pizzicati* from **Sylvia (La nymphe de Diane)** (1876), 1P6H
- P,T (©1928) (*9)
  IU-M213.D35.S3
  b)   *Valse lente* from **Coppelia**, 1P6H
- P,T
2) *FPQC*, arr.
  Passe pied from **Le roi s'amuse**, 4P8H
- *FPQC*-No.126

DENNÉE, Charles F., French
PARLOW, Edmund (1855-?), arr.
  Rondo villageois, Morceau facile, Op.12, No.3, 2P8H

- Schm (©1907)
  LC-M213.D413

DIETRICH, M.
EBERS, W., arr.
  Galop de bravoure, Op. 43, 1P6H
  Presto
- And (©1913)
  LC-M213.D

DINICU, Grigoras (1889-1949), Rumanian
HEIFETZ, Jascha (1901-1989), arr; *First Piano Quartet Collection*,
  arr.
  Hora Staccato, 4P8H
- *FPQC*-No.157

DITMARS, F.R., American
FENIMORE, W.P., arr.
  Dream of Happy Days, Polka, 1P6H
- Nor (©1888)
  LC-M213.D6.D7

DONIZETTI, Gaetano (1797-1848), Italian
1) FASANOTTI, F., arr.
  Viva il Madera from **Lucrezia Borgia** (1883), 2P8H
- Car (©1882)
  BrM-h.3277.a.(34.)
2) FOWLER, J.A., arr.
  Grand March from **Norma**, 2P8H
- Dit (©1891) (*5)
  LC-M216.D65
3) LERMAN, J.W., arr.
  Sextette from **Lucia di Lammermoor**, 1P6H
- Mol (©1913)
  LC-M213.D

DRESHER, D.A., American
LOSSÉ, F., arr.
  Lehigh Polka, 1P6H

- Nor (©1885)
  LC-M213.D

DRESSLER, William, arr.
1)   *Innosence*
- Dit
  LC-M213.H
2)   *Little Romp Quickstep*, 1P6H
- Dit
  LC-M213.H

DRUMHELLER, Charles, American
1) MORRIS/BARNET, arrs.
        Merry Bells of Morning, Reverie, 1P6H
- Chu (©1922)
  LC-M213.D
2) PARLOW, Edmund (1855-?), arr.
        Bridal Bells, 2P8H
- P,T:1P6H; 2P8H
- Witz (©1895)
  LC-M216.B9

DUKAS, Paul (1865-1935), French
FPQC, arr.
        The Sorcerer's Apprentice, 4P8H
- *FPQC*-No.37

DURAND, Charles, American
STREABBOG, (Jéan) Louis, arr.
        Fast Mail Galop, Op. 91, 1P6H
- Witz
  LC-M213.D

DURAND, Marie Auguste (1830-1909), French
1) ROQUES, Léon, arr.
   a)   *Chaconne, Op. 62*, 2P8H
- Dur (©1910) (*11)
  LC-M216.D87
- *PRG*:440

b) *Première valse, Op. 83*, 2P8H
- Dur (©1909)
  LC-M216.D88
  UR-M216.D949.v.1
2) STEIGER, Charles
   Première valse, Op. 83, 1P6H
   Presto
- Dur
  LC-M213.D

DVOŘÁK, Antonín (Leopold) (1841-1904), Bohemian
1) KELLER, Robert, arr.
   Slavische Tänze, Op. 46, 2P8H
- Sim
  UR-M216.D98.vols.1-3
2) KRAEHENBUEHL, David (*b* 1923), arr.
   Ecossaises, Op. 41, 2P8H
- Su-B
- *PRG*:440
3) MORROW, Sidney, arr.
   Moderato, quasi marcia from **Serenade in D Minor, Op. 44**
   (1878), 2P8H
- F,C (©1973), 1878
  LC-M216.D93.Op.44.M7
  PCM-M216.D988.Op.44.1973
4) RIHM, Alexander, arr.
   Symphony No. 9 in E Minor, Op. 95 (New World), 2P8H
- Sim (©1907)
  UMic-M216.D97.S99.1907
  UR-M216.D988.sy.9R
5) *First Piano Quartet Collection*, arrs.
   a) *Finale* from **American String Quartet**, 4P8H
- *FPQC*-No.121
   b) *Humoresque*, 4P8H
- *FPQC*-No.92
   c) *Polka*, 4P8H
- *FPQC*-No.117
   d) *Silhouettes, Op. 8, Nos. 2, 4* and *12*, 4P8H
- *FPQC*-Nos.133,148,123

e)   *Slavonic Dance No.6*, 4P8H
- *FPQC*-No.105
    f)   *Songs My Mother Taught Me*, 4P8H
- *FPQC*-No.122
    g)   *Symphony No. 4 (New World), I*, 4P8H
- *FPQC*-No.150
6) Arr. by ?
            Humoreske in G-Flat Major, Op. 101, No.7, 1P6H
- CMP
- *PRG*:440

EGGELING, Georg
PARLOW, Edmund (1855-?), arr.
1)   *La capricieuse, Valse, Op. 120*, 2P8H
- Schm (©1907; ©1923)
    LC-M216.E33.C2 and C3
2)   *Menuetto scherzando*, 1P6H (Moderately difficult)
- Schm
3)   *Summer Morn, Gavotte, Op. 203*, 1P6H
- P,T
    LC-M213.E
4)   *Valse Intermezzo*, 2P8H (Moderately difficult)
- Schm (©1927)
    LC-M216.E33.V2
5)   *Zur Maienzeit (In Maytime), Op. 168*, 1P6H
- Schm (©1913)
    LC-M213.E

ELGAR, Sir Edward (William) (1857-1934), English
CARPER, Virginia Speiden, arr.
            *Pomp and Circumstance, Military March No. 1, in D
            Major, Op. 39* (1901), 2P8H
- CPP/Bel (©1985)
- S,G
- *PRG*:440

EMMETT, Daniel Decatur (1815-1904), American
LERMAN, J.W., arr.
1)   *Dixie*, 1P6H

- Mol (©1908)
  LC-M213.E
2)   *Dixie Land*, 1P6H
- P,T (©1903)
- Witz
  LC-M213.E

ENESCO [or ENESCU], Georges (1881-1955), Rumanian
        Rumanian Rhapsody No. 1, 4P8H
- *FPQC*-No.78

ENGELBRECHT, J.C., American
MÜLLER, Julius E., arr.
        March of the Videttes, 1P6H
- Wil (©1880)
  LC-M213.E

ESTALIÈRES
REISSIGER, C.G., arr.
        Overture to *Die Felsenmühle, Op. 71*, 2P8H
- Sim
  LC-M216.R37.F3

ETTERLEIN, A., American
MICHEUZ, Georges, arr.; rev. and fing. by Reginald BARRETT
1)   *Pan American Galop*, 1P6H
- F,J (©1902)
  LC-M213.E
2)   *Troopers on Parade*, 1P6H
- F,J (©1902)
  LC-M213.E

FALLA (Y MATHEU), Manuel de (1876-1946), Spanish
FPQC, arr.
1)   *Jota*, 4P8H
- *FPQC*-No.262
2)   *Polo*, 4P8H
- *FPQC*-No.264
3)   *Ritual Fire Dance*, 4P8H

- *FPQC*-No.145
4)   *Sequidille Murciana*, 4P8H
- *FPQC*-No.263
5)   *Serenata Andaluza*, 4P8H
- *FPQC*-No.192
6)   *Spanish Dance No. 1* from **La Vida Breve**, 4P8H
- *FPQC*-No.269

FAURÉ, Gabriel-Urbain (1845-1924), French
FPQC, arr.
        Romance sans paroles, 4P8H
- *FPQC*-No.181

FINK, Wilhelm, German
PARLOW, Edmund (1855-?), arr.
        Klange vom Ebro-Strand, Bolero (Sounds from the Ebro),
        Op. 355, 2P8H (Moderately difficult)
- Schm (©1905)
  LC-M216.F
  UR-M216.F499.K

FIRST PIANO QUARTET COLLECTION, arr.
1)   *Classical Cocktail No.1*, 4P8H
        1. **STRAUSS**, Johann, Jr., *Blue Danube Waltz*
        2. **STRAUSS**, Johann, Jr., *Voices of Spring*
        3. **CHOPIN**, *Minute Waltz*
        4. **STRAUSS**, Johann, Jr., *Die Fledermaus* (abridged)
        5. **CHOPIN**, *Waltz in C-Sharp Minor*
        6. Anon., *Chopsticks*
- *FPQC*-No.69
2)   *Classical Cocktail No.2*, 4P8H
        1. **SCHUBERT**, *Symphony No.8 (Unfinished)*
        2. **TCHAIKOVSKY**, *Symphony No. 4, I*
        3. **BIZET**, *Habanera* from **Carmen**
- *FPQC*- No.83
3)   *Classical Cocktail No.3*, 4P8H
        1. **MOZART**, *Overture* to **The Marriage of Figaro**
        2. **WAGNER**, *Overture* to **The Flying Dutchman**
        3. **WAGNER**, *Choir of the Sailors* from **The Flying**

Dutchman
4. **BEETHOVEN**, *Turkish March* from *The Ruins of Athens, Op. 113*
5. **BRAHMS**, *Hungarian Dance No. 5*
- *FPQC*-No.107
4) *Classical Cocktail No. 4*, 4P8H
   1. **OFFENBACH**, *Barcarole* from *The Tales of Hoffman*
   2. **GRIEG**, *Morning Mood* from *Peer Gynt Suite*
   3. **BIZET**, *Seguiduilla* from *Carmen*
   4. **WAGNER**, *Sword Motif* from *The Ring*
   5. **VERDI**, *Triumphant March* from *Aida*
   6. **WAGNER**, *Pilgrim's Chorus* from *Tannhäuser*
   7. **TCHAIKOVSKY**, *Symphony No. 5, IV*
- *FPQC*-No.132
5) *Classical Cocktail No. 5*, 4P8H
   1. **SCHUMANN**, *The Happy Farmer*
   2. **BEETHOVEN**, *Presto*
   3. **TCHAIKOVSKY**, *Concerto No. 1, I*
   4. **TCHAIKOVSKY**, *Symphony No. 4, IV*
   5. **TCHAIKOVSKY**, *Chinese March* from *The Nutcracker Suite*
   6. **FOSTER**, S., *Oh! Susannah*
- *FPQC*-No.172
6) *Classical Cocktail No. 6 in 3/4 Time*, 4P8H
   (Happy Birthday Theme)
   1. **TCHAIKOVSKY**, *Flower Waltz* from *The Nutcracker Suite*
   2. **STRAUSS**, Johann, Jr., *Fledermaus Waltz*
   3. **STRAUSS**, Johann, Jr., *Blue Danube*
   4. **TCHAIKOVSKY**, *Piano Concerto No. 1*
   5. **LIADOV**, *Music Box*
- *FPQC*-No.178
7) *Classical Cocktail No. 7*, 4P8H
   (Children's Version--"Non-alcoholic")
   1. *Three Blind Mice*
   2. *London Bridge is Falling Down*
   3. *Twinkle, Twinkle Little Star*
   4. *Jingle Bells*
   5. *Long Long Ago*

6. *The Stars and Stripes Forever*
7. *Anchors Aweigh*
8. **MOZART**, *Sonata in C Major, I*
- *FPQC*-No.231
8)   *Funiculì, Funiculà (Italian Folk Song)*, 4P8H
- *FPQC*-No.9
9)   *God Save the King*, 4P8H
- *FPQC*-No.347
10)   *Happy Birthday*, 4P8H
- *FPQC*-No.394
11)   *Scrambled Classics (24 composers)*, 4P8H
- *FPQC*-No.74
12)   *United Nations Cocktail Medley*, 4P8H
     1. *The Stars and Stripes Forever*
     2. *Marseillaise*
     3. *Tipperary*
     4. *Meadowlands*
     5. *United Nations March*
     6. *Anchors Aweigh*
     7. *Caissons Go Rolling Along*
- *FPQC*-No.283

FISCHER, George H., American
HAMMEREL, Victor, arr.
1)   *Knights of Columbus March*, 1P6H
- F,J (©1899)
   LC-M213.F
2)   *Patriotic American, Two-step*, 1P6H; 2P8H
- F,J (©1899)

FLAGLER, I.V., American
FERBER, Richard, arr.
     With Song and Jest, Polka élégante, 2P8H
- P,T (©1916)
   LC-M216.F57.W4

FLOTOW, Friedrich (Adolf Ferdinand) von (1812-1883), German
1) Arr. by ?
     Martha Fantasy, 2P8H

- P,CF
- *PRG*:440
2) Arr. by ?
    Overture to *Martha* (1847), 2P8H
- P,CF
- *PRG*:440
3) BURCHARD, Carl (1820-1896), arr.
    Overture to Rübezahl (1852), 2P8H
- And (©1924)

FONDEY, Charles F., American
GOEDELER, Richard, arr.
    Girard Gavotte, 1P6H
- P,T (©1895)
  LC-M213.F

FOSTER, Stephen Collins (1826-1864), American
FPQC, arr.
    Medley, 4P8H
      1. *Beautiful Dreamer*
      2. *Oh! Susannah*
      3. *Old Folks at Home*
- *FPQC*-No.87

FRANCK, César (Auguste Jean Guillaume Hubert) (1822-1890),
    Belgian
FPQC, arr.
    Organ Prelude in C Minor, arr. 4P8H
- *FPQC*-No.289

FRANKE, J. Max (1896-?), American
PARLOW, Edmund (1855-?), arr.
1)   *Bajaderen-Tanz, Op. 58*, 2P8H (Moderately difficult)
- Schm (©1906)
  LC-M216.F7
  UR-M216.F829b
2)   *In the Boat*, 1P6H (Easy)
- Schm

FUMAGALLI, A.
FPQC, arr.
>   *Grand fantasia militaire, Op. 60*, 4P8H
>   1. *Ronda Notturna*
>   2. *Una Notte al Campo*
>   3. *Segnal d'allarme*
>   4. *Imno Trionfale*
>   5. *Funeral March*
- *FPQC*-No.322

GADE, Niels Wilhelm (1817-1890), German
1) BRUNNER, C.T., arr.
>   *Sinfonie No. 1 in C Minor, Op. 5*, 2P8H
- Kis (©1862)
   NYPL
2) *FPQC*, arr.
>   *Scherzo*, 4P8H
- *FPQC*-No.76
3) Arr. by ?
>   *Nachklänge von Ossian, Ouvertüre für Orchester, Op. 1*,
>   2P8H
- Br&H (©1862)
   NYPL
   UR-M216.G12

GAUTIER, Léonard, French
GURLITT, Cornelius (1820-1901), arr.; Ed. by Fanny
>   WATERMAN
>   *Le secret, Intermezzo pizzicato*, 1P6H
- Aug
- Fab (©1983)   (*11)
- P,T
- S,G
- W-S (Grade 3)
- *PRG*:440

GEIBEL, Adam (1855-1933)
FENIMORE, W.P., arr.
1)   *Hunting Song*, 1P6H

- Nor (©1888)
  LC-M213.G4.H7
2)   *Starlight Schottische*, 1P6H
- Nor (©1887)
  LC-M213.G4.H7

GERMAN, Edward
WITHROW, Miriam Fox, arr.
1)   *Morris Dance* from *Henry. VIII Dances*, 2P8H
          Allegro giocoso
- Su (©1940)
  LC-M216.G
2)   *Shepherd's Dance* from *Henry VIII Dances*, 2P8H
          Allegro quasi andantino
- Su (©1949)
  LC-M216.G4.S5
3)   *Torch Dance* from *Henry VIII Dances*, 2P8H
- Su (©1949)
  LC-M216.G4.T6

GERSHWIN, George (1898-1937), American
1) GRAINGER, Percy Alderidge (1882-1961), arr.
   a)   *Oh, I Can't Sit Down*, 1P6H
- S,G (©1950)
- Hin-*PGTAP*:57
   b)   *Rhapsody in Blue*, abridged version, 50P100H
- performed at 1984 Summer Olympic Opening Ceremonies in
          Los Angeles, California, with fifty pianists on fifty
          white grand pianos.
2) *FPQC*, arr.
   a)   *An American in Paris*, 4P8H
- *FPQC*-No.370
   b)   *Fascinatin' Rhythm*, 4P8H
- *FPQC*-No.406
   c)   *I Got Plenty of Nuttin'* from *Porgy and Bess*, 4P8H
- *FPQC*-No.371
   d)   *It Ain't Necessarily So*, 4P8H
- *FPQC*-No.372
   e)   *The Man I Love*, 4P8H

- *FPQC*-No.373
  f)   *Rhapsody in Blue*, 4P8H
- *FPQC*-No.237
  g)   *Somebody Loves Me*, 4P8H
- *FPQC*-No.407
  h)   *Strike Up the Band*, 4P8H
- *FPQC*-No.374
  i)   *Summertime* (including some of the *Overture* and *Bess You Is My Woman Now*) from *Porgy and Bess*, 4P8H
- *FPQC*-No.369

GETZE, Jacob Alfred, arr.
    Mocking Bird Echoes (Variations on *Auld Lang Syne*), 1P6H
- L&W (©1869)
  LC-M213.G

GIESE, Theodore, American
PAUL, Oscar, arr.
    Joyful March, Op. 160, No.6, 1P6H
- Lam (©1902)
  LC-M213.G

GILBERT-JESPERSEN, Charlotte, arr., Norwegian
    Lette stykker, 1P6H
    1. *Festkanon*
    2. *Tre danske børnesange*
    3. a) **MOZART**, W.A., *March*
       b) **MOZART**, L., *Polonaise*
    4. *Kehraus*
- HanG
  LC-M213.G

GILLET, Ernest (1856-1940), American
1) MOELLING, Theodore, arr.
   a)   *Loin de bal (Echoes of the Ball)*, 1P6H
- Dit (©1899)
  LC-M213.G
2) ROEDER, C., arr.

        Recollections of the Ball, 1P6H; 2P8H
- Witz (©1901)
  LC-M213.G;M216.G45

GLAZUNOV, Aleksandr Konstantinovich (1865-1936), Russian
TSCHERNOV, K., arr.
        La forêt, Fantaisie pour grand orchestre, Op.19, 2P8H
- Bel (©1889)
  UR-M216.G553f

GLIÈRE, Reinhold (1875-1956), Russian
FPQC, arr.
        Russian Sailor's Dance from *The Red Poppy* (Ballet), 4P8H
- *FPQC*-No.79

GLINKA, Mikhail Ivanovitch (1804-1857), Russian
1) LANGER, Edward Leontevich (1835-1905), arr.
        Souvenir d'une nuit d'été à Madrid, Fantaisie sur des
        thèmes espagnols, 2P8H
- Jur (©189-?)
  NYPL
2) LIÂPUNOV, Sergei Mikhailovitch (1859-1924), arr.
  a)   *La jota aragonesa, Caprice brillant*, 2P8H
- En
  UR-M216.G561j
  b)   *Overture* to *Ruslan und Ludmila* (1837-1842), 2P8H
- Jur (©1910)
  NYPL
- *TPR*:155
3) SILVER, Alfred J., arr.
        Mazurka russe, 1P6H
- F,J (©1915)
  LC-M213.G
4) TSCHERNOV, K., arr.
  a)   *Komarinskaja*, 2P8H
- Jur (©1909)
  NYPL
  b)   *Marsch des Tschernovnor* from *Ruslan und Ludmila*, 2P8H
- *Jur* (©1910)

NYPL
- See 1. Nineteenth-Century Works: Liszt
  c)   *Tänze in den Zaubergärten Naina's* from *Ruslan und*
          Ludmila, 2P8H
- Jur (©1910)
  NYPL
  UR-M216.G561.RT
  d)   *Valse-fantaisie*, 2P8H
  NYPL

GLUCK, Christoph Willibald von (1714-1787), German
1) *FPQC*, arr.
  a)   *Andantino* from *Orfeo ed Euridice*, 4P8H
- *FPQC*-No.170
  b)   *Gavotte* from *Iphigénie en Aulide*, 4P8H
- *FPQC*-No.59
  c)   *Larghetto* from *Echo et Narcisse*, 4P8H
- *FPQC*-No.281
2) Arr. by ?
          Air from *Orfeo ed Euridice* (1762; 1774), 1P6H
- P,T
- *PRG*:440

GODARD, Benjamin
ROQUES, Léon, arr.
          Deuxième valse, Op. 56, 2P8H
- Dur (©1910)
  LC-M216.G63

GOLDMARK, Karl (1830-1915), Hungarian, of Austrian origin
FPQC, arr.
          Entrance and *March* from *Die Königin von Saba*, 4P8H
- *FPQC*-Nos.182,180

GOSSEC, François Joseph (1734-1829), Belgian
FPQC, arr.
          Gavotte in D Major, 4P8H
- *FPQC*-No.253

GOTTSCHALK, Louis Moreau (1829-1869), American
1) SILVER, Alfred J., arr.
   a)   *La gallina (The Hen)*, 1P6H
- F,J (©1916)
  LC-M213.G
   b)   *Ojos Criollos (Creole Eyes)*, 1P6H
- F,J (©1916)
  LC-M213.G
   c)   *Radieuse, Grande valse de concert*, 2P8H
- F,J (©1916)
  LC-M216.G66.R3
2) ESPADERO, N.R., arr. *La nuit des tropiques*, 2P or 3P, 4H or
      6H (unfinished arrangement)
  UCLA
NB--Ralph Kirkpatrich has arr. this for 2P4H
*According to Gottschalk, any number of pianos could be used in a
performance of any one of his piano pieces.

GOUNOD, Charles François (1818-1893), French
1) CRÉMER, Henry, arr.; rev. and fing. by Reginald BARRETT
     Faust Fantasia, 1P6H
- F,J
  LC-M213.C
2) LÉMOINE, Léon, arr.
   a)   *Fête de Jupiter, Grande marche*, 2P8H
- Lem (©1895)
  UR-M216.G711f
   b)   *Passacaille; Sérénade*, 2P8H
- Lem (©1895)
  UR-M216.G711P
3) LISZT/*FPQC*, arrs.
     Waltz from *Faust*, 4P8H
- *FPQC*-No.314
4) MÜLLER, William F., arr.
     Grand March from *Faust*, 2P8H
- Pon (©1892)
  LC-M216.G6B
5) PAUL, Oscar, arr.
     Romaine March, 1P6H

- Lam (©1910)
  LC-M213.G
6) SARTORIO, Arnoldo (1853-1936), arr.
      Waltz from *Faust*, 1P6H; 2P8H
- Dit
- P,T
  LC-M213.G(©1927); M216.G681(©1925)
7) TIMM, Henry Christian (1811-1892), arr.
      Waltz and Chorus from *Faust*, 2P8H
- S,G (©1892)
  LC-M216.G682
8) VILBACK, Renaud de (1829-1884), arr.; Ed. by American
      Piano Quartet (Pollei, Wilberg, Shumway, Parkinson)
      Waltz from *Faust*, 2P8H
- Kj (©1990), WP 310, American Piano Quartet Series
9) Arr. by ?
    a)   ***Philémon et Baucis**, Fantasy* (1860), 2P8H
- P,CF
- *PRG*:440
    b)   ***Queen of Sheba**, Fantasy* (1862), 2P8H
- P,CF
- *PRG*:440
    c)   ***Sapho**, Fantasy* (1851; rev. 1884), 2P8H
- P,CF
- *PRG*:440
    d)   *Soldier's Chorus* from *Faust* (1859), 2P8H
- P,CF
- *PRG*:440
    e)   *Valse* from *Faust (1859)*, 2P8H
- P,CF
- *PRG*:440

GRAINGER, Percy Alderidge (1882-1961), American, of
Australian origin
FPQC, arr.
 Molly on the Shore, 4P8H
- *FPQC*-No.271

GRANADOS, Enrique (1867-1916), Spanish
FPQC, arr.
1) *Playera, Spanish Dance No. 5*,
 4P8H
- *FPQC*-No.14
2) *Villanesca, Spanish Dance No. 4*, 4P8H
- *FPQC*-No.220

GREENWALD, M.
1) *Barbara, Waltz*, 1P6H
- CMP; c/o Ash
- *PRG*:440
2) *The Home Guard*, 1P6H
- CMP; c/o Ash
- *PRG*:440

GRIEG, Edvard (Hagerup)(1843-1907), Norwegian
1) CARPER, Virginia Speiden, arr.
 Triumphal March from **Sigurd Jorsalfar**, *Op. 22* (1872),
 2P8H (Difficult Class I)
- CPP/Bel (©1985)
 SBTS
- P,T (©1949)
 LC-M216.G75.Op.56.C3
2) JOHNSON, Thomas A., arr.
 Piano Concerto in A Minor, Op. 16 (1868), 2P8H
- Hin (©1960)
 Cur-M216.G848.Op.16.1960
 UR-M216.G848c
- P,CF
- *PRG*:430;440

3) RUTHARDT, Adolf (1849-1934), arr.

   Peer Gynt, Suite No. 1, Op. 46 (1876), 2P8H

   Vol. 1 *Morning Mood*

   Vol. 2 *Death of Aase; Anitra's Dance*

   Vol. 3 *In the Hall of the Mountain King*

- P,CF (©1957)

 ASU-M216.G8.P4x

 BBC

 BrM-e.378.a.(1.)

 UR-M216.G848.PS.no.1(1895)

- *PRG*:440

- *TPR*:155

4) THRESHER, Muriel, arr.

   Elverdans (Elfin Dance) from *Lyric Pieces, Book I, Op. 12, No. 4* (1867), 1P6H

- WM

- *PRG*:440

5) WEBB, F.R., arr.

   Norwegian Bridal Procession, Op. 92, 2P8H

- Chu (©1901)

 LC-M216.G72

- P,T

- *PRG*:440

6) *FPQC*, arr.

 a) *Anitra's Dance*, 4P8H

- *FPQC*-No.62

 b) *In the Hall of the Mountain King*, 4P8H

- *FPQC*-No.36

 c) *March of the Dwarfs*, 4P8H

- *FPQC*-No.355

GRIMM, Carl William (1863-?), American
   Anniversary Processional, 2P8H
- Chu (©1922)
   LC-M216.G755.A5

GROSSMANN, I.
WAGNER, E.D. and F. BRISSLER, arrs., Op. 80, No. 57
   Czardas aus der Op Der geist des woiwaden, 2P8H
- Rie

GUION, David (Wendell Fentress)(1892-1981), arr., American
FPQC, arr.
   Arkansas Traveller, 4P8H
- *FPQC*-No.173

GUIRAUD, Ernest (1837-1892), American, active in France
STEIGER, Charles, arr.
   Carnaval, 2P8H
- Dur (©1887)
   BrM-h.3291.a.(6.)
- *PRG*:440
- See 8. Transcriptions/Arrangements: Saint-Saëns, No. 1

GUNGL
BARKER, George, arr.
   En avant!, 1P6H
- P,AC
   LC-M213.G

GURLITT, Cornelius (1820-1901), German
PARLOW, Edmund (1855-?), arr.
   Wiener Waltzer, Op. 178, No.10, 2P8H (Easy)
- Schm (©1905)
   LC-M216.P
   UR-M216.G979W

HACKH, Otto Christoph (1852-1917)
PARLOW, Edmund (1855-?), arr.
> *Sevillana, Morceau de genre*, 2P8H
- Schm (©1905)
  LC-M216.H13

HÄNDEL, George Frideric (1685-1759), German
1) CARPER, Virginia Speiden, arr.
   a) *Allegro Deciso* from *The Water Music* (1717), 2P8H
       (Moderately difficult)
- CCP/Bel (© 1985)
- Cha
  BU
  LC-M216.H
- S,G (©1964)
- *PRG*:440
   b) *Three Pieces* from *The Water Music* (1717), 2P8H
           1. *Allegro in F Major*
           2. *Minuet in D Major*
           3. *Minuet in F Major*
- S,G (©1972)
  LC-M216.H14.W43
   c) *Two Minuets* from *Music for the Royal Fireworks* (1749),
       2P8H
- Cha
- S,G (©1965)
  WSU
- *PRG*:440
2) CZERNY, Carl (1791-1857), arr.
   Hallelujah Chorus from *Messiah*, 1P6H
- Dit (©184-?)
  LC-M213.C99.T7
3) EASDALE, Brian, arr.
   Arrival of the Queen of Sheba from *Solomon* (1749), 2P,
   6H or 8H
- Ox (©1937)
  SBTS
4) SARTORIO, Arnoldo (1853-1936), arr.
   Largo from *Xerxes*, 2P8H

- P,T (©1925)
  LC-M216.H14.x3.S3
5) WAGNER, E.D. and F. BRISSLER, arrs., Op. 80, No. 46
     Chorus from *Judas Makkabäus*, 2P8H
- Rie
6) *FPQC*, arr.
   a)   *Hornpipe* from *Water Music Suite*, 4P8H
- *FPQC*-No.48
   b)   *Passacaglia* from *Suite No. 7 in G Minor*, 4P8H
- *FPQC*-No.275

HANSON, Howard (1896-1981), American
FPQC, arr.
     Love Duet from *Merry Mount Suite*, 4P8H
- *FPQC*-No.409

HARPER, Frederick J., arr., English
     [6]Trios, 1P6H
- Dona (©1888)
  BrM-h.3071.(5.)

HARTUNG, C.F.
PARLOW, Edmund (1855-?), arr.
     Home Again, Waltz, Op. 48, No. 5, 2P8H (Easy)
- Schm (©1913)
  LC-M216.H17

HAUSE, Carl, German
WAGNER, E.D. and F. BRISSLER, arrs., Op. 80, No. 48
     Die fliegenden Clauen, Bravour-galopp, Op. 92, 2P8H
- Rie

HAYDN, Franz Joseph (1732-1809), Austrian
1) BILBRO, Mathilde, arr.
     Andante Theme from *Symphony No. 94 in G Major*
     (Surprise) (1791), 1P8H
- WM (©1938)
2) BURCHARD, Carl (1820-1896), arr.
     Symphony No. 102 in B-Flat Major (1795), 2P8H

- Hoff (©186-?)
  Cur-M216.H415.H.I.102.186-
3) KIRCHER, Theodor (1823-1903), arr.
   a)   _Symphonien, Nos. 1-3_, 2P8H
- P,CF
  UR-M216.H415.S9.K.v.1
   b)   _Symphonien, Nos. 4-6_, 2P8H
- P,CF
  UR-M216.H415.S9.K.v.2
   c)   _Symphonien, Nos. 103, 104, 94, 102, 100, 88_, 2P8H
- P,CF (©1887)
  Cur-M216.H415.H.I.S46.1887
4) KRAEHENBUEHL, David, arr.
     Minuetto, 2P8H
- Su-B
- _PRG_:440
5) KRAMER, Wilhelm, arr.
   a)   _Finale aus der **16**. Symphonie_, 1P6H
- And (©1893)
  LC-M213.H
   b)   _[III.] Rondo all 'Ongarese_ from _Piano Trio in G Major,_
        Hob. XV:25(Gypsy) (1793-1796), 1P6H
- And (©1893)
  LC-M213.H
6) MARCIANO, Ernesto, arr.
     Overture to _Orlando Palandino_, 2P8H
- Ric
  LC-M216.H26.074
7) REHBERG, Willi (1863-1937), arr.
     [II.] Serenade from _String Quartet in F Major, Hob._
     III:17, [2P8H]
- Scho
- _PRG_:440
8) SARTORIO, Arnoldo (1853-1936), arr.
     Menuet from _Symphony No. **100** in G Major (Military)_,
     2P8H
- Schm (©1927)
  Cur-M216.H415.H.I.100.1927
  LC-M216.H26.P2

9) WEST, G.F., arr.

> *Gloria in excelsis* from the *Mass No.la: Rorate coali desuper in G Major, Hob XXII:3*, 1P6H

- Coc (1890)
  BrM-h.3035.b.(35.)

10) *FPQC*, arr.

   a)   *Finale* from *String Quartet, Op. 76, No. 5*, 4P8H

- *FPQC*-No.64

   b)   *Gypsy Rondo* from *Trio in G Major,* **Hob. XV:25 (Gypsy)**, 4P8H

- *FPQC*- No. 326

   c)   *Ox-minuet*, 4P8H (erroneously attributed to Haydn; see 8. Transcriptions/Arrangements: Seyfried)

- *FPQC*-No.260

11) Arr. by ?

> *Symphony No. 94 in G Major (Surprise)*, 2P8H

ASU-M216.H3.M94.B8.v.1 and v.2

(Arr. 6te Symphonie: mit den Pauken schlage)

HAYS, F. Clifton, American
MOELLING, Theodore, arr.

1)   *Cooing Dove Polka*, 1P6H

- Ell
  LC-M213.H

2)   *Lotta Mazurka*, 1P6H

- Ell
  CM-M213.H

HAYS, William Shakespeare (1837-1907), American
DRESSLER, William (1826-?), arr.

> *Pretty as Pink, Barcarole*, 1P6H

- Dit (©1870)
  LC-M213.D

HERBERT, Victor (1859-1924), Irish
FPQC, arr.

> *March of the Toys*, 4P8H

- *FPQC*-No.239

HÉROLD, (Louis Joseph) Ferdinand (1791-1833), French, of
     Alsatian origin
1) BURCHARD, Carl (1820-1896), arr.
     Overture to *Zampa*, 2P8H
- And (©1924)
2) LUX, F., arr.
     Overture to *Zampa*, 2P8H
- Scho
   UR-M216.H561.Za
3) WEST, G.F., arr.
     Overture to *Zampa (La fiancée de marbre)*(1831), 1P6H
- Coc (©1891)
   BrM-h.3292.(3.)(see Lot, no.11)
4)   *Overture* to *Zampa*, 4P8H
- *FPQC*-No.378
5) Arr. by ?
     Overture to *Pré aux clercs*, 2P8H
- Lem

HEWITT, James (1770-1827), American
GUNTHER, Phyllis, arr.
     Early American Suite, 2P4H 2P or 6H or 8H
      1. *Washington March*
      2. *Fitzjames*
      3. *Rondo*
- CPP/Bel (©1975)
   LC-M216.H533.E2
   SBTS

HOFFMAN, Edward (fl.1866), arr., American
     Grand Fantasia on the Popular Theme The Mocking Bird
     [Auld Lang Syne], 2P8H
- L&W
   LC-M216.H55

HOLT, Henry (*b* 1934) American, of Austrian origin
FPQC, arr.
1)   *Scherzo*, 4P8H
- *FPQC*-No.70

2) *There Was a Lover and His Lass* from *Incidental Music* for
   Shakespeare's *As You Like It*, 4P8H
- *FPQC*-No.142

HOWELL, C.R., American
PAUL, Oscar, arr.
   Rustic Dance, 1P6H
- Lam (©1912)
   LC-M213.H78.R6

HUMPERDINCK, Engelbert (1854-1921), German
1) SINGER, Otto, arr.
   Vorspiel und Traum; Pantomime from *Hänsel und Gretel*
   (1893), 2P8H
- Scho
   UR-M216.H926.HV
2) *FPQC*, arr.
   Introduction to *Act I* from *Children of the King*, 4P8H
- *FPQC*-No.183

ICHYINSKI
FPQC, arr.
   Cradle Song, Op. 13, from *Noure and Anitra Suite*, 4P8H
- *FPQC*-No.140

JENSON, Adolf (1837-1879), German
1) KRONKE, Emil (1865-?), arr.
   Hochzeitsmusik (Wedding Music), Op. 45, 2P8H
   1. *Festzug*
   2. *Brautgesang*
   3. *Reigen*
   4. *Nocturno*
- SteV (©1910)
   LC-M216.J352
2) TIMM, Henry Christian (1811-1892), arr.
   Hochzeitsmusik (Wedding Music), Op. 45, 2P8H
- S,G (©1892)
   LC-M216.J35

JESSEL, Léon (1871-1942), German
1) GLOVER, David Carr, arr.
    Parade of the Tin Soldiers, 2P8H
- Mark (©1968)   1905
  ASU-M216.J48x.Op.123.1968
2) *FPQC*, arr.
    Fantasy on Parade of the Wooden Soldiers, 4P8H
- *FPQC*-No.319

JOKL, Otto
FPQC, arr.
    Dance of the Puppets, 4P8H
- *FPQC*-No.94

JOSEFFY, Rafael (1852-1915), American, of Hungarian origin
FPQC, arr.
    Mill-clack, 4P8H
- *FPQC*-No.77

JULLIEN, E.
FOWLER, J.A.
    The Prima Donna Waltz, 2P8H
- Dit (©1890)
  LC-M216.J75

KENNETH, Alford
GRAINGER, Percy Alderidge (1882-1961), arr.
    Bridge on the River Kwai--Marches, 1P6H
        c.1959

KEY, Francis Scott (1779-1843), American
1) PAUL, Oscar, arr.
    The Star Spangled Banner March, 1P6H
- Lam (©1903)
  LC-M213.P
2) *FPQC*, arr.
    The Star Spangled Banner, 4P8H
- *FPQC*-No.137

KHACHATURIAN, Aram (1903-1978), Russian
FPQC, arr.
1)   *Galop* from *Masquerade Suite*, 4P8H
- *FPQC*-No.367
2)   *Sabre Dance* from *Gayne Suite* (Ballet), 4P8H
- *FPQC*-No.331

KIEFFER, American
LOSSÉ, L., arr.
        Orange Grove Schottische, 1P6H
- Nor (©1885)
   LC-M213.K

KINKEL, Charles (1832-?), American
DRESSLER, William, arr.
1)   *Holiday March*, 2P8H
- Dit (©1898)
   LC-M216.K45
2)   *Wild Flowers*, 2P8H
- Dit (©1898)
   LC-M216.K452

KISTLER, Cyrill (1848-1907), German
REINHARD, August (1831-1912)
        *Vorspiel zum 3. Akte der Oper **Kunihild und der Brautritt
        auf Kynast** (1882)*, 2P8H
- Sim (©1897)
   LC-M216.K49

KJERULF, Halfdan (1815-1868)
REINHARD, August (1831-1912), arr.
        Wiegenlied, Op. 4, No. 3, 2P8H
- Sim (©1898)
   LC-M216.K;M216.K53

KNIPPER, Lev (1898-1974), Russian
FPQC, arr.
        *Meadowland, Song of the Plains (Red Army Marching
        Song)*, 4P8H

- FPQC-No.236

KODÁLY, Zoltán (1882-1967), Hungarian
FPQC, arr.
1)   *Entrance of Emperor and His Court* from *Háry János*
        Suite, 4P8H
- FPQC-No.361
2)   *Viennese Musical Clock* from *Háry János Suite*, 4P8H
- FPQC-No.360

KOELLING, Carl
LIFTL, Friedrich J., arr., Op. 186
        Hungary, Rhapsodie mignonne, Op. 410, 1P6H
- P,T (©1929)
  LC-M213.K76

KONTSKI, Anton [or Antoine de] (1817-1899)
HORN, August, arr.
        Reveil du lion, Caprice héroïque, Op. 115, 2P8H
- Schl (*15)
  NYPL

KORNGOLD, Erich Wolfgang (1897-1957), Austrian
FPQC, arr.
        Hornpipe from *Much Ado About Nothing*, 4P8H
- FPQC-No.57

KRAUSS, Anne McClenny and Maurice HINSON, arrs.
        Dances of the Young Republic: Duets-Trios-Quartets,
        1P4H, 1P6H, 1P8H
        TRIOS, Marine Cotillions
        1. *The Constitution* (Alexander REINAGLE)
        2. *The Chesapeake* (Alexander REINAGLE)
        3. *The Virginia Reel* (Anonymous)
           Paddy Carey (Anonymous)
        QUARTETS, Cotillions, Set 7
        Deidania (Francis JOHNSON)
        Is There a Heart (Francis JOHNSON)
        March in Rob Roy Country (Francis JOHNSON)

The Campbells Are Comin' (Anonymous)
- Alf (© 1991)

KREISLER, Fritz (1875-1962), Austrian
FPQC, arr.
1)   *Liebesfreud*, 4P8H
- *FPQC*-No.28
2)   *Liebeslied*, 4P8H
- *FPQC*-No.29

KREUTZER, Conradin (1780-1849), German
1) BUCHARD, Carl (1820-1896), arr.
    Overture to *Das Nachtlager von Granada* (1834) 1P6H
- S,G (©1895)
   LC-M213.K
2) EBERS, W., arr.
    Overture to *Das Nachtlager von Granada* (1834), 2P8H
- Hofm (©186-?) (*19)
- PCM-Rarebook.M216.A3.18--
   (*Achthändig Ouvertüren, No. 8*)

KRONKE, Emil
PARLOW, Edmund (1855-?),arr.
    Marcia giocosa, Op. 48, No. 3, 2P8H (Moderately difficult)
- Schm (©1913)
   LC-M216.K76

KÜCKEN, Friedrich W. (1810-1882)
BERG, Albert W. (1825-1906), arr.
    Chant du bivovac, 2P8H
- Pon (©1867)
   LC-M216.K94.B3

LABIZKY
FOWLER, J.A., arr.
    Germania (Imperial Waltz! Imported from the Rhine), 2P8H
- Pon   1871
   LC-M216.L

LAMBERT
FPQC, arr.

   Variations on **When Johnny Comes Marching Home**, 4P8H
- *FPQC*-No.272

LATOUR, T. (1766-1837)
LOSSÉ, L., arr.
   Notre Dame Waltz, 1P6H
- Nor (©1885)
   LC-M213.L

LECUONA, Ernesto (1896-1963), Cuban
FPQC, arr.
1)   *Andalucía*, 4P8H
- *FPQC*-No.11
2)   *Aragonesa*, 4P8H
- *FPQC*-No.306
3)   La Comparsa, 4P8H
- *FPQC*-No.5
4)   *Concert Conga (Here Comes the Chinaman)*, 4P8H
- *FPQC*-No.72
5)   *Danza de Los Nanigos*, 4P8H
- *FPQC*-No.68
6)   *Danza Lucumi*, 4P8H
- *FPQC*-No.17
7)   *Danza Negra*, 4P8H
- *FPQC*-No.75
8)   *No Puedo Contigo (I Cannot Make You Understand)*, 4P8H
- *FPQC*-No.210
9)   *En Tres por cuatro (In Three-Quarter Time)*, 4P8H
- *FPQC*-No.212
10)   *Lola está de Fiesta (Lola is Celebrating)*, 4P8H
- *FPQC*-No.211
11)   *Malagueña*, 4P8H
- *FPQC*-No.20
12)   *Speak No More*, 4P8H
- *FPQC*-No.176
13)   *¿Porqué te vas? (Why Do You Go?)*, 4P8H
- *FPQC*-No.208

LENZBERG, Julius
PAUL, Oscar, arr.
> *Little Hero's March*, 1P6H
- Lam (©1903)
  LC-M213.P

LÉONARD, Robert
BURCHARD, Carl (1820-1896), arr.
> *Königs-Husaren, Marche brillante, Op. 16*, 2P8H
- And (©1924)

LEONCAVALLO, Ruggiero (1858-1919), Italian
1) MAILAND, Sonzogno, arr.
> *Der Bajazzo*, 2P8H
>> 1. *Prolog*
>> 2. *Intermezzo*
>> 3. *Fantasie*
>> 4. *Tempo di Menuetto e Gavotta*
>> 5. *Serenata*
- Fur (©1893)
  LC-M216.L37
2) WAGNER, E.D. and F. BRISSLER, arr., Op. 80, No. 56
> *Pantins vivants*, 2P8H
- Rie

LERMAN, J.W., composer and arr.
George Molineaux Collection (New York Pub.), Library of
Congress:
1) *American Patriotic Medley*, 1P6H
- (©1908)
  LC-M213.L
2) *Birthday March*, 1P6H
- (©1908)
  LC-M213.L
3) *Blue Bells of Scotland*, 1P6H
- (©1911)
  LC-M213.L472
4) *Cupids Contest*, 1P6H

- (©1900)
  LC-M213.L472
5) MEACHAM-LERMAN, *Cyclone Galop*, 1P6H
- (©1913)
  LC-M213.M
6) SCHUBERT-LERMAN, *Les dames de Seville*, 1P6H
- (©1914)
  LC-M213.L472
7) MEACHAM-LERMAN, *Drill March*, 1P6H
- (©1913)
  LC-M213.L
8) *Elfin Pranks*, 1P6H
- (©1905)
  LC-M213.L471
9) *E.Z. Gavotte*, 1P6H
- (©1914)
  LC-M213.L472
10) *E.Z. March*, 1P6H
- (©1914)
  LC-M213.L472
11) *E.Z. Mazurka*, 1P6H
  (©1913)
  LC-M213.L
12) *E.Z. Polka*, 1P6H
- (©1913)
  LC-M213.L
13) *E.Z. Schottische*, 1P6H
- (©1914)
  LC-M213.L472
14) *E.Z. Waltz*, 1P6H
- (©1905)
  LC-M213.L47
15) LANG-LERMAN, *Flower Song*, 1P6H
- (©1900)
  LC-M213.L47
16) *Harum Scarum Galop*, 1P6H
- (©1908)
  LC-M213.L

17) *Hazel March*, 1P6H
- (©1905)
  LC-M213.L471
18) *High Spirits, Two-step*, 1P6H
- (©1905)
  LC-M213.L471
19) DVOŘÁK-LERMAN, *Humoreske*, 1P6H
- (©1914)
  LC-M213.L472
20) KJERULF-LERMAN, *Last Night*, 1P6H
- (©1911)
  LC-M213.L472
21) *Linwood Waltz*, 1P6H
- (©1914)
  LC-M213.L472
22) *Lots O'Fun Polka*, 1P6H
- (©1911)
  LC-M213.L472
23) MOLLOY-LERMAN, *Loves Old Sweet Song*, 1P6H
- (©1908)
  LC-M213.M
24) SMITH, S.-LERMAN, *Marchedes tambours*, 1P6H
- (©1905)
  LC-M213.L47
25) MEACHAM-LERMAN, *March of the Juniors*, 1P6H
- (©1913)
  LC-M213.M
26) WORK, H.C.-LERMAN, *Marching Through Georgia*, 1P6H
- (©1908)
  LC-M213.W
27) *Medley of March Masterpieces*, 1P6H
- (©1914)
  LC-M213.L472
28) CARL-LERMAN, *National Guard Grand Parade March*
       1P6H
- (©1914)
  LC-M213.L472

29) *Off to School March*, 1P6H
- (©1905)
     LC-M213.L47

30) FOSTER,S.-LERMAN, *Old Folks at Home*, 1P6H
- (©1905)
     LC-M213.L471

31) FAURÉ-LERMAN, *The Palms*, 1P6H
- (©1905)
     LC-M213.L471

32) *Pell Mell Galop*, 1P6H
- (©1905)
     LC-M213.L47

33) *Playfellows Waltz*, 1P6H
- (©1911)
     LC-M213.L472

34) *Playful Pickaninnies*, 1P6H
- (©1905)
     LC-M213.L47

35) *Pleasant Recollections, Reverie*, 1P6H
- (©1911)
     LC-M213.L472

36) *Russian Peasant Dance*, 1P6H
- (©1914)
     LC-M213.L472

37) *Sacred Melody of Hymn Tunes*, 1P6H
- (©1911)
     LC-M213.L472

38) *Silvery Thistle (L'Argentine)*, 1P6H
- (©1914)
     LC-M213.L472

39) *Slap Bang Galop*, 1P6H
- (©1905)
     LC-M213.L471

40) GOUNOD-LERMAN, *Soldier's Chorus* from *Faust*, 1P6H
- (©1911)
     LC-M213.L472

41) *Tambourine Dance*, 1P6H
- (©1914)
     LC-M213.L472

42) BIZET-LERMAN, *Toreador's Song* from **Carmen**, 1P6H
- (©1905)
  LC-M213.L471
43) WAGNER-LERMAN, *Under the Double Eagle*, 1P6H
- (©1900)
  LC-M213.L47
44) *Waltz of the Elves*, 1P6H
- (©1913)
  LC-M213.M

LIADOV, Anatoli (1855-1914), Russian
FPQC, arr.
     Musical Snuff Box, 4P8H
- *FPQC*-No.56

LICHNER, Heinrich (1829-1898), German
MÜLLER, Julius E., arr.
     Au revoir, 1P6H
- Will (©1885)
  LC-M213.L

de LIMA VIANNA
FPQC, arr.
     Dansa de Negros, 4P8H
- *FPQC*-No.25

LINDERS, Karl
HEARTZ, H.L., arr.
     Floating Water-lilies, Gavotte, 1P6H (Grade 3)
- W-S

LISZT, Franz (1811-1886), Hungarian
1) HERBERT, Theodore, arr.
     La regata veneziana, notturno [par] F. Liszt, 2P8H
- Sch   1888
  NYPL
2) HORN, August (1825-1870), arr.
     Rákóczy-Marsch, G. 117, 2P8H
- Schl

BBC:4572
3) KLEINMICHEL, Richard (1846-1901), arr.
    Hungarian Rhapsodie No. 2, 2P8H
- Cha
S,G (©1937)
BrM-g.547.j.(4.)
PCM-M216.L774.R2.1937
SBTS
- *PRG*:441
4) KRONKE, Emil, arr.
  a)   *Les préludes, Symphonic Poem No. 3*, 2P8H
- Br&H (©1906)
LC-M216.L57
UR-M216.L77.P
  b)   *Rapsodie hongroise IX: Le carnival de pesth*, 2P8H
- Scho (©1909)
NYPL-JMG 77-194
UR-M216.L77.R9
5) SITT, Hans, arr.
    Hungarian Rhapsody No. 2, 2P8H
- Scho
UR-M216.L77.U2.S
6) *FPQC*, arr.
  a)   *La Campanella* from *Paganini Etudes* (No. 3), 4P8H
- *FPQC*-No.98
  b)   *Don Juan Fantasy*, 4P8H
- *FPQC*-No.379
  c)   *Galop chromatique*, 4P8H
- *FPQC*-No.274
  d)   *Liebestraum*, 4P8H
- *FPQC*-No.38
  e)   *Mephisto Waltz*, 4P8H
- *FPQC*-No.392
  f)   *Räkóczy March*, 4P8H
- *FPQC*-No.4
  g)   *Hungarian Rhapsody No. 2*, 4P8H
- *FPQC*-No.234
  h)   *Hungarian Rhapsody No. 12*, 4P8H
- *FPQC*-No.333

i) *Waldesrauschen*, 4P8H
- *FPQC*-No.50

LONGAS, Federico (1893-1968), Spanish
FPQC, arr.
   Catalina (An Impression of Spain), 4P8H
- *FPQC*-No.215

LORTZING, (Gustav) Albert (1801-1851), German
BURCHARD, Carl (1820-1896), arr.
   Overture to *Der Wildschütz (oder Die Stimme der Natur)*
   (1842), 2P8H
- Br&H (©1873 or ©1874) (*15)
   PCM-Rare book. M216.A3.18--
   (Achthändig Ouverturen, No. 1)

LOUMEY, August, American
LOSSÉ, F., arr.
1)   *Pussy's Concert Waltz*, 1P6H (Grade 2)
- Nor (©1885)
   LC-M213.L
2)   *Woodland Pleasures March*, 2P8H (can be played with the
       addition of an organ)
- Nor

LÖW, Joseph, German
PARLOW, Edmund (1855-?), arr.
   Russicher Kosaken Tanz, Op. 570, No. 3, 2P8H
- Schm (©1906)
   LC-M216.L64

LYNES, Frank (1858-1913), American
PARLOW, Edmund (1855-?), arr.
1)   *The Hunter's Song, Op. 14, No. 3*, 1P6H (Easy)
- Schm (©1890; ©1909)
   LC-M213.L
2)   *Die Marionetten Waltzer, Op. 14, No. 6*, 2P8H (Easy)
- Schm (©1906)
   LC-M216.L95

UR-M216.L988.M
3)   *The Paper Chain, Waltz,* 1P6H (Easy)
- Schm

MACDOWELL, Edward Alexander (1860-1908), American
FPQC, arr.
1)   *From Uncle Remus, Woodland Sketch, Op. 51, No. 7,* 4P8H
- *FPQC*-No.328
2)   *To a Water Lily, Woodland Sketch, Op. 51, No. 6,* 4P8H
- *FPQC*-No.337
3)   *To a Wild Rose, Woodland Sketch, Op. 51, No. 1,* 4P8H
- *FPQC*-No.327

MAHLER, Gustav (1860-1911), Austrian
BOCKLET, Heinrich von, arr.
          Symphony No. 2 in C Minor/E-Flat Major (Resurrection)
          (1888-1894; rev. 1903) 2P8H (Mahler arr. for 2P4H in
          1895)
- UE (©1914)
- *TPR*:155

MARCELLO, Benedetto (1686-1739), Italian
HORNIBROOK, Wallace, arr.
          Psalm XIX from *Estro poetico-armonico, No. 18, para fasi*
          sopra di primi [secondi] 25 salmi [Psalm 18 of the Latin
          Vulgate numbering used by Marcello; arr. of the 1st verse
          only] (Originally for 4 voices--ATTB--and continuo) (1724-
          1726), 2P4H or 8H or 12H
- Photocopy of manuscript
  IU-M215.M3.E7

MARCOTTE, Don and Zequinha ABREU
FPQC, arr.
          Tico-Tico, 4P8H
- *FPQC*-No.375

MARIE, Gabriel (1852-1926), French
FPQC, arr.
    Cinquantaine, 4P8H
- *FPQC*-No.301

MARTINI
ZILCHER, Paul (1855-1943), arr.
    Gavotte in F Major, 1P6H
- Schm (©1928)

MASCAGNI, Pietro (1863-1945), Italian
MOELLING, Theodore, arr.
    Intermezzo from *Cavalleria Rusticana*, 1P6H
- Dit (©1898)
    LC-M213.M

MASSENET, Jules (Emile Frédéric) (1842-1912), French
FPQC, arr.
    The Dream of Des Grieux from *Manon*, 4P8H
- *FPQC*-No.332

MATTEI, Tito (1841-1914)
1) BLASSER, Gustav (1857-?), arr.
    Bouquet de fleurs, Deuxième valse de concert, Op. 27,
        2P8H
- And (©1924)
2) WOLFF, Bernhard, arr.
    Le tourbillon, Grande valse de concert, Op. 22, 2P8H
- And (©1924)

MEACHAM, Frank W., American
STONE, Alonzo, arr.
    Restless Galop, 1P6H (3rd Grade)
- W-S (©1899)
    LC-M213.M

MEALE, J.A.
AUSTIN, Ernest, arr.
    Crimson Sunset, Pièce caractéristique, 1P6H
- (©1916)
  LC-M213.M

MÉHUL, Étienne Nicolas (1763-1817), French
BURCHARD, Carl (1820-1896), arr.
1)   *Jagd-Ouverture: La chasse* from *Le jeune Henri* (1797),
    2P8H
- Hofm (©186-?)(*23)
  PCM-Rare book.M216.A3.18--
  (Achthändig Ouvertüren, No. 10)
2)   *Overture* to *Josephin Aegypten*, 2P8H
- Hofm (©186-?)(*11)
  PCM-Rare book.M216.A3.18--
  (Achthändig Ouvertüren, No. 3)

MEIGS, Alice H., American
MOELLING, Theodore, arr.
    Gladsome Love Yorke, 1P6H
- Ell (©1893)
  LC-M213.M

MENDELSSOHN-BARTHOLDY, (Jacob Ludwig) Felix (1809-
    1847), German
1) BEY, Adolf, arr.
    Elfenmarsch aus dem Sommernachtstraum, 2P8H
- Scho
  PCM
2) BISSELL, Thomas, arr.
    Wedding March from *A Midsummer Night's Dream*, 1P6H
- Dit (©1885)
  LC-213.M
3) BRISSLER, Franz, arr.
  a)   *Ouverture in C Major (Trumpet Overture), Op. 101*, 2P8H
      Allegro vivace
- Br&H (©1875)
  LC-M216.M3.Op.101

b) *Ouverture: Heimkehr aus der Fremde, Op. 89*, 2P8H
- Br&H (©1873 or ©1874)
  LC-M216.M3.H562
4) BURCHARD, Carl (1820-1896), arr.
  Overture to *Ein Sommernachtstraum, Op. 21* (1826), 2P8H
- And (©1924)
5) BUSONI, Ferruccio (Dante Michelangelo Benvenuto)(1866-1924), arr.
  Symphony No. 1 in C Minor, Op. 11 (1824), 2P8H
- Br&H
6) CESI, Beniovrino, arr.
  Notturno, Scherzo, Marcia Nuziale, 2P8H
- Ric
  M216.M3.S583
7) HERBERT, Theodor, arr.
  a) *Venetianisches Gondellied in A Minor*, from **Lieder ohne Worte**, *Op. 62, No. 5, Vol. VI* (1824-1844), 1P6H
- Scho (Kzd)
  b) *Venezianisches Gondellied* from **Lieder ohne Worte**, *Op. 19, No. 6, Vol. I* (1829-1830), 1P6H
     Andante sostenuto
- Scho (Kzd)
8) HERMANN, Friedrich, arr.
  a) *Ouverture:* **Die Hochzeit des Comacho**, *Op. 10*, 2P8H
- Br&H
  LC-M216.M3.H664
  b) *[5] Ouvertüren*, 2P8H
     1. *Ein Sommernachtstraum, Op. 21* (1826)
     2. *Fingals Höhle, Op. 26* (1830)
     3. *Meeresstille und glückliche Fahrt, Op. 27* (1828)
     4. *Märchen von die schönen Melusine, Op. 32* (1833)
     5. *Ruy Blas, Op. 95* (1839)
- P,CF (©187-?)
  ASU-M216.M54.H4P.P
  Cur-M216.M537.096.187-
  UR-M216.M5.0
- *TPR*:155
9) HORN, August (1825-1893), arr.
  a) *Kriegsmarsch der Priester aud **Athalia**, Op. 74*, 2P8H

- Br&H
  NYPL
  b)   *Symphony No. 2 in B-Flat Major, Op. 52*, 2P8H
- Br&H
  BBC-5984
  c)   *Symphony No. 3 in A Minor, Op. 56 (Scottish)* (1830-1842), 2P8H
- Br&H (©1855)
  BrM-g.635.h.(2.)
  d)   *Symphony No. 4 in A Major, Op. 90 (Italian)*, 2P8H
- Br&H
  UR-M216.M53.4H

10) KELLER, Robert, arr.
       Overture to *Ein Sommernachtstraum, Op. 21*, 2P8H
- Sim (©1913)
  UR-M216.M53.M

11) KIRCHNER, Theodor (1823-1903), arr.
  a)   *Symphony No. 3 in A Minor, Op. 56 (Scottish)*, 2P8H
- Br&H
  UR-M216.M53.3
  b)   *Symphony No. 4 in A Major, Op. 90 (Italian)*, 2P8H
- P,CF
  UR-M216.M53.SK

12) PAUER, Ernest (1826-1905), arr.
       Overture to *Ruy Blas (*1839), *Op. 95*, 2P8H
- Aug (©1894)
  BrM-e.378.(11.)
  UR-M216.M53.rP

13) SARTORIO, Arnoldo (1853-1936), 1841-1844, arr.
  a)   *Allegretto grazioso in A Major, Op. 62, No. 6, Vol. VI (Spring Song)* (1842-1844), 1P6H
- P,T (©1924)
  LC-M213.M5.S3
  b)   *Wedding March* from *Ein Sommernachtstraum*, 2P8H
- P,T (©1925)
  LC-M216.M3.S5.S3

14) SCHUBERT, Ferdinand Lukas (1794-1859), arr.
  a)   *Overture* to *Athalia, Op. 74*, 2P8H
- Br&H (©1862)

LC-M216.M3.A868

b)   *Overture* to *den Hebriden (Fingals Höhle), Op. 26* (1830), 2P8H
- Br&H (©1846 or 1874)

c)   *Overture* to *Mährchen von der schönen Melusine, Op. 32,* 2P8H
- Br&H (©1847?)

LC-M216.M3.M3

d)   *Overture* to *Meeresstille und glückliche Fahrt, Op. 27,* 2P8H
- Br&H (©1848)

LC-M216.M3.M4

e)   *Overture* to Shakespeare's *Ein Sommernachtstraum, Op. 21,* 2P8H
- Br&H (©1846)

LC-M216.M3.S568

f)   *Ouvertüren,* 2P8H

Band 1:
1. *Ein Sommernachtstraum, Op. 21*
2. *Fingals Höhle (Hebriden), Op. 26*
3. *Meeresstile und glückliche Fahrt, Op. 27*

Band 2:
4. *Märchen von der schönen Melusine, Op. 32*
5. *Ruy Blas, Op. 95*
- Br&H

NYPL--Nos.1,2,3(Band 1)

UR--No.1:M216.M53.so

   No.4:M216.M53.sm

15) WAGNER, E.D. and F. BRISSLER, arrs.

a)   *Presto in C Major, Op. 67, No. 4, Vol. VI (Spinning Song)*(1843-1845), 2P8H
- Rie (*7)

PCM-M216.M537.Op.67.No.4B (See *Beliebte Compositionen für zwei Pianoforte zu acht Händen,* No. 36)

b)   *Capriccio in E Major/Minor, Op. 118* (1837), 2P8H
- Rie (Op. 50, No. 58)

16) *FPQC*, arr.
   a)   *II. Canzonetta* from **String Quartet in E-Flat Major, Op.**
         12, 4P8H
- *FPQC*-No.357
   b)   *Fingal's Cave Overture*, 4P8H
- *FPQC*-No.199
   c)   *On Wings of Song*, 4P8H
- *FPQC*-No.45
   d)   *Overture* to **A Midsummer Night's Dream**, 4P8H
- *FPQC*-No.131
   e)   *Prelude and Fugue, Op. 35, No. 3*, 4P8H
- *FPQC*-Nos.40,67
   f)   *Scherzo* from **Octet, Op. 20**, 4P8H
- *FPQC*-No.41
   g)   *Scherzo in E Minor*, 4P8H
- *FPQC*-No.1
   h)   *Scherzo* from **A Midsummer Night's Dream**, 4P8H
- *FPQC*-No.66
   i)   *Spinning Song*, 4P8H
- *FPQC*-No.112
   j)   *Spring Song, Op. 62, No.6*, 4P8H
- *FPQC*-No.258
   k)   *Tarantella* from **Songs Without Words, No. 45**, 4P8H
- *FPQC*-No.95
   l)   *Venetian Boat Song, Op. 30, No. 2*, from **Songs Without**
         Words, No. 6, 4P8H
- *FPQC*-No.190
17) Arr. by ?
         Kinderstück in G Minor, Op. 72, No. 5 (1842-1847), 2P8H
- P,T (©1847)
- *PRG*:441

MERCADANTE, Saverio Raffaele Francesca Donato (1797-
         1870), Italian
DRESSLER, Theodore, arr.
         Era Stella del Mattino from **Il Guiramento**, 1P6H
- Dit (©1887)
   LC-M213.M

MERO, W.P., arr.
   Norwegian Hunter's March, 2P8H
- P,T (©1910)
   LC-M216.M37

MESSONIER
FENIMORE, W.P., arr.
1)   *Bon Ton Gavotte*, 2P8H (ad. lib. organ)
- Nor
2)   *Merry Woodbird Polka*, 1P6H
- Nor (©1889)
   LC-M213.M

MEYER
1) *Kirmes Waltzes*, 2P8H (ad. lib. organ)
- Nor
2) FENIMORE, W.P., arr.
   Rêve des fées, Grande valse, 2P8H
- Nor (©1886)
   LC-M216.093
3) *The Village Band; Rustic Dance*, 2P8H (ad. lib. organ)
- Nor
4) LOSSE, F., arr.
   Young May Queen March, 2P8H (ad. lib. organ)
- Nor (©1885)
   LC-M216.093

MEYERBEER, Giacomo (Jakob Liebmann) (1791-1864), German
1) AUZENDE, A.M., arr.
   Pas de cinq from **Robert le diable** (1831), 2P8H
- Brau (©1886)
   BrM-h.3291.a.(10.)
2) FOWLER, J.A., arr.
   [Coronation] March from **Le prophète**, 2P8H
- Hal
   LC-M216.F68.M9
3) KRAMER, arr.
   Coronation March from **Le prophète** (1849), 1P6H
- S,G

- *PRG*:441
4) SARTORIO, Arnoldo (1853-1936), arr.
   a)   *Coronation March* from *Le prophète* (1849), 1P6H; 2P8H
- S,G (1P6H)
- WM (©1929)
- *PRG*:441
   b)   *Coronation Waltz* from *Le prophète* (1849), 2P8H
- WM
- *PRG*:441
5)   *Krönungsmarsch aus der Oper Der Prophet*, 2P8H
- Br&H (*7)
  NYPL

MICHEUZ, G.
BIEDERMANN, Edward J., arr.
      Attention! Military March, 1P6H
- F,J (©1900)
  M213.M

MILES and ZIMMERMAN, Americans
FPQC, arr.
      Anchors Aweigh, 4P8H
- *FPQC*-No.404

MILHAUD, Darius (1892-1974), French
FPQC, arr.
      III. Brazileira from *Scaramouche, Op. 165b*, 4P8H
- *FPQC*-No.238

MITTLER, F., American
FPQC, arr.
1)   *Barnyard Polka*, 4P8H
- *FPQC*-No.259
2)   *Christmas Vision*, 4P8H
- *FPQC*-No.246
3)   *First Piano Quartet March*, 4P8H
- *FPQC*-No.410
4)   *Jumping Beans (A Novelty)*, 4P8H
- *FPQC*-No.286

5)   *Lazy Susie's Music Box*, 4P8H
- *FPQC*-No.299
6)   *Polonaise*, 4P8H
- *FPQC*-No.257
7)   *Tango Desperado*, 4P8H
- *FPQC*-No.303
8)   *Valse sentimentale*, 4P8H
- *FPQC*-No.250

MOELLING, Theodore, arr., American
1)   **CZIBULKA**, Stephanie, *Gavotte de la princesse*, 1P6H
2)   **DELIBES**, L., *Pizzicati* from *Sylvia*, 1P6H
3)   **MEYERBEER**, G., *Coronation March* from *Le prophète*,
        1P6H
4)   **MICHAELIS**, Theodore, *The Turkish Patrol March*,
        1P6H
5)   **WAGNER**, R., *Bridal Chorus* and *March* from *Lohengrin*,
        1P6H
6)   **WAGNER**, R., *March* from *Tannhaüser*, 1P6H
- Dit (©1884)
  LC-M213.M7.N3

MONTI
FPQC, arr.
1)   *Czardas*, 4P8H
- *FPQC*-No.125
2)   *Spanish Dances, Op. 12, Nos. 1* and *5*, 4P8H
- *FPQC*-Nos.138,46

MOSZKOWSKI, Moritz (1854-1925),
  Polish
1) GURLITT, Cornelius (1820-1901), arr.
        Valse brillante in A-Flat Major, 2P8H
- S,G (©1902)
  ASU-M216.M635.V3.P
  PCM-M216.M916
  UR-M216.M916.V214.1902
- *PRG*:441
- *TPR*:155

2) REINHARD, August, arr.

    Wälzer-Suite, Fünf Walzer, Op. 8, 2P8H

    1. *Allegro moderato*

    2. *Pesante e lugubre*

    3. *Allegro grazioso (In Canonischer Weise)*

    4. *Vivace assai*

    5. *Pomposo ed energico, ma non troppo allegro*

- Sim (©1898)

  LC-M216.784

3) STOUGHTON, R.S., arr.

    Valse in E Major, op. 31, No.1, 2P8H

- P,T (©1940)

  LC-M216.M

4) WAGNER, E.D. and F. BRISSLER, arrs. (Op. 80, Nos. 45 and 47)

    a)   *Mazurka, Op. 60, No. 3*, 2P8H

- Rie (©1902)

  LC-M213.M78

    b)   *Minuetto, Op. 56, No. 6*, 2P8H

- Rie (©1902)

  LC-M216.M782

5) WOLFF, Bernhard, arr.

    Spanische Tänze, Op. 12, 2P8H

- P,CF(*35)

  ASU-M216.M635.Op.12.1900

  UR-M216.M916.sw

6) Arr. by ?

    a)   *Serenata*, 2P8H

- P,T

    b)   *Spanish Dance, Op. 12, No. 1*, 2P8H

- Hin

  BBC-12737

- P,CF (1990 catalogue listing)

- *PRG*:440

    c)   *Waltzer*, 1P6H

- MAU

MOZART, Wolfgang Amadeus (1756-1791), Austrian
1) BENDEL, Franz (1833-1874), arr.
    Menuet favori, 2P8H
- Rie (*6)
  PCM-M215.6.B458
2) BRUNNER, Christian Traugott (1792-1874), arr.
    *Quintet für Pianoforte, Hoboe, Clarinette, Horn und Fagott
    in E-Flat Major, K.452* (1784), 2P8H
- Hofm (©1862)
  NYPL
- *TPR*:155
3) BURCHARD, Carl (1820-1896), arr.
    a)   *Octett für 2 Oboen, 2 Clarinetten, 2 Hörner und 2 Fagotts*,
         2P8H
- H,G (©186-?)
  NYPL
    b)   *Symphony No. 39 in E-Flat Major, K.543*, 2P8H
- Br&H
  UR-M216.M93.39
    c)   *Symphony No. 40 in G Minor, K.550*, 2P8H
- Br&H
  UR-M216.M93.40
    d)   *Symphony No. 41 in C Major, K.551 (Jupiter)*, 2P8H
- Br&H (©188-?)
  Cur-M216.M939.K.551.188-(piano part I only)
    e)   *III. Rondo alla Turca* from **Sonata in A Major, K.331**,
         2P8H
- And (©1924)
4) BUSONI, F./*FPQC*, arrs.
    Rondo Duettino Concertante (last movement from the **Piano
    Concerto No. 19 in F Major** by Mozart), 4P8H
- *FPQC*-No.163
5) CARPER, Virginia Speiden, arr.
    German Dance in C Major, K.605, No.3, 2P8H
    (Elementary class IV)
- CPP/Bel
- S,G (©1970)

6) CLARKE, Mary Elisabeth, arr.
   Wind Serenade, 2P8H (Intermediate)
- Myk (1990 catalogue listing)
7) HERBERT, Theodore, arr.
   III. Minuet from *Symphony No. 39 in E-Flat Major, K.543*
   (1788), 1P6H
- F,C (©1908)
  Cur-M213.M939.K.543c
  LC-M213.M939
  MAU
- *PRG*:441
8) KELLER, Robert, arr.
   Overture to *The Marriage of Figaro*, 2P8H
- Sim
  UR-M216.M93n
9) KIRCHNER, Theodor (1823-1903), arr.
   a)   *Symphony No. 39 in E-Flat Major, K.543*, 2P8H
- P,CF
  UR-M216.M93.39K
   b)   *Symphony No. 40 in G Minor, K. 550*, 2P8H
- P,CF (©188-?)
  Cur-M216.M939.K.550.188-
   c)   *Symphony No. 41 in C Major, K. 551 (Jupiter)*, 2P8H
- Br&H
  UR-M216.M93.41
- P,CF
  UR-M216.M93.41K
10) LAST, Joan, arr.
   III. Minuet and Trio from *Symphony No. 40 in G Minor,*
   K. 550, 2P6H or 8H
- Aug (©1962)
  SBTS
11) PARLOW, Edmund (1855-?), arr.
   Minuetto giocoso from *Eine kleine Nachtsmusik Serenade*
   in G Major, K. 525, 2P8H
- Schm (©1906)
  PCM-M215.6.M939.K525.1907
  LC-M216.M85

12) PERRIER, arr.
    III. Minuet from *Symphony No. 39 in E-Flat Major, K.*
    543, 1P6H
- H,F
13) RÖSLER, Gustav, arr.
    Ouvertüren, 2P8H
    1. *Don Juan*
    2. *Die Hochzeit des Figaro*
    3. *Die Zauberflöte*
    4. *Titus*
- P,CF (Lit)
  PCM-No.1:M216.M939.K.527.19--
  UR-M216.M93.O
14) SCHMIDT, Gustav Martin, arr.
    Six grandes sinfonies de Mozart: [No. 41 in C Major, K.
    551 (Jupiter)], 2P8H
- Kle
  LC-M216.M85.S2
15) TIMM, Henry Christian (1811-1892), arr.
  a)   *Vedrai Carino* from *Don Giovanni, K. 527* (1787), 2P8H
- Hofm;S,G (©1891)
  LC-M216.T58.C5
  b)   *Serenade* from *Don Giovanni*, 2P8H
- Hofm;S,G (©1891)
  LC-M216.T58.C5
  c)   *Batti, batti* from *Don Giovanni*, 2P8H
- Hofm;S,G (©1891)
  LC-M216.T58.C5
16) ZILCHER, Paul (1855-1943), arr.
    Gavotte from *Idomeneo* (1781), 2P8H
- Schm (©1937)   1781
  Cur-M216.M939.K.367.1937
17) *FPQC*, arr.
  a)   *Air with Variations*, 4P8H
- *FPQC*-No.268
  b)   *Sonata in D Major, K. 448, III. Allegro molto*, 4P8H
- *FPQC*-No.387
  c)   *Sonata in D Major, K. 381, II. Andante* and *III. Presto*,
    4P8H

- *FPQC*-No.265a,b
  d)   *Canzonetta* from *Don Juan*, 4P8H
- *FPQC*-No.241
  e)   *Little Jig*, 4P8H
- *FPQC*-No.273
  f)   *Minuet* from *Divertimento No. 17 in D Major*, 4P8H
- *FPQC*-No.251
  g)   *III. Rondo alla Turca* from *Sonata in A Major, K. 331*, 4P8H
- *FPQC*-No.19
  h)   *Rondo* (*last movement* from *Haffner Serenade in D Major*), 4P8H
- *FPQC*-No.12
  i)   *Sonata in C Major, I*, 4P8H
- *FPQC*-No.266
18) Arr. by ?
     Gloria from *Mass No. 12*, 1P6H
- Dit

MÜLLER, Julius E., arr., American
1) **BAUMANN**, A., *Hope March*, 1P6H
- Witz (©1877)
  LC-M213.M96.T6
2) **BECKER**, O., *Demerara Polka Mazurka*, 1P6H
- Witz (©1877)
  LC-M213.M96.T6
3) **EVERSMAN**, Fred, Jr., *Le cuirassier, Galop*, 1P6H
- Witz (©1877)
  LC-M213.M96.T6
4) **HERZOG**, A., *Black Key Mazurka*, 1P6H
- Witz (©1877)
  LC-M213.M96.T6
5) **JUNGMANN**, Albert, *The Blacksmith*, 1P6H
- Witz (©1877)
  LC-M213.M96.T6
6) **LIEBACH**, Manuel, *Musical Box*, 1P6H
- Witz (©1877)
  LC-M213.M96.T6

7) **MAGRUDER**, *Centennial Schottische*, 1P6H
- Witz (©1877)
  LC-M213.M96.T6
8) **MÜLLER**, Julius E., *Consecration March*, 1P6H
- Witz (©1877)
  LC-M213.M96.T6
9) **MÜLLER**, Julius E., *Excelsior Polka*, 1P6H
- Witz (©1877)
  LC-M213.M96.T6
10) **MÜLLER**, Julius E., *Les bords du Danube*, 1P6H
- Witz (©1877)
  LC-M213.M96.T6
11) **MÜLLER**, Julius E., *Evergreen Waltz*, 1P6H
- Witz (©1877)
  LC-M213.M96.T6
12) **MÜLLER**, Julius E., *March of the Videttes*, 1P6H
- Witz (©1877)
  LC-M213.M96.T6

MÜLLER, Julius S., American
DRESSLER, William, arr.
   Coming Step March, Marche sentimentale, 1P6H
- Dit (©1870)
  LC-M213.M

MUSORGSKY, Modest Petrovich (1839-1881), Russian
1) KRAEHENBUEHL, David (*b* 1923), arr.
   Bydlo (The Ox-cart) from **Pictures at an Exhibition, Op. 11**
   (1874), *No. 4*, 2P8H
- WM (©1984)
- *PRG*:441
2) SILVER, Alfred J. (1870-?), arr.
   Hopak, Russian Dance, 1P6H
- F,J (©1912)
  LC-M213.M928

3) *FPQC*, arr.
   a)   *Coronation Scene* from **Boris Godunov**, 4P8H
- *FPQC*-No.40
   b)   *Hopak*, 4P8H
- *FPQC*-No.43
   c)   *Kinderscherz*, 4P8H
- *FPQC*-No.151
   d)   From *Pictures at an Exhibition, Op. 11*, 4P8H
         2.   *The Old Castle*
         3.   *Tuileries: Children Quarrelling after Play*
         4.   *Bydlo*
         5.   *Ballet of the Unhatched Chicks in their Shells*
         9.   *The Hut on Hen's Legs (Baba-Yaga)*
- *FPQC*-Nos.141,169,233,252,115

NESVADBA, Joseph, American
BURCHARD, Carl (1820-1896), arr.
      Loreley Paraphrase, Op. 17, 2P8H
- And (©1924)

NEVIN, Ethelbert (Woodbridge)(1862-1901), American
TREHARNE, Bryceson (1879-1948), arr.
      The Rosary, 1P6H (originally a women's club song on a
      text by R.C. Rogers)
- BMC
- *PRG*:441

NEWTON, Ernest, American
PARLOW, Edmund (1855-?), arr.
      Minuet in G Major, 1P6H (Easy)
- Schm (©1913)
  LC-M213.N

NICOLAI, (Carl) Otto (Ehrenfried)(1810-1849), German
1) EBERS, arr.
      Overture to **Die lustigen Weiber von Windsor** (1849), 2P8H
- And (©1924)

2) MOSENTHAL, H.S., arr.
   Overture to *Die lustigen Weiber von Windsor* (1849), 2P8H
- Bo&Bo (©185-?)
  NYPL
- P,CF
- *PRG*:441
3) PAUER, Ernst (1826-1905), arr.
   Overture to *Die lustigen Weiber von Windsor* (1849), 2P8H
- Aug
  UR-M216.N636m

NOEL, Henri
BENFORD, Robert T. (1898-?), arr.
1)   *March*, 1P6H
- S,G (©1961)   (*7)
- Cha
- *PRG*:441
2)   *Waltz*, 1P6H
- S,G
- *PRG*:441

NOHYNEK
THORNTON, Hans, arr.
      Quatre pièces, 2P8H
      1. *Capriccietto*
      2. *Valse mélancolique*
      3. *Rusticana*
      4. *Valse-Intermezzo*
- Bos (©1906)
  LC-M216.N75.T4

OFFENBACH, Jacques (1819-1880), French, of German   origin
1) LEEFSON, Maurits, arr.
   Barcarole from *Les contes d'Hoffman*, 1P6H
- Fau (©1915)
  LC-M213.032.Č5
2) ROSENAUER, A., arr.
   Offenbach, Les contes d'Hoffman, Op. 33, No. 2.
   Transcriptions petites sur des motifs des opéras les plus

       célèbres, 1P6H
- Forb (©1911)
  LC-M213.0
3) SILVER, Alfred J., arr.
       Barcarole from *Les contes d'Hoffman* (1881), 1P6H
- F,J (©1912)
  LC-M213.044
- Also P,T, 1P6H
4) Arr. by ?
       Les contes d'Hoffman Fantasy, 2P8H
- P,CF
- *PRG*:441
5) *FPQC*, arr.
    a)   *Orpheum (Sylophon)*, 4P8H
- *FPQC*-No.31
    b)   *Menuet à l'antique*, 4P8H
- *FPQC*-No.219
6) Arr. by ?
       La fille du tambour-major (1879) Fantasy, 2P8H
- P,CF
- *PRG*:441

OLDENBERG, Susanne, American
MOELLING, Theodore, arr.
       Rushing Torrent, March-galopade, 1P6H
- Ell (©1893)
  LC-M213.0

ORTH, Lizette Emma (Blood)(1858-1913), American
PARLOW, Edmund (1855-?), arr.
       In Uniform, March, Op. 29, No. 5, 2P8H (Easy)
- Schm (©1905)
  LC-M216.078

PADEREWSKI, J.J.
WAGNER, E.D. and F. BRISSLER, arrs.

Tatra-album, Op. 12, Nos. 1,4,6, 2P8H
- Rie

PADWA, V.
FPQC, arr.
    Electric, 4P8H
- *FPQC*-No.203

PAËR, Ferdinando (1771-1839), Italian
BURCHARD, Carl (1820-1896), arr.
    Sargines (1803), 2P8H
- And (©1924)

PAGANINI, Nicolò (1782-1840), Italian
LISZT, Franz (1811-1886), arr.; *FPQC*, arrs.
    La chasse, Paganini Etude No. 5, 4P8H
- *FPQC*-No.16

PALDI, Mari
PARLOW, Edmund (1855-?), arr.
    Neath Sunny Skies, Tarantelle, 1P6H
- Schm (©1922)
    LC-M213.P22.N3

PARLOW, Edmund (1855-?), American
DURAND, A., arr.
    Flying Squadron Galop, 1P6H; 2P8H
- Witz (©1890)
    LC-M216.P27
- P,T

PERGOLESI, Giovanni Battista (1710-1736), Italian
FPQC, arr.
    Nina, 4P8H
- *FPQC*-No.209

PETRELLA, Errico, Italian
TROMBERTA, G., arr.
    Sinfonia dell'opera Jone, 2P8H

- Luc (*24)
  NYPL

PIERNÉ, (Henri Constant) Gabriel (1863-1937), French
GUNTHER, Phyllis, arr.
> *Marche des petits soldats de plomb (March of the Little Tin*
> *Soldiers)* from ***Album pour mes petits amis**, Op. 14, No. 6*,
> 2P8H
- WM (©1984)

PLANQUETTE, Robert (1848-1903), French
PAUL, Oscar, arr.
> *Reverie* from ***Bells of Corneville***, 1P6H
- Lam (©1908)
  LC-M213.P713

POLDINI, Ede (Eduard)(1869-1957), Hungarian
FPQC, arr.
> *Murmuring Brook*, 4P8H
- *FPQC*-No.134

PORTER, Frank Addison (1859-1941), American
PARLOW, Edmund (1855-?), arr.
> *With Light Hearts, Waltz*, 1P6H (Easy)
- Schm (©1909)
  LC-M213.P

PRESS, Jacques
FPQC, arr.
> *Freilachs (Wedding Dance)*, 4P8H
- *FPQC*-No.385

PROKOFIEV, Sergei (Sergeyevitch)(1891-1953), Russian
1) *FPQC*, arr.
   a)   *Finale* from ***Classical Symphony**, Op. 25*, 4P8H
- *FPQC*-No.227
   b)   *Gavotte in D Major* from ***Classical Symphony**, Op. 25*,
        4P8H
- *FPQC*-No.101

c)   *II. Larghetto* from **Classical Symphony, Op. 25**, 4P8H
- *FPQC*-No.225
d)   *March* from **Love of Three Oranges**, 4P8H
- *FPQC*-No.146
e)   *Prelude in C Major, Op. 12, No. 7*, 4P8H
- *FPQC*-No.186
2) Arr. by ?
        Humorous Sketch. 2P8H
- NKAA
- *PRG*:441

PUCCINI, Giacomo (1858-1924), Italian
FPQC, arr.
        Fantasy based on **Madame Butterfly**, 4P8H
- *FPQC*-No.80

RACHMANINOV, Sergei Vasilevich (1873-1943), Russian
1) REBNER, Wolfgang Edward (*b* 1910), arr.
        Prelude in G Minor, Op. 23, No. 5 (1901), 2P8H
        Alla Marcia
- S,G (©1939)
  IU-M216.R119.P7
- *PRG*:441
2) *FPQC*, arr.
   a)   *Italian Polka*, 4P8H
- *FPQC*-No.193
   b)   *Prelude in C-Sharp Minor*, 4P8H
- *FPQC*-No.102
   c)   *Prelude in G Minor, Op. 23, No.5*, 4P8H
- *FPQC*-No.376

RAFF, Joseph Joachim (1822-1882), American
1) BURCHARD, Carl (1820-1896), arr.; rev. and fing. by William
        SCHARFENBERG
- P,T
- S,G (©1893)
  LC-M216.R15
- Rie,Op.80,No.50

2) MÖLLING, Theodore, arr.
    Polka de la reine, 1P6H; 2P8H
- Ell (©1893)
- LC-M213.R
  B.Nor

RAMEAU, Jean Philippe (1683-1764), French
FPQC, arr.
1)   *Musette*, 4P8H
- *FPQC*-No.202
2)   *Tambourin* (arr. in part by Godowsky), 4P8H
- *FPQC*-No.255

RATHBURN, Frederic G., American
PARLOW, Edmund (1855-?), arr.
    Festival Procession, 1P6H; 2P8H
- P,T (©1904)
  LC-M213.R;M216.R23.F3

RAVEL, Maurice (1875-1937), French
FPQC, arr.
1)   *Boléro*, 4P8H
- *FPQC*-No.171
2)   *Daybreak* from *Daphnis et Chloë, Deuxième suite*, 4P8H
- *FPQC*-No.356
3)   *La valse*, 4P8H
- *FPQC*-No.395

REDDINGTON, Katherine Wells, American
MÖLLING, Theodore, arr.
1)   *Dance of the Imps, Caprice*, 1P6H
- Ell (©1893)
  LC-M213.R
2)   *Moonlight on the Breakers, Presto*, 1P6H
- Ell (©1893)
  LC-M213.R
3)   *Twilight Wooing Reverie*, 1P6H
- Ell (©1893)
  LC-M213.R

REINECKE, Carl (Heinrich Carsten)(1824-1910), German
KÖLLING, Theodore, arr.
1)   *Ballet Music* from *König-Manfred*, 2P8H
- S,G (©1892)
   LC-M216.R35
2)   *Rustic Dance, Op. 266, No. 3*, 1P6H; 2P8H
- P,T (©1907)
   LC-M213.R36.K5

REISSIGER, Carl Gottlieb (1798-1859), German
BURCHARD, Carl (1820-1896), arr.
   Overture to *Die Felsenmühle*, 1P6H
- S,G (©1893)
   LC-M213.R

RICHTER, H. Ernst Friedrich (Edward)(1808-1879), German
BURCHARD, Carl (1820-1896), arr.
   Fest-Ouvertüre in D Major, Op. 100, 2P8H
- And (©1924)

RIES, Ferdinand
BERG, Albert W., arr.
   *Grande marche triomphale et finale tirées de l'ouverture
   solennelle*, (1863) 2P8H
- Pon (©1891)   1863
   LC-M216.R4.B3 and B32

RIMSKY-KORSAKOV, Nikolai Andreievich (1844-1908),
       Russian
1) LANGER, Eduard Leontevich (1835-1905), arr.
   Sadko, tableau musical pour orchestre, Op. 5 (1867; rev.
   1869 & 1892), 2P8H
- Jur (©1893)
   BBC-4570
   NYPL
   UR-M216.R577.SaL

2) WITHROW, Miriam Fox, arr.
   Dance of the Buffoons from *The Snowmaiden*, 2P8H
- Su (©1939)
  LC-M216.R
3) *FPQC*, arr.
   a)   *Capriccio Espagnol (Scene* and *Gypsy Song)*, 4P8H
- *FPQC*-No.204
   b)   *Dance of the Buffoons* from *The Snow Bride*, 4P8H
- *FPQC*-No.130
   c)   *Flight of the Bumble Bee*, 4P8H
- *FPQC*-No.3

RINGUET, Leon
LERMAN, J.W., arr.
1)   *Le carillon, Polka brillante, Op. 19*, 2P8H
- P,T (©1916)
  LC-M216.R
2)   *Promenade-Polka-March*, 1P6H
- P,T (©1908)
  LC-M213.R582

ROSSINI, Gioacchino (Antonio)(1792-1868), Italian
1) BURCHARD, Carl (1820-1896), arr.
   a)   *Overture* to *Barbier de Séville* (1816), 2P8H
- And (©1924)
   b)   *Overture* to *Elisabetta, regina d'Inghilterra* (1815), 2P8H
- Hofm (©185-?)
  PCM-Rare book.M216.A3.18--(See *Achthändig Ouvertüren, No. 4*)
   c)   *Overture* to *Die Italienerin in Algier* (1813), 2P8H
- Hofm (©186-?)(*17)
  PCM-Rare book.M216.A3.18--(See *Achthändig Ouvertüren, No. 11*)
   d)   *Overture* to *Othello (ossia Il Moro di Venezia)* (1816), 2P8H
- And (©1924)
   e)   *Overture* to *Semiramide*, 2P8H
- Hofm (©186-?)(*23)
  PCM-Rare book.M216.A3.18--(See *Achthändig Ouvertüren, No. 6*)

f)   *Overture* to *Siège de Corinthe* (1826), 2P8H
- And (©1924)
g)   *Overture* to *Tancrède* (1813), 2P8H
- And (©1924)
- Chu (1P6H)
2) CZERNY, Carl (1791-1857), arr.
   a)   *Overture* to *Guillaume Tell* (1828-1829), 8P32H
- Dia (©1830)   1830
   b)   *Overture* to *Semiramide* (1823), 8P32H
- Dia (©1830)   1830 (11½*)
  BBC-6148
  BU
  LC-M216.R63.C8 (incomplete)
  UCol-M216.R6.S4
3) DECOURCELLE, arr.
        Overture to *La Gazza Ladra*, 3P12H
- P,T
4) EBERS, arr.
        Overture to *Guillaume Tell* (1828-1824), 2P8H
- And (©1924)
5) LISZT, F./*FPQC*, arrs.
        La dansa (Tarantella), 4P8H
- *FPQC*-No.13
6) SCHMIDT, G.M., arr.
        Overture to *Guillaume Tell* (1828-1829), 2P8H
- Dit (12 3/4*)
  NYPL (from *Eight Hands: A collection of music well arranged for
        two pianos*)
- *TPR*:155
7) THALBERG, Sigismund (1812-1871), Swiss
        Overture to *Semiramide, ?*

RUBINSTEIN, Anton (Grigorievich)(1829-1894), Russian
1) BRISSLER, Friedrich, arr.
   a)   *Cosaque et petite russienne* from *Bal costumé* (1879) *Op.
        103, No. 11*, 2P8H
- Bo&Bo (©1886)
  PCM-M216.R896.Op.103.No.11
   b)   *Toréador et Andalouse* from *Bal costumé* (1879), *Op. 103,*

      No. 7, 2P8H
- Bo&Bo (©1886)
    PCM-M216.R896.Op.103.No.7
2) KLEINMICHEL, Richard (1846-1901), arr.
    a)   *No. 2: Lichtentanz der Bräute von Kaschmir* from
        Feramors, 2P8H
- Senf (©1902)
    LC-M216.R72.F3
    UR-M216.R896.Fli
    b)   *Melody in F*, 2P8H
- P,T (©1925)
    LC-M216.R72.M3
3) LANGER, Eduard Leontevich (1835-1905), arr.
    a)   *Cosaque et petite russienne* from *Bal costumé* (1879), *Op.*
        103, No. 11, 2P8H
- Jur
    UR-M216.R896.BC
    b)   *Danse des bayadères 1* from *Feramors*, 2P8H
- Jur
    UR-M216.R896.FL
    c)   *Finale* from *Bal costumé* (1879), *Op. 103, No. 20*, 2P8H
- Jur
    UR-M216.R896.BF
    d)   *Les ghinka* from *Le démon*, 2P8H
- Bes
    UR-M216.R896.DL
    e)   *Pêcheur napolitain et napolitaine* from *Bal costumé* (1879),
        Op. 103, No. 5, 2P8H
- Jur
    UR-M216.R896.BPel
    f)   *Pélerin et fantaisie (Etoile du soir)* from *Bal costumé*
        (1879), *Op. 103, No. 8*, 2P8H
- Jur
    UR-M216.R896.BPel
    g)   *Polonais et polonaise* from *Bal costumé* (1879), *Op. 103,*
        No. 9, 2P8H
- Jur
    UR-M216.R896.BPo
    h)   *Toréador et espagnole* from *Bal costumé* (1879), *Op. 103,*

　　　　No. 7, 2P8H
- Jur
　UR-M216.R896.BT
　i)　　*Trot de cavalerie, Morceau de salon* from **Bal costumé**
　　　　　(1879), *Op. 103, No. 7*, 2P8H
- Bo&Bo (©1886)
　PCM-M216.R896.Op.103,No.7
- Jur (©1890)
　TPR:155
4) SARTORIO, Arnoldo (1853-1936), arr.
　　　　Melody in F, 1P6H; 2P8H
- P,T (©1927)
　LC-M213.R89.S2
5) *FPQC*, arr.
　　　　Kamenoi Ostrow, 4P8H
- *FPQC*-No.61

SAINT-SAËNS, (Charles) Camille (1835-1921), French
1) GUIRAUD, Ernest (1837-1892), arr.
　　　　Danse macabre, Op. 40 (1874), 2P8H
- Dur (©1875) (*19)
　UR-M216.S152d
- Schoe
　NYPL
　PRG:442
2) ROQUES, Léon, arr.
　a)　　*Suite algérienne, Op. 60* (1880), 2P8H
- Dur (©1881)
　UR-M216.S152s
- *PRG*
- *TPR*:155
　b)　　*Symphony No. 3 in C Minor, Op. 78*, 2P8H
- Dur (©1910)
　UR-M216.S152.sy.3R
3) *FPQC*, arr.
　a)　　*Danse macabre*, 4P8H
- *FPQC*-No.113
　b)　　*The Swan* from **Carnival of the Animals**, 4P8H
- *FPQC*-No.108

4) Arr. by ?
   a)   *Overture* to *La princesse jaune, Op. 30* (1872), 2P8H
- Dur; Schoe (©1887)
  BrM-h.3181.c.(1.)
   b)   *Le rouet d'omphale, Op. 31* (1871), 2P8H
- Dur (©1872)
  UR-M216.S152r
  PRG:442

SANDOVAL, Miguel
FPQC, arr.
          Tacha-Tacha (Guaracha), 4P8H
- *FPQC*-No.382

SARASATE, Pablo de (1844-1908), Spanish
FPQC, arr.
          Zigeunur Weisen (Gypsy Airs), 4P8H
- *FPQC*-No.18

SARTORIO, Arnoldo (1853-1936), American
PARLOW, Edmund (1855-?), arr.
          Siegeszug, Marsch (The Victor's Return), Op. 174, No. 5,
          2P8H (Easy)
- Schm (©1905)
  LC-M216.S18

SAUER, Emil von (1862-1942), German
FPQC, arr.
          Music Box, 4P8H
- *FPQC*-No.174

SCARLATTI, (Giuseppe) Domenico (1685-1757), Italian
FPQC, arr.
1)   *Capriccio*, 4P8H
- *FPQC*-No.15
2)   *Pastorale*, 4P8H
- *FPQC*-No.21
3)   *Sonata No. 23*, 4P8H
- *FPQC*-No.188

SCHARWENKA, Xavier (1850-1924), Polish
KIRCHNER, F., arr.
  a)   *Gavotte*, 1P6H
- S,G (©1900)
  b)   *Polish Dance, Op. 3, No. 1*, 1P6H
- Aug
- P,T (©1906)
  LC-M213.S

SCHUBERT, Franz (Peter) (1797-1828), Austrian
1) BRUNNER, C.F., arr.
        Overture to *Rosamunde, Op. 26*, 2P8H
- Cra
  UR-M216.S384.Z0
2) BURCHARD, Carl (1820-1896), arr.
  a)   *Balletmusik* from *Rosamunde*, 2P8H
- Gla
  UR-M216.S384.RB
  b) *Symphony No. 8 in B Minor, D. 759*
     (Unfinished) (1822), 2P8H
- And (©1924)
3) DIETER, Bernard, arr.
        Moment Musicale in F Minor, Op. 94, No. 3, 2P8H
        Allegro moderato
- Su (©1939)
  LC-M216.S
4) HERBERT, Theodore, arr.
        Marche héroïque, Op. 27, No.3, 1P6H
- Dit (©1887)
  LC-M213.S
5) HORVÁTH, G., arr.
        Marche militaire in D Major, Op. 51, No. 1 (1818), 1P6H;
        2P8H
- P,T
  LC-M213.S
- S,G
- *PRG*:442
6) JANSEN, F.G., arr.
        Overture to *Rosamunde, D. 797* (1823), 2P8H

- Schl (©1885)
NYPL
- *TPR*:155
7) JELLY, arr.
    Minuet, 1P (3 or 4 parts), with an optional part for a second
    P
- S,G
- *PRG*:442
8) KIRCHNER, Theodor (1823-1903), arr.
    Symphony No. 8 in B Minor (Unfinished), 2P8H
- P,CF (©1888)
NYPL
UR-M216.S384.S8K
9) KRAEHENBUEHL, David (*b* 1923), arr.
    Four Country Dances, D. 814, K.7 (1824), 2P8H
- NKAA (©1969)
LC-M216.S28
10) KRONKE, Emil, arr.
    Soirée de Vienne, 4 Vols., 2P8H
- Schm (©1910)
LC-M216.S28.S6
11) LAST, Joan (*b* 1908), arr.
    Incidental Music to **Rosamunde, D. 797**, 2P8H
- Aug (©1961)
12) LIBA, Carl, arr.; ed. and fing. by William SCHARFENBERG
    Serenade in D Minor, 1P6H
    Moderato
- S,G (©1900)
UR-M213.S384s
13) MAHAN, Frederick Augustus (1847-1918), arr.
    Symphony in C Major (Great), 2P8H
- Autograph manuscript (©1896)
NYPL
14) PARLOW, Edmund (1855-?), arr.
    a)   *Children's March*, 2P8H (Easy)
- Schm (©1910)
LC-M216.S28.K52
    b)   *Deutsche Tänze, Op. 33*, 2P8H
- Kis (©1907)

UR-M216.S38.D

15) PAUER, Emil (1826-1905), arr.
      6 Celebrated Marches, 2P8H
- Aug
  UR-M216.S38.mP

16) SARTORIO, Arnoldo (1853-1936),
   arr.
   a)   *Marche militaire in D Major, Op. 51, No. 1*, 2P8H
- Dit
  LC-M213.S
- P,T
   b)   *Rustic Dance*, 1P6H
- Schm (©1951)
  LC-M213.S

17) TAYLOR, Colin, arr.
      Scherzo from **String Quartet in C Major, Op. 163, No. 2**,
      2P8H
- Aug (©1949) (*12)
  LC-M215.S

18) ZILCHER, Paul (1855-1943), arr.
      Children's March, 1P6H
- Aug (©1929)
  LC-M213.S39.C4

19) *FPQC*, arr.
   a)   *Andante* from **Sonatina, Op. 137, No. 1**, 4P8H
- *FPQC*-No.267
   b)   *Ballet Music* from **Rosamunde**, 4P8H
- *FPQC*-No.300
   c)   *Impromptu in B-Flat Major, Op. 142, No.3*, 4P8H
- *FPQC*-No.317
   d)   *Marche caractéristique, Op. 121, No.2*, 4P8H
- *FPQC*-No.362
   e)   *Marches militaires, Op. 51, Nos. 1* and *3*, 4P8H
- *FPQC*-Nos.8,111
   f)   *Moment musicale*, 4P8H
- *FPQC*-No.27
   g)   *Trout Variations (Die Forelle)*, 4P8H
- *FPQC*-No.26
   h)   *Variations and Fugue*, 4P8H

- *FPQC*-No.351
20) Arr. by ?
   a)   *Ballet Music* from *Rosamunde*, 1P6H
- P,T (©1930)
  LC-M213.S39.B2
   b)   *Four Country Dances*, 2P8H
- CMP
PRG:442
   c)   *Symphony in C Major (Great)*, 2P8H
- Br&H
  UR-M216.S384.S7

SCHUMANN, Robert (1810-1856), German
1) BILBRO, Mathilde, arr.
      Soldier's March, 1P8H
- WM (©1938)
2) HERMANN, Friedrich, arr.
      Overture zu Manfred, Op. 115, 2P8H
- Br&H (©1874-1879)
  Cur-M216.S392.Op.115.187-
3) HORN, August (1825-1893), arr.
   a)   *Symphony No. 1, Op. 38*, 2P8H
- Br&H
  UR-M216.S39.1
   b)   *Symphony No. 2, Op. 61*, 2P8H
- Br&H
  UR-M216.S39.2
   c)   *Symphony No. 3, Op. 97*, 2P8H
- Br&H (©1887)
  NYPL
   d)   *Symphony No. 4, Op. 120*, 2P8H
- Br&H
  UR-M216.S39.4
4) KIRCHNER, Theodor (1823-1903), arr.
   a)   *Overture zu Genoveva, Op. 81*, 2P8H
- P,CF (©1888)
  NYPL
   b)   *Overture zu Manfred, Op. 115*, 2P8H
- P,CF (©1888)

NYPL

   c)   *Symphony No. 1 in B-Flat Major, Op. 38*, 2P8H
- P,CF (©1895)
   PCM-M216.1.S392
   UR-M216.S392.Syk

   d)   *Symphony No. 2, Op. 61*, 2P8H
- P,CF
   UR-M216.S392.Syk

   e)   *Symphony No. 3 in E Major, Op. 97*, 2P8H
- P,CF (©1895)
   PCM-M216.1.S392
   UR-M216.S39.3K

   f)   *Symphony No. 4 in D Minor, Op. 120*, 2P8H
- P,CF (©1895)
   PCM-M216.1.S392.Op.120
- *PRG*:442

5) NAUMANN, Ernest Karl (1832-?), arr.
       Andante und Variationen in B-Flat Major, Op. 46 , 2P8H
- Br&H (©1875)(*17)
   PCM-M216.S392.Op.46.1875
   UR-M216.S392an

6) PARLOW, Edmund (1855-?), arr.
       Knecht Ruprecht from ***Album für die Jugend***, *Op. 68, No. 12*, 2P8H
- P,T (©1908)
   LC-M216.S38.Op.68
- *PRG*:442

7) REINHARD, August, arr.
       Piano Concerto in A Minor, Op. 54, 2P8H
- Scho
   PCM-M216.S392.C

8) RIEDEL, August, arr.
   a)   *Drei kleine Stücke aus Schumann's **Jugend Album**, Op. 68: Knecht Ruprecht*, 2P8H
- Pic (©1887)
   M216.S329.Op.68.1887
   b)   *Orgelfugue über B-A-C-H, Op. 60, No. 2*, 2P7H
- Sie (©1887) (*9)
   PCM-M216.S392.Op.60.No.2.1887

9) SARTORIO, Arnoldo (1853-1936), arr.

   a)   *Traveller's Song*, 2P8H
- WM
- *PRG*:442

   b)   *Wanderer's Song, Op. 35*, 1P6H
- P,T (©1924)
   LC-M213.S40.Op.35S3

10) WAGNER, E.D. and F. BRISSLER, arrs., Op. 80, Nos. 44 and 43

   a)   *Jagdlied, Op. 82, No. 8*, 2P8H
   Rie

   b)   *Scherzino, Op. 26, No. 3*, 2P8H
   Rie

11) *FPQC*, arr.

   a)   *Traumeswirren*, 4P8H
- *FPQC*-No.33

   b)   *The Fountain*, 4P8H
- *FPQC*-No.52

   c)   *Spanish Romance (The Smuggler)*, 4P8H
- *FPQC*-No.191

   d)   *Traumerei*, 4P8H
- *FPQC*-No.63

   e)   *Warum, Op. 12, No. 2*, 4P8H
- *FPQC*-No.139

12) Arr. by ?

       Sketch, 2P8H
- NKAA
- *PRG*:442

SCHYTTE, Ludwig Theodore (1848-1909)
WAGNER, E.D. and F. BRISSLER, arrs. Op. 80, No. 51

   a)   *Aubade, Op. 77, No. 1*, 2P8H
- Rie (©1904)
   LC-M216.S44

   b)   *Sylphs and Nixies, Rondo*, 1P6H (Moderately difficult)
- Rie

SCOTT, Sebastian, arr., American

   a)   *Three English Folk Tunes*, 1P6H

1. *Billy Boy*
2. *Waly, Waly*
3. *Dashing Away With the Smoothing Iron*

- Fr/En; c/o EAMD (1988 catalogue listing)
  b)   *Three Scottish Folk Tunes*, 1P6H
- RCM

SEROV, A.N.
SHEFER, A.N., arr.
>*Rognyeda, Dance of the Buffoons*, 2P8H

- Gut
  UR-M216.S486.Rd

SEYBOLD, Arthur (1868-1948)
PARLOW, Edmund (1855-?), arr.
>*Pierrot, Impromptu-valse, Op. 135*, 2P8H (Moderately difficult)

- Schm (©1913)
  LC-M216.S49

SEYFRIED, Ignaz Xaver Ritter von (1776-1841) (formerly attributed to Haydn)
PARLOW, Edmund (1855-?), arr.
>*Oxen Minuet*, 2P8H

- P,T (©1914)
  LC-M216.S495.0246

SHOSTAKOVICH, Dmitri (1906-1975), Russian
FPQC, arr.
1)   *Polka* from *The Golden Age*, 4P8H
- *FPQC*-No.194
2)   *Russian Dance* from *The Golden Age*, 4P8H
- *FPQC*-No.295
3)   *United Nations on the March (Thousands Cheer)*, 4P8H
- *FPQC*-No.282

SIBELIUS, Jean [or Johan] (Julius Christian)(1865-1957), Finnish
1) SCHAUM, John W. (*b* 1905), arr.
>*Finlandia, Op. 26, No. 7*, 2P8H

- CPP/Bel (©1959)
2) *FPQC*, arr.
  a) *Study*, 4P8H
- *FPQC*-No.55
  b) *Finlandia*, 4P8H
- *FPQC*-No.47

SIEWERT, Heinrich
BURTON, G., arr.
> *Chiming May Bells*, 1P6H
- F,J (©1899)
  M213.S

SINDING, Christian (1856-1941), Norwegian
FPQC, arr.
> *Rustle of Spring*, 4P8H
- *FPQC*-No.34

SMETANA, Bedřich [or Friedrich] (1824-1884), Bohemian
1) RIHM, Alexander, arr.
> *Overture* to *Die verkaufte Braut (The Bartered Bride)*,
> 2P8H
- Bo&Bo (©1909)
  LC-M216.S63.R6
2) *FPQC*, arr.
> *Polka*, 4P8H
- *FPQC*-No.32

SOEDERMANN, A., Swedish
FPQC, arr.
> *Swedish Wedding March*, 4P8H
- *FPQC*-No.81

SOUSA, John Philip (1854-1932), American
1) CAMPIGLIO, Paolo F., arr.
  a) *The Liberty Bell March*, 1P6H
- Chu (©1894)
  LC-M213.S68.L4
  b) *The Manhattan Beach March*, 1P6H

- Chu (©1894)
  LC-M213.S
2) CARPENTER/SMITH, eds.
    The Star Spangled Banner, 2P8H
- BMC
- *PRG*:442
3) CARPER, Virginia Speiden, arr.; John S. SMITH, ed.
    The Star Spangled Banner, 2P8H
- BMC (©1943)
  SBTS
4) GOULD, Morton (*b* 1913), arr.
    The Stars and Stripes Forever (1897), multiple pianos and
    orchestra
- S,G;Cha (NY rental library)   1953
- Letter from Gould, August 30, 1990
5) HOFMAN, Joseph, arr.
    The Star Spangled Banner, 10P20H
6) JORDAN, Harry C., arr.
  a)   *The Directorate March*, 1P6H
- Chu (©1894)
  b)   *King Cotton March*, 1P6H
- Chu (©1895)
  LC-M213.S
7) MERO, W.P., arr.
    El Capitán, 1P6H
- Chu (©1937)
  LC-M213.S
8) MITTLER, Franz (*b* 1893), arr.
    King Cotton March, 1P6H
- Chu (©1948)
  LC-M213.S
9) OREM, Preston Ware, arr.
    Keeping Step With the Union, 1P6H
- P,T (©1921)
  LC-M213.S68.K3
10) WILBERG, Mack (member of the American Piano Quartet), arr.
    The Stars and Stripes Forever, 2P8H
- Kj (©1988), WP 180, American Piano Quartet Series
11) *FPQC*, arr.

The Stars and Stripes Forever, 4P8H
- *FPQC*-No.393
12) Arr. by ?
   a)   *The Beau Ideal March*, 1P6H
- Cole (©1894)
  LC-M213.S
   b)   *The Bride-elect March*, 1P6H
- Chu (©1898)
  LC-M213.S
   c)   *The Charlatan March*, 1P6H
- Chu (©1898)
  LC-M213.S
   d)   *Hands Across the Sea*, 1P6H
- Chu (©1891)
  LC-M213.S
   e)   *The Stars and Stripes Forever*, 1P6H
- Chu (©1897)
  LC-M213.S
- P,T
- *PRG*:442
   f)   *The Washington Post*, 1P6H
- Cole (©1893)

SPINDLER, Fritz (1817-1905)
1) BERG, Albert W. (1825-1906), arr.
     Trot du cavalier, Caprice marzial, 2P8H
- Pon (©1902)
  LC-M216.S75
2) HERBERT, arr.
     Charge of the Huzzars, Galop, Op. 140, No. 3, 1P6H
- Dit (©187-?)
  LC-M213.S757.Op.140.H4
- F,C

SPOHR, Louis (1784-1859), German
1) BURCHARD, Carl (1820-1896), arr.
     Polonaise aus der Oper Faust, 2P8H
- Nau (©184-?)
  NYPL

2) TIMM, Henry Christian (1811-1892), arr.
   Notturno, Op. 34 (1815), 2P8H
- S,G (©1891)
  LC-M216.T58.C5
  PCM-M216.S762.Op.34.1891

SPONTINI, Gaspard (1774-1851)
BURCHARD, Carl (1820-1896), arr.
   Ballets et choeur from *Cortez*, 2P8H
- Schl
  UR-M216.S763.Co

STRAUSS, Eduard (1835-1916), Austrian
FPQC, arr.
   Bahn Frei, Polka, Op. 35, 4P8H
- *FPQC*-No.359

STRAUSS, Johann, Jr. (1825-1899), Austrian
1) TAUSIG, Carl (1841-1871), arr.; *FPQC*, arr.
   One Lives But Once; 4P8H
- *FPQC*-No.119
2) *FPQC*, arr.
   a)   *Blue Danube*, 4P8H
- *FPQC*-No.22
   b)   *Emperor Waltz*, 4P8H
- *FPQC*-No.200
   c)   *Overture* from *Die Fledermaus*, 4P8H
- *FPQC*-No.156
   d)   *Perpetual Motion*, 4P8H
- *FPQC*-No.51
   e)   *Wine, Women and Song*, 4P8H
- *FPQC*-No.100

STRAUSS, Johann, Sr. (1804-1849), Austrian
CHOTCH, Francis Xavier, arr.
1)   *Alexandra-Waltzer*, 1P6H
- Has (©183-?)
  LC-M213.S9.M56
2)   *Die Berggeister*, 1P6H

- Has (©1839)
  LC-M213.S

STRAUSS, Josef (1827-1870), Austrian
FPQC, arr.
> *Music of the Spheres*, 4P8H
- *FPQC*-No.287

STRAUSS, Richard (Georg) (1864-1949), German
1) BOCKLET, Heinrich von, arr.
   a) *Till Eulenspiegel's lustige Streiche, nach alter
      Schelmenweise, Op. 18* (1895), 2P8H
- Aid
  UR-M216.S91.E
- P,CF
- *PRG*:442
   b) *Tod und Verklärung, Op. 24* (1889), 2P8H
- Aib
  UR-M216.S91.to
- P,CF
- *PRG*:442
2) *FPQC*, arr.
> *Rosenkavalier Fantasy*, 4P8H
- *FPQC*-No.82
3) Arr. by ?
> *Also sprach Zarathustra, Op. 30* (1896), 2P8H
- P,CF
- *PRG*:442

STRAVINSKY, Igor (1882-1971), Russian
FPQC, arr.
> *I. Danse russe* from ***Petroushka***, 4P8H
- *FPQC*-No.155

STREABBOG, (Jéan) Louis (pseud. Jéan Louis GOBBAERTS)
       (1835-1886), France
1) CLARK, Mary Elisabeth, arr.
> *Carnival*, 3 keyboard parts, six rhythm parts (Late
> elementary)

- Myk
2) DURAND, August, arr.
    Fast Mail Galop, 2P8H
- Witz (©1891)
  LC-M216.S93
3) PAUL, Oscar, arr.
  a)   *Do Re Me Fa Waltz*, 1P6H
- Lam (©1906)
  LC-M213.S
  b)   *Little Fairy Waltz*, 1P6H
- Lam (©1905)
  LC-M213.S

STREAT, Sexteenz S., American
BOLLAN, H., arr.
    Chrysaline Caprice, 1P6H
- Bol (©1892)
  LC-M213.S

SUPPÉ, Franz von [or Francesco Ezechiele Ermenegildo Cavaliere
        Suppé Demelli] (1819-1895), Austrian, of Belgian origin
1) RIEDEL, August, arr.
    Light Cavalry, Overture, 1P6H; 2P8H
- F,J
- S,G
- P,T
- *PRG*:442
2) SARTORIO, Arnoldo (1853-1936), arr.
    Light Cavalry, Overture, 2P8H
- P,T (©1925)
  LC-M216.S98.S3
3) Arr. by ?
  a)   *Overture* to **Dichter und Brauer** (1846), 2P8H
- Aug (©1887; ©1894)
  BrM-e.379.d.(8.)
  UR-M216.S959p
  b)   **Poet and Peasant**, *Overture*, 1P6H; 2P8H
- F,J (1P6H)
- P,T (2P8H)

SWINNEN, Firmin (1885-1972), American
MILLER, Victor, arr.
   Chinoiserie, 1P6H
- F,J (©1921)
   LC-M213.S97.C4

TCHAIKOVSKY, Peter Ilich (1840-1893), Russian
1) BRÜLLOV, W. and LENS, N., arrs.
   Manfred; symphonie en quatre tableaux d'après le poème
   dramatique de Byron, Op. 58
- Jur (©188-?)
   UR-M216.T87.Ma
2) LANGER, Eduard Leontevich (1835-1905), arr.
   a)   *Capriccio italien, Op. 45* (1880), 2P8H
- Jur (©189-?)
   LC-M216.C36.P45.L3
   NYPL
- *TPR*:156
   b)   *1812 Overture, Op. 49*, 2P8H
- Rah
   UR-M216.T87e
   c)   *Entr'acte et valse* from *Eugène Onéquine*, 2P8H
- Jur
   UR-M216.T87.EV
   d)   *Marche slave, Op. 31*, 2P8H
- Jur
   UR-M216.T87m
- S,G (©1880)   (*19)
   P,CM-M216.T3.Op.31.19--
- *PRG*:442
- *TPR*:156
   e)   *The Sleeping Beauty Waltz, Op. 66, No. 6* (1888-1889),
       2P8H
- Jur
   LC-M216.T
   NYPL
- *TPR*:156
   f)   *Sérénade, Op. 48*, 2P8H
- Jur

UR-M216.T87sc

    g)   *Symphony No. 1, Op. 13 (Winter Dreams)*, 2P8H
- Jur
    UR-M216.T87.1L

    h)   *Symphony No. 3, Op. 29 (Polish)* (1875), 2P8H
- Jur (©1877; ©1903)
    NYPL
    UR-M216.T87.3
- *TPR*:156

    i)   *Symphony No. 4, Op. 36*, 2P8H
- Jur (©1900)
    LC-M216.C36.Op.36.L3
- Rod
    UR-M216.T87.4L

    j)   *Symphony No. 5, Op. 64*, 2P8H
- Jur
    UR-M216.T87.5L;M216.T87.5L.cl-c4
- Rah

    k)   *Symphony No. 6, Op. 74 (Pathétique)*, 2P8H
- Forb (©1887)
    UR-M216.T87.6L
- Jur (©1894)
    LC-M216.C36.Op.74.L3.1894
    UR-M216.T87.6L

    l)   *La tempête, fantaisie d'après Shakespeare, Op. 18* (1873), 2P8H
- Jur (©1891; ©1889)
    LC-M216.T
    NYPL
    UR-M216.T87t
- *TPR*:156

    m)   *Waltzer aus dem Ballet* **Dornröschen***, Op. 66, No. 6*, 2P8H
- Rah
    UR-M216.T87.DW

3) PARLOW, Edmund (1855-?), arr.

    a)   *Chanson napolitaine* from *24 pièces faciles (à la Schumann), Op. 39, No. 18* (1878), 2P8H
- P,T (©1910)
    Cur-M216.T877,Op.39.1910

b)   *Chant sans parole, Op. 2, No. 3*, 2P8H
- P,T (©1922)
  LC-M216.T83.C5
4) SCHAEFER, A.N., arr.
  a)   *Polonaise* from *Eugène Onéguine*, 2P8H
- Jur (©1922)
  LC-M216.T
  UR-M216.T87.EV
  b)   *Romeo et Juliette, Overture--Fantaisie d'après Shakespeare*,
     2P8H
- Bes
  LC-M216.T
5) THORNTON, Hans, arr.
  a)   *Chant sans parole, Op. 40, No. 6*, 2P8H
      Allegro moderato
- Bos
  LC-M216.T83.C4
  b)   *Danse russe, Op. 40, No. 10*, 2P8H
      Andantino
- Bos
  LC-M216.T83123
6) *FPQC*, arr.
  a)   *Finale* from *Symphony No. 4*, 4P8H
- *FPQC*-No.166
  b)   *Humoresque*, 4P8H
- *FPQC*-No.135
  c)   *None But the Lonely Heart*, 4P8H
- *FPQC*-No.147
  d)   From *Nutcracker Suite*, 4P8H
      1. *Chinese March*
      2. *Dance of the Sugar-plum Fairies*
      3. *Dance of the Toy Pipes*
      4. *March*
      5. *Trepak*
- *FPQC*-Nos.136,89,88,168,42
  e)   *I. Piano Concerto in B-Flat Minor, No. 1*, 4P8H
- *FPQC*-No.154
  f)   *Scherzo: Pizzicato ostinato* from *Symphony No. 4*, 4P8H
- *FPQC*-No.165

g)   *Waltz* from *Serenade for Strings*, 4P8H
- *FPQC*-No.127
h)   *Waltz of the Flowers*, 4P8H
- *FPQC*-No.90

THOMAS, Ambroise
ISAMBERT, Maria, arr.
   Overture to *Mignon*, 2P8H
- Men
- Heu
   UR-M216.T454.Mo

THOMÉ, François (1850-1909), French
1) LÉMOINE, Léon (1855-1916), arr.
   a)   *Marche croate*, 2P8H
   b)   *Menuet la vallière*, 2P8H
2) ROQUES, Léon, arr.
   Simple aveu, Romance sans paroles, Op. 25, 2P8H
- Dur (©1909)
   LC-M216.T36

THOMSON, Virgil (*b* 1896), American
FPQC, arr.
   Ragtime Bass, 4P8H
- *FPQC*-No.320

THONY, Charles, American
SOURILAS, Theodore, rev. & arr.; fing. by Reginald BARRETT
   On the Scent, Galop, 1P6H
- F,J (©1902)
   LC-M213.T

THUILLE, Ludwig [François Lucien Joseph](1861-1907)
RIHM, Alex
   Romantische Ouverture für grosses Orchester, Op. 16,
      2P8H
- Kis (©1912)
   LC-M216.T49

TOCH, Ernst (1887-1964), American, of Austrian origin
FPQC, arr.
>   *The Juggler, Op. 31, No. 3*, 4P8H
- *FPQC*-No.261

VASSEUR, Jules, American
SOURILAS, Theodore, arr.; rev. & fing. by Reginald BARRETT
>   *To the Circus! Galop Brillant*, 1P6H
- F,J (©1902)
  LC-M213.V

VERDI, Giuseppe (Fortunino Francesco) (1813-1901), Italian
1) HAUSSER, H., arr.
>   *Triumphal March* from *Aida*, 1P6H
- P,T (©1906)
  LC-M213.V
2) LÉMOINE, Léon (1855-1916), arr.
>   *Overture* to *Nabucco*, 2P8H
- Lem
  UR-M216.V484.N
3) MAYER, F.C., arr.
>   *Beauties of Verdi's Operas*, 1P6H (Potpourri)
- Chu (©1883)
  LC-M213.V48.B3
4) PAUL, Oscar, arr.
>   *Anvil Chorus* from *Il Travatore*, 1P6H
- Mol (©1908)
  LC-M213.V
5) Arr. by ?
>   *Miserere* from *Il Trovatore*, 2P8H
- P,T (©1926)
  LC-M216.V48.M5

VILLA-LOBOS, Heitor (1887-1959), Brazilian
FPQC, arr.
1)   *Alnitah* from *The Three Maries*, 4P8H
- *FPQC*-No.318
2)   *Moreniuha (The Little Paper Doll)* from *Prolo de Bébé, No. 2*, 4P8H

- *FPQC*-No.197
3)   *Polichinelle*, 4P8H
- *FPQC*-No.110

VIVIANI, F., American
DRESSLER, William, arr.
     Silver Trumpets, Grand Processional March, 2P8H
- Dit (©1890)
  LC-M216.V85.S5

VOLKMANN, Robert Friedrich (1815-1883), German
ZILCHER, Paul (1855-1943), arr.
1)   *The Shepherd, Op. 11, No. 6*, 1P6H
- Aug (©1929)
  LC-M213.V4.S4
2)   *Under the Linden Tree, Op. 24, No. 7*, 1P6H
- Aug (©1929)
  LC-M213.V5.U5

WACHS, Paul, American
HAMMEREL, Victor, arr.
     Madrileña, 1P6H
- F,J (©1904)
  LC-M213.W

WAGNER, Josef, American
FPQC, arr.
     Metropolitan Round-up, 4P8H
- *FPQC*-No.313

WAGNER, (Wilhelm) Richard (1813-1883), German
1) BURCHARD, Carl (1820-1896), arr.
   a)   *Gros Ballets* from *Rienzi*, 2P8H
- Fur (©188-?)
  PCM-M216.W134.G
   b)   *Overture* to *Tannhäuser*, 2P8H
- Mes (©1845;©1859)
  LC-M216.W15(NB--Piano I score missing)
  NYPL

- *PRG*:442
- *TPR*:156
2) CHEVILLARD, Camille (1859-1923), arr.
    Der Ritt der Walküren from *Die Walküre*, 2P8H
- Scho (©1901)
  NYPL
  UR-M216.W134.WR
- *TPR*:156
3) DEPROSSE, Anton (1838-1878), arr.
    Vorspiel from *Die Meistersinger von Nürnberg*, 2P8H
- Scho (©1870)
  Cur-M216.W134.M4V.1870
  UR-M216.W134.Mc
4) HEINTZ, Albert, arr.
  a)   *Isolde's Liebes-Tod* from *Tristan und Isolde*, 2P8H
- Br&H
  UR-M216.W134.TrI
  b)   *Vorspiel* from *Tristan und Isolde*, 2P8H
- Br&H
  LC-M216.W14.T74
5) HERMANN, Friedrich, arr.
  a)   *Einleitung zum dritten Akt* from *Lohengrin*, 2P8H
- Br&H
  UR-M216.W134.LE
  b)   *Elsa's Dream* from *Lohengrin*, 2P8H
Arranged from Franz Liszt's transcription
- Br&H (©1886) (*9)
  PCM-M216.W134.LE.1886
  c)   *Richard Wagner Album, Band II*, 2P8H
             1.   *Spinnerlied* from *Der fliegende Holländer*
             2.   *Einzug der Gäste auf Wartburg* from *Tannhäuser*
             3.   *Einzug der Götter Walhall* from *Das Rheingold*
- Br&H (©1914)
  LC-M216.W144
  d)   *[4]Stücke* from *Lohengrin*, 2P8H
- Br&H (©1887)
  BrM-h.356.j.(7.)
6) HORN, August (1825-1893), arr.
  a) *Einzug der Götter in Walhall* from *Das Rheingold*,   2P8H

- Scho (©1879)(*23)
  PCM-M216.W134.E.1879
  UR-M216.W134.RhE
  b)　*Wotan's Abschied von Brünhilde und Feuerzauber* from *Die Walküre*, 2P8H
- Scho (©1878)
  PCM-M216.W134.W.1878
  UR-M216.W134.WW
7) KLAUSER, Karl, arr.
  　Eine Faust--Ouvertüre, 2P8H
- Br&H
  UR-M216.W134.F.O.
8) KLINDWORTH, Karl (1830-1916), arr.
  　Overture to *Die fliegende Holländer*, 2P8H
- Fur (©1887)
  BrM-h.356.j.(3.)
9) LIVONIUS, arr.
  　Vorspiel from *Die Meistersin ger von Nürnburg*, 3P12H
- P,T
10) PARLOW, Edmund (1855-?), arr.
  a)　*Richard Wagner Album, Band II*, 2P8H
  　　1.　*Spinnerlied* from *Der fliegende Holländer*
  　　2.　*Einzug der Gäste auf Wartburg* from *Tannhäuser*
  　　3.　*Einzug der Götter in Walhall* from *Das Rheingold*
- Br&H (©1914)
  LC-M216.W144
  b)　*Richard Wagner Album, Band III*, 2P8H
  　　1.　*Isoldens Liebestod* from *Tristan und Isolde*
  　　2.　*Der Ritt der Walküren* from *Die Walküre*
  　　3.　*Wotans Abschied und Feuerzauber* from *Die Walküre*
- Br&H (©1914)
  LC-M216.W144
  c)　*Richard Wagner Album, Band IV*, 2P8H
  　　1.　*Siegfried-Idyll*
  　　2.　*Waldweben* from *Siegfried*
  　　3.　*Trauermarsch* from *Götterdämmerung*
  　　4.　*Charfreitagszauber und Schluss* from *Parsifal*
- Br&H

LC-M216.W142 (©1914)
d)   *Richard Wagner Overture Album, Band I*, 2P8H
       Overture to **Rienzi**, 2P8H
- Br&H (©1914)
LC-M216.W146
UR-M216.W134.0
e)   *Richard Wagner Overture Album, Band II*, 2P8H
       1.   *Overture* to **Der fliegende Holländer**
       2.   *Overture* to **Die Meistersinger von Nürnberg**
       3.   *Overture* to **Parsifal**
- Br&H (©1914)
UR-M216.W134.0.v.2
f)   *Richard Wagner Overture Album, Band III*, 2P8H
       1.   *Prelude* to **Tristan und Isolde**
       2.   *Overture* to **Tannhäuser**
       3.   *Prelude* to **Lohengrin**
- Br&H (©1914)
UR-M216.W134.0.v.3
g)   *Richard Wagner March Album*, 2P8H
       1.   *Huldigungs-Marsch zum 19. Geburtstage Seiner*
            Majestät des Königs Ludwig II von Bayern
       2.   *Kaiser-Marsch*
- Br&H (©1914)
LC-M216.W142
11) PAUER, Ernst (1826-1905), arr.
   a) *Marche de paix* from **Rienzi**, 2P8H
- Aug
UR-M216.W134.RF
   b) *Marche de Tannhäuser*, 2P8H
- Aug
UR-M216.W134.M
12) RAY, A., arr.
         Overture to **Vaisseau fantôme**, 2P8H
- Dur
UR-M216.W134.fR
13) ROQUES, Léon, arr.
   a) *Choeur des fileuses* from **Vaisseau fantôme**, 2P8H
- Dur
UR-M216.W134.Fls

b) *Marche et choeur des fiançailles* from ***Lohengrin***, 2P8H
- Dur (©1887)
  BrM-h.356.j.8
14) RUPP, H., arr.
   Trauermarsch beim Tode Siegfried's from
   Götterdammerung, 2P8H
- Scho (©1877)
  PCM-M216.W134.G.T.1877
  UR-M216.W134.G.T
15) SARTORIO, Arnoldo (1853-1936), arr.
   Tannhäuser March, 1P6H
- P,T (©1924)
  LC-M213.W2.T3.S3
16) *FPQC*, arr.
   a) *Bacchanale* from ***Tannhäuser***, 4P8H
- *FPQC*-No.222
   b) *Isoldes Liebestod* from ***Tristan und Isolde***, 4P8H
- *FPQC*-No.310
   c) *Forest Murmurs* from ***Siegfried***, *Act II*, 4P8H
- *FPQC*-No.128
   d) *Magic Fire Music* from ***Die Valkyrie***, 4P8H
- *FPQC*-No.104
   e) *Ride of the Valkyries*, 4P8H
- *FPQC*-No.221

WALDTEUFEL
1) BROWNOLD, Max, arr.
   Bella Bocca, Polka, Op. 10, No. 1, 2P12H
- Ell (©1890)
  LC-M213.W
2) *FPQC*, arr.
   Les patineurs (Skater's Waltz), 4P8H
- *FPQC*-No.377

WARREN, George William (1828-1902), American
DRESSLER, William (1826-1914), arr.
   Tam O'Shanter, 1P6H
- F,J
- Pon (©1905)

LC-M213.W

WEBER, Carl Maria (Friedrich Ernst) von (1786-1826), German
1) BUCHARD, Carl (1820-1896), arr.
     Overture to *Der Freischütz*, 1P6H
- Brau; S,G (©1895)
  LC-M213.W
2) CHWATAL, Franz Xavier, arr.
     ·Collection Litolff: Nos. 623 and 624: *Overtures* to *Der
     Freischütz* and *Oberon*, 2P8H
- Lit
  UR-M216.W373.FC;M216.W373.0C
3) DRESEL, Otto, arr.
     Invitation à la valse, 2P8H
- Dit (©1890)
  LC-M216.W37
4) GURLITT, Cornelius (1820-1901), arr.
     Mazurka, 1P6H
- S,G (©1900)
- Aug
5) HORN, August (1825-1870), arr.
     Aufforderung zum Tanz, *Op. 65*, 2P8H
- Schl
  UR-M216.W373A
6) KELLER, Robert, arr.
     Overtures to *Euryanthe, Der Freischütz, Oberon*, 2P8H
- Simr
  UR-
  M216.W373.E;M216.W373.F;M216.
  W373.0
7) MEREUX, arr.
     Overture to *Oberon*, 3P12H
- P,T
8) RÖSLER, Gustav (1819-1882), arr.
     Overtures of Weber, 2P8H
     1. *Der Freischütz*
     2. *Oberon*
     3. *Euyanthe*
     4. *Jubelouvertüre*, Op.59

- P,CF
NYPL
PCM-M216.W374
9) SARTORIO, Arnoldo (1853-1936), arr.
    Invitation to the Dance, Op. 65, 2P8H
- P,T (©1924)
LC-M126.W37.S3
10) WITTMAN, R., arr.
    Overture to *Euryanthe*, 2P8H
- Hofm (©186-?)
PCM-Rare book.M216.W374.E. (From *Achthändig Ouvertüren, No. 7*)
11) Collection Litolff
    Aufforderung zum Tanz, Op. 65, 2P8H
- P,CF
UR-M216.W373AG
12) *FPQC*, arr.
  a)   *Invitation to the Dance*, 4P8H
- *FPQC*-No.7
  b)   *Momento Capriccioso, Op. 12*, 4P8H
- *FPQC*-No.179
  c)   *Overture* to *Euryanthe*, 4P8H
- *FPQC*-No.230
  d)   *Perpetual Motion*, 4P8H
- *FPQC*-No.240

WEBSTER, American
FENIMORE, W.P., arr.
    Home Sweet Home, 1P6H (Grade 2)
- Nor (©1887)
LC-M213.W

WEINBERGER, Jaromir (1896-1967), Czechoslovakian
FPQC, arr.
1)   *Dupak*, 4P8H
- *FPQC*-No.129
2)   *Polka* from *Schwanda the Bagpiper*, 4P8H
- *FPQC*-No.99

WILKING, Frank Oscar (*b* 1895), American
BURKETTE, Burton B., arr.
>   *Romanita, Gypsy Airs*, 2P8H
- (©1937)
     LC-M216.W

WILSON, G.D., American
ROODE, R. de, arr.
1)   *Dance of the Haymakers, Morceau de concert, Op. 37*,
     1P6H; 2P8H
- Dit (©1900; ©1905)
     LC-M213.W; M216.W59.D3
2)   *Moonlight on the Hudson, Morceau de salon, Op. 60*,
     1P6H; 2P8H
- Dit (©1902; ©1905)
     LC-M213.W;M216.W59.M6
PARLOW, Edmund, (1855-?), arr.
1)   *Rustic Dance, Op. 230, No. 4*, 2P8H (Easy)
- Schm
     LC-M216.W55
2)   *Through Field and Forest*, 1P6H (Moderately difficult)
- Schm
     LC-M216.W55

WINNER, Septimus (1827-1902), Irish
GETZE, J.A., arr.
>   *Listen to the Mocking Bird: Mocking Bird Echos*,
>   *Air on the Popular Theme **Auld Lang Syne***, 1P6H
- L&W (©1867)
     LC-M213.W

WOLLENHAUPT, Hermann Heinrich Adolf (1827-1865), German
1) BERG, Albert W., arr.
>   *Grande marche de concert*, 2P8H
- Pon (©1866)
     LC-M216.W74;M216.W75
2) HERBERT, arr.

Grand Galop Brillant, Op. 71, 1P6H
- P,T (©1907)
  LC-M213.W

WUESTLAND, George W.
ITZEL, John, arr.
Chaperon March, 1P6H
- Will (©1905)
  LC-M213.W

ZADORA
FPQC, arr.
Cakewalk, 4P8H
- *FPQC*-No.153

ZAREMBSKI, Jules (1854-1885), Polish
REINHARD, August, arr.
Danses polonaises, I. Série: Danses galiciennes, Op. 2,
2P8H
1. *Danse polonaise in G Minor*
2. *Danse polonaise in D Minor*
- Sim (©1899)
  LC-M216.Z27

ZIEHRER, Carl Michael (1843-1922)
PAUL, Oscar, arr.
Flower Polka, 1P6H
- Lam (©1912)
  LC-M213.Z

9. PEDAGOGICAL/GRADED PIECES FOR CLASS PIANO

ALT, Hansi Magdalen (*b* 1911), American, of Austrian origin
1)   *The Cat Sat on a Chair of Gold*, 1P-3P,4H-12H
- P,T (©1972)
  LC-M1389.A495.C4
- *PRG*:439(1990 catalogue listing)
2)   *Secondo Scales* from *The Early Virtuoso*, 2P6H (duet
       accompaniments for the 12 major scales)
- Lan
- Su-B (©1962)

ANSON, George (1903-1985), American
       In the Toy Shop, 1P6H
- SMP
- *PRG*:439

BACH, Johann Sebastian (1685-1750), German
1) FROTHINGHAM, Frances, arr.
       Musette in D Major from *Clavierbüchlein* for *Anna
       Magdalena, No. 21* (1725), 2P8H
- F,C (©1934)
  UR-M216.B11.mF
- *PRG*:439
2) LUCKTENBERG, arr.
   a)   *Minuet in G Major* from *Clavierbüchlein* for *Anna
        Magdalena, No. 4* (1725), 2P8H (Primary Class II)
- CPP/Bel
   b)   *Polonaise*, 2P8H (Elementary Class I)
- CPP/Bel
3) PARLOW, Edmund (1855-?), arr.
       March in F Major, 2P8H (Easy)
- Schm (©1910) (*5)
  LC-M216.B13;M216.B13.P2
4) PARSENS-POOLE, Clifford, arr.
       Jesu, bleibet meine Freunde (Jesu, Joy of Man's Desiring)
- H,F
  LC-M216.B

BAINES, William (1899-1922), English
LIFTL, Franz J. (1874-?), arr.
    The King's Review, Op. 189, 1P6H
- P,T (©1931)
  LC-M213.B13.K4
- *PRG*:439

BALKIN, Alfred, American
    Six For Eight, 4P8H
      1. *Allegro vivace*
      2. *Allegro cantabile*
      3. *Moderato*
      4. *Allegro--marcato*
      5. *Allegro, with a strong jazz beat*
      6. *Allegro moderato*
- GMP;c/o Kj (©1971)   1971 (*4)
  LC-M216.B286.S5
- *PRG*:439

BARRET, Betsy, arr., American
    Two Folk Tunes, 2P8H (Elementary)
      1. *Rowing Gently Down the Stream*
      2. *Brother John and the Bells*
- S,H,M (©1972)   1972
  LC-M216.B26.F6
- *PRG*:439

BASSET, Beth, arr., American
    Ten Little Indians, 2 or more P, 10 keyboard parts
    (Intermediate)
- Myk

BASTIEN, Jane Smisor, arr., American
    Christmas Carols For Multiple Pianos, 2P8H (Elementary)
      1. *We Wish You a Merry Christmas*
      2. *Jingle Bells*
      3. *Silent Night*
      4. *O Little Town of Bethlehem*

- GMP;Kj (©1971)
- *PRG*:439

BEARD, Katherine K.
      Pin Wheels, 1P6H (Elementary)
- WM (© 1988)

BENSON, Esher C., American
1)   *Circus Day*, 2P8H
- WM
- *PRG*:439
2)   *Gay Butterflies*, 2P8H
- WM
- *PRG*:439
3)   *Spring Breezes*, 1P6H
- WM
- *PRG*:439
BERKOVYCH, Isaak Iakovlevych (*b* 1902), Russian
      Forte pianniansambli, zoshyt 2, piano ensembles
           1966 (*42)
  NYPL-JMF 78-424

BILBRO, Mathilde, American
1)   *Dance of the Moonbeams*, 1P8H
- Schm
2)   *Dancing in the Sunshine*, 1P6H
- Chu (©1926)
3)   *Forward March*, 1P6H
- S,G (©1923)
- *PRG*:439
4)   *Hear the Bells Ring!*, 1P8H
- WM (©1936)
5)   *March of the Jumping Jacks*, 1P6H; 2P12H
- WM (©1932)
  MAU
- *PRG*:439
6)   *Marching*, 1P6H
- S,G
- S&G (©1936)

7)   *Spring Violets*, 1P6H
- S,G (©1923)
- *PRG*:439
8)   *Sunbeams at Play*, 1P8H
- Schm

BILLEMA
      Children's Concerto, Op. 68, 1P6H
- Col; c/o Bel
- *PRG*:428;439

BISSEL, T., arr.
      Home Sweet Home, 1P6H (Very easy)
- Dit (©1885)
  LC-M213.B

BLEACH, Lindsay, English
      Four Little Trios, 1P6H
- Free (©1962)
  BrM-h.3292.b.(7.)

BLISS, Paul, American
1)   *Conquerers*, 1P6H
- WM (©1919)
  LC-M213.B65.C5
- *PRG*:439
2)   *Dreams*, 1P6H
- WM (©1919)
  LC-M213.B65.D6
- *PRG*:439

BLON, Franz von (1861-1945)
      Jubilee March, 2P8H (Grade 3 1/2)
- P,T (©1924)
  LC-M216.B62.J

BORDELEAU, Paul and Wilma, arrs., Americans

> *Fun and Play at the Keyboards: an Easy Chord Ensemble Book*, adaptable from 2 to 6 or more players in any combination of organ and/or piano

- Bor (©1974)

  LC-M185.F86

BRADLEY, Richard, arr., American

1)   *Bradley's Ensembles For Kids*, 1P6H or multiple keyboards
   1. **VALENS**, *La Bamba*
   2. **WITHERS**, *Lean On Me*
   3. **BEETHOVEN/SCHILLER**, *Ode to Joy*
   4. **BRADLEY**, *Waltzing Bears*
   5. *Three Mice in a Boat (Three Blind Mice* with *Row, Row, Row Your Boat)*

- BP (©1989)

2)   *Bradley's Ensembles For Kids: Fun For 3 or More (Blue Series)*, 1P6H or multiple keyboards
   1. **DUKAS**, Paul, *The Sorcerer's Apprentice*
   2. **DAVID**, Mack and Jerry **LIVINGSTON**, *This Is It! (Theme* from *The Bugs Bunny Show)*
   3. **COHAN**, George/SUTTON, Betty and R. BRADLEY, arrs., *You're A Grand Old Flag*
   4. **SUTTON**, Betty, *Puppet Dance*
   5. **SUTTON**, Betty, *Sultan's Dance*
   6. **BEETHOVEN**, Ludwig van/BRADLEY, R. and B. SUTTON, arrs., *Symphony No. 5 (First Movement Theme)*
   7. **SCHUBERT**, Franz, *Marche militaire in D Major*

- BP (©1990)

BROWN, Veronica

1)   *From the East: Pianoforte Trio for Six Hands*, 1P6H
- Ash (©1961) (*5)

2)   *Waltz: Pianoforte Trio for Six Hands*, 1P6H
- Ash (©1961)   (*11)

BURROWS

> *First Rounds for Piano*, 1P6H or 8H

- CMP; c/o Ash
- *PRG*:439

BUTCHER, Vernon (*b* 1909), arr.
　　Two French Tunes, 1P6H
　　1. *Frère Jacques*
　　2. *Il était une bergère*
- Hin (©1955)　　(*3)
　Cur-M213.B983.F8

CARDIN, Joy and Kevin **RAYBUCK**, Americans
1)　　*Easy Ensembles for Multiple Keyboards*, for any number or combination of acoustic/electronic keyboards
- Leo
- S,G (©1990)
2)　　*Intermediate Ensembles for Multiple Keyboards*, for any number or combinations of acoustic/electronic keyboards
- S,G (©1990)

CHALFANT, Scott
　　Pom-Pom, 1P6H
- WM (©1920)
　LC-M213.C43.P5

CHEADLE, William
　　Skip to My Lou and Others Too, 2P8H (Intermediate)
- Myk (1990 catalogue listing)

CHEVALLIER, Heinrich
　　Kinderfest-Marsch in C Major, Op. 27, 2P8H
- Sim (©1901)　　(*5)
　LC-M216.C43

CHURCHILL, Virginia, arr., American
　　Partner Quartets, 2P8H (Grade 3), based on folk tunes
　　1.　　*Love Somebody, Yes I Do* (American); *Sound the Flute* (Russian)
　　2.　　*The Galway Piper* (Irish); *Skip to My Lou* (American)
　　3.　　*Peter, Peter, Paul* (Czechoslovakian); *A Dancing*

       Song (Swabian)
4.   *Captain Jinks* (American); *Push the Business On*
       (English)
- BMC
- *PRG*:439

CITATI-BRACCI, Clelia (1895-?), Italian
1)   *Shall We Play a Trio*, 1P6H
- Col
- *PRG*:439
2)   *Suoniamo in tre?* **2 Canti popolari tedeschi**, 1P6H
       1. *Canto di Natale*
       2. *Un nano danza*
- Ric (©1954)
  LC-M213.C
3)   *Three Children at One Keyboard*, 1P6H
- Col
- *PRG*:439
4)   *Tre Bimbi e una Tastiera:* **2 Canti Regionali Italiani**, 1P6H
       1. *La Biondina in Gondoletta*
       2. *Danza Siciliana*
- Ric (©1956)
  LC-M213.C

CLARKE, Henry, English
    Trefoil Leaves: *Twelve Easy Trios*, 1P6H
     1. *Annie Laurie*
     2. *Ah che la morte*
     3. *Bonny Breast-knots*
     4. *Canadian Boat Song*
     5. *Deh conte*
     6. *Evening Bells*
     7. *Garry Owen*
     8. *Home, Sweet Home*
     9. *O dolce concento*
    10. *St. Patrick's Day*
    11. *There's Nae Luck*
    12. *The Minstrel Boy*
- Aug

CLARKE, Mary Elizabeth (Eastridge) (*b* 1918), arr., American
1)   *Folk I*, (Grade 2)
                1. *The Lonesome Road*
                2. *Charlie Is My Darling*
                    1 keyboard, 6H
                3. *Worried Man Blues*
                4. *I Know Where I'm Going* 6 keyboards, 12H
                5. *Aura Lee*
                6. *Green Grow the Lilacs*
- Lew (©1971)
  LC-M216.C59.F61
- Myk (1990 catalogue listing)
2)   *Kum Ba Ya*; *Scarborough Fair*, 6 keyboards, 12 H (late first
        year piano class)
- Lew (©1971)
  LC-M216.C59.K8
- Myk (1990 catalogue listing)
3)   *Sweetly Sings the Donkey*, 2 keyboards, 8H (Grade 2)
- Myk (1990 catalogue listing)

CLARKE, Mary Elizabeth (Eastridge) (*b* 1918), American
KLICKER, arr.
       Schottische, 2 keyboards, 8H (4 keyboard and rhythm parts)
- Myk (1990 catalogue listing)

COLLINS, Hilary, English
1)   *The Three Friends*, 1P6H
- Pat (© 1935)
2)   *The Three Students*, 1P6H
- Pat (©1976)

DAY, Ruth E. (*b* 1901), American
1)   *Fluttering Butterflies*, 2P8H
- WM (©1938)
  WSU
- *PRG*:439
2)   *Friendly Frolics*, 2P8H
- [CPP]Bel
- *PRG*:439

3)   *Happy Dancers*, 2P8H
- WM
- *PRG*:439

DENNYS, Phil, American
1)   *Fantasy Dance*, 1P6H
- Nov (©1989)
2)   *Three-way Stretch*, 1P6H
- Nov (©1985)   (*8)

DEPUE, Wallace
1)   *A Knight Waltz*, 4P8H (Early intermediate)
- Kj (©1972)
  LC-M216.D46.K6
- *PRG*:439
2)   *Sixteen Pawns*, 4P8H (Intermediate)
- Kj (©1971)
  LC-M216.D46.S6
- *PRG*:439

ELLEN, Barbara, American
1)   *Ski Slope*, 1P6H (Early intermediate)
- Myk (1990 catalogue listing)
2)   *Triplicity in Black*, 1P6H (Grade 2 1/2)
- Myk (©1975)
  LC-M213.E

ELLINGER, Ruth, American
        Balloon Pop Polka, 2P8H (and 12 balloons)
- CPP/Bel (©1986)

ENOCH, Yvonne, arr., American
1)   *Six Nonsense Songs*, 1P2H or 4H or 6H
- Bos (©1972) (*18)
2)   *Three Carols for Three Pianists*, 1P6H
- EAMD (1988 catalogue listing)
- Fr-En (1989 catalogue listing)
3)   *Three Easy Tunes for Three Pianists*, 1P6H
- Fr-En (1989 catalogue listing)

4)   *Three More Carols for Three Pianists*, 1P6H
          1. *Here We Come A-Wassailing*
          2. *Infant Holy*
          3. *Ding Dong*
- Fr-En (©1989)

EWING, Montague George (1890-?), American
1)   *Harvest Dance*, 1P6H
- H,F (©1953)
    LC-M213.E
2)   *March of the Clockwork Soldiers*, 1P6H
- H,F (©1953)
    LC-M213.E
3)   *A Mysterious Tale*, 1P6H
- H,F (©1956)
    LC-M213.E
4)   *Red Shoes*, 1P6H
- H,F (©1953)
    LC-M213.E
5)   *Serenade to the Moon*, 1P6H
- H,F (©1953)
    LC-M213.E

EZELL, Helen Ingle, American
          Toy Shop Band: Music Box, 1P6H
- WM (©1964)
    PRG:440

FERREL, Billie (*b* 1921), American
          Bom Bom Boogie, 1P6H (Early intermediate)
- Myk (1990 catalogue listing)

FICHTER
MCWHERTOR, arr.
          'Cause It's Christmas, any number of pianos
- Vol
- *PRG*:440

FOESTER, A.

>   *At the Dancing Masters, Gavotte*, 1P6H (Easy)
- Schm

FOSTER, Stephen Collins (1826-1864), American
KRAFT, Carrie, arr.
>   *Camptown Races* (1850), 1P6H (Primary Class I)
- CPP/Bel

FRANKLIN-PIKE, Eleanor (1890-?), arr., American
1)   *The Bells of Aberdovey*, 1P6H
- Ash (©195-?)
2)   *Golden Slumbers; Hot Cross Buns, Op. 22, Nos. 1* and *2*,
>   3P6H
- Ash (©1957)
3)   *Greensleeves, Op. 21*, 1P6H
- Ash (©1956) (1½*)
  RCM
4)   *The Keel Row*, 1P6H
- Ash (©195-?)
5)   *Oranges and Lemons*, 1P6H
- Ash (©195-?)
  RCM
6)   *The Princess Dances*, 1P6H
- Ash (©195-?)
7)   *A Slow March and a Quick March*, 1P6H
- Ash (©195-?)

GEORGE, arr.
>   *Twinkle, Twinkle, Little Star*, 1P6H
- Su-B
- *PRG*:440

GILLOCK, William (*b* 1917), American
1)   *Champagne Toccata*, 2P8H
>   *Allegro*
- WM (©1977)
  LC-M216.G54.C5
2)   *The Little Sparrow (homage to Edith Piaf)*, 1P6H
- WM (©1987)

3)   *Oriental Bazaar*, 1P6H
- WM (©1986)

GOTLIB, M., ed. and arr.
        Teaching Repertoire of Children's Music School, Grades 4-7:
        Pieces for Two Pianos, Eight Hands, 2P8H
1. **MAKAROW**, E., *Solemn Prelude*
2. **TCHAIKOVSKY**, P., *Dance fei ligeur* from the ballet
   Shchelkunchik
3. **BACH**, J.S., *Largo* from the *Trio Sonata in A Major*
- MCA (©1966)
   UR-M216.G685.P

GREIM, Helen A.
1)   *Goblins*, 1P6H
- F,C (© 1935)
- *PRG*:440
2)   *March of the Lead Soldiers*, 1P6H
- F,C (© 1936)
- *PRG*:440

GUNTHER, Phyllis, American
        Patriotic Medley, 2P8H (Elementary Class III)
        1. *Battle Hymn of the Republic*
        2. *Yankee Doodle*
        3. *America the Beautiful*
- CPP/Bel (©1975)
   LC-M216.G86.P4

HALL, Marian L., American
1)   *And Four to Go*, 1P6H
- WM (©1977)
2)   *Boogie--In Five*, 1P6H
- WM (©1983)

HALL, Marie F.
1)   *The Jolly Sailor Man*, 1P8H
- Schm
2)   *The Robin's Morning Song*, 1P8H

- Schm

HAYDN, Franz Joseph (1732-1809), Austrian
BILBRO, Mathilde, arr.
    Andante Theme from the *"Surprise" Symphony*, 1P8H
- WM (©1938)

HOPKINS, Harry Patterson (*b* 1900), composer and arr., American
1)   *Big Bass Fiddle Humoresque*, 1P6H
- CMP
- *PRG*:440
2)   *The Big Drum Major March*, 1P6H
- CMP
- *PRG*:440
3)   *Golden Rod Waltz*, 1P6H
- CMP
- *PRG*:440
4)   *Little French Doll*, 1P6H
- CMP
- *PRG*:440
5)   *Sunshine Waltz*, 1P6H
- CMP
- *PRG*:440
6)   *Sweet Moments, Reverie*, 1P6H
- CMP
- *PRG*:440
7)   *We Three Kings of the Orient Are*, 1P6H
- CMP
  MAU

HOPKINS, J.
SCHAUM, John W., arr.
    We Three Kings of Orient Are, 1P6H
- CPP/Bel (© 1944)

HORVATH, Geza
1)   *The Acrobat*, 1P6H (Easy)
- Schm
2)   *Minuet in E-Flat Major*, 1P6H

- Aug

HUBICKI, Margaret (*b* 1915), arr., American
      Double Duets, 2P8H (Easy)
-S,G
PRG:440

HYSON, Winfred Prince (*b* 1925), arr., American
1)   *Eight Light-Hearted Variations on The Jolly Miller*, 1P8H
- Kj
- *PRG*:440
2)   *Fantasy on Three English Folksongs*, 1P8H
- Kj
- *PRG*:440

ISAACS, Leonard (*b* 1909), Canadian
1)   *The Grasshopper*, 1P6H
- Elk (©1954)
- S,G; Curw
  BBC-11996
2)   *The Village March* and *The Lake*, 1P6H
- Curw (©1955)

KEENE, A.B., American
      Miniature Waltz, 2P8H (Easy)
- Schm

KING, Patricia, American
1)   *Festivities*, 2P8H
- Available from composer 1983 (4½*)
  32 Hill Lane
  Roslyn Heights, NY 11577
2)   *Humoresque*, 2P8H; 2P16H
- Available from composer 1982 (3¼*)
3)   *Theme and Variations for 40 Fingers*, 2P8H
- Available from composer 1984 (3 ¾*)

KNÄBEL, Alphonse M.
1)   *Op. 5*, 1P6H

1. *Playing Soldier, March*
2. *Rustling Leaves, Schottische*
3. *Under the Arbor, Melodie*
4. *At the Picnic, Polka*
5. *Dancing on the Lawn, Waltz*
6. *Sleigh Bells, Galop*
7. *Romance sans paroles*
   - F,J
2) *Galop di Bravura, Op. 24*, 1P6H
- F,J
  LC-M213.K

KRAEHENBUEHL, David, composer and arr., American
1) *Ten Little Indians*, 1P8H
- Su-B (©1961)　(*7)
  M213.K89.T2
- *PRG*:440
2) *The Drunken Sailor*, 1P8H
- Su-B (©1961) (*5)
  IU-M213.K89.D7
3) *There and Back; A Strange Procession*, 2P8H
- NKAA
- *PRG*:440
4) *The Wayfaring Strange*, 1P6H
- Su-B (©1961)　(*5)
  IU-M213.K89.W3
- *PRG*:440

KRAFT, Carrie, composer and arr., American
Keyboard Ensemble Series (CPP/Bel)
1) *Amazing Grace*, 1P6H
2) *Brother John*, 1P6H (Primary Class I)
- (© 1986)
3) *Jesus Loves Me*, 1P6H (Early elementary level)
4) *A Christmas Medley: Away in a Manger/The First Noel*,
   1P6H (Elementary)
- CPP/Bel (© 1990)
5) *March of the Mice*, 1P6H (Primary Class II)
- (© 1986)

6)   *My Hat, It Has Three Corners*, 1P6H (Primary Class II)
7)   *Oh Where, Oh Where*, 1P6H (Primary Class I)
8)   *Scarborough Fair*, 1P6H (Primary Class II)
9)   *This Old Man*, 1P6H (Primary Class I)
- (© 1986)
10)   *Up On the Housetop*, 1P6H (Elementary)
- (©1990)
11)   *What A Beautiful Savior*, 1P6H

KROGMANN, C.W.
         Zephyrs from Melodyland, Op. 15, 1P6H
         1.   *Little Prince*
         7.   *Little Patriot*
         12.   *Robin's Lullaby*
- S,G
- *PRG*:440

LAST, Joan Mary (*b* 1908), English
         Waltz For Three, 1P6H
- GME (©1963) (*7)
  BrM-h.3292.b.(6.)

LÁSZLÓ, Sáry
         Pebble Playing in a Pot, 1-4 keyboards (or percussion
         instruments)
- Edi (©1980)
  UR-M216.S251.K87

LEE, Julia
1)   *Ready to Go*, 1P6H (Very easy)
- Bo&H (©1986) (*22)
  Three in a Row, 1P6H (Easy)
- Bo&H (©1984) (*16)
  RCM

LOVELL, Joan (*b* 1915), English
1)   *Lilliburlero*, 1P6H
- Aug
2)   *Scherzino*, 1P6H

- Aug (©1958)   (*5)
  LC-M213.L
3)   *Twos and Threes*, 1P,4H or 6H
- Aug

LUCKTENBERG, George, arr., American
    [J.S.] Bach for Piano Ensemble, 1P8H (4 parts with 1 pianist
    per line)
- Bel (©1971)
- Lan

LYKE, James, American
    Ensemble Music for [Adult] Group Piano, pieces of 1P4H; 2P,
    4H and 8H; 3P to 6P (Bk.I Easy; Intermediate; Bk.II--
    Intermediate, Moderately advanced)
- Sti (©1976)
- Lan

MACGREGOR, Helen, composer and arr., American
1)   *Frère Jacques (Brother James)*, 1P6H
- WM (© 1933)
2)   *Double Melodies*, 1P6H
- WM (© 1933)
3)   *Follow Me*, 1P6H
- WM
4)   *Humoreske* [1st player]; *Old Folks at Home* [2nd player];
        accompaniment [3rd player], 1P6H
- WM
5)   *Italian Dance*, 2P8H
- S,G
6)   *Lazy Mary* [1st player]; *Oh! Dear! What Can the Matter Be?*
        [2nd player]; *accompaniment* [3rd player], 1P6H
- WM (©1932)
7)   *London Bridge* [1st player]; *Merrily We Roll Along* [2nd
        player]; *accompaniment* [3rd player], 1P6H
- WM (©1932)
8)   *Piano Quartet: Medley of American Tunes: Oh! Susannah,
        Ten Little Indians, and Yankee Doodle*, 1P8H
- WM (©1933)

9)   _Pije Kuba; Bohemian Dance_, 2P8H
- S,G
10)   _Row, Row, Row Your Boat_, 1P6H
- WM (© 1933)
11)   _So Merrily Dancing_ [1st player]; _Poor Old Augustin_ [2nd player]; _accompaniment_ [3rd player], 1P6H
- WM
12)   _Spinning Song; Dutch Bride's Dance_, 2P12H
- S,G
13)   _Three Blind Mice_, 1P6H
- WM
14)   _Tunes of the USA_, 1P6H
- WM
- _PRG_:441

MARWICK, Marion and Maryanne **NAGY**, arrs., Americans
        Popular Duets for Two or More Pianos
- Screen Gems-CPP (©1975)
  LC-M215.P

MATTINGLY, Jane M. (1872- ?), American
1)   _Dancing Fairies, Op. 16, No. 1_, 1P6H
- WM (©1925)
2)   _The Merry-makers, Op. 16, No. 2_, 1P6H
- WM
3)   _Jack Frost, Op. 16, No. 3_, 1P6H
- WM
See _PRG_:441

MCBRIDE, Robert, arr., American
        Folk Tunes, 1P4H or piano ensemble
        1. _Kum Ba Ya_
        2. _On Top of Old Smokey_
        3. _Smarty_
        4. _Down in the Valley_
        5. _Jacob's Ladder_
        6. _La Cucaracha_
        7. _Sweet Betsy From Pike_
        8. _Green Grow the Lilacs_

9. *Polly-Wolly-Doodle*
10. *Greensleeves*
11. *Brother John*
12. *The Rovin' Gambler*
13. *I Ride an Old Paint*
14. *The Girl I Left Behind*
15. *Hangman; Sinner Man*
16. *Home on the Range*

- Facsimile of manuscript
  1976
  NYPL-JNG 81-285 (Donated by the Inez Barbour Hadley Fund for the Henry Hadley Memorial Library.)

MCCLENNEY, Ann and Maurice **HINSON**, arrs., Americans
    Dances of the Young Republic, 1P4H, 1P6H and 2P8H
- Hin (©1977)   (*31)
  NYPL-JNF 78-116

MÉTIS, Frank, composer and arr.
1)   *Africasian Affair*, 2P to 4P (Intermediate) ; or 1P and tape recorder
- Vol (©1970) (*4)
  LC-M214.M542.A4
- *PRG*:441
2)   *Easy/Rock Sketches*, 4-part ensembles (Late elementary to intermediate)
- Pied (©1970)
3)   *Easy Together*, 4-part ensembles (Late elementary to intermediate)
- Pied (©1970)
4)   *Festival Fingers*, 2P to 4P, or 1P and tape recorder
- (©1976) (*31)
  NYPL-JNG 77-222
5)   *Good'n Groovy*, 4-part ensemble (Late elementary to intermediate)
- Mark
- Pied (©1972)
- *PRG*:441
6)   *Happiness Hill*, 2P to 4P (Easy); or 1P and tape recorder

- Vol
  LC-M214.M542.H3
7)   *Kids 'n Keyboards*, 4-part ensembles (Late elementary to intermediate)
- Mark
- Pied (©1972)
- *PRG*:441
8)   *Parisian Polka*, 2P to 4P (Intermediate)
- Vol
- *PRG*:441
9)   *Rock Modes and Moods*, 2P to 4P; or 1P and tape recorder
- Mark
10)   *Scarborough Fair*, 2P to 4P or 1P and tape recorder
- Mark (*4)
  LC-M216.M47.S3
- *PRG*:441
11)   *Wicked World Waltz*, 2P to 4P (Intermediate)
- Vol
- *PRG*:441

MEWS, Douglas
      Pastorale and Polka, 1P6H
      1.   *Andantino con moto*
      2.   *Allegro con brio*
- Aug (©1960) (*13)
  LC-M213.M

MILLER, Dawn, American
      Fresh Mix, multiple keyboards and players (Intermediate)
- Kj

MOREY, F.L.
      Away to the Woods, 1P6H (Easy)
- Sohm

MUNGER, Shirley, American
      4 for 6: 4 Easy Pieces for Piano 6 Hands, 1P6H
      1.   *Barcarole*
      2.   *Six Galloping Riders*

      3.   *Street Dance in Holland*
      4.   *Whistling Hikers*
- GMC (©1960)
  LC-M3190.M
  MAU

OGILVY, Jim and Susan, composers and arrs., Americans
1)   *Ogilvy Piano Multiples--Bluezette: for any Level and Combination of Piano Ensemble*
      1.   Jim, *Blue All Through*
      2.   Susan, *Blue Boogie*
      3.   Jim, *Blue Circle*
      4.   Jim, *Blue Slider*
      5.   Jim, *Disco Blues*
      6.   Jim, *Minor Bird Blue*
      7.   Susan, *Suspended Blues*
      8.   Susan, *Sweet Blue*
2)   *Ogilvy Piano Multiples--Jazz Vignettes: for any Level and Combination of Piano Ensemble*
      1.   Jim, *Bob Motif*
      2.   Jim, *Ode to C.C.*
      3.   Jim, *Ode to H.H.*
      4.   Susan, *A Scott Rag*
      5.   Jim, *A Shorter 3/4*
      6.   Susan, *Waltz for Bill*
- BP (©1983)

OGILVY, Susan, composer and arr., American
1)   *Ogilvy Piano Multiples--Book 1: for any Level and Combination of Piano Ensemble*
      1.   *After a Fashion*
      2.   *Bein' Blue*
      3.   *The Chordal Hook*
      4.   *A Gaelic Melody*
      5.   *Fast Motion*
      6.   *Meatball Boogie*
      7.   *Slow Movement*
- BP (©1983)
2)   *Pops for Piano Ensemble: for any Level and Combination of*

     Piano Ensemble, 6 parts
     1.   **JOPLIN**, Scott, *The Entertainer*
     2.   **MANN**, Barry, *Here You Come Again*
     3.   **DEVORSEN**, Barry and Perry **BLOTKIN**, *Nadia's Theme* from *The Young and the Restless*
     4.   **HAMLISCH**, Marvin, *The Way We Were*
     5.   **WONDER**, Stevie, *You Are the Sunshine of My Life*
     6.   **BROOKS**, Joe, *You Light Up My Life*
- BP (©1983)

PAGE, Cleveland L., arr., American
     [Folk-Tune Arrangements] *Ensemble Music for Group Piano*, for multiple piano/keyboard ensemble
- Can (©1970)

PARFREY, Raymond John (*b* 1928), English
1)   *Carol in a Mode*, 1P6H
     Andante
- Available from composer (©196-?)
  53 Longley Road
  Harrow, HA1 4TG
  Middlesex, England
- Letter from Parfrey, November 14, 1990
2)   *For Three and a Keyboard*, 1P6H
     Alla marcia
- Available from composer (©196-?)
- Letter from Parfrey, November 14, 1990
3)   *Southern Sun*, 1P6H
     Not too fast, but boldly
- CPE (©1969)
- Letter from Parfrey, November 14, 1990

PARSENS (or **PERSENS**), Charles [pseud. for Clifford **POOLE**] (*b* 1916), Canadian
1)   *Swaying Willows*, P6H
- H,F
2)   *Tango*, 1P6H
- H,F

PIERPONT, J., American
MACGREGOR, Helen, arr.
>*Jingle Bells*, 1P8H
- WM (©1931)

POTTER, Archibald James (1918-1980), Irish
>*Finnegan's Wake*, 10P20H
- ConMC   1957 (3*)

PURCELL, Henry (1659-1695), English
1) CARPER, Virginia Speiden, arr.
>*Two Trumpet Voluntaries* from *Ten Select [Harpsichord]*
>*Voluntaries, Z.S. 124* (c.1780), 2P8H
- S,G (©1968)
LC-M216.C585.T8 (from *Ten Select Voluntaries)*
NB--*No.1*(or *No. 9* may not be by Henry Purcell, but by Jeremiah
Clarke (1673-1707). [See C.L. Cudworth, "Some New Facts About
the *Trumpet Voluntary.*" *The Musical Times* (September, 1953).]
2) RABINOF, Sylvia, arr.
>*Air: When I Am Laid in Earth (Dido's Lament)* from *Dido*
>*and Aneas, Z. 628* (1689), 2P8H (Moderately Difficult Class
>II)
- CPP/Bel (©1990)

RABINOF, Sylvia
>*The Happy Farmer (and His Family)* [Variations on Robert
>Schumann's *Frohlicher Landmann* from *Album für die*
>*Jugend, Op. 68, No. 10*], 2P8H (Very difficult class)
>CPP/Bel (©1990)

REID
>*Three Pals*, 1P6H
- P-AP
- *PRG*:441

RENNICK, Esther
>*Let's Play Trios*, 1P6H
- CPP/Bel
- *PRG*:442

RISTAD, Eloise
1)   *Storm Gods*, 1P6H (Grade 3)
- Myk
2)   *Sunlight on the Water*, 1P6H (Grade 4)
- Myk (©1975)
  LC-M213.R

RODGERS, Irene (1891-?), American
COBB, Harold Courtland (*b* 1903), arr.
1)   *Moon Mist*, 1P6H; 2P8H
- S,G (©1941)
- Su (©1948)
  LC-M213.R; M216.R
- *PRG*:442
2)   *Six Little Hands at One Keyboard*, 1P6H
- S,G
- *PRG*:442

ROLSETH, Bjarne
      Little Princess (Waltz), 1P6H or 2P12H
- S&G (©1938)

ROWLEY, Alec (1892-1958), English
1)   *Bells*, 1P6H
- Curw (©1952) (*3)
- S,G
  BrM-g.1236.1.(12.)
  LC-M213.R
- *PRG*:442
2)   *Tambourin*, 1P6H
- Curw (©1952)
- S,G
  LC-M213.R
- *PRG*:442

RUSSEL, H.M.
HARTS, H.L., arr.
      The Witch's Flight, Galop, 1P6H (Grade 3)
- W-S (©1920)

LC-M213.R92.W4

SATTÉLMAIR, Eugene
    Mignon, Gavotte, Op. 84, 1P6H (Moderately difficult)
- Schm (©1913)
  LC-M213.S

SCHAUM, John W. (*b* 1905), arr., American
1)   STEEFE, William-SCHAUM, arr.
    The Battle Hymn of the Republic, 2P8H
- Bel (©1952)
  LC-M216.S82.B3
- *PRG*:442
2)   *Four Bells and All's Well*, 1P8H
- CPP/Bel
  LC-M213.S
- *PRG*:442
3)   WORK, H.C.-SCHAUM, arr.
    Grandfather's Clock, 2P8H (Grade 1)
- CPP/Bel
4)   *Mexican Clap Hands Dance*, 2P8H
- CPP/Bel (©1947)
  WSU
- *PRG*:442
5)   *Three Blind Mice*, 1P6H (Grade 1)
- CPP/Bel
- *PRG*:442
6)   *The Three Musketeers*, 1P6H (Grade 1)
- CPP/Bel (©1946)
- *PRG*:442
7)   *We Three Kings of* [the] *Orient Are*, 1P6H (Grade 1)
- CPP/Bel (©1944)
  WSU

SCHUMANN, Robert (1810-1856), German
BILBRO, Mathilde, arr.
    Soldier's March, 1P8H
- WM (©1938)

SCOTT, Sebastian, American
      Three Scottish Tunes, 1P6H
      1. *Bonnie Lassie*
      2. *A Red, Red Rose*
      3. *Skye Boat Song*
- Fr-En (©1989)

SEUEL, Marie
HOLST, arr.
  a)   *Forest Lullaby*, 1P6H or 2P12H
- S&G (©1938)
  b)   *Round and Round*, 1P6H or 2P12H
- S&G (©1938)

SHUR, Laura, arr., American
1)   *Christmas Tunes for Three*, 1P6H
- Nov (©1987)
2)   *Tunes for Three*, 1P6H
- Nov (©1985) (*17)
3)   *More Tunes for Three*, 1P6H
- Nov (©1986)

STECHER, Melvin and Norman **HOROWITZ**, arrs., Americans
1)   *Ensemble Repertoire, Book 1A, K* from *Keyboard Strategies*
       (duets, for two to six pianos)
- S,G (1990 catalogue listing)
2)   *Ensemble Repertoire, Book 1B*, from *Keyboard Strategies*
       (duets, for two to four pianos)
- S,G (1990 catalogue listing)
3)   *Textures for Multiple Pianos*, from *Keyboard Strategies (duets,*
       for three to six pianos)
- S,G (1990 catalogue listing)

STEINER, Eric (*b* 1911), arr., American
      Chopsticks For Three, 1P6H
- CPP/Bel (©1963)
- *PRG*:442

TANSMAN, Alexandre (1897-1986), French, of Polish origin

Reverie from *Nous jouons pour maman*, piano ensemble
- S,G (1990 catalogue listing)

THIMAN, Eric H., English
Pastourelle, 1P6H
- Elk (© 1956)

TROJELLI, A.
1)   *Marche des trois frères*, 1P6H
- En (©1896)
    LC-M213.T
2)   *Valse des trois soeurs*, 1P6H
- En (©1896)
    LC-M213.T

TURNER, Cecil
Three Times Three, 1P6H
- Aug (©1955)
    LC-M213.T

VANDALL, Robert D., composer and arr., American
1)   *Amazing Grace*, for up to 6 parts/players (Elementary)
- Kj (©1977)
2)   *Cindy*, for up to 6 parts/players (Elementary)
-Kj (©1977)
    LC-M213.V
3)   *Down in the Valley*, for up to 4 parts/players (Late
        elementary)
- Myk (1990 catalogue listing)
4)   *Five Will Get You Four*, for up to 5 parts/players (Elementary)
- Kj (©1977)
    LC-M213.V
5)   *Greensleeves*, for up to 4 parts/players (Elementary)
- Kj (©1977)
6)   *Hush-A-Bye*, for up to 6 parts/players (Late elementary)
- Myk (1990 catalogue listing)
7)   *Jingle Bells*, for up to 6 parts/players (Intermediate)
- Myk (1990 catalogue listing)
8)   *Looby Loo*, for up to 4 parts/players (Late elementary)

- Myk (1990 catalogue listing)
9)   *Michael, Row the Boat Ashore*, for up to 4 parts/players (Late
        elementary)
- Myk (1990 catalogue listing)
10)   *Old Joe Clark*, for up to 4 parts/players (Late elementary)
- Myk (1990 catalogue listing)
11)   *On the Bridge of Avignon*, for up to 4 parts/players (Late
        elementary)
- Myk (1990 catalogue listing)
12)   *Riddle Song*, for up to 6 parts/players (Late elementary)
- Myk (1990 catalogue listing)
13)   *Scarborough Fair*, for up to 6 parts/players (Elementary)
- Kj (©1977)
14)   *Shenandoah*, for up to 6 parts/players (Elementary)
- Kj (©1977)
15)   *Sleep, Baby, Sleep*, for up to 6 parts/players (Elementary)
- Kj (©1977)
16)   *Silent Night*, for up to 5 parts/players (Elementary)
- Kj (©1977)
17)   *Theme and Variations on **Skip to My Lou***, for up to 6
        parts/players (Elementary)
- Kj (©1977)

VANDEVERE, J. Lillian
1)   *Gay Gondoliers, Barcarole*, 1P6H
- S,G
- *PRG*:442
2)   *The Gnome and the Fairy*, 1P6H or 2P12H
- S&G (©1936)
3)   *A Summer Concert*, 1P6H or 2P12H
- S&G (©1936)
4)   *The Three Bears*, 1P6H or 2P12H
- S&G (©1938)
5)   *We Follow the Band*, 1P6H
- BMC
- *PRG*:442
6)   *We Go Hiking*, 1P6H
- BMC
- *PRG*:442

7)　　*We Go Sailing*, 1P6H
- BMC
- *PRG*:442
8)　　*We Waltz*, 1P6H
- BMC
- *PRG*:442

WAXMAN, Donald, American
　　　Parade of the Gingerbread Army, 1P6H
- GMC (©1967)

WEBER, Reinhold (*b* 1927), German
　　　Vier Miniaturen, 1P6H
- Scho　　　　　　　1983
- *Kzd* (Pub. No. ED7258)

WEISER, Philipp, American
　　　Blossom-time, Gavotta, 2P8H (Easy)
- Schm

WERDIN, Eberhard (*b* 1911), German
　　　Familienmusik--eine kleine musikalische Szene: Beachte die
　　　Spielanweisung in der Erklärrung der einzelnen Stücke, S. 58,
　　　1P6H
- Scho　　　　　　　1983
- *Kzd* (Pub. No. ED7257)

WEYBRIGHT, June, composer and arr., American
1)　　*Book of Trios*, 1P6H (Grade 2)
- CPP/Bel
- *PRG*:442
2)　　*Branle*, 1P6H (Grade 3 1/2)
- CPP/Bel
3)　　*Carpenters*, 1P6H (Grade 1)
- CPP/Bel
4)　　*Dusty Roads*, 1P6H (Grade 1 1/2)
- CPP/Bel
5)　　*The Elephant Speaks*, 1P6H (Grade 2)
- CPP/Bel

6)   *Feet in the Jungle*, 1P6H (Grade 1 1/2)
- CPP/Bel
7)   *In Time*, 1P6H (Grade 1 1/2)
- CPP/Bel
8)   *Little Hill*, 1P6H (Grade 1 1/2)
- CPP/Bel
9)   *Mary's Other Lambs*, 1P6H (Primary Class I)
- CPP/Bel
- *PRG*:442
10)   *Pictures*, 1P6H (Grade 1 1/2)
- CPP/Bel
11)   *Pond in the Wood*, 1P6H (Grade 2)
- CPP/Bel
12)   *Rigaudon*, 1P6H (Grade 3)
- CPP/Bel
13)   *Thousands of Millions of Stars*, 1P6H (Grade 2)
- CPP/Bel
14)   *Three On One*, 1P6H (Primary Class I)
- CPP/Bel
- *PRG*:442
15)   *Yankee Doodle*, 1P6H (Grade 1?)
- CPP/Bel

WILLIAMS, Madge, arr., American
1)   *Oh Dear! What Can the Matter Be?*, 1P6H
- WM
- *PRG*:442
2)   *Twinkle, Twinkle, Little Star*, 1P6H
- WM (©1988)
- *PRG*:442

WILSON, Dorothy (*b* 1904), American
       My Turn!, 1P6H
- facsimile of manuscript (*1)
  AMC-M213.W7472.M9

WILSON, M., American
1)   *Op. 98*, 2P8H
       1. *At the Photographers*

      2. *Grandma and Grandpa*
      3. *Aunt Susannah*
- CMP
- *PRG*:442
2) MELLICHAMP, N., ed.
      Soldier's March, 1P8H
- CMP
- *PRG*:442

WOLFF, Bernhard (1835-1906), German
NICHOLL, H.W., ed.
1)   *Festival Polonaise*, 1P6H (Moderately difficult)
- Schm
2)   *Tanzstück, Op. 138*, 1P6H
- Schu (©1888)
  LC-M213.W85.T3
3)   *Waltz, Op. 137*, 1P6H
- Schu (©1888)
  LC-M213.W85.T3

ZAPFF, Oskar, German
     Die kleinen Musikanten (Little Musicians), Op. 19, 1P6H
     Gavotte
- And (©1906)
  LC-M213.Z

ZILCHER, Paul (1855-1943), German
1)   *Drei leichte Stücke, Op. 75*, 1P6H
      1. *Kindermarsch*
      2. *Melodie*
      3. *Auf dem Ball*
- Kis (©1909)
  LC-M213.Z
2)   *Vier leichte Stücke, Op. 80*, 1P6H
      1. *Barcarole*
      2. *Waltzer*
      3. *Alla Marcia*
      4. *Schlummerlied*
      5. *Am Bache (Ruisseau dans la forêt)*

      6. *Alla Tarantella*
- Scho (©1985)
- *Kzd*
3)   Individually Published Pieces:
  a)   *Along the Garden Path, Op. 172, No. 2*, 1P6H
- Schm
  b)   *At the Ball, Op. 75, No. 3*, 2P8H
- S,G
  c)   *At the Fountain*, 1P6H
- S,G (©1929)
  LC-M213.Z69.P4
  d)   *A Dance on the Lawn, Op. 172, No. 3*, 1P6H
- Schm
  e)   *Merry Andrew, Morris Dance*, 1P6H
- P,T
  f)   *On Parade*, 2P8H
- S,G
- *PRG*
  g)   *Playtime*, 1P6H (Easy)
- Schm
  h)   *Sevilla, Bolero*, 1P6H
- P,T
  LC-M213.Z69.S3
  i)   *Village Carnival, Op. 241, No. 6*, 1P6H
- Schm
  j)   *Wandering*, 1P6H
- S,G (©1929)
  LC-M213.Z69.P4

10. SOME ANTHOLOGIES AND COLLECTIONS *

1. *Achthändig Ouvertüren*, Leipzig: F. Hofmeister, 186-? (PCM: rare book, M216.A3.186-?)

2. Offenbach am Main: Johann André

* Many of the works listed on the backs of scores that were available in various libraries were not available for examination. This section illustrates some of these obscure works.

3. Bey, Adolf, arr.,   *Die ersten Versuche im Ensemblespiel.*
                         Achte leichte Stücke aus klassichen Meistern.
                         Mainz: B. Schott's Söhne, 1883. (Pl. No.
                         23372)

4. Berlin: Ed. Bote & G. Bock

5. Leipzig: Breitkopf & Härtel

Breitkopf und Härtel in Leipzig.

Breitkopf & Härtels Klavierbibliothek.

 Für 2 Klaviere zu 8 Händen. Nach Gruppen geordnet.

Heftausgabe.

Die Preise sind bei jeder Gruppe angegeben, die der Volksausgabe bleiben unberührt.

Kleinere Vortragsstücke.

Symphonien.

Phantasien u. Kammermusikwerke.

Ouvertüren.

6. Boston: Oliver Ditson Company

EIGHT HAND PIANO MUSIC

FOUR PERFORMERS ON TWO PIANOS

Ascher, Joseph	Mazurka des Traineaux. (Arr. by T. Bissell)	1.25
Auber, D. F. E.	Overture to *Masaniello*. (Arr. by G. M. Schmidt)	1.50
Baker, Fred T.	Danse Écossaise. (Arr. by F. Lasso)	1.25
Behr, Franz	Roguish Kitten (*Mutsi Katschen*) (Scherzo-Polka.) Op. 443. (Arr. by Gustav Blasser).	.60
Bohm, Carl	La Grâce. Op. 312, No. 5. (Arr. by W. P. Fasimore)	1.00
Flotow, F. von	Overture to *Martha*. (Arr. by A. Horn)	1.50
Gounod, Charles	Soldiers' Chorus, from *Faust*. (Arr. by F. L. Schubert)	.85
Herold, L. J. F.	Overture to *Zampa*. (Arr. by Lattenberg)	2.00
Kéler Béla	Lustspiel Overture. Op. 73. (Arr. by Theodor Herbert)	1.25
Kinkel, Charles	Wild Flower March. (Arr. by Wm. Dressler)	.60
Mendelssohn, Felix	Priests March, from *Athalie*. (Arr. by August Horn)	.60
do	Overture to *Midsummer Night's Dream*. (Arr. by G. M. Schmidt)	2.00
do	Wedding March	.60
Milde, L.	Galop de Concert. Op. 10	2.00
Raff, Joachim	La Polka de la Reine. Op. 95. (Arr. by W. P. Fasimore)	2.50
Rossini, G. A.	Overture to *William Tell*. (Arr. by G. M. Schmidt)	2.50
Schubert, Franz	Marche Militaire. (Arr. by Wm. Dressler)	1.00
Schumann, Robert	Gipsy Life. (Arr. by Arnoldo Sartorio)	1.00
Spindler, Fritz	Charge of the Hussars (*Husarenritt*). Op. 110, No. 3. (Arr. by Theodor Herbert).	1.25
Suppé, F. von	Overture to *Poet and Peasant*. (Arr. by C. T. Brunner)	2.00
Wagner, Richard	Prelude to *Lohengrin*. (Arr. by Léon Roques)	.50
Weber, Carl Maria von	Invitation to the Dance (*Invitation à la Valse*). Op. 65. (Arr. by Otto Dresel).	2.00
Wilson, G. D.	Dance of the Haymakers. (Morceau de Concert.) Op. 57. (Arr. by R. de Roode).	2.25
do	Moonlight on the Hudson. (Morceau de Salon.) Op. 60.	2.25

OLIVER DITSON COMPANY, BOSTON

C. H. DITSON & CO.   LYON & HEALY
New York   Chicago

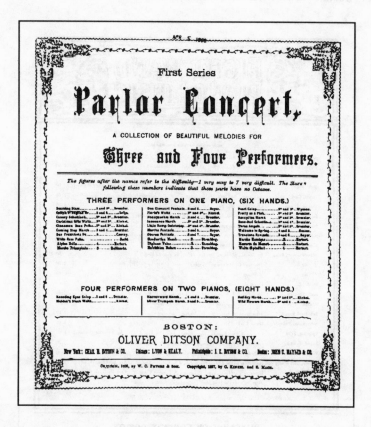

7. Paris: A. Durand & Fils

8. *The First Piano Quartet Collection.*

The manuscript collection of music for four pianos (original works and arrangements)--31 boxes (ca.1200 items)--located in Special Collections (JOB 76-14) of the New York Public Library at Lincoln Center (111 Amsterdam Avenue, New York, NY, 10023). The file includes a letter from the donor of the collection, Mrs. Fadiman, stating that any of these manuscripts can be photocopied for use (in performance) by four piano ensembles. (The donor's husband, Edwin Fadiman, was the founding member of the First Piano Quartet in the 1940s.)

9. Leipzig: Robert Forberg

10. Berlin: Adolph Fürstner

COMPOSITIONEN
für 2 Pianoforte zu   8 Händen
und
für Pianoforte zu 6 Händen.

GOBBAERTS. Op. 83. Marche triomphale zu 6 Hdn

SCHUBERT, F. Ständchen „Leise flehen meine Lieder" zu 6 Hdn. (Liba)

WAGNER, R. Marsch und Chor „Einzug der Gäste" (Tannhäuser) für 2 Pfte. zu 8 Hdn. (Burchardt) .

GHYS. Air Louis XIII. für 2 Pfte. zu 8 Hdn. (Brissler) . . . .

WAGNER, R. Ouverture Rienzi für 2 Pfte. zu 8 Hdn. (Burchardt) . . . .

WAGNER, R. Ballet Rienzi für 2 Pfte. zu 8 Hdn. (Burchardt) . . . .

WAGNER, R. Ouverture-Tannhauser für 2 Pfte. zu 8 Hdn. (Burchardt) . . . .

MÉTRA, O. Sérénade, Valse Espagnole für 2 Pfte. zu 8 Hdn. (Brissler)

WAGNER, R. Spinnerlied aus „Der fliegende Holländer" für 2 Pfte. zu 8 Händen. (Kallser)

GOBBAERTS. Op. 113. Polonaise für 2 Pfte. zu 8 Hdn

WAGNER, R. Ouverture „Der fliegende Holländer" für 2 Pfte. zu 8 Händen. (Klindworth) . . . .

SCHUMANN, R. Op. 124. № 16. Schlummerlied (Esdur) für 2 Pfte. zu 8 Hdn. (Brissler)

SCHUMANN, R. Op. 99. № 9. Novellette (Hmoll) für 2 Pfte. zu 8 Hdn. (Brissler)

SCHUMANN, R. Op. 99. № q. Abendmusik (Bdur) für 2 Pfte. zu 8 Hdn. (Brissler)

SCHUMANN, R. Op. 99. № 13. Scherzo (Gmoll) für 2 Pfte. zu 8 Hdn. (Brissler)

Eigenthum des Verlegers.

BERLIN, ADOLPH FÜRSTNER
(C F MESER)
Königl. Sächs. Hof-Musikalien-Handlung.
Den Verträgen gemäss deponirt.
ENT. STAT. HALL.

11. Leipzig: Friedrich Hofmeister

Ausgewählte

Klaviermusik-Werke

für mehrere Spieler.

Für 1 Klavier zu 6 Händen.

Bohr, Franz, Festival-March
Liebich, Im., Op. 73. Fantasien üb. Themen beliebt. Opern.
 No. 1. *Mozart*, Don Juan
 No. 2. *Meyerbeer*, Hugenotten
 No. 3. *Weber*, Oberon
Winterberg, E., Op. 49. Ein Klavierquartett. (4 Spieler) n.

Für 2 Klaviere zu 8 Händen.

Auber, D. F. E., Ouvertüre: Maurer und Schlosser, f.
 2 Pfte zu 8 Händen, arr. v. *C. Burchard*
Beethoven, L. v., Op. 18. Quintett (Es), f. 2 Pfte zu
 8 Händen, arr. v. *Rob. Wittmann*
Bellini, V., Ouvertüre zur Oper: Norma, f. 2 Pfte zu
 8 Händen, arr. v. *C. Burchard*
Berlioz, H., Op. 4. Ouvertüre zu König Lear für 2 Pfte
 zu 8 Händen, arr. v. *Alexander Fiske*
Beutel v. Lattenberg, F. V., Op. 13. Air national
 „God save the Queen", varié p. 2 Pianos à 8 Mains
Henselt, Ad., Op. 2. No. 6. Etude: Si Oiseau j'étais,
 f. 2 Pfte zu 8 Händen
Kreutzer, Conr., Ouvertüre zur Oper: Das Nachtlager
 in Granada, f. 2 Pfte zu 8 Händen arr. v. *R. Wittmann*
Liszt, Franz, Grand Galop chromatique, f. 2 Pfte zu
 8 Händen arr. v. *Joh. v. Vegh*
Marschner, H., Op. 42. Ouvertüre (Dm) zur Oper: Der
 Vampyr, arr. f. 2 Pfte zu 8 Händen v. *H. Enke*
 — Op. 60. Ouvertüre: Templer und Jüdin, f. 2 Pfte zu
 8 Händen arr. v. *Rob. Wittmann*
 — Op. 78. Fest-Ouvertüre (gr. Ouv. solenelle) (D), arr. f.
 2 Pfte zu 8 Händen von *K. Wittmann*
 — Op. 80. Ouvertüre (F) zur Oper: Hans Heiling, f. 2
 Pfte zu 8 Händen arr. v. *G. M. Schmidt*
Méhul, E. H., Ouvertüre zur Oper: Heinrich IV. (La
 Chasse du jeune Henri), arr. f. 2 Pfte zu 8 Händen v.
 C. Burchard
 — Ouvertüre zur Oper: Joseph in Aegypten, arr. f. 2 Pfte
 zu 8 Händen v. *C. Burchard*
Mozart, W. A., Op. 39. Quintett f. Pfte, Hoboe, Kla-
 rinette, Horn und Fagott, arr. f. 2 Pfte zu 8 Händen
 v. *C. T. Brunner*
 — Op. 38. Sinfonie (C) mit der Fuge, arr. f. 2 Pfte zu
 8 Händen v. *Brissl von Lattenberg*
Rosplini, G., Ouvertüre zur Oper: Elisabeth (Barbier von
 Sevilla), arr. f. 2 Pfte zu 8 Händen von *C. Burchard*
 — Ouvertüre zur Oper: Semiramis, arr. f. 2 Pfte zu 8 Hän-
 den v. *C. Burchard*
 — Ouvertüre zur Oper: Die Italienerin in Algier, arr. f.
 2 Pfte zu 8 Händen von *C. Burchard*
Schnyder, X., von Wartensee, Ouvertüre zur Oper: For-
 tunat, f. 2 Pfte zu 8 Händen arr. v. *H. Näyeh*
Weber, C. M. v., Ouvertüre zur Oper: Euryanthe, f.
 2 Pfte zu 8 Händen arr. von *R. Wittmann*
Winter, P. v., Ouvertüre zur Oper: Das unterbrochene
 Opferfest, arr. f. 2 Pfte zu 8 Händen

Eigentum des Verlegers für alle Länder.

LEIPZIG ■ FRIEDRICH HOFMEISTER.

12. Moscow: P. Jürgenson

Compositions célèbres

pour deux PIANOS à 8 mains.

Balakirew, M. Ouverture sur trois thèmes russes. . . . . (*A. Petrow*).
Dargomijsky, A. Cosatschoque . . . . (*E. Langer*).
Gillet, E. Loin du bal . . . . (*A. Kündinger*)
Glinka, M. Polonaise . . . . (*E. Messer*).
    "   Ouv. espagnolos: 1) Jota Aragonesa. . . . . (*E. Langer*).
    "   "   2) Nuit d'été à Madrid . . . . " (*E. Langer*).
Henselt, A. Nicolai-Marche . . . . (*par l'auteur*)
Lwoff, A. Hymne national russe . . . . (*A. Kontels*).
Rimsky-Korsakow, M. Sadko . . . . (*E. Langer*).
Rubinstein, A. Op. 103. │ № 5. Pêcheur et Napolitaine
   "   │ " 7. Toréador et Andalouse
   "   *Bal Costumé* │ " 8. Pèlerin et Fantaisie
   "   │ " 9. Polonais et Polonaise.
   "   │ " 11. Cosaque et Petite-Russienne
   "   │ " 20. Finale.
   "   Trot de Cavalerie.
   "   Feramors. № 1. Danse des bayadères I. . . . . (*E. Langer*).
   "   "   " 2. Danse des fiancées de Cachemir . (*E. Langer*).
   "   "   " 3. Danse des bayadères II. . . . . (*E. Langer*).
   "   "   " 4. Le cortège de noces. . . . . . (*E. Langer*).
Tschaikowsky, P. Op. 2. № 3. Chant sans paroles . . . .
   "   " 13. 1-re Symphonie. . . . . (*E. Langer*).
   "   " 18. Tempête. Fantaisie d'après Shakespeare . (*E. Langer*).
   "   " 29. 3-me Symphonie D-dur . . . . . . (*E. Langer*).
   "   " 29ᵃ „Alla Tedesca", tirée de la 3-me Symphonie. (*S. Liapounow*)
   "   " 31. Marche slave. . . . . (*E. Langer*).
   "   " 32. Francesca da Rimini. Fantaisie . . . (*A. Schaefer*).
   "   " 36. 4-me Symphonie (F-moll) . . . . . (*E. Langer*).
   "   " 45. Capriccio italien. . . . . (*E. Langer*).
   "   " 48. Sérénade pour Orchestre à cordes . . (*E. Langer*).
   "   " 48ᵃ Valse, tirée de la Sérénade. . . . . (*E. Langer*).
   "   " 48ᵃ   "   "   . . . . . (*A. Schaefer*).
   "   " 49. Ouverture Solennelle 1812 . . . . . (*E. Langer*).
   "   " 58. Manfrède. Poëme symphonique . . . (*W. Brüllow*).
   "   " 64. 5-me Symphonie (E-moll). . . . . . (*E. Langer*).
   "   " 66. № 6. La belle au bois dormant. Valse . (*E. Langer*).
   "   " 74. 6-me Symphonie (H-moll). . . . . . (*E. Langer*).
   Oneguine. Valse. . . . . (*E. Langer*).
   Oneguine. Polonaise. . . . . (*A. Schaefer*).

Propriété de l'éditeur

P. JURGENSON à MOSCOU,

Commissionnaire de la Chapelle de la Cour, de la Société Impériale Musicale russe
et du Conservatoire de Moscou.

St.-Pétersbourg, chez J. Jurgenson. | Varsovie, chez E. Wende & Cᵒ.
Kiew, chez L. Idzikowski.
Imprimerie de musique P. Jurgenson à Moscou.

13. Lott, E.M. *A Series of Overtures*, for one piano, six hands
    (BrM: h.848.c., 1877).

14. *Neue Compositionen*, for two pianos, eight hands. Berlin,
    [1878] [BrM:h.1448.d.(4.)]

15. Philadelphia: F.A. North & Co.

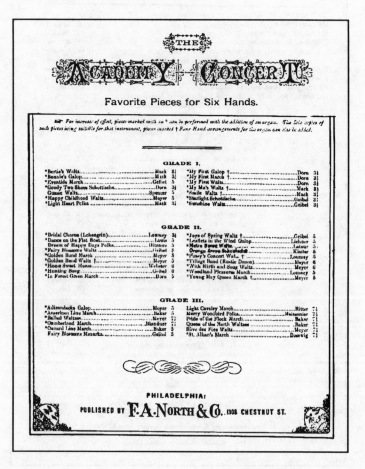

16. *L'orchestre au salon*, collection of pieces for one piano, six hands, Paris, [1874]. (BrM:h.1427)

17. *Piano Trio Collection*, 1P6H, Boston Public Library:
    1. **ABRREN**(Sp?), George W., *Tam O'Shanter*
    2. **MOSZKOWSKI**, Moritz, *Spanish Dance, Op. 12, No. 1*
    3. **SINNHOLD**, Rudolf, *Under the Palm Trees, Waltz*
    4. **STREABBOG**, L., *At the School Festival, Waltz*
    5. **WACHS**, Paul, *Madrilèna, Spanish Fantaisie*
    6. **YEN**, S. Constantino, *Knickerbocker, Intermezzo-Gavotte*

18. Some Pedagogical Collections:
    a) Bradley, Richard, arr., *Bradley's Ensembles for Kids.* New York: Bradley Publications, 1989.
    b) Cardin, Joy and Kevin Raybuck. *Easy Ensembles for Multiple Keyboards.* New York: G. Schirmer, 1990.
       _____. *Intermediate Ensembles for Multiple Keyboards.* New York: G. Schirmer, 1990.
    c) *Easy Pieces, for one piano, six hands.* [European Music Distributors Catalogue (©1988): Vol. 1-ST07257; Vol.2-ST 07258.]
    d) *The Family Music Book (252 pieces of piano and vocal music of moderate difficulty), for two pianos, eight hands.* Boston; New York: G. Schirmer; Boston: The Boston Music Co., [1914]. 790 p. (PCM:Mbl.F198)
    e) *Klavierspiel zu dritt [easy pieces for one piano, six hands by Cornelius Gurlitt, Felix Mendelssohn-Bartholdy, Paul Zilcher, Eberhard Werdin and Reinhold Weber]* Herausgegeben von Franzpeter Goebels. 2 Vols. Mainz; London: Schott, ©1985. (Pub. Nos. ED7257; ED7258)

19. a) New York; London; Frankfurt; Leipzig: C.F. Peters Corp.

Collection Henry Litolff (UR) also published by:
  a) New York: The Arthur P. Schmidt Co.
  b) London: Enoch & Sons
  c) Paris: Enoch et Cie.
  d) Milan: Carisch & Jünichen
  e) St. Petersburg: J. Jurgenson
  f) Moscow: P. Jurgenson
NB--Henry Litolff (1818-1891) was the "English Liszt."

b) **SCHULTZE**, Max, arr.
Les trois inséparables, compositions célèbres, 1P6H
Vol. 1. *Album classique*
Vol. 2. *Danses et marches*
- Lit (No. 2105) (©1894)
  BrM-g.375
  NYPL
  UR-M216.S387q

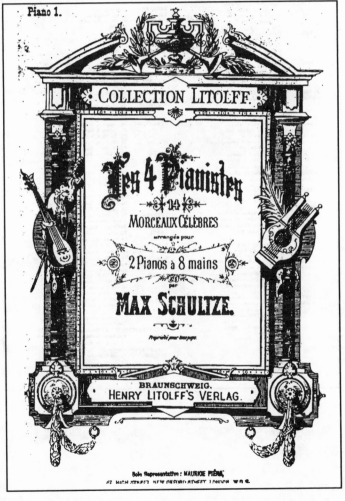

20. Philadelphia: Theodore Presser

SIX HAND PIANO MUSIC

ANDRÉ,	Op.146, Christi Kind'l, Gavotte. *Kramer.*
"	Op.118, Krausköpfchen. *Kramer.*
ANSCHER,	Op.40, Fanfare Militaire. *Herbert*
BEHR,	Op.2v5, No.2. Spring Flowers (Polka in Thirds)
BERLIOZ,	Marche Hongroise. *Alder.*
BEETHOVEN,	Turkish March, *Strausog.*
BELLINI,	Norma, Overture. *Herbert.*
BACH, S.	Awakening of Spring. *Herbert*
BACHMANN,	Sorrento. *Beyer.*
BEHR,	Birthday Gavotte.
"	Sparrows' Chirping. *Löw.*
-BRAHMS,	Hungarian Dances Nos.1 and 2. *Czerny*
"	Cradle Song. *Czerny.*
"	Hungarian Dances Nos. 3, 4 and 5. *Czerny*
"	Hungarian Dances Nos. 6, 7 and 9. *Czerny*
"	Hungarian Dances Nos. 8 and 10. *Czerny*
CLARK,	Torchlight Procession, March.
FLOTOW,	Martha, Fantasy. *Beyer.*
FUNDEY,	Girard Gavotte
FELIX,	Rustic Dance
GUSSET,	From Olden Days, Gavotte
GOLDE,	Prussian March.
GABRIEL-MARIE,	La Cinquantaine.
"	Serenade Badine. *Alder*
GAUTIER,	Secret. *Garliti.*
GOBBAERTS,	Op.58, Marche Triomphale
GURLITT,	Husarenmarsch.
"	Op.192, No.2, Gavotte.
"	Op.192, No.3, Capriccietta
"	Op.192, No.4, Ballata.
GOUNOD,	Faust, Fantasy. *Krug.*
PAGNONCELLI, G B.	Ballata.
"	Bizzarria.
KOELLING, C	Op.413, Marche Militaire
"	Op.414, Marche Lyreus
HOFMANN,	Rosebud
HAYDN,	Two Menuets. *Herbert.*
"	Gipsy Rondo. *Kramer.*
HORVATH,	Vis-a-vis, Children's Quadrille.
HUFMANN,	March with Trio.
HORVATH,	Menuet.
HIRSCH,	Friendship Polonaise
KELLER,	An open air dance.
KOLLING,	Op.362, From Norway
ÁELEK BÉLA,	Op.73, Lustspiel Overture. *Alpes.*
KRAMER,	Op.19, Glockenspiel.
"	Op.7, Jubelfeier, Polonaise.
"	Op.19, Pensionatsfreuden, Waltzes
"	Op.9, im Flügelkleide.
LFL,	Polonaise.
LORTZING,	Czaar and Zimmermann, Fantasy. *Krug*
MISSA,	Les Coquets du Moulin.
"	Gavotte Printanière.
"	Patrouille Mauresque.
"	Petite Parade Militaire.
"	Les Petits Tirailleurs.
"	Prière des Derviches.
"	Repos du Berger.

MAYER,	Op.117, Galop Militaire. *Herbert.*
MENDELSSOHN,	Hunting Song and Venetian Barcarolle. *Herbert*
"	Midsummer Night's Dream, Overture. *Herbert.*
MOZART,	Magic Flute, Fantasy. *Krug.*
"	Magic Flute, Overture. *Burchard*
"	Menuet in E flat. *Herbert.*
MENDELSSOHN,	Hebrides Overture. *Herbert*
"	Wedding March. *Herbert.*
LEONARD,	A tour in an Auto
LEONARD,	At the Telephone
OESTEN,	Op.175, Alpine Bells. *Herbert*
"	Op.193, Alpine Glow. *Herbert*
"	Op.305, Three Sisters. *Herbert.*
"	Op.319, Arrival of Spring. *Herbert*
RATHBUN	A May Day
RAVINA,	Op.69, Tyrolienne Variee.
ROSSINI,	Barber of Seville, Overture. *Herbert*
"	La Gazza Ladra, Overture. *Herbert.*
"	Tancredi, Overture. *Czerny*
SANDRÉ,	Op.54, Marche de Fête.
"	Op.55, Bleue Matinee.
SUPPÉ,	Boccaccio, Fantasy. *Alberti.*
SPINDLER,	Op.264, No.1, Waltz. *Herbert.*
SCHUBERT,	Op.27, No.2, March in D. *Herbert.*
"	Op.27, No.1, March in B min. *Herbert.*
SPINDLER,	Op.140, No.3, Charge of the Hussars. *Herbert*
STREABBOG,	Op.100, No.3, Galop.
"	Op.100, No.4, Ronde.
"	Op.100, No.5, Polonaise
"	Op.100, No.6, Bolero.
"	Op.183, No.1, Marche.
"	Op.183, No.2, Valse.
"	Op.75, March.
"	Op.100, No.2, Valse.
"	Op.100, No.7, Le Départ.
"	Op.100, No.8, Les Amazones
"	Op.100, No.9, La Fileuse
"	Op.100, No.10, Rondino.
"	Op.100, No.11, Chanson Napolitaine.
"	Op.100, No.12, Echo des Montagnes.
TUTSCHEK,	Op.87, Frühlingsmarsch. *Herbert.*
THUILLIER,	A Day in Seville.
"	The Feast of the Rose.
VERDI,	Trovatore, Fantasy. *Beyer.*
VOYE,	Op.34, Roses of Spring. *Kramer.*
STREABBOG,	Op.75, March
SCHARWENKA,	Op.3, No.1, Polish Dance. *Kirchner*
RICHTER,	Op.87, Spring Flowers
"	Op.88, Wedding Day
"	Op.89, On Parade
WEBER,	Euryanthe, Overture. *Herbert.*
"	Freischütz, Overture. *Herbert.*
"	Oberon, Overture. *Herbert.*
"	Oberon, Fantasy. *Herbert.*
"	Freischütz, Fantasy. *Krug.*
"	Invitation to the Dance. *Herbert.*
"	Jubel Overture. *Herbert.*
"	Op.10, No.6, Rondo in E flat. *Horvath*
"	Preciosa, Overture. *Burchard.*
WOLLENHAUPT,	Op.71, Grand Galop brillant. *Herbert.*
VERDI,	Triumphal March from "Aida" *Hummer*
ZPAFF,	Op.19, Little Musician
SCHARWENKA,	Gavotte.
STRAUSS,	Radetzky March

PHILADELPHIA: **THEODORE PRESSER** 1712 CHESTNUT STR.

THREE FRIENDS

FAVORITE PIANOFORTE
COMPOSITIONS FOR
SIX HANDS

4772	THE GOLDEN WEDDING, La Cinquantaine	GABRIEL MARIE
6924a	BALLATA	G. B. PAGNONCELLI
6924b	BIZZARRIA	G. B PAGNONCELLI
8518	MOONLIGHT IN THE BREAKERS	K. W. REDDINGTON
8520	ASSEMBLY MARCH	A. M. COHEN
8531	MARCH MILITANT	G. W. BRYANT
8530	POLKA DE LA REINE	J. RAFF
11033	MARCHE, Op. 75	L. STREABBOG
1829	GIRARD GAVOTTE	C. F. FONDEY
4773	A MAY DAY	F. G. RATHBUN
5125	FROM NORWAY, Op. 362	C. KOELLING
6815	RUSTIC DANCE, Op. 266, No. 2	C. REINECKE
7261	PROMENADE- Polka March	L. RINGUET
7656	MARCHE MILITAIRE, Op. 413	C. KOELLING
7674	MARCHE LYRIQUE, Op. 414	C. KOELLING
8516	DANCE OF THE IMPS- Caprice	K. W. REDDINGTON
9060	SYLVAN SPRITES- Waltz	H. ENGELMANN
9943	UNDER THE MISTLETOE- Waltz	H. ENGELMANN
9974	THE TRUMPET CALL- March	MATILEE LOEB-EVANS
9977	IN THE ARENA- March	H. ENGELMANN
9983	TWILIGHT IDYL	P. A. SCHNECKER
11005	TWILIGHT SONG	F. N. SHACKLEY
11006	THE YOUNG RECRUIT	F. G. RATHBUN
11007	EN ROUTE MARCH	H. ENGELMANN
11008	TWO FLOWERS	C. KOELLING
11012	BETROTHAL MARCH	CHAS. LINDSAY
11013	HOMEWARD MARCH	CHAS. LINDSAY
11023	IRIS - Intermezzo	PIERRE RENARD
12098	SUMMER NIGHT- Waltz	F. A. FRANKLIN
15043	PAGEANT- Marche Brillante	GEO. L. SPAULDING
13373	MARCHE HEROIQUE	GEO. L. SPAULDING
9193	MARCHE Op. 183 No. 1	L. STREABBOG
19362	WHEN ROBINS SING	DANIEL ROWE
4770	SPRING FLOWERS. Op. 295, No. 2	FRANZ BEHR
19620	WE'RE PLAYING TOGETHER	GEO. L. SPAULDING
19680	THE BROOKLET	PAUL ZILCHER
19681	AT THE BALL	PAUL ZILCHER
3636	MARCHE TRIOMPHALE Op. 59	L. GOBBAERTS
6717	GRAND GALOP BRILLANT, Op. 71, *Herbert*	WOLLENHAUPT
1918	CZAR and ZIMMERMANN, Op. 316, N⁰ 3	D. KRUG
23163	WEDDING MARCH	F. MENDELSSOHN
1916	MAGIC FLUTE, Fantasy. *Krug*	MOZART
12175	MEADOW QUEEN, Schottische, Op. 40, N⁰4	FRED. A. FRANKLIN

Philadelphia
Theodore Presser Co
1712 Chestnut Str.

MUSIC FOR
TWO PIANOS, EIGHT HANDS

NO SURRENDER MARCH	R. S. MORRISON
COMMENCEMENT MARCH	C. KOELLING
DANCE OF THE WINDS	A. JACKSON PEABODY Jr.
CONCERT POLKA	A. W. LANSING
OXEN MINUET	J. HAYDN
LE CARILLON, Op. 10	L. RINGUET
INSTALLATION MARCH	G. K. ROCKWELL
CROWN OF TRIUMPH, Op. 221	F. P. ATHERTON
TARANTELLA From "MASANIELLO"	D. F. E. AUBER
CARMEN	G. BIZET
CONCERT POLONAISE	H. ENGELMANN
GERMAN-AMERICAN FESTIVAL MARCH	H. ENGELMANN
GRAND FESTIVAL MARCH	H. ENGELMANN
IN THE ARENA, Op. 608	H. ENGELMANN
OVER HILL AND DALE, Op. 270	H. ENGELMANN
PARADE REVIEW, Op. 207	H. ENGELMANN
ON TO PROSPERITY	R. FERBER
COMRADES IN ARMS, TWO STEP	F. C. HAYES
REUNION MARCH	G. W. HEWITT
MARCH, Op. 39, No. 1	A. HOLLAENDER
HUNGARY, Op. 410, RAPSODIE MIGNONNE	C. KOELLING
MARCHE LYRIQUE, Op. 414	C. KOELLING
MARCHE MILITAIRE, Op. 412	C. KOELLING
SAILORS' SONG AND HORNPIPE	C. KOELLING
PERSIAN MARCH, Op. 360	A. de KONTSKI
IMPROMPTU A LA HONGROISE	P. LACOME
RUSSIAN HYMN	A. LVOFF
CHILDREN'S PIECE, Op. 5, No. 5	F. MENDELSSOHN
KNIGHT RUPERT, Op. 68, No. 12	R. SCHUMANN
NORWEGIAN HUNTERS' MARCH	W. F. MERO
FESTIVAL PROCESSION, MARCH	F. G. RATHBUN
MARCHE TRIOMPHALE	F. G. RATHBUN
MAZURKA, Op. 39, No. 10	P. TSCHAIKOWSKY
NEAPOLITAN DANCE SONG, Op. 39, No. 18	P. TSCHAIKOWSKY
SOLDIERS' MARCH, Op. 39, No. 5	P. TSCHAIKOWSKY
VALSE, Op. 39, No. 8	P. TSCHAIKOWSKY
MODERN CHIVALRY MARCH, Op. 108	F. R. WEBB
THE NEW WOMAN, Op. 79b	F. R. WEBB

Philadelphia
Theodore Presser Co
1712 Chestnut Str

MAY-6'26

MUSIC FOR
TWO PIANOS, EIGHT HANDS

12449 FAST MAIL GALOP	. .	L. STREABBOG	20
11450 LOVE BY MOONLIGHT	.	C. DURAND	60
11451 BRIDE'S WELCOME MARCH	.	C. DURAND	85
11452 PEERLESS WALTZ	. .	C. DURAND	75
11502 FAMOUS TWO STEP	.	C. DURAND	75
11500 FLYING SQUADRON GALOP	.	A. PARLOW	80
14817 CAMP OF GLORY	. .	E. HOLST	1.25
14818 BRIDAL BELLS	. .	C. DRUMHELLER	85
14821 MOONLIGHT SERENADE	.	O. LANGE	75
14822 FLIGHT OF THE SWALLOWS	.	O. LANGE	75
14823 JOYOUS SHEPHERD	.	O. LANGE	75
15280 SERENATA	. .	M. MOSZKOWSKI	60
14846 DIXIE DOODLE	.	E. HOLST	85
14849 SOUTHERN BEAUTY MARCH	.	E. SCHREIDER	1.00
15940 MILITARY MARCH	. .	F. SCHUBERT	50
15941 TROT DE CAVALERIE	.	A. RUBINSTEIN	75
15820 MARCH AND CHORUS from "TANNHÄUSER"	.	R. WAGNER	1.00
16313 PARTING, MARCH from LENORE SYMPHONY	.	J. RAFF	1.00
16951 GRANDE VALSE CAPRICE	.	H. ENGELMANN	1.75
18012 MENUET IN G	. .	BEETHOVEN-PARLOW	60
18013 CHANT SANS PAROLES, Op. 2, No. 3	.	TSCHAIKOWSKY-PARLOW	60
19044 INVITATION TO THE DANCE	.	v. WEBER-SANTORIO	1.50
22581 HUNGARIAN DANCE No. 6	. .	J. BRAHMS	60
22582 LARGO, from "XERXES"	.	G. F. HANDEL	60
22583 WEDDING MARCH, from "MIDSUMMER NIGHT'S DREAM"			
		F. MENDELSSOHN	90
22652 MELODY IN F	. .	A. RUBINSTEIN	60
22653 WALTZ, from "FAUST"	.	CH. GOUNOD	1.00
22828 LIGHT CAVALRY, OVERTURE	.	F. von SUPPÉ	1.25
23144 POET AND PEASANT, OVERTURE	.	F. von SUPPÉ	1.50
23184 INTERMEZZO AND MINUET	.	G. BIZET	1.25
23215 MISERERE, from "IL TROVATORE"	.	G. VERDI	75

Philadelphia
Theodore Presser Co
1712 Chestnut Str

TWO PIANOS EIGHT HANDS

BERLIOZ, Marche Hongroise. *Lutende*
BEETHOVEN, Turkish March. *Burchard*
BEHR, Op.443, Hittei Klätschen. *Plotnel*
BELLINI, Norma, Fantasy. *Alberti*
BOCCHERINI, Menuet in A. *Burchard*
BOIELDIEU, Calif of Bagdad, Overture. *Burchard*
BIZET G., Carmen. *Parlow*
CHEVALLIER, Kinderlust March
Abu le du 2 ? Fanatella from "Bal am Da" Parlow
Mendelssohn ? Pageant of Triumph, Military March .

ENGELMANN, Op. 270, Over Hill and Dale.
" Op. 307, Parade Review
" Op. 452, Grand Festival March.
" Op. 608. In the Arena March.
" Concert Polonaise.
In time American Festival March

GOUNOD, March and Soldiers Chorus, "Faust." *Nebhart*
GOUNOD-BACH, Ave Maria *Herbert*

HAYES, Comrades in Arms. *Swilling*
HEROLD, Zampa, Overture. *Ins*
HOLLAENDER, Op.89,No 1, March
HOWITZ,G.W Neuman Marck
HAYDN PARLOW Alter Minuet
KELER BELA, Op. 73, Lustspiel, Overture. *Herbert*
KONTSKI,de Awakening of the Lion. *Horn.*
" Op. 394, Persian March. *Koordsler*
KOWALSKI, Op. 13, Hungarian March.
KRAMER, Op. 7, Jubelfeier, Polonaise. *Burchard*
KÖCKEN, Op. 73, Fest-Polonaise. *Jansen*
KOELLING, Hungary, Rhapsodic Mignonne
" Sailors' Song and Hornpipe
" Op. 413, Marche Militaire
" Op. 414. Marche Lyrique
LACOME, Impromptu a la Hongroise
LACHNER, March from Suite Op 114.
LISZT, Op.12, Grand Galop Chromatique. *Pach*
" Rakoczy March. *Horn.*
" Second Hungarian March. *Horn.*
" Hungarian Rhapsodie No. 2. *Kirinmichel*
LVOFF, Russian Hymn

MATTEI, Tourbillon, Grande Valse, A flat. *Wolff.*
MENDELSSOHN, Midsummer Night's Dream. Overture. *Jansen*
" Op.95, Ruy Blas, Overture. *Jansen*
" Spring Song. *Wagner*
" War March of the Priests. *Jansen*
" Wedding March. *Jansen*
MILDE, Op. 10. Galop de Concert.
MOSZKOWSKI, Op.18, Serenata. *Blone.*

RAFF, Op.174,No.8, Polka. *Ertester*
" Valse Impromptu a la Tyrolienne. *Herbert*
ROSSINI, Barber of Seville, Overture. *Andre*
" Barber of Seville, Fantasy. *Alberti*
" Semiramide, Overture. *Burchard*
" Tancredi, Overture. *Burchard*
" William Tell, Overture. *Schmidt*
RUBINSTEIN, Trot de Cavalerie. *Brinster*
RATHBUN, Festival Procession March
RAFF, March from Leonore Symphony
ST. SAËNS, Op.40, Danse Macabre. *Parord .*
SCHMIDT, Op.9, Polonaise No.1.
" Op.28, Polonaise No.2.
SCHUBERT, Op.51, No.1, Marche Militaire. *Wagne.*
" Op. 51, Trois Marches Militaires. *Brunner*
" Op.78,No.2, Menuet. *Wagner.*
" Rosamunde, Overture. *Jansen.*
" Rosamunde, Ballet Music. *Burchard.*
SCHULHOFF, Op.4, Valse Brillante, A flat. *Herg..*
" Op.20, Valse Brillante, D flat. *Horn.*
SCHUMANN, Op.99, No.8, Hunting Song. *Brinster*
" Op.124, No.16, Slumber Song. *Brinster.*
SPINDLER, Op.140, No.3, Charge of Hussars. *Herbert*
SUPPÉ, Light Cavalry, Overture. *Model*
" Poet and Peasant, Overture. *Brunner*
SCHUMANN, Op.68, No.12, Knight Rupert *B. Parlow*
MENDELSSOHN,Op. 72, No. 9, Children's Piece

THOMAS, Raymond, Overture. *Herbert*
TSCHAIKOWSKY, P. Op.39,No.5, Soldiers' March. *Parlow*
" Op.39, No.8, Valse. *Parlow*
" Op.39,No.10, Mazurka. *Parlow*
" Op.39,No.14, Neapolitan Dance-Song. *Parlow*
WAGNER, Lohengrin, Prelude. *Bogane*
" March and Bridal Chorus,"Lohengrin." *Bogane*
" Meistersinger, Overture. *De Prosse*
" Ride of the Valkyrie. *Chevalliere*
" Spinning Song, "Flying Dutchman." *Keller*
" Tannhäuser, Overture. *Burchard*
" Tannhäuser, March and Chorus. *Reinhard*
WEBER, Euryanthe, Overture. *Wiliomas*
" Freischütz, Fantasy. *Alberti*
" Invitation to the Dance. *Born*
" Oberon, Overture. *Wrede*
" Oberon, Fantasy. *Alberti*
WEBB, The New Woman March
" Modern Chivalry March

NICOLAI, Merry Wives of Windsor, Overture. *Sate. . .*

PHILADELPHIA: **THEODORE PRESSER** 1712 CHESTNUT STR.

21. Berlin: Ries & Erler

Beliebte Compositionen

für zwei Pianoforte zu acht Händen

bearbeitet von

E.D. Wagner und F. Brissler.

Op. 80.

21. Schubert, Franz, Scherzo A dur
22. Schumann, Robert, Grillen, Op.12 Nº 4
23. ———— Novellette, Op.21 Nº 7
24. ———— Traumeswirren, Op.12 Nº 7
25. ———— Intermezzo aus dem Clavierconcert, Op.54
26. ———— Kreisslen Op.130 Nº 4
27. Chopin, F. Valse (E moll) Oeuvre posthume
28. ———— Op.26. Nº 1. Polonaise in Cis moll
29. Gluck, Ch. Ballet
30. Alföldy, Imre, Ungarischer Tanz A dur
31. ———— Ungarischer Marsch
32. ———— : Ungarischer Tanz F dur
33. Schumann, Robert, Am Springbrunnen, Op. 85 Nº 9
34. Mozart, W. A. Alla Turca
35. Schumann, Robert, Op.13. Finale aus den Etudes symphoniques
36. Mendelssohn - Bartholdy, Felix, Spinnerlied C dur
37. Silas, E. Op. 79. Bourrée (G moll)

22. **SAVLER**, Roberta, ed., American
Ensemble at Two Pianos: a Collection of Pieces for ... Two
Pianos, Eight Hands, 2P8H
- Su (©1955)(*38)
  LC-M215.S

23. New York: G. Schirmer

Piano Ensemble Music

ONE PIANO—SIX HANDS

Three Performers

Bohr, Frans
Festival March 70

Bilbro, Mathilde
Forward March 50
Spring Violets 50

Czerny, C.
Air de Chasse (*C. Gurlitt*) 50

Ducelle, Paul
Alpine Song. Op. 16, No. 11 50
Dance of the Dewdrops. Polka. Op. 16, No. 4 . .50
Dancing Stars. Waltz. Op. 16, No. 1 . . .60
Hand in Hand. March. Op. 16, No. 10 . .50
Lilliputian Parade. March. Op. 16, No. 2 . .61
Queen of Drowsy-Land. Cradle Song. Op. 16,
  No. 7 60
Souvenir Valse. Op. 16, No. 5 60

Gautier, Léonard
Le Secret. Intermezzo (*C. Gurlitt*) 50

Gebhoorn, L.
Triumphal March. Op. 83 50

Gurlitt, Cornelius
March of the Hussars 40

Kragmann, C. W.
Zephyrs from Melodyland. Op. 15:
  Evening Song. No. 11 50
  The Little Patriot. March. No. 7 . . .50
  The Little Prince. No. 1 50
  The Merry Bobolink. No. 10 50
  The Pony Race. No. 8 40
  Primrose Dance. Polka. No. 6 50
  The Rainbow Fairy. Mazurka. No. 4 . .50
  The Robin's Lullaby. Waltz. No. 12. . .60
  Santa Claus Guards. March. No. 2 . . .50
  Song of the Sea Shell. No. 3 50

MacGregor, Helen
National Dance Tunes:
  Highland Fling (Scotch) 30
  Irish Jig (Irish) 30

MacGregor, Helen
National Dance Tunes:
  Kamarinskaia (Russian) 40
  Morris On (English) 30
  Tannenbaum (German) 30
  Thanksgiving Day (American) 30

Moszkowski, Moritz
Walzer (*C. Gurlitt*) 40

Rodgers, Irene and McGrath, Doris
Six Little Hands at One Keyboard. A Preparatory
  Book on Ensemble-Playing and a First Approach
  to Sight-Reading 1.00

Scharwenka, Xaver
Gavotte, in F (*C. Gurlitt*) 35

Schubert, Frans
Serenade (*Carl Lile*) 30

Strassbog, L.
Waltz. Op. 100, No. 2 40

Thuillier, E.
Feast of the Rose. Triumphal March 70

Vandevere, J. Lilian
Gay Gondoliers. Barcarole 40
The Princess Dances. Waltz 40

Weber, C. M. von
Mazurka (*C. Gurlitt*) 65

Zilcher, Paul
At the Fountain 40
Barcarolle. Op. 109, No. 1 40
Bolero. Op. 211, No. 3 50
By the Bubbling Spring. Op. 109, No. 2 . .
Melody. Op. 211, No. 2 . . . .
Minuet. Op. 211, No. 1 . . . .
Serenade . . . .
→Tarantella. Op. 109, No. 3 . . . . .
Wandering . . . .

(Prices apply to U. S. A.)

G. SCHIRMER, INC.   ©1423   **NEW YORK**

24. Leipzig: C.F.W. Siegel's Musikalienhandlung

25. Berlin: Carl Simon

Den Musikschulen gewidmet.

Neue Kompositionen

und

Übertragungen

für

zwei Klaviere zu acht Händen,

zum Teil mit Begleitung von Streichinstrumenten.

Erste Sammlung.

1. Bach, Emanuel. Frühlings Erwachen. Romanze in F dur, arr. von *F. Brissler* *
2. Beethoven, L. v. Op. 69. Sonate in A dur, übertr. von *Aug. Reinhard*
3. Kjerulf, H. Op. 4 Nr. 3. Wiegenlied, übertr. von *Aug. Reinhard* *
4. Kleffel, Arno. Op. 6 Nr. 10. Marsch der Wichtelmänner, arr. von *Bernh. Wolff* *
5. Mohr, Herm. Op. 29 Nr. 1. Sonatine in G dur
6. — Op. 29 Nr. 2. Marsch in C dur. . . . . } (leichte Original-Kompositionen)
7. — Op. 29 Nr. 3. Rondo Allegro in G dur. . . }
8. Op. 48. Polacca in D dur. (Original.) Ausgabe A *
9. — Ouverture zur Kantate: Handwerkerleben. (Original.) Op. 7a *
10. Moszkowski, M. Op. 8. Fünf Walzer, übertr. v. *A. Reinhard*. Nr. 1, 2, 3, 4, 5 M. 1.80 bis
11. — Op. 12. Spanische Tänze Nr. 1/2, arr. von *Bernh. Wolff* *
12. — Op. 12. Spanische Tänze Nr. 3/4, arr. von *Bernh. Wolff* *
13. — Op. 12. Spanische Tänze Nr. 5 (Bolero). arr. von *Bernh. Wolff* *
14. — Valse brillante in A sdur, arr. von *C. Gurlitt*
15. Rubinstein, Ant. Op. 3 Nr. 1. Melodie in F dur, arr. von *Wilh. Popp* *
16. Scharwenka, Phil. Op. 54 Nr. 6. Menuett in D dur, arr. von *F. Brissler*
17. Schubert, Franz. Ungarischer Marsch in C moll, arr. von *Bernh. Wolff*
18. Schultz, Edwin. Op. 64. Polonaise in C dur. (Original-Komposition)
19. — Op. 157. Serenade in F dur. (Original-Komposition)
20. — Op. 182 Nr. 1. Kleiner Festmarsch, C dur } (leichte Original-
21. — Op. 182 Nr. 2. Menuett, G dur . . . . . } Kompositionen)
Op. 198 Nr 2.Lustige Musikanten in D dur (C. 2900)
22. Schumann, R. Chor und Finale aus Paradies und Peri, bearb. von *Aug. Reinhard*
23. — Op. 21 Nr. 1. Novellette, F dur, übertr. von *Aug. Reinhard*
24. Söderman, A. Op. 12. Schwedischer Hochzeitsmarsch. Idylle, arr. v. *Bernh. Wolff* *
25. — Op. 13. Bröllops-Marsch (Bauernhochzeit), arr. von *H. Schramke* *
26. Tschaikowsky, P. Op. 2 No. 3. Chant sans Paroles (Lied ohne Worte) arr. von *F. Brissler* *
27. Weber, C. M. v. Adagio und Rondo, übertr. von *Aug. Reinhard* *
28. Zarembski, J. Op. 2. Danses galiciennes, übertr. v. *A. Reinhard*. Nr. 1 M. 3. Nr. 2 u. 3 je

*) Zu den mit einem Stern * bezeichneten Werken sind Streichquartett- (ad. Quintett-) Stimmen zu haben.

Eingetragen gemäss den Vorschriften der internationalen Verträge.

In das Vereinsarchiv eingetragen.   *Eigentum des Verlegers für alle Länder.*

Carl Simon, Musikverlag, Berlin SW.

Hofmusikalienhändler Sr. Hoh. des Erbprinzen von Anhalt

Markgrafenstrasse 21.

Generalvertretung und Lager von Schiedmayer-Harmonium.

Auslieferungslager bei F. Volckmar in Leipzig.

26. Berlin: N. Simrock

Verlag von N. SIMROCK in Berlin.
G. m. b. H.

WERKE

für

zwei Pianoforte zu acht Händen.

Nº 1. **Auber, D. F. E.** Ouvertüre zur Stummen v. Portici.
Nº 2. **Beethoven, L. van,** Sinfonie Nº 1. *C dur,* Op. 21
Nº 3. — Sinfonie Nº 2. *D dur,* Op. 36
Nº 4. — Sinfonie Nº 3. (Eroica) *Es dur,* Op. 55
Nº 5. — Sinfonie Nº 4. *B dur,* Op. 60
Nº 6. — Sinfonie Nº 5. *C moll,* Op. 67
Nº 7. — Sinfonie Nº 6. (Pastoral) *F dur,* Op. 68
Nº 8. — Sinfonie Nº 7. *A dur,* Op. 92
Nº 9. — Sinfonie Nº 8. *F dur,* Op. 93
Nº 10. — Sinfonie Nº 9. *D moll,* Op. 125
Nº 11. — Ouvertüre zu Coriolan
Nº 12. — idem zur Leonore
Nº 13. — idem zu Fidelio
Nº 14. — idem zu Egmont
Nº 15. **Boieldieu, A.,** Ouvertüre zum Calif von Bagdad
Nº 16. — idem zur weissen Dame
Nº 17. **Brahms, Joh⁹,** Op. 68. Erste Symphonie, *C moll*
Nº 18. — Op. 73. Zweite Symphonie, *D dur*
Nº 19. — Op. 80. Akademische Fest-Ouverture
Nº 20. — Op. 81. Tragische Ouverture
Nº 21. — Op. 90. Dritte Symphonie *F dur*
Nº 22. — Op. 98. Vierte Symphonie, *E moll*
Nº 23. — Ungarische Tänze, Erstes Heft
Nº 24. — idem, Zweites Heft
Nº 25. — idem, Drittes Heft
Nº 26. — idem, Viertes Heft
Nº 27. **Cherubini, L.,** Ouvertüre zu Anacreon
Nº 28. — idem zum Wasserträger
Nº 29. — idem zu den Abencerragen
Nº 30. **Dvořák, Anton,** Op. 59. Legenden, Erstes Heft
Nº 31. — idem Zweites Heft
Nº 32. — Slavische Tänze, Erstes Heft
Nº 33. — idem, Zweites Heft
Nº 34. — idem, Drittes Heft
Nº 35. — idem, Viertes Heft
Nº 36. **Gluck, J. C. de,** Ouvertüre zu Iphigenia in Aulis
Nº 37. — idem zu Alceste
Nº 38. **Herold, F.,** Ouvertüre zu Zampa
Nº 39. **Mehul, F.,** Ouvert. „La Chasse du jeune Henri"
Nº 40. **Mendelssohn-Bartholdy, F.,** Ouvt. z. Sommernachtstr.
Nº 41. — Ouvertüre zu den Hebriden (Fingals-Höhle)
Nº 42. — idem zum Märchen v. d. schönen Melusine
Nº 43. — idem zu Meeresstille u. glückl. Fahrt
Nº 44. — idem zu Athalia
Nº 45. — idem zu: Die Heimkehr a. d. Fremde
Nº 46. **Mozart, W. A.,** Ouvertüre zu Don Juan
Nº 47. — idem zu Figaro's Hochzeit
Nº 48. — idem zur Zauberflöte
Nº 49. **Reissiger, C. G.,** Ouvertüre zur Felsenmühle

Nº 50. **Rossini, G,** Ouvertüre zum Barbier von Sevilla
Nº 51. — idem zur Gazza ladra
Nº 52. — idem zu Tancred
Nº 53. — idem zu Othello
Nº 54. — idem zur Belagerung von Corinth
Nº 55. **Schumann, Robert,** Sinfonie Nº 3. *Es dur,* Op. 97
Nº 56. **Weber, C. M. von,** Ouvertüre zum Freischütz
Nº 57. — idem zu Oberon
Nº 58. — idem zur Euryanthe
Nº 59. — Jubelouverture
Nº 60. — idem zu Preciosa
Nº 61. **Brahms, Joh⁹,** Op. 56ᵃ Variationen über ein Thema von Jos. Haydn.
Nº 62. — Op. 11. Serenade, *D dur*
Nº 63. — Op. 16. Serenade, *A dur*
Nº 64. — Op. 18. Sextett, *B dur*
Nº 65. — Op. 36. Sextett, *G dur*
Nº 66. **Dvořák, Anton,** Op. 95. Symphonie (Nº 5 *E moll*)
Nº 67. **Brahms, Joh⁹,** Op. 83. Klavierkonzert Nº 2.

27. a) *Piano Music for Six Hands.* Chicago; New York: Clayton F. Summy Company, n.d.

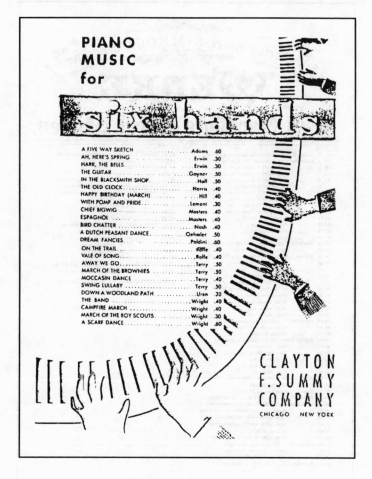

27. b) *Ensemble at Two Pianos: a Collection of Pieces*, 2P8H
Evanston, Illinois: Summy-Birchard, 1959.
(UR-M216.S955e)

Piano 1

REVISED EDITION

ENSEMBLE
at two pianos

a collection of pieces for 2 pianos / 8 hands

Contents

SUMMY-BIRCHARD PUBLISHING COMPANY EVANSTON/ILLINOIS

27. c) *Eight Hands at Two Pianos*. Ed. by Harry Watts (formerly of
        the Eastman School of Music). Evanston, Illinois: Summy-
        Birchard, 1961. (UR)

EIGHT HANDS
at
TWO PIANOS

ensembles selected and edited

by HARRY WATTS

Eastman School of Music

- transcriptions by Edmund Parlow
	Country Dances — *Beethoven*	6
	Children's March — *Schubert*	16
- transcriptions by Harry Watts
  and H. Maxwell Ohley
	Promenade — *Moussorgsky*	2
	Menuetto — *Grieco*	14
	Chorale Preludes by J. S. Bach	
	Christ Lay in Bonds of Death	22
	I Call to Thee	24
	Arisen Is the Holy Christ	26
	Hark, a Voice Saith All Is Mortal	28
	Now Is Salvation Come to Us	30

SUMMY-BIRCHARD PUBLISHING COMPANY

EVANSTON ● ILLINOIS

BIBLIOGRAPHY

Musical Works Discussed

Antheil, George. *Ballet mécanique* (1952 version). Dubuque, Iowa; Delaware Water Gap, PA: Templeton Publishing Co., Inc., 1959.

Bach, Johann Sebastian. *Neue Ausgabe samtlicher Werke (Neue Bach-Ausgabe)*. Ed. by Johann-Sebastian-Bach-Institut, Gottingen and Bach-Archiv. Leipzig: Kassel and Basel, 1954-?; ser. I/viii.

Behrens, Jack. *Aspects, for Three Pianos in Sixths of Tones*. Toronto: Canadian Music Centre, 1983.

Bentzon, Niels Viggo. *Chamber Concert No. 1 for 11 Instruments, Op. 52*. Copenhagen: Wilhelm Hansen, 1950.

Brown, Earle. *Corroboree*. London: Universal Edition, 1970.

_____. *December 1952* from *Folio*. New York: Associated Music Publishers, Inc., 1961.

_____. *Twenty-five Pages*. Toronto: Universal Edition, 1975.

Cage, John. *Music for Piano 4-19*. New York: Henmar Press, Inc., 1960.

_____. *Music for Piano 21-36; 37-52*, New York: Henmar Press, Inc., 1960.

_____. *Music for Piano 53-68*. New York: Henmar Press, Inc., 1960.

_____. *Music for Piano 69-84*. New York: Henmar Press, Inc., 1960.

_____. *Winter Music*. New York: Henmar Press, 1960.

Cage, John and Lejaren Hiller. *HPSCHD: Solo VII*. New York: Henmar Press, 1969.

Casadesus, Robert. *Concerto for Three Pianos and String Orchestra, Op. 65*. Paris: Durand, 1966; Paris: Editions de l'Oiseau-Lyre, 1938.

Crumb, George. *Celestial Mechanics* from *Makrokosmos IV: Cosmic Dances for Amplified Piano, Four Hands*. New York: C.F. Peters Corp., 1979.

Czerny, Carl. *Quatuor concertant, Op. 230*. Vienna: Anton Diabelli & Co., [c.1830].

_____. *Rondeau brillant, Op. 227 Book 1*. Rotterdam: L. Plattner, Imprimeur & Marchand de Musique [c.1831].

_____. *Les trois amateurs: Fantaisies brillantes, Op. 141, Nos. 2 and 3*. Mayence; Anvers; Brussels: B. Schott, [184-?].

Dahl, Ingolf. *Quodlibet on American Folk Tunes*. New York: C.F. Peters Corp., 1957.

Feldman, Morton. *Extensions IV*. New York: C.F. Peters Corp., 1962.

_____. *Piece for 4 Pianos*. New York: Trio Music Co., Inc., 1958.

Fritsch, Johannes. *Ikonen*. Cologne: Feedback Studio Verlag, 1971.

Grainger, Percy Alderidge. *J.S. Bach for Keyboard Team-Work: Toccata in F Major (Originally composed for Organ)*. Foreword by P.A. Grainger (May, 1938). New York: G. Schirmer, Inc., 1940.

Ives, Charles Edward. *Vote For Names.* New York: Peer International Corp., 1968.

Kagel, Mauricio. *Der Eid des Hippokrates.* Frankfurt; New York; London: C.F. Peters Corp., 1984.

Kupkovič, Ladislav. *Happy-End.* Facsimile edition sent by composer, 1976.

_____. *Präludium und Fuga in Form einer Clavierübung.* Facsimile edition sent by composer, 1977.

Milhaud, Darius. *Paris, suite pour quatre pianos.* Paris: Editions Max Eschig, 1959.

Moscheles, Ignaz. *Les contrastes, Grand duo, Op. 115.* Leipzig: Friedrich Kistner, [184-?].

Mozart, Wolfgang Amadeus. *Three Fortepiano Concerto No. 7 in F Major, K. 242a ("Lodron").* Ed. Marius Flothius. Kassel; Basel; Tours; London: Bärenreiter Verlag, 1972: V/15/i.

Orff, Carl. *Der gute Mensch.* Mainz: B. Schott's Sons, 1931.

_____. *Veni Creator Spiritus.* Mainz: B. Schott's Sons, 1931.

_____. *Vom Frühjahr, Öltank und vom Fliegen.* Mainz: B. Schott's Sons, 1968.

_____. *Valse and Romance.* Ed. by Maurice Hinson. Miami, FL: CPP/Belwin, Inc., 1988.

Ravel, Maurice. *Frontispice.* Paris: Editions Salabert, 1975.

Smetana, Bedřich. *Rondo.* Ed. Kurt Hermann. London; Frankfurt; New York: C.F. Peters Corp., 1990.

———. *Sonata in One Movement.* Ed. by Georg Kuhlmann. London; Frankfurt; New York: C.F. Peters Corp., 1938.

Vivaldi, Antonio. *Le opere de Antonio Vivaldi.* Ed. by Gian Francesco Malipiero. Milan: Edizione Ricordi & Co., 1965. [*Concerto in B Minor, Op. 3, No. 10 (L'estro armonico), F. IV, 10; Tomo 415; RV580; P148: 1717; 1722.*]

Wyschnegradsky, Ivan. *Ainsi parlait Zarathoustra, Symphonie en système de quarts de ton, Op. 17.* Paris: Editions l'Oiseau-Lyre, 1938.

Monographs

Abraham, Gerald. *The Concise Oxford History of Music.* Oxford: Oxford University Press, 1985.

Alcaraz, Jose Antonio. *Luigi Dallapiccola.* n.p.: Cuadernos de Musica Nueva Serie, 1977.

Altmann, Wilhelm. *Verzeichnis von Werken für Klavier vier-und sechshändig, sowie für zwei und mehr Klaviere.* Leipzig: Verlag von Friedrich Hofmeister, 1943.

Antheil, George. *Bad Boy of Music.* Intro. by Charles Amirkhanian. New York: Da Capo Press, 1981.

Apel, Willi. *The History of Keyboard Music to 1700.* Trans. and rev. by Hans Tischler. Bloomington; London: Indiana University Press, 1972.

Balough, Teresa, ed. *A Complete Catalogue of the Works of Percy Grainger.* Nedlands, Western Australia: University of Western Australia, 1975.

Bartoš, František. *Bedřich Smetana: Letters and Reminiscences.* Trans. Daphne Ruebridge. Prague: Artia, 1955.

Belaiev, Victor. Igor Stravinsky's *Les noces*: The Outline (Trans. S. Pring). London, 1928.

Blume, Friedrich. *Renaissance and Baroque Music: A Comprehensive Survey*. Trans. by M.D. Herter Norton. New York: W.W. Norton and Co., Inc., 1967.

Boroff, Edith. *The Music of the Baroque*. Dubuque, Iowa: William C. Brown Co., 1970.

Borovsky, Victor and Alexander Schouvalov. *Stravinsky on Stage*. London: Stainer and Bell, 1982.

Bukofzer, Manfred. *Music in the Baroque Era*. New York: W.W. Norton and Co., Inc., 1947.

Burbank, Richard. *Twentieth-Century Music*. London: Thames & Hudson, Ltd., 1984.

Cage, John. *Silence*. Middletown, Conn.: Wesleyan University Press, 1961.

Caldwell, John. *English Keyboard Music Before the Nineteenth Century*. New York: Dover Publications, Inc., 1973.

Carrell, Norman. *Bach the Borrower*. London: George Allen and Unwin, Ltd., 1967.

Carse, Adam. *The Life of Jullien*. Cambridge: W. Heffer and Sons, 1951.

Chang, Frederic Ming and Albert Faurot. *Team Piano Repertoire: A Manual of Music for Multiple Players at One or More Pianos*. Metuchen, N.J.: The Scarecrow Press, Inc., 1976. 201p.

Clapham, John. *Smetana*. London: J.M. Dent & Sons, Ltd., 1972.

Clarkson, Austin. *Stefan Wolpe: A Brief Catalogue of Published Works*. Islington, Ontario: Sound Way Press, 1981.

Collaer, Paul. *Darius Milhaud*. Geneva; Paris: Slatkine Edition, 1982.

Cope, David H. *New Directions in Music*. Dubuque, Iowa: William C. Brown Co., Pub., 1980.

Czerny, Carl. *Complete Theoretical and Practical Piano- Forte School, Op. 500*. Trans. by J.A. Hamilton. 3 Vols. London: Cocks & Co., c.1860: 55-76.

―――. *Erinnerungen aus meinem Leben*. Baden-Baden: Verlag Valentin Koerner, 1968.

―――. "Recollections from My Life (1842)." Trans. by Ernest Sanders. *The Musical Quarterly,*, Vol. 13 (1956): 302-17.

Dallin, Leon. *Techniques of Twentieth-Century Composition: A Guide to the Materials of Modern Music*. 3rd ed. Dubuque, Iowa: William C. Brown Co. Pub., 1981.

Davison, J.W. *From Mendelssohn to Wagner*. London: n.p., 1912.

Doyle, John G. "The Piano Music of Louis Moreau Gottschalk." Unpub. diss. New York: New York University, 1960.

Dubal, David. *The Art of the Piano: Its Performers, Literature, and Recordings*. New York: Summit Books, 1989.

Fanna, Antonio. *Antonio Vivaldi Catalogo Numerico-Termatico Delle Opere Strumentali*. Milan: Ricordi, 1968.

Ferguson, Howard, ed. *Style and Interpretation: an Anthology of Keyboard Music: Keyboard Duets (I) [of the] 17th-18th Century*. Vol. 5. London; New York; Toronto: Oxford University Press, 1971.

Foreman, Lewis, ed. *The Percy Grainger Companion*. London: Thames Publishing, 1981.

Geiringer, Karl. *The Bach Family*. London: George Allen Unwin, Ltd., 1959.

_____. *Johann Sebastian Bach: The Culmination of an Era*. New York: Oxford University Press, 1966.

Gill, Dominic, ed. *The Book of the Piano*. Oxford: Phaidon Press Ltd., 1981.

Gillespie, Don, ed. *George Crumb: Profile of a Composer*. New York; London; Frankfurt: C.F. Peters Corp., 1986.

Gillespie, John and Anna. *A Bibliography of Nineteenth-Century American Piano Muisc*. Westport, Conn.: Greenwood Press, 1984.

Gilmore, Patrick Sarsfield. *History of the National Piece Jubilee*. Boston: n.p., 1871.

Gottschalk, Louis Moreau. *Notes of a Pianist*. Translated and Ed. by Jeanne Behrend. New York: Alfred A. Knopf, 1964. (Reprint of the 1881 edition, pub. in Philadelphia.)

Griffiths, Paul. *The Thames and Hudson Encyclopedia of Twentieth-Century Music*. London: Thames and Hudson, 1986.

Grout, Donald. *A History of Western Music*. Rev. ed. New York: W.W. Norton and Co., Inc., 1973.

Hansen, Peter S. *An Introduction to Twentieth Century Music*. 3rd ed. Boston: Allyn and Bacon, Inc., 1971.

Hellyer, Roger. Jacket notes for *Mozart: Wind Concertos/Early Piano Concertos*. Alexandria, Virginia: Time-Life Records, 1981.

Hensel, Octavia. *Life and Letters of Louis Moreau Gottschalk.* Boston: Oliver Ditson Co., 1870.

Heusser, I. "Ignaz Moscheles in seinen Klavier-Sonaten, Kammermusikwerken, und Konzerten." Diss. University of Marburg, 1963.

Hinson, Maurice. *Music for Piano and Orchestra.* Bloomington, IN: Indiana University Press, 1981. 327 p.

――――. *Music for More Than One Piano: An Annotated Guide.* Bloomington, IN: Indiana University Press, 1983. 218 p.

――――. *The Pianist's Guide to Transcriptions, Arrangements, and Paraphrases.* Bloomington, IN: Indiana University Press, 1990. 160 p.

――――. *The Pianist's Reference Guide: A Bibliographical Survey.* Los Angeles: Alfred Publishing Co., Ltd., 1987.

――――. *The Piano in Chamber Ensemble.* Bloomington, IN: Indiana University Press, 1978. 570 p.

Hitchcock, H. Wiley. *Music in the United States: An Historical Introduction.* 2nd ed. Englewood Cliffs, New Jersey: Prentice-Hall, Inc., 1974.

Hünten, Franz. *A Complete Book of Instruction for the Pianoforte, Op. 60.* Mainz: n.p., 1835.

Hutchings, Arthur. *The Baroque Concerto.* New York: W.W. Norton and Co., Inc., 1965.

――――. *A Companion to Mozart's Piano Concertos.* 2nd ed. London: Oxford University Press, 1980.

_____. *Mozart: The Man--The Musician.* New York: G. Schirmer Books, 1976.

Joseph, Charles M. *Stravinsky and the Piano.* Ann Arbor, Mich.: UMI Research Press, 1983.

Kallmann, Helmut. *A History of Music in Canada, 1534-1914.* 3rd ed. Toronto: U of Toronto Press, 1960.

Kamper, Dietrich. *Gefangenschaft und Freiheit: Leben und Werk des Komponisten Luigi Dallapiccola.* Cologne: Gitarre & Laute, 1984.

Karásek, Bohumil. *Bedřich Smetana.* Trans. by Joy Kradečková. Prague: Suprahon, 1967.

Kelting, Knud. *Danish Music After Carl Nielsen.* Copenhagen: Danish Music Information Center, 1990.

Kendall, Alan. *Vivaldi.* London: Chappell and Co., 1978.

Kirby, F.E. *A Short History of Keyboard Music.* New York: G. Schirmer Books, 1966.

Korf, William, E. *The Orchestral Music of Louis Moreau Gottschalk.* Henryville; Ottawa; Binningen: Institute of Mediaeval Music, Ltd., 1983.

Kostelanetz, Richard, ed. *John Cage: Documentary Monographs in Modern Art.* New York: Penguin Press, 1970; New York: R.K. Editions, 1971.

Krummel, D.W. *Querhändig.* Urbana: University of Illinois Press, N.d. (Piano music for 3, 5 or more hands.)

Landon, H.C. Robbins, ed. *The Mozart Compendium: A Guide to Mozart's Life and Music.* London: Thames and Hudson, Ltd., 1990.

Lang, Paul Henry, ed. "Preface." *The Concerto: 1800-1900.* New
York: W.W. Norton and Co., Inc., 1969.

──────. *Stravinsky: A New Appraisal of His Work.* New York:
W.W. Norton and Co., Inc., 1963.

Large, Brian. *Smetana.* New York: Praeger, 1970.

Lederman, Minna, ed. *Stravinsky in the Theatre.* New York: Da
Capo Press, 1975.

Levine, Michael. *The Music Address Book.* New York: Harper &
Row, Pub., 1989.

Liess, Andreas. *Carl Orff.* Trans. by Adelheid and Herbert Parkin.
Zürich, Freiburg: Atlantis, 1977.

List, Eugene. Jacket notes for Eastman's *Monster Concert: Ten
Pianos/Sixteen Pianists* (Columbia Masterworks, M 31726).
[Review: Robert Offergeld, "A Monster Concert in the Great
American Tradition," *Stereo Review* (April, 1973): 108-109.]

Longyear, Rey M. *Nineteenth-Century Romanticism in Music.* 2nd
ed. Englewood Cliffs, NJ: Prentice-Hall, Inc., 1973.

Lubin, Ernest. *The Piano Duet: A Guide for Pianists.* New York:
Da Capo Press, 1976.

──────. *Introduction to Contemporary Music.* 2nd ed. New York:
W.W. Norton and Co., 1979.

Malaurent, Jacqueline. Jacket notes for *J.S. Bach: The Concertos for
Three and Four Claviers* (EMI/Angel Records, DS 37897).

Mather, Bruce. Program notes for *Poème du délire.* Montréal:
Canadian Music Centre, 1983.

Mather, Bruce and Jack Behrens. Jacket notes for *Music for Pianos in Sixths of Tones* (Montréal: McGill University Records, 83017, 1983).

Mazoe, Margarita. "Stravinsky's *Les noces* and Russian Folk Wedding Ritual." *Journal of the American Musicological Society*, Vol. XLIII, No. 1 (Spring 1990):99-142.

McGee, Timothy J. *The Music of Canada*. New York: W.W. Norton and Co., 1985.

McGraw, Cameron. *Piano Duet Repertoire*. Bloomington, IN: Indiana University Press, 1981.

Metzger, Heintz-Klaus. Jacket notes for *Avant Garde* (Cologne: Electrole-Studio, 137009).

Morgan, Robert P. *Twentieth-Century Music: A History of Musical Style in Modern Europe and America*. New York; London: W.W. Norton & Co., 1991.

Morley, Thomas. *A Plaine and Easie Introduction to Practikall Musicke*. Ed. by R. Alec Harman, New York: W.W. Norton & Co., 1953.

Moscheles, Ignaz. *Aus Moscheles Leben nach Briefen und Tagebücher*. 2 Vols. Leipzig: n.p., 1872; Ed. by C. Moscheles. Eng. Trans. by A.D. Coleridge. London: Hurst and Blackett, 1873. (Includes catalogue of works.)

Myers, Rollo Ho. *Ravel: Life and Works*. London: Gerald Duckworth & Co., Ltd., 1960.

The New Grove Dictionary of Music and Musicians. *See* Sadie, Stanley.

Nicolodi, Fiamma. *Luigi Dallapiccola: saggi, test imonianze, carteggio, biografia e bibliografia.* Milan: Suivi Zerboni, n.d.

Norris, Geoffrey. *Rakhmaninov.* London: J. M. Dent and Sons, Ltd., 1976.

Opiénski, Henryk. *Chopin's Letters.* New York: Vienna House,1971.

Orenstein, Arbie. *Ravel: Man and Musician.* New York; London: Columbia University Press, 1975.

Pace, Robert Lee. *Piano for Classroom Music.* Englewood Cliffs, NJ: n.p., 1971.

Palisca, Claude. *Baroque Music.* Englewood Cliffs, NJ: Prentice-Hall, Inc., 1968.

Palmieri, Robert. *Piano Information Guide: An Aid to Research.* New York: Garland Publishing, Inc., 1989.

Pheimister, William. *American Piano Concertos: A Bibliography.* Detroit: Information Coordinators, Inc., 1985.

Pincherle, Marc. *Antonio Vivaldi et la musique instrumentale.* Vol. II, *"Inventaire thèmatique."* Paris: Librarie Floury, 1948.

―――. *Vivaldi, Genius of the Baroque.* Translated by C. Hatch. New York: W.W. Norton and Co., Inc., 1962.

Radcliffe, Philip. *BBC Music Guide: Mozart Piano Concertos.* London: British Broadcasting Corp., 1978.

Randel, Don Michael, ed. *The New Harvard Dictionary of Music.* Cambridge, Mass.: Belknap Press of Harvard University Press, 1986.

Ratcliffe, Ronald V. *Steinway.* San Francisco: Chronicle Books, 1989.

Raynor, Henry. *Music and Society Since 1815.* New York: Barrie & Jenkins, 1976.

Reich, Steve. *Writings About Music.* Ed. by K. Koenig. New York: New York University Press, 1974; Halifax, Nova Scotia: Nova Scotia College of Art and Design Press, 1974.

Rezits, Joseph and Gerald Deatsman. *The Pianist's Resource Guide, 1978-79: Piano Music in Print and Literature on the Pianistic Art [by] Joseph Rezits and Gerald Deatsman.* Parke Ridge, Illinois: Pallma Music Company, Neil A. Kjos, 1978. 1491 p.

Rupert, Mary Jane. *The Piano Music of Darius Milhaud.* Doc. diss. Bloomington, IN: Indiana University, 1974.

Ruthardt, Adolf. *Wegweiser durch die Klavier-Literatur 10. Aufl.* Leipzig; Zürich: Hug and Co., 1925.398p. (First published in 1888.)

Sadie, Stanley, ed. *The New Grove Dictionary of Music and Musicians.* 20 Vols. London: Macmillan Publishers, Ltd., 1980.

_____. *The Norton/Grove Concise Encyclopedia of Music.* New York: W.W. Norton and Co., 1988.

Salzman, Eric. Jacket notes to *Igor Stravinsky's Les noces* (Zürich: Nonesuch, H-71133).

_____. *Twentieth-Century Music: an Introduction.* 2nd ed. Englewood Cliffs, NJ: Prentice-Hall, Inc., 1974.

Schickel, Richard and Michael Walsh. *Carnegie Hall: The First One Hundred Years.* New York: Harry N. Abrams, Inc.,

Publishers, 1987.

Schonberg, Harold C. *The Great Pianists from Mozart to the Present*. New York: Simon and Schuster, 1963.

Schweitzer, Albert. *J.S. Bach*. Vol. 1. Trans. by Ernest Newman. London: Adam & Charles Black, 1964.

Siff, Nancy K. Jacket notes to *Casadesus's Triple Piano Concerto: First Recording* (Columbia Masterworks, M30946; Mono 3211 0025).

Simms, Bryan R. *Music of the Twentieth Century: Style and Structure*. New York: G. Schirmer Books, 1986.

Slattery, Thomas C. *Percy Grainger, The Inveterate Innovator*. Evanston, Ill.: Instrumentalist Co., 1974.

Slonimsky, Nicholas, ed. *The Concise Baker's Biographical Dictionary of Musicians*. New York: Schirmer Books, 1958, 1984 and 1988.

Smidak, Emil F. *Isaak-Ignaz Moscheles*. Town of publication is unknown, Hampshire, England: Scolar Press, 1988.

Spitta, Philipp. *J.S. Bach*. Vol. I. Leipzig: Breitkopf and Härtel, 1873.

Sternfeld, F.W., ed. *Music in the Modern Age*. New York; Washington, D.C.: Praeger Publishers, 1973.

Stravinsky, Igor and Robert Craft. *Memories and Commentaries*. Los Angeles: University of California Press, 1981.

Stravinsky, Vera and Robert Craft. *Stravinsky in Pictures and Documents*. New York: Simon and Schuster, 1978.

Strunk, Oliver. *The Baroque Era*. *Vol. III of Source Readings in*

Music History. New York: W.W. Norton and Co., Inc., 1984.

Stuckenschmidt, H.H. *Twentieth Century Music*. New York; Toronto: World University Library, 1976.

Suermondt, R.P. *Smetana and Dvořák*. Stockholm: Continental Book Co., 1949.

Talbot, Michael. "Antonio Vivaldi," *The New Grove Italian Baroque Masters*. New York: W.W. Norton and Co., Inc., 1984.

——. *Vivaldi*. London: J.M. Dent and Sons, Ltd., 1978.

Teige, K. *Smetana's Works*. Prague: n.p., 1893.

Van Den Toorn, Pieter C. *The Music of Igor Stravinsky*: New Haven and London: Yale University Press, 1983.

Veinus, Abraham. *The Concerto*. London: Cassell 1948; 2nd ed., rev. New York: Dover, 1964.

Vinton, John, ed. *Dictionary of Contemporary Music*. New York: E.P. Dutton & Co., Inc., 1974.

Von Gunden, Heidi. *The Music of Pauline Oliveros*. Metuchen, NJ: Scarecrow Press, Inc., 1983.

Walsh, Stephan. *The Music of Stravinsky*. London; New York: Routledge, 1988.

White, Eric Walter. *Stravinsky: The Composer and His Works*. Los Angeles: University of California Press, 1966.

Whitesitt, Linda. *The Life and Music of George Antheil: 1900-1959*. Ann Arbor, Mich.: UMI Research Press, 1983.

Williams, Adrian. *Portrait of Liszt: By Himself and His Contemporaries.* Oxford: Clarendon Press, 1990.

Wolff, Christoph, Walter Emery and Nicolas Temperley. *The New Grove Bach Family.* 3rd ed. New York: W.W. Norton and Co., 1985.

Wolters, Klaus and Franz Peter Goebels. *Handbuch der Klavierliteratur.* Zürich: Atlantis Verlag, 1967. 650 p.

Yates, Peter. *Twentieth Century Music.* New York: Pantheon Books, 1967.

Catalogues

BBC [Central] Music Library: Piano and Organ Catalogue. 2 Vols. London: British Broadcasting Corp., 1965.

The Boston Public Library: Dictionary Catalog of the Music Collection. Vol. 15. Boston, Mass.: G.K. Hall and Co., 1972.

The British Catalogue of Music: Chamber Music. 2nd ed. Ed. by A.J. Wells. London: British Museum, 1957-88.

Canadian Chamber Music. Calgary; Montréal; Toronto; Vancouver: Canadian Music Centre, 1980.

Canadian Music Centre Biographies. Toronto: Canadian Music Centre, 1986-88.

Hauptkatalog des Musikalien-Verlags Johann André. Aus-gegeben am 1. Januar 1924.

The New York Public Library: Dictionary Catalog of the Research Libraries, Supplement. A Cumulative List of Authors, Titles, and Subjects Representing Materials Added to the Collections

Beginning January 1, 1972. Vols. 43 and 51 (Set 43). New York Public Library: Astor, Lennox & Tilden Foundations, 1980, 1989; Vols. 8 and 32. 2nd ed. Boston: G.K. Hall, 1982.

Ohmura, Noriko. *A Reference Concordance Table of Vivaldi's Instrumental Works.* Japan: n.p., 1972.

The Pianist's Library: für 2 Klaviere zu 8 Händen. Leipzig; New York: Breitkopf & Härtel (No. 13379), n.d.

Ryom, Peter. *Verzeichnis der Werke Antonio Vivaldi's.* Complete version. Leipzig: VEB Deutscher Verlag für Musik, 1975.

Articles

"Awakening the Monster: October [27 and 28] Massey Hall Concerts Continue Multi-Piano Performance Tradition." *Music Magazine, Royal Conservatory of Music, Toronto,* 13, (September/October 1990):30.

Berger, Salome. "Group Piano as an Introduction to Chamber Music." *Clavier* (May/June, 1982):50-51.

Blasch, Robert E. "The Challenge of Monster Concerts." *American Music Teacher* (February/March, 1987):34-35.

Blesche, Eulalie. "Interaction of Equals." *Clavier* (November, 1976):23.

Boas, H. "über Joh. Seb. Bachs Koncerte für drei Klaviere." *Bach-Jahrbuch* (1913):31-38.

Brown, Anthony. "An Introduction to the Music of Morton Feldman." *Asterisk I* (December 1974).

Brown, Earle. "Form in New Music." *Source I,* No. 1 (January

1967):49-51. (Excellent discussion of the "event" concept, mobile structure and open form in music.)

Busse, Ralf. "Ein donnerndes Riesending: Orchester zum 13. Ton spielte das *Ballet mécanique.*" *Südwesbpesse*, (April 7, 1989).

Cage, John. "To Describe the Process of Composition in *Music for Piano 21-52.*" *Die Reihe*, 3:41.

Czerny, Carl. "Recollections from My Life." Trans. by Ernest Saunders, *The Musical Quarterly*, 42, (July 1956): 302-317.

Dallapiccola, Luigi. "On the Twelve-Note Road." *Music Survey* (October 1951):318-332.

Dery, Mark. "The Eclectic Odyssey of Otto Luening: Something Old, Something New." *Keyboard*, Vol. 17, No. 1 (January 1991):36-50.

Elder, Dean. "Gaby Casadesus Perspective." *Clavier* (February 1979):12-13.

Emery, Walter, Christopher Wolff and Nicholas Temperly. "Johann Sebastian Bach," *The New Grove Bach Family.* New York: W.W. Norton and Co., Inc., 1985.

Faurot, Albert. "Team Playing." *Clavier* (November 1976):19-21.

Grainger, Percy Alderidge. "Community Music." *Playground*, 24 (July 1930):235.

Helm, Eugene. "Carl Philipp Emanuel Bach." *The New Grove Bach Family.* New York; London: W.W. Norton and Co., 1985.

Hinson, Maurice. "Carl Czerny Remembered (1791-1857)." *Clavier* (October 1985):15-19.

Howard, Leslie. "The Keyboard Music [of Percy Grainger]." *Studies in Music*, 16 (1982):62-68.

———. ("Piano Teams") Gilles Potvin, and Kenneth Winters, eds. *Encyclopedia of Music in Canada*. Toronto: University of Toronto Press, 1981.

Karp, David A. "Teaching Musicianship Through Piano Ensemble." *Clavier* (May/June 1982):30-31.

Lancaster, E.L. "Ensemble Repertoire for Class Piano." *Clavier* (November 1976):42-44.

Lange, F.C. "Vida y muerte de Louis Moreau Gottschalk en Rio de Janeiro (1869)." *Revista de estudios musicales II*, 5, (Mendosa, Argentina, 1953), np.

Leopard, Barbara. "Organizing a Multi-Piano Ensemble Program." *Clavier* (April 1980):52-53.

Mellers, Wilfred. "Music Matters. New Worlds for Old, Old Worlds for New: Percy's [Grainger] Paradox." *Music and Musicians International*, 39, (October 1990):14-16.

Miller, Hugh M. "The Earliest Keyboard Duets." *The Musical Quarterly*, 29 (October 1943):438-457.

Offergeld, Robert. "The Gottschalk Legend: Grand Fantasy for a Great Many Pianos." *The Piano Works of Louis Moreau Gottschalk*. 5 Vols. Ed. Vera Brodsky Lawrence. New York, 1969.

Pattison, Lee. "Ensemble Piano Playing." *Pacific Coast Musical Review* (n.d.):72.

Schramm, Harold, ed. "Editorial [Morton Feldman's *Two Pieces for Three Pianos*]." *The Piano Quarterly*, 16, (1968):3.

Schuessler, Annemarie. "Two-Piano Transcriptions of Orchestral Works." *Clavier*, 29, (March 1990):16-19.

Shanaphy, Ed. "Monsters Invade Norfolk: *Sheet Music Magazine's* Publisher Joins Eugene List in the Gottschalk Tradition." *Sheet Music Magazine* (April/May 1985):6-7.

Solomon, Maynard. "Charles Ives: Some Questions of Veracity." *Journal of the American Musicological Society*, XL, (Fall 1987):443-470.

Stuckenschmidt, H.H. "Umschau: Ausblick in die Musick." *Das Kunstblatt VII* (July, 1923):221-23.

Taubman, Howard. "Thirty-four Pianists Render Steinway Tribute." *New York Times*, October 20, 1953.

Tetley-Kardos, Richard. "Piano Transcriptions--Back for Good?" *Clavier*, 25, (February 1986):18-19.

Walker, Alan. "In Defense of Arrangements." *The Piano Quarterly*, 143 (Fall 1988):26;28.

Weaver, William. "The Unknown Smetana." *Hi-Fi/Musical America*, 15 (May 1965):44-47.

Yoder, Alene. "The Excitement of Multi-Piano Concerts." *Clavier*, 18, (April 1979):27-29.

Letters from Composers to Dr. Grant L. Maxwell[1]

Beckwith, John. November 15, 1990.

---

[1]   These letters have been donated by Dr. Grant Maxwell to the Bruce Peel Special Collections Library at the University of Alberta.

Behrens, Jack. January 21, 1991.

Cage, John. October 20, 1990; November 18, 1990.

Casadesus, Gaby. December 12, 1990.

Chapple, Brian. November 18, 1990.

Crumb, George. November 19, 1990.

Diemer, Emma Lou. December 4, 1990.

Gould, Morton. August 30, 1990.

Hart, Jane Smith. November 17, 1990.

Horwood, Michael. November 20, 1990.

Kenins, Talivaldis. November 14, 1990.

King, Patricia W. January 10, 1991.

Kupkovič, Ladislav. November 17, 1990.

Lanza, Alcides. December 5, 1990.

Luening, Otto. December 11, 1990.

Mather, Bruce. November 13, 1990; February 15, 1991.

Melnyk, Lubomyr. January 3, 1991.

Mozetich, Marjan. November 28, 1990.

Parfrey, Raymond. November 14, 1990.

Reich, Steve. November 26, 1990.

Riepe, Russel. January 9, 1989.

Schickele, Peter. December 5, 1990.

Schwartz, Elliot. November 20, 1990.

Winiarz, John. December 20, 1990.

Discography[2]

ANTHEIL, George. *Ballet mécanique*
1.   (*Columbia Special Products, ML 4956). New York
       Percussion Group; Carlos Surinach, conductor. (LC)
2.   (*Telefunken, 642196, 1977). Netherlands' Percussion
       Ensemble. (LC)
3.   (*Urania, USD1034; UR 134). Los Angeles Contemporary
       Music Ensemble; Robert Craft, conductor. (LC)

BACH, Johann Sebastian. *Concerto for 3 Claviers, BWV 1063*
1.   (CBS, DC-MK 45579; cassette: MT-45579). Synthesized
       orchestra; Bob James; Gunner and Sunner Pekinel, pianists.
2.   (Philips, CD-426084-2 PM; cassette: 426084 4 PM). English
       Chamber Orchestra; Leppard, Andrew Davis, Ledger,
       harpsichordists; Leppard, conductor.

────── . *Concerto for 3 Claviers, BWV 1064*(*CBS Masterworks, 32 11
       0025, 1967). Orchestre des Concerts Cologne; Robert, Gaby
       and Jean Casadesus, pianists; Pierre Dervaux, conductor.
       (Also *Philadelphia Orchestra, Eugene Ormandy, conductor:
       Odyssey/Columbia, V31531, 1972). (LC)

────── . *Concertos for 3 and 4 Claviers*
1.   (Charlin, SLC-2; CD-SCL-2). Milan Angelicum Chamber
       Orchestra; Tagliavini, Canino, Ballista and Abbado; Zedda,
       conductor.

---

2   Recordings marked with an asterisk are no longer in print.

2. (Claves, D-614). Dähler, Gerber, Daxelhofer and Meystre, harpsichordists; Dähler, conductor.

3. (Deutsche Grammophon, 400--041-2AH;400--041-4AH;2534/3311 001;CD-(ARC-413634-2 AH3). English Consort; Pinnock, Gilbert, Mortensen and Kraemer, harpsichordists. (LC)

4. (Deutsche Grammophon, CD-415655-2 GH). Hamburg Philharmonic; Frantz, Eschenbach, Oppitz and Schmidt, pianists; Eschenbach, conductor.

5. (Elektra/Nonesuch, H-71019; cassette:NS-71019). Saar Chamber Orchestra; Newmayer, Berger, Burr and Urbuteit, harpsichordists; Ristenpart, conductor.

6. (EMI/Angel, CDC-74063;DS-37897, 1981). Ensemble Orchestral de Paris; Michel Béroff, Jean-Phillipe Collard, Bruno Rigutto and Gabriel Tacchino, pianists; Jean-Pierre Wallez, conductor. (LC)

7. (Fideleo, CD-1815). Liszt Chamber Orchestra; Rohmann, Falvai, Kocsis and Schiff, pianists; A. Simon, conductor. (Hungaroton, LP:SLPX-11752; cassette: MK-11752).

8. (5-Intercord, INT-185.816;CD-820738 and 860954). Stuttgart Chamber Orchestra; Kipnis, Schell-Pluth, Schader and Hertzberg, harpsichordists; Münchinger, conductor.

9. (London, STS-15075; cassette: 410136-4LT;CD-ARC 413634-2 AH3). English Chamber Orchestra; Malcolm, Aveling, Parsons and Leppard, harpsichordists; Leppard, conductor (*BWV 1063;1065*).

10. (Serenus, 12051). Baroque Chamber Orchestra; Marlowe, Cook, Conant and Saidenberg, harpsichordists; Saidenberg, conductor. (*BWV 1064;1065*)

11. (3-Teledec, 35778 DX; CD-35778 XD). Leonhardt Consort; Müller, Leonhardt, Wering and Uittenbosch, harpsichordists; Leonhardt, conductor.

12. (Turnabout, CT-4106). Mainz Chamber Orchestra; Galling, Bilgram, Lehrndofer and Stolz, harpsichordists; Kehr, conductor.

BACH, Wilhelm Friedrich Ernst. *Das Dreyblatt*, for 1P6H (*Boston Records, BUA-1). (UR)

BROWN, Earle. *Corroboree* (*Mainstream, 5000).

———. *Four Systems* (*Columbia, MS-7139).

CAGE, John. *Winter Music*
1.   (*Deutsche Grammophon, 137009, 1990). Ensemble Musica
        Negative; Riehe, conductor; Bauer, Gerstein, Metzger,
        Meyer-Denkmann and Venzago, pianists. (UR)
2.   (*Kew Gardens, NY: Mode Records; Albany, NY: Classical
        Music, Inc.; Finnabar 9006).

CAGE, John and Lejaren Hiller. *HPSCHD* (Elektra/Nonesuch
        Records, H-71224). Vischer, Bruce and Tudor,
        harpsichordists; Johnston, conductor.

CASADESUS, Robert Marcel. *Three Piano Concerto, Op. 65* (*CBS
        Masterworks, 3211 0025, 1967). Orchestre des concerts
        Colonne; Pierre Dervaux, conductor. Robert, Gaby and Jean
        Casadesus, pianists. (Also *Philadelphia Orchestra, Ormandy,
        conductor: Odyssey/Columbia, V31531, 1972) (LC)

CRUMB, George. *Celestial Mechanics (Makrokosmos IV)*.
1.   (Smithsonian Collection, N-027; Pro Arte Records, re-
        release). Orkis and Primosch, pianists.
2.   (*AMU Records). Degenhardt and Kent, pianists.
3.   (Attacca, 8740). Nasveld and Bogaart, pianists.

CZERNY, Carl. *Music for 2, 4 and 6 Hands at One Piano.* (*St.
        Albans, Herts, Four Hands Music, 1985).

———. *Piano Music for Four Hands* (Sony, SK 45936, 1991). Quotal
        and Groethuysen, pianists.

DALLAPICCOLA, Luigi. *Music Per Tre Pianoforti (Inni)* (*La
        musica moderna n. 75, Fratelli Fabbri Editiori). Bruno
        Canino, Massimo Toffoletti and Antonio Ballista, pianists.

FELDMAN, Morton. *Extension IV; Piece for Four Pianos* (*Columbia, ML 5403). Tudor, Shermann and Hywovitz, pianists; (Odyssey, 32160302).

——. *False Relationships and the Extended Ending.* (New York: Composer's Recordings, Inc., S-276).

FIRST PIANO QUARTET. *Dances Not For Dancing* [Waltzes from the Classics] (*RCA Victor, LM 1165). (UCol)

——. *First Piano Quartet Encores* (*RCA Victor: Red Seal Records, 2SJ482). Adam Garner, Edward Edson, Glauco D'Attili and Frank Mittler, pianists. (LC)

——. *First Piano Quartet* (*RCA Victor, ERA-70). (LC;UR)

——. *[Russian Melodies and Rhythms]* (*RCA Victor, ERA-96). (LC)

FORTNER, Wolfgang. *Triplum* (*Wergo, WER60 035, 1970). Alfons, Aloys and Bernhard Kontarsky, pianists.

GOTTSCHALK, Louis Moreau. *A Gottschalk Festival* (Vox Box, CDX 5009, 1990). Vienna State Opera Orchestra; Berlin Symphony Orchestra; Trinidad Paniagua, soprano, Jose Alberto Esteves, tenor and Pablo Garcia, baritone; Eugene List, Cary Lewis and Brady Millican, pianists; Igor Buketoff and Samuel Adler, conductors.

HAMPTON, Calvin. *Catch-up* (*Odyssey, 32160161-2). Pappastavrou and Lanning, pianists (two piano version).

HIDALGO, Juan. *Tamaran; grocce di sperma per dodici pianoforti* (*Cramps, SRCLP 6102, 1974). Nova Musicha. (LC) (Chance composition for twelve pianos in which all parts are performed by Juan Hidalgo.)

HILLER, Lejaren. *Fantasy for Three Pianos* (Spectrum, SR-190). S. & F. Manes, Mikhashoff, pianists.

JAZZ PIANO QUARTET. *Let It Happen* (*RCA Victor, CPL 1-0680, 1974). Hyman, Jones, McPartland and Hanna, pianists. (LC)

KUPKOVIČ, Ladislav. *Präludium und Fuga in Form einer Clavierübung* (*EMI/Electrola, IC 066-45 424).

LEWIS, Meade Lux (1905-1964). *Boogie Woogie Prayer* for three pianos (*NYPL ScAudio CM-45, Side 1, Nos. 3-4). (LC)

MARIÉTAN, Pierre. *Perspectives romandes et jurassienne:* Un âge va, un âge vient pour récitant, soli, choeur, et orchestre (New York: Qualiton Imports, 1984; Switzerland: Gallo, 30-417). Christen Giger sound recording. (HU) Italian-Swiss Radio Orchestra and Chorus.

THE MARTY PAICH PIANO QUARTET (RCA Victor LPM-2259, 1961) Johnny Williams, Jimmy Rowles, Pete Jolly, Marty Paich, pianists.

MILHAUD, Darius. *Paris, Suite pour quatre pianos*
1.   (*Paris: IME Pathé Marconi, LPS 512076).
2.   (*La voix de son maître, 2C065 12076, 1972). Ivaldi, Béroff, Collard and Lee, pianists.

MONSTER CONCERT: TEN PIANOS/SIXTEEN PIANISTS (*Columbia Masterworks, M 31726, 1973). Members of the Eastman School of Music Piano Faculty and Eastman School Graduates, Samuel Adler, Conductor. Featuring Eugene List, Frank Glazer, Barry Snyder and Maria Luisa Faini. The following works are performed: Sousa-Morton Gould/Russel Riepe, *The Stars and Stripes Forever*; Rossini-Gottschalk, *William Tell Overture*; J. Strauss, Jr.-Russel Riepe, *Thunder and Lightening Polka*; Joplin-Russel Riepe, *Maple Leaf Rag*; J. Strauss, Jr.-Schultz/Evler/Chasins, *Blue Danube Waltzes*;

Rossini-Czerny, *Semiramide Overture*; Gottschalk, *La Gallina* (The Hen); Gottschalk, *Ojos Criollos* (Creole Eyes). (LC;UR) [Review: Robert Offergeld, "A Monster Concert in the Great American Tradition," *Stereo Review* (April, 1973):108-109.]

MOZART, Wolfgang Amadeus. *Three Piano Concerto No. 7 in F Major, K. 242 (Lodron)*
1. (*Ambassador Record Corp., JAS 19027).
2. (*CBS Masterworks, M32173, 1973). New York Philharmonic; Bernstein, Gold and Fizdale, pianists; Bernstein, conductor.
3. (Denon, CD-C37-7600). Vienna Capella Academia; Dreyfus, Baumont and Kiss; Melkus, conductor.
4. (Deutsche Grammophon, CD-ARC-427317-2 AH). English Baroque Soloists; Bilson, Levin and Tan, pianists; Gardiner, conductor.
5. (*Epic, LC 3259). Vienna Symphony Orchestra; Alpenheim, Helen and Karl Ulrich Schnabel, pianists; Paumgartner, conductor.
6. (Fidelio, 3353; CD-1812; cassette: C-3353). Hungarian State Orchestra; Kocis, Ránki and Schiff, pianists; Ferencsik, conductor.
7. (London, 430 232-4). English Chamber Orchestra. Schiff, Barenboim and Solti, pianists; Solti, conductor.
8. (*Musical Heritage Society, Inc., MHS 1123). Vienna Chamber Orchestra; Kann, Rivera-Aguilar and Marciano, pianists; Seipenbusch, conductor.
9. (*Nonesuch, H-71028; H-1028, mono). Orchestre de l'Association des Lamoureaux Concerts; Sancan, Pommier, and Silic, pianists; Chorofas, conductor.
10. (*Odyssey/Columbia, V31531, 1972). Philadelphia Orchestra; Robert, Gaby and Jean Casadesus, pianists; Eugene Ormandy, conductor. (LC)
11. (*Seraphim, S-60072). London Philharmonic Orchestra; Hephzibah, Yaltah and Jeremy Menuhin, pianists; Yehudi Menuhin, conductor. (LC)

12.   (Time-Life Records, STL-M11:CSL-1074B, 1981). English
         Chamber Orchestra; Ashkenazy, Barenboim and Fou Ts'ong,
         pianists; Barenboim, conductor.

MUSIC FOR THREE PIANOS IN SIXTHS OF TONES (*Montréal:
      McGill University Records, 83017, 1985). Louis-Philippe
      Pelletier, Paul Helmer and François Couture, pianists; Bruce
      Mather, conductor. Works included: Jack Behrens, *Aspects*
      (1983); Bruce Mather, *Poème du délire* (1982);
      Wyschnegradsky, *Dialogue á trois, Op. 51* (1982), and
      Composition, Op. 46, No. 1 (1961). (UA;LC)

NEW MUSIC FOR PIANOS (Mainstream, MS 5000). Yuji
      Takahashi, pianist. (Includes Earle Brown's *Corroboree*.)
      (UCol)

THE ORIGINAL PIANO QUARTET (Adam Garner, Frank Mittler,
      Edward Edson and William Gunther, pianists). *The Original
      Piano Quartet* (*Decca, 710047, 1962). (LC) (Later became
      the First Piano Quartet.)

————. *The Original Piano Quartet, Vol. 2* (*Decca, DL 10047,
      10055, 1962). (LC)

————. *A Pops Concert* (*Decca, DL10 D98, 1964). (LC)

————. *The Original Piano Trio Plays 20's-Style Nostalgia* (*Klavier
      Records, KS-128, 1975). (LC)

PIANO CIRCUS. *Steve Reich, Six Pianos*; *Terry Riley, In C*
      (London: Arco, 430380-2, January, 1990). Kirsteen
      Davidson-Kelly, Richard Harris, Kate Heath, Max Richter,
      Ginny Strawson and John Wood, pianists.

RACHMANINOV, Sergei. *Valse; Romance* (*Harmonica Mundi,
      HMC-901301/02). Engerer, Maisenberg and Bachkirova,
      pianists.

RASMUSSEN, Karl Aage. *Genklang (Echo)* (*Odeon, MOAK 30009).

RAVEL, Maurice. *Frontispiece*
1. (Angel, CDM-63156). Collard, Béroff and Katia Labèque, pianists.
2. (*Dischi Ricordi, 1979). (LC)
3. (*Japan: Denon, 1986). (LC)
4. (*Nonesuch, H-71355, 1978). Jacobs, Kalish and Sterne, pianists. (LC)

REICH, Steve. *Drumming* for 6 Pianos (*Deutsche Grammophon, 2740 106, 1974). (LC)

————. *Four Organs*
1. (*Angel, S-36059, 1973). Michael Tilson Thomas, Grierson, Kellaway and Raney, organists. (LC)
2. (*Disques Shandor, 10005, 1971). Philip Glass, Murphy, Chambers and Gibson, organists. (Recorded live at the Guggenheim Museum.) (LC)

————. *Music for Eighteen Instruments* (ECM 821-417-2).

————. *Six Pianos* (Deutsche Grammophon, 427 428-2 GC 2, 1974). Steve Reich and musicians. (LC)

RUSH, Loren. *The Contemporary Piano Project, Vol. 2* (*Serenus, SRS 12070, 1977). (LC)

STRAVINSKY, Igor. *Les noces*
1. (*CBS Masterworks, ML 6391, 1967; MS 6991, 1967; M 33201, 1974). Orpheus Chamber Ensemble; Gregg Smith Singers; Robert Craft, conductor. (LC) NB--1917 orchestral version.
2. (Deutsche Grammophon, 3300 880, 1977; CD-423251-2 GC, 1988). Members of English Bach Festival Orchestra; English Bach Festival Chorus; Mory, Parker, Mitchinson and Hudson, singers; Argerich, Zimerman, Katsaris and Francesch,

pianists; Leonard Bernstein, conductor. NB--1923 version. (LC)
3.   (Elektra/Nonesuch, H-71133). Orchestre Theatre National de l'Opera; Pierre Boulez, conductor.
4.   (*Epic, LC 3231, 1956). (LC)
5.   (Hungaroton, SLPD-12989 (D); CD-HCD-12989). Amadinda Percussion Ensemble; Slovak Philharmonic Chorus; Ablaberdyeva, Ivanova, Martinov and Saflulin, singers; Hansen, Kocsis, Chen and Rohmann, pianists; P. Eötvös, conductor. NB--the 1917 and 1923 versions.
6.   (*London, CS 6219, 1961). (LC)
7.   (Newport Classic, CD-NCD-60118). Choral Guild of Atlanta; Crowder, Busching, Oosting, Colleys and O'Hearn, singers; W. Noll, conductor.
8.   (Supraphon, CD-110273-2, 1962). Czech Philharmonic and Chorus; V. Neumann, conductor.
9.   (Vanguard, VRS 452, 1954). (LC)
10. (Pierre Vernay, CD-PV-787032). Strasbourg Percussion Ensemble; Choeur Contemporain; Quercia, Cooper, Capelle and Marinov, singers; Vieuxtemps, Conil, Arzoumanian and Raynaut, pianists; Hayrabedian, conductor. NB--1923 version.
11. (Vox, PL 8630, 1954). (LC)

TAKEMITUS, Tōru. *Complete Piano Works (1952-1990): Corona* (Et cetera, 1990). Roger Woodward, pianist.

VIVIER, Claude. *Pulau Dewata* (*Toronto: Centre-discs, 39931759, 1984).

WOLPE, Stefan. *Enactments* (Los Angeles, CA:Elektra/Nonesuch, H-780241; 178024-4, 1984).

WYSCHNEGRADSKY, Ivan.
1.   [*The first long playing recording of his music.*] (*Montréal: McGill University Records, 77002, 1978).
2.   *Vier tettonmusik* (Music in 1/4-tones) (*Berlin: Block, 1983). (See *Music for Three Pianos in Sixths of Tones.*)

INDEX TO THE CATALOGUE

One Piano Four Hands

One Piano Five Hands

One Piano Six Hands

One Piano Eight Hands

Two Pianos Eight Hands

Two Pianos Ten Hands

Two Pianos Twelve Hands

Three Pianos Three Hands

Three Pianos Six Hands

Three Pianos Eight Hands

Three Pianos Twelve Hands

Four Pianos Eight Hands

Five Pianos Ten Hands

Six Pianos Ten Hands

Six Pianos Twelve Hands

Ten Pianos Twenty Hands

Twelve Pianos Twenty-four Hands

Thirteen Pianos Twenty Six Hands

CAGE, John 180

Fifty Pianos One Hundred Hands

GRAINGER, Percy Aldridge
269

ABOUT THE AUTHOR

Pianist and author Grant Lyle Maxwell received his musical education at the University of Alberta (Canada). A recipient of numerous scholarships and awards, including the prestigious Alberta Heritage Trust Fund Award for excellence in his field, he was furthermore granted scholarships to pursue musical studies at the Banff Centre, the Mozarteum Academy and in Leeds, England.

Grant Maxwell is a highly regarded pianist in Canada, as winner of many competitions, as a performer in many radio and television recitals, and as a solo and chamber music pianist. His musical mentors include Ernesto Lejano (the University of Alberta), Gyorgy Sandor and Hans Graf (the Mozarteum Academy) and Menahem Pressler (the Banff Centre).

The publication of *Music for Three or More Pianists: A Historical Survey and Catalogue* is the first book on the important, little-known literature for multiple pianos. This document is the culmination of Dr. Grant Maxwell's many years of study, research, as well as his practical experience in multiple piano performances.